T0389109

Corruption, Economic Growth and Globalization

Corruption is increasingly placed on top of the agenda of national governments and supra national institutions, such as the OECD, UN or the World Bank. A necessary condition for promoting sustainable economic growth is the pre-existence of a stable political system which is able to control corruption. Corruption, however, is a very complex issue, associated with institutional and cultural specificities, personality traits related to individualistic values, and criminal personalities. In this book the social, political and economic realities that prevail in particular settings are viewed from an interdisciplinary, multidimensional and a multi-country perspective.

This book is divided into three parts. The first part presents a comprehensive, theoretical and empirical framework of corruption with an overview of literature on economic growth and corruption. Part two encompasses the in-depth analysis of several countries, ranging from middle corrupted contexts like Portugal, to highly corrupted countries including Serbia, Russia, Thailand and China—the latter viewed from the perspective of firms from a very low corruption country such as Finland. The final part explores the prevention and control of corruption, looking at the public sector in Thailand and fighting corruption with different strategies.

This volume is of the interest of those who study international economics, development economics or organized crime.

Aurora A.C. Teixeira is Associate Professor at Faculdade de Economia, Universidade do Porto, Portugal.

Carlos Pimenta is Full Professor at Faculdade de Economia, Universidade do Porto, Portugal.

António Maia is Researcher at OBEGEF (Observatório de Economia e Gestão de Fraude), Inspector of Judicial Police, and Lecturer at the Institute of Judicial Police and Criminal Sciences, Portugal.

José António Moreira is Assistant Professor at Faculdade de Economia, Universidade do Porto, Portugal.

Routledge Studies in the Modern World Economy

For a complete list of titles in this series, please visit www.routledge.com.

Corruption, Economic Growth and Globalization

Edited by
Aurora A.C. Teixeira, Carlos Pimenta,
António Maia and José António Moreira

Routledge
Taylor & Francis Group

LONDON AND NEW YORK

First published 2016
by Routledge
2 Park Square, Milton Park, Abingdon, Oxon OX14 4RN

by Routledge
711 Third Avenue, New York, NY 10017

Routledge is an imprint of the Taylor & Francis Group, an informa business

British Library Cataloguing in Publication Data
A catalogue record for this book is available from the British Library

Library of Congress Cataloging in Publication Data
  Corruption, economic growth and globalization /
  edited by Aurora Teixeira, Carlos Pimenta, António Maia and
  José António Moreira.
    pages cm
  1. Corruption. 2. Corruption–Prevention. 3. Economic development.
  4. International cooperation.
  I. Teixeira, Aurora, editor. II. Pimenta, Carlos, editor.
  HV6768.C6756 2015
  364.1'323–dc23   2015010143

ISBN: 978-1-138-02287-4 (hbk)
ISBN: 978-1-315-77682-8 (ebk)

Typeset in Times New Roman
by Sunrise Setting Ltd, Paignton, UK

Printed and bound by CPI Group (UK) Ltd, Croydon, CR0 4YY

Contents

Figures

Tables

Contributors

Joseph Attila, Maître de Conférences, Laboratoire EQUIPPE, Université d'Artois – UFR EGASS, France.

Vanja Bajović, Lecturer at University of Belgrade, Law School, Serbia.

Frederico Cavazzini, Researcher at Instituto Superior de Economia e Gestão (ISEG), Universidade de Lisboa, Portugal.

Fátima de Souza Freire, Professor at Faculdade de Economia, Administração e Contabilidade, Universidade de Brasília – UnB, Brazil.

Andrey Ivanov, Acting Chief Researcher, Centre for PPP Studies, Graduate School of Management, St Petersburg State University, Russia.

Päivi Karkuhnen, Academy Research Fellow, Center for Markets in Transition (CEMAT), Aalto University School of Business, Finland.

Sirilaksana Khoman, Advisor to Commissioner, National Anti-Corruption Commission, Thailand.

Riitta Kosonen, Professor at Aalto University School of Business and Director of the Center for Markets in Transition (CEMAT), Aalto University School of Business, Finland.

António Maia, Researcher at OBEGEF (Observatório de Economia e Gestão de Fraude), Inspector of Judicial Police, and Lecturer at the Institute of Judicial Police and Criminal Sciences, Portugal.

Savo Manojlović, Junior fellow at the Constitutional Court of Serbia.

Rodrigo Fontanelle Miranda, Analyst of Finance and Control at Controladoria Geral da União, Brazil.

Pedro Nevado, Assistant Professor, Instituto Superior de Economia e Gestão (ISEG), Universidade de Lisboa, Portugal.

Gabrielle Poeschl, Associate Professor at Faculty of Psychology and Educational Sciences, Universidade do Porto, Portugal.

Raquel Ribeiro, Researcher at Centro de Estudos Sociais (CES), Universidade de Coimbra and Invited Assistant Professor at Faculdade de Psicologia e de Ciências da Educação, Universidade do Porto, Portugal.

César Silva, Professor at Universidade de Brasília – UnB, Brazil.

Sandra Tavares Silva, Assistant Professor at Faculdade de Economia, Universidade do Porto. Associate Research at CEF.UP (Center in Economics and Finance).

Orapin Sopchokchai, Professor at Far East University, South Korea.

Aurora A.C. Teixeira, Associate Professor at Faculdade de Economia, Universidade do Porto. Associate Research at CEF.UP (Center in Economics and Finance), INESC Tec, and OBEGEF (Observatório de Economia e Gestão de Fraude).

Sirirat Vasuvat, Director, Research Center, Office of the National Anti-Corruption Commission, Thailand.

1 Corruption, economic growth and globalization

An introduction

Aurora A.C. Teixeira

> Corruption is a severe impediment to economic growth, and a significant challenge for developed, emerging and developing countries.
>
> (G20 Seoul Summit 2010)[1]

The attention of society, in general, and policy-makers, in particular, has increasingly focused on public sector corruption—the abuse of public office for personal economic gain (Rose-Ackerman 1978)[2]—as a key determinant of countries' economic performance (Hessami 2014; Oberoi 2014).

A European Commission report revealed that corruption affects all EU countries and costs the bloc's economies around 120 billion euros ($150 billion) a year (EC 2014). Other estimates show that the cost of corruption equals more than 5 percent of global GDP (US$2.6 trillion) with over US$1 trillion paid in bribes each year (OECD 2014).

In a context of economic austerity and increasing social inequalities, citizens are less and less indifferent to corruption (Gómez Fortes *et al.* 2013; Hessami 2014). Protests against corruption, both on the Internet and in street demonstrations, have gathered massive support and followers all over the world (Sloam 2014), especially in countries recently hit by corruption scandals (e.g., Australia, Brazil, Bulgaria, Czech Republic, Greece, Hungary, Italy, Japan, Portugal, Romania, Spain, Slovakia, Thailand, Turkey and Ukraine).[3]

A basic premise is that corruption tends to occur where rents exist and public officials have discretion in allocating them (Mauro 1998b). The essentials about corruption are neatly revealed in Klitgaart's (1988) formula: *corruption = monopoly + discretion − accountability*. For instance, the processes of privatization (of public or state companies) have themselves produced situations whereby some individuals (e.g., ministers, high-ranking political officials) have the *discretion* to make key decisions while others (most notably, managers and other insiders) have information that is not available to outsiders, thus enabling them to use privatization to their benefit in a context deprived of transparency and *accountability*. Such abuses have been particularly significant in the transition economies (Tanzi 1998; Achwan 2014; Duvanova 2014), where chaotic corruption seems to prevail (Mauro 1998b).

As shown in Chapter 2, theory is divided over the effects of corruption on economic growth—the "grease the wheel"/"efficient corruption" argument (Leff 1964; Beenstock 1979) versus the "sanders"/private and public investment misallocation argument (Mauro 1998a) or, more recently, the "gamble" hypothesis (Saastamoinen and Kuosmanen 2014). However, there is a growing consensus based on the empirical literature that corruption is detrimental to economic growth (Bose 2010; Ahmad *et al.* 2012). While the causality underlying this relationship is likely to run both ways, the majority of researchers contend that it is primarily running from corruption to economic growth rather than in the opposite direction (Grochová and Otáhal 2013). Notwithstanding, the two-way relationship has the potential of setting in motion a virtuous circle, where product and productivity gains from curtailing corruption can be invested in human and civic capital necessary to make further progress in reducing corruption, leading to more production and productivity gains (Mehanna *et al.* 2010; Dzhumashev 2014).

The negative impact of corruption on economic performance can occur through a host of key transmission channels, most notably investment, including Foreign Direct Investment (Pellegrini and Gerlagh 2004), competition (Jain 2001b), entrepreneurship (Ugur 2014), government efficiency (Otáhal 2014), and human capital formation (Mauro 1998b). Additionally, corruption affects other important indicators of economic performance such as the quality of the environment (Johnson *et al.* 2011), personal health and safety status (Ahmad *et al.* 2012), equity (income distribution) (Tanzi 1998), and various types of social or civic capital ("trust") (Boycko *et al.* 1996)—which impact significantly on economic welfare and a country's development potential (Aidt 2009).

Corruption undermines public trust in the government, hampering its ability to fulfill its core task of providing acceptable public services and an adequate environment for private sector progress (Bjørnskov 2011). The delegitimization of the state associated with corruption leads to political and economic instability (Khan 2007), resulting in general uncertainty which negatively impacts on the willingness and ability of private business to commit to a long-term development strategy, hindering the countries' sustainable development paths (Saastamoinen and Kuosmanen 2014).

Corruption may be more prevalent in poor, non-democratic or politically unstable countries (Cason and Ramaswamy 2003; Odi 2014). However, given increasing globalization, corruption in less developed countries is likely to affect not only their economic growth but also that of more developed countries through the impact it has on investments from foreign-owned firms in less developed countries (Keig *et al.* 2014). Thus, the issues of corruption and globalization are profoundly interconnected (Asongu 2014), and are characterized by nonlinearities (Lalountas *et al.* 2011), as established in Chapter 3. Indeed, as a result of globalization and the growing awareness among multinational companies of the hazardous impact of corruption on investment, growth and poverty reduction and, therefore, on successfully achieving their goals, the phenomenon of corruption has come to be regarded as an effective barrier to global, regional and local economic development (Tanzi 1998; Javorcik and Wei 2009; Teixeira and Grande 2012; Ugur

2014). Thus, corruption is not only an obstacle to social development but also to economic growth because it drives the private sector out (Tanzi 1998). When it does not, in most cases, it makes investing in a corrupt country more expensive than in a transparent one (Saastamoinen and Kuosmanen 2014). By lowering economic growth, it breeds poverty and inequality over time (Mauro 1998b; Gupta *et al.* 2002; Oberoi 2014). At the same time, poverty itself might foster corruption (see Chapter 9) as poor countries are unable to devote enough resources to setting up and enforcing an adequate legal framework and/or developing an education infrastructure conducive to cultivating better informed and ethically aware individuals (Pitsoe 2013; Justesen and Bjørnskov 2014).

The present volume offers a novel, coherent, and multidisciplinary–multidimensional–multi-country account of corruption, addressing the complex linkages between corruption, economic growth and globalization (see Figure 1.1).

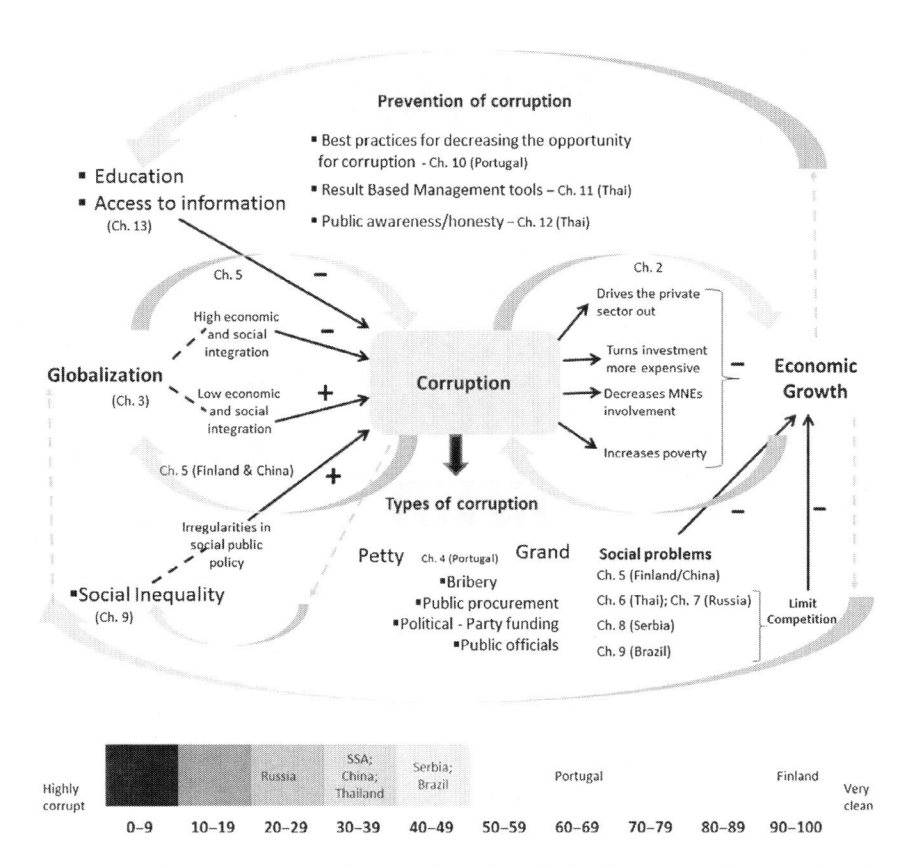

Figure 1.1 Corruption, economic growth and globalization—portraying the book's structure.

Note: The classification of corruption is based on the Corruption Perception Index, 2012–14.

Source: Transparency Index.

The book combines distinct perspectives by analyzing corruption through the lenses of economics, international business, law, criminology, psychology and sociology, highlighting the nonlinearities and two-way causality among these three phenomena (cf. Chapters 2–3), as well as the relevance of taking into account the types of corruption (cf. Chapters 4–9) when assessing its impact on the economic performance of countries. It provides in-depth, empirical insights into quite disparate contexts in terms of perceived corruption, including very high (Russia, sub-Saharan African countries, China, Thailand), middle-high (Serbia, Brazil), middle (Portugal), and very low (Finland) corruption contexts. Finally, it addresses the topic of corruption prevention based on the evidence and experiences of some countries that have been facing noticeable corruption problems for a long time (Tanzi 1998): Portugal (Chapter 10), Thailand (Chapters 11 and 12) or sub-Saharan African (SSA) countries (Chapter 13).

In terms of structure, the book is divided into three parts. Part one provides a theoretical and empirical account of the linkages between corruption, economic growth and globalization. Part two, focusing on distinct mechanisms, presents evidence on how different types of corruption (grand versus petty) are likely to impact on the economic performance of countries. Part three describes the measures and policies deployed in some countries to prevent and control corruption setting the path for sustainable growth strategies.

Within part one, Chapter 2 provides a theoretical overview on the "tribes" of (the economics of) corruption and (endogenous) economic growth based on Hoover's (1991) "Tribe and Nation" perspective. Aurora Teixeira and Sandra Silva then complement this theoretical account with a bibliometric exercise which details the main contributions from research in these fields, and assesses the possible emergence of an intersecting research pattern between both "tribes." In Chapter 3, Joseph Attila thoroughly scrutinizes the nonlinearity between globalization and corruption, demonstrating that the relationship between corruption and globalization might not be as simple as suggested in the current literature. Applying econometric tools to a sample of 122 countries from 1990 to 2006, Attila shows that globalization did not benefit most sub-Saharan African countries because their participation in the internationalization process has not been sufficiently high. He further stipulates that countries need to achieve a minimum level of economic and social integration before they can take advantage of the reducing effect of globalization on corruption and, ultimately, on sustainable economic development.

The effect of corruption on growth tends to vary among countries and the type of corruption (Ugur 2014). Little evidence exists, however, on which types of corruption are more deleterious and should be tackled first (Shah and Schacter 2004; Winters *et al.* 2012). Country-specific studies and anecdotal evidence suggest that high-level and low-level corruption tend to coexist and reinforce each other (Mauro 1998a; Mashali 2012). One of the most well-known and widely used taxonomies of corruption is the one that distinguishes between bureaucratic or "petty" corruption and political or "grand" corruption (Mauro 1998b; Jain 2001b; Nystrand 2014). Specifically, bureaucratic corruption includes "corrupt acts of the appointed bureaucrats in their dealings with either their superiors (the political elite) or with the public" (Jain 2001b: 75). Petty corruption is the most common form of bureaucratic corruption often involving the payment of a bribe to bureaucrats by the public either to receive a service to which they are eligible or to speed up a bureaucratic procedure; it usually involves smaller sums of money (than grand corruption) and typically more junior officials. Political or grand corruption is generally considered the corrupt acts of high-ranking officials or "the political elite by which they exploit their power to make economic policies" (Jain 2001b: 73), usually involving substantial amounts of money.[4]

Corruption as "the way things are" or petty corruption is, in general, less condemned by citizens than grand corruption (Nystrand 2014). Indeed, the former is often seen as a system of which everyone is part and therefore people do not judge each other's involvement in this type of corruption, while grand corruption benefits a few by considerable amounts of money, which greatly distresses people. This also seems to be the case in Portugal. Gabrielle Poeschl and Raquel Ribeiro (Chapter 4) analyzed the responses of 182 Portuguese individuals and found that people are not fully aware of the social costs of corruption (both petty and grand). In general, Portuguese citizens tend to disapprove of corrupt practices, especially involving grand corruption, "and reluctantly accept lenient verdicts in the cases of grand corruption," but fail to demonstrate a "shared social responsibility" able to overcome such alarming and growth inhibiting phenomena.

Mauro (1998b) further distinguishes well-organized/predictable corruption from chaotic corruption. He claims that the latter may be the most deleterious in terms of private investment and entrepreneurship and, ultimately, for the economic growth of countries. This is justified on the basis that under a well-organized/predictable system of corruption, "entrepreneurs know whom they need to bribe and how much to offer them, and are confident that they will obtain the necessary permits for their firms;" moreover, "a corrupt bureaucrat will take a clearly defined share of a firm's profits, which gives him an interest in the success of the firm" (Mauro 1998b: 13).

The characteristic of the predictability of corruption in China explains, according to Päivi Karkuhnen and Riitta Kosonen (Chapter 5), why corruption does not have a stronger negative impact on (foreign) investment in this country. These authors, adopting the neo-institutional organization theory, identify the strategic responses that Finnish firms (originating from a country recurrently ranked among the world's least corrupt) take in their Chinese subunits to cope with corruption as a feature of the local institutional environment. Based on 60 interviews with the management of Chinese subsidiaries of Finnish firms, collected between 2003 and 2011, they discovered that although "corruption is recognized as a common feature of Chinese society and economy, its influence on foreign firms is not as significant as could be expected." Additionally, it is recognized that "few firms can afford to completely ignore the external pressures from the corrupted institutional environment." However, instead of engaging in corrupt practices, foreign firms "substitute corruption with reliance on personal networks." Thus, "good personal relations with high-level public sector officials can be used to shortcut the bureaucracy as an alternative to speed-up payments." An important strategy by Finnish firms investing in China to circumvent corruption is to delegate the interactions with potentially corrupt Chinese stakeholders to the local staff. Such a strategy "helps Finnish firms and their potential expatriate management in China to simultaneously conform to the home country's anti-corruption institutional pressures and the external pressures from the host environment to do business 'in the local way.'"

Networks and, more precisely, interpersonal relationships for social, business, and other activities are also key to understanding corrupt activity in Thailand, as Sirilaksana Khoman (Chapter 6) insightfully establishes. Resorting to cases studies to determine the pattern of patron–client networks that affect procurement, the author shows that the network relationship in Thai public procurement constitutes "fertile ground" for both petty and grand corruption. It is important to underline that procurement spending, that is, the purchase of goods and services on the part of the government, has traditionally lent itself to frequent acts of high-level corruption (Tanzi 1998). Such acts escalate government expenditures and distort allocation of government expenditure away from education, health and maintenance infrastructure (Ahmad *et al.* 2012), which is likely to severely undermine the growth prospects of countries.

Andrey Ivanov (Chapter 7) also deals with public procurement corruption, in this case, in Russia. With the expectation of fostering suppliers' involvement in "the procurement process, to reduce corruption, and to hinder the possibility of collusion by suppliers, which would subsequently lead to improved competition in auctions and to larger price reductions," Russian government changed from outcry auctions to e-auctions in public procurement. Such expectations, however, were not fully met, as Ivanov demonstrates. According to the author, the strong decline in competition at auctions and the significant number of failed auctions could be explained by dishonest actions by public buyers restricting competition in favor of a pre-selected "favorite," conveying a "quasi-corrupt" behavior by the contracting authority. In his modified version of the principal–agent model, Ivanov postulates that "competition may be limited by both the mala fide and bona fide public buyers. The first seeks to obtain bribes, the second tries to achieve other goals." Considering that "competition . . . can be expected to fuel increases in productivity, employment, international competitiveness, innovation, overall economic growth and average living standards" (Crampton 2003: 24), such competition and efficiency distorting measures experienced in Russia create an enormous impediment to economic growth and development.

As wittily recognized by Susan Rose-Ackerman (1997a: 40), "[d]emocracy is not necessarily a cure for corruption." In the transition countries, namely those from Europe, the shift from command economies to free market economies has created massive opportunities for the appropriation of rents (Mauro 1998b; Boerner and Hainz 2009). In many of these countries, some proceeds from corruption go to finance the activities of political parties (Tanzi 1998; Achwan 2014). Departing from the general belief that the political system in Serbia fosters political corruption, Vanja Bajović and Savo Manojlović (Chapter 8) examine the connection between political party funding and corruption. The authors show that although some progress has occurred with the creation (mostly as a result of international pressure) of the 2011 law on financing political activities—which provided more effective control mechanisms and a more appropriate combination of public and private funding, prohibited political party participation in for-profit, commercial activities, and certain prima facie suspicious donations, and granted the Anti-Corruption Agency more powers, providing for its financial independence—many critical problems persist. In particular, the politicization of the judicial system, as well as the partisanization of public companies, institutions and state-owned enterprises, have contributed to continuous, unnecessary administrative obstacles and discretionary decision-making, which has hampered Serbia's sustainable economic growth. The authors conclude that legal efforts, albeit important, are not sufficient; there is instead a need for "the combined efforts of legislative, institutional and social mechanisms, otherwise, even the best law is only a decoration without real impact."

Institutional and social mechanisms lie at the heart of the novel analysis conducted in Chapter 9. Rodrigo Miranda, César Silva and Fátima de Souza Freire examine a flagship social welfare program by the Brazilian government, the *Bolsa Família Program* (BFP) or Family Allowance Program. This program was considered by *The Economist* (2008) as an "anti-poverty scheme invented in Latin America [which] is winning converts worldwide." According to the United Nations (United Nations 2011), Brazil's *Bolsa Família* conditional cash transfer scheme is the biggest social transfer scheme in the world, covering (data from 2011) 26 percent of the population, 50 million people, and has contributed by one-third to the decline in income inequality over the past decade. Departing from the premise that corruption is the main cause of poverty as well as a barrier to its eradication, Miranda, Silva and Freire address the relationship between the social indicators of 717 Brazilian municipalities and the number of irregularities found in each of them in the management of the BFP. Although the authors are cognizant that "not all irregularities found should be deemed as corruption ... irregularities indicate lack of control over municipal resources, and it is this negligence or inefficiency in management that cloaks corruption, hinders accountability and facilitates the actions of corrupt officials."

Given the intricate relationship that corruption maintains with other relevant dimensions of a society, "[undermining] good governance and the rule of law, ... negatively impact[ing] service quality and efficiency, and pos[ing] threats to principles of democracy, justice and the economy" (Graycar and Sidebottom 2012: 384), preventing and controlling corruption, although a challenging task, constitutes an imperative. The final part of the book is devoted to these issues, examining the viewpoints of practitioners (Chapters 10 and 12) and researchers (Chapters 11 and 13).

António Maia (Chapter 10) considers "opportunity" as an important dimension in understanding the phenomenon of corruption in the public sector and therefore useful to establish preventive strategies in this area. Based on the content analysis of 60 judicial sentences for corruption over an eight-year period (2003–10), complemented by interviews with qualified informants (judicial decision-makers and directors of auditing departments of public administration services), the author examines the importance of the opportunity factor to explain corruption and fraud in Portuguese public services. He found that corrupt public servants tend to act in isolation, lack supervision and come from all hierarchical levels. Maia concludes that the Portuguese public administration's control mechanisms over administrative action are not as effective as they should expectedly be. Thus, he recommends the development of strategies to create codes of conduct in each public service. Such documents "should include the values of the public service and ... lead to the creation and dissemination, within the organization, of best practices manuals for all positions and for all administrative procedures."

Prevention of public sector corruption is also the focus of Chapter 11. Orapin Sopchokchai discusses and examines the Thai public sector reform, addressing particularly how strategic planning and results-based management has been introduced and implemented in Thai public organizations. Notwithstanding the convergence of several key factors that enabled the implementation of strategic and results-based management in the Thai public sector—sufficient technical knowhow; committed political leaders; regular disclosure of procurement information; development of training programs to educate public officers; setting internal auditing systems to monitor performance; political, civil society and private sector support—some critical obstacles remain, preventing the Thai economy from reaping the fruits of such efforts in terms of increased development. Among these obstacles stand some systemic opportunities for corruption (in line with Graycar and Sidebottom (2012), see Figure 1.2): the lack of a culture of integrity and that patronage and nepotism are widely accepted ("weakness of civil society and lack of civic participation in monitoring and evaluation, and in accessing the necessary information"); complexity of regulations/complexity of systems and weak legal regimes ("public organizations and public managers operate under complex and difficult contexts such as policy ambiguity, political uncertainty and intervention, media scrutiny, lateral coordination, and citizen and stakeholder demands"); and weak institutions of governance ("resistance to change and negative mentality among those who must implement the system").

Education and information dissemination are the "weapons" selected by the authors of Chapters 12 and 13 to control and fight corruption, respectively, in Thailand and sub Saharan African (SSA) economies. Sirirat Vasuvat (Chapter 12) encourages governments to invest in the education of young people which is likely to be the basis to "build up attitudes, values, morals and ethics concerning integrity" that, in the long run, "successfully eradicate corruption." Establishing the background of corruption in Thailand, and the current problems relating to corruption in the criminal justice system and their solutions at the investigation, prosecution and trial levels, Vasuvat proposes solutions for these problems and general measures to prevent corruption. Among these, and again resorting to Graycar and Sidebottom's (2012) opportunities taxonomy, we might find measures to overcome some systemic and localized opportunities for corruption. Regarding the former (systemic opportunities), we can mention measures to overcome the

Corruption prevention and control

Understanding and overcoming opportunities for corruption

Systemic opportunities	Localised opportunities
Lack of integrity among leaders (in both the public and private sectors) **(Ch. 12)**	Supervision and oversight is not taken seriously **(Ch. 10)**
Lack of culture of integrity **(Ch. 10) (Ch. 11) (Ch. 12)**	Specialised knowledge/high discretion **(Ch. 10)**
Ethical codes do not exist, or are not enforced **(Ch. 10)**	Activity remote from supervision **(Ch. 10)**
Patronage and nepotism are accepted **(Ch. 11) (Ch. 12)**	No capable guardian **(Ch. 10)**
Complexity of regulations/complexity of systems **(Ch. 11)**	Low decision monitoring **(Ch. 10)**
Weak legal regimes **(Ch. 11) (Ch 12)**	Silencing of whistleblowers **(Ch. 12)**
Weak financial controls **(Ch. 10)**	Low risk of being caught **(Ch. 10)**
Weak institutions of governance **(Ch. 11) (Ch. 12)**	

Figure 1.2 Corruption prevention and control—overcoming systemic and localized opportunities.

Source: Adapted from Graycar and Sidebottom (2012).

lack of integrity among leaders ("review and rationalize legislation and administration to enable them to deal with the change in their environment that leads to increasing demands and expectations from the private and public sectors"), the lack of culture of integrity ("educate the people to understand the detrimental effect of corruption," "instill citizens with awareness of sound values and self-esteem," "implement strong social sanctions against corruption"), acceptance of patronage and nepotism ("create social mechanisms that will make corruption a very difficult and risky business"), weak legal regimes ("to improve the system of oversight that unwaveringly enforces the regulations and laws"), and the weak institutions of governance ("install good governance by reforming the bureaucracy for transparency, efficiency, and accountability"). The measures addressing localized opportunities, much lower in number, include "to establish rewards and protection for witnesses" and "to stimulate the public to be the clean alliance and have the confidence to cooperate in reporting information and giving evidence," avoiding therefore the silencing of whistle-blowers.

Highlighting that "corruption is not only an obstacle to social development but also to economic growth," Pedro Nevado and Frederico Cavazzini (Chapter 13) present a framework to understand and fight corruption in which the level of education combined with access to information play a pivotal role in sustaining the ability to claim political and social accountability. Based on a sample of 45 SSA countries, the authors show that education and freedom of expression have significant effects on the countries' perceptions of corruption. The underlying explanation is simple: "education and information strengthen personal integrity and empower individuals to make effective use of accountability and good governance mechanisms;" additionally, "the control of corruption enables more effective resource allocation" fostering economic growth and development. This requires, in the authors' own words, "fighting corruption with strategy."

Notes

1 In www.oecd.org/daf/anti-bribery/G20_Anti-Corruption_Action_Plan.pdf (accessed April 15, 2015).

2 Corruption includes acts of bribery, embezzlement, nepotism or state capture, and it is often associated with and reinforced by other illegal practices, such as bid rigging, fraud or money laundering (OECD 2014). However, it is important to note that illegal acts such as fraud, money laundering, drug trafficking, and black market operations do not constitute corruption in and of themselves because they do not involve the use of public power (Jain 2001b).

3 For brief accounts of these scandals, see: Australia https://wikileaks.org/aus-suppression-order/press.html; Brazil www.npr.org/2014/11/20/365516363/corruption-scandal-engulfs-brazils-state-oil-company; Greece www.dw.de/greek-bankers-embroiled-in-corruption-scandal/a-17387888; Italy www.reuters.com/article/2014/05/23/us-italy-corruption-idUSBREA4M0DC20140523; Japan http://globalvoicesonline.org/2014/10/27/japans-cabinet-members-are-falling-like-dominoes-to-corruption-scandals/; Philippines www.businessinsider.com/philippines-corruption-scandal-2014-6#ixzz3O2fYXBYe; Portugal http://article.wn.com/view/2014/11/30/Corruption_scandals_fuel_public_anger_at_politicians_in_aust_z/; Spain www.theguardian.com/world/2014/oct/27/spanish-authorities-arrest-51-anti-corruption-swee; Thailand http://thediplomat.com/2014/10/thai-junta-beset-by-corruption-scandals/; and Bulgaria, Czech Republic, Hungary, Romania, Slovakia, Turkey, Ukraine http://blog.transparency.org/2014/12/03/europe-central-asia-and-the-state-of-corruption-in-2014-the-gold-standard/ (all accessed April 15, 2015).

4 As mentioned earlier, corruption, in its varied forms, might include bribery, extortion, misappropriation, self-dealing, patronage, abuse of discretion, creating or exploiting conflicts of interest, nepotism, clientelism and favoritism, etc. (see also Graycar and Sidebottom 2012).

Part I

Corruption, economic growth and globalization

The linkages

2 Economic growth and the economics of corruption

A merge between tribes?

Aurora A.C. Teixeira and
Sandra Tavares Silva

2.1 Introduction

The attention of society, in general, and policymakers, in particular, has increasingly focused on public sector corruption—the abuse of public office for personal economic gain (Rose-Ackerman 1978)[1]—as a key determinant of the economic performance of countries (Hessami 2014; Oberoi 2014).

In a poll conducted in September 2010 for BBC World Service by GlobeScan, over 13,000 individuals from 26 countries were interviewed and out of 14 possible global problems, corruption stood as the most talked-about problem and was considered one of the most serious problems, particularly in countries from Africa, Latin America and the Asia-Pacific regions.[2] In North America, corruption is a major issue for US citizens whereas in Europe and Asia-Pacific, corruption is considered a particularly acute problem in Russia, China and the Philippines.

The research on the causes and consequences of corruption has greatly benefited from the theoretical contributions done in the 1970s by Anne Krueger (1974) and Susan Rose-Ackerman (1975, 1978), or Jagdish Bhagwati (1982). In particular, after Rose-Ackerman's seminal (1978) book, *Corruption: A Study in Political Economy* (with about 2,000 citations in Google Scholar), corruption became a central research topic in economics during the 1980s.

Given that corruption affects the entire economy, it has become a prominent issue within economic growth literature (Ugur 2014). The intersection of corruption with economic growth has been systematically investigated since the mid-1990s, particularly with Mauro's (1995, 1998a) influential empirical studies. Within this stream of research, several authors have argued that a necessary condition for promoting sustainable economic growth is the pre-existence of a stable political system, able to control corruption (e.g., Tebaldi and Mohan 2010). Most commonly, the relevant literature points out the need to reduce/eliminate corruption, sustaining there is a negative vicious circle between corruption and growth and development (e.g., Aidt *et al.* 2008; Gundlach and Paldam 2009).

One might argue that (endogenous) economic growth and (the economics of) corruption "tribes" have been gradually converging. Seeking to go beyond a mere review of the relevant literature on this research area—corruption and economic growth—we offer, in the present chapter, what may comprise a portrayal of such wide-ranging and somewhat disperse theoretical reasoning.

Since (the economics of) corruption covers a large array of research areas, such as economic growth, industrial organization, game theory, organization theory, financial markets, and the interactions between economics, law, culture and psychology (Jancsics 2014), our analysis aims to achieve a clearer definition of the economics of corruption and economic growth.

To attain our goal, it is important to adopt an appraisal criterion of the history and methodology of science. We resort to Hoover's (1991) "Tribe and Nation" perspective, which we contend will bring more consistency into the discussion of a possible combination between the literature on endogenous growth theory and the contributions from the economics of corruption. The use of this criterion serves to deal with important questions about the nature and growth of economic knowledge (Backhouse 1998). Then, a bibliometric exercise is presented to help us to describe and analyze the structure and process of science involved in our discussion, by providing an independent corroboration of the tribes and family trees. Before detailing the corruption and economic growth tribes, the next section sets the context for the present chapter by examining the theoretical debate on the impact of corruption on economic growth.

2.2 Corruption and economic growth: the "sand the wheels," the "grease the wheels," and the "gamble" hypotheses

The debate on the impact of corruption on economic growth encompasses two contrasting viewpoints. On the one hand, there is the "sand/grit on the wheels" argument (Mauro 1995, 1998a; Tanzi 1998; Mo 2001; Ugur 2014), according to which corruption would be expected to reduce economic growth by lowering incentives to invest, lowering the quality of public infrastructure and services, decreasing tax revenue, causing talented people to engage in rent-seeking rather than productive activities, and distorting the composition of government expenditure (Wei 1999). In a longer run perspective, Tanzi (1998) stresses the cost-increasing nature of corruption which tends to reduce public revenue and increase public spending, contributing to larger fiscal deficits, making it more difficult for the government to run a sound fiscal policy. Additionally, corruption is likely to increase income inequality, because it allows well-positioned individuals to take advantage of government activities at the cost of the rest of the population, and is likely to increase poverty because it reduces the income earning potential of the poor. Corruption might be particularly damaging for the entrepreneurship potential of a country (and thus its economic growth) as it is often coercive for small firms. Pressures on new firms often come from local government officials, who impose high pecuniary costs for licenses and authorizations. Since small firms are the engine of growth in most countries (Mayer-Haug *et al.* 2013), obstacles to their creation and growth cause economies to deteriorate, especially in developing countries and increasingly in economies in transition (Zhuplev and Shtykhno 2009).

On the other hand, it has been suggested that corruption might be efficiency-enhancing because it removes government-imposed rigidities that hinder investment and interfere with other economic decisions favorable to growth (Leff 1964; Huntington 1968), thus "greasing the wheels" of growth. As Leff (1964: 11) posits: "[i]f the government has erred in its decision, the course made possible by corruption may well be the better one." In the same line of reasoning, corruption can be efficient because it saves time for those (e.g., the entrepreneurs) for whom time has the greatest value (Lui 1985) or may "grease the wheels" in rigid public administrations (Beenstock 1979). As Huntington (1968: 386) notes: "[i]n terms of economic growth, the only thing worse than a society with a rigid, over-centralized, dishonest bureaucracy is one with a rigid, over-centralized, honest bureaucracy." Corruption can also constitute useful political glue by allowing politicians to get funds that can be used to hold a country together, which is a necessary condition for growth (Graziano 1980). A final pro-corruption argument sustains that bribes can supplement low wages, allowing the government to maintain a lower tax burden, which can favor growth (Tullock 1996; Becker and Stigler 1974).

More recently, Saastamoinen and Kuosmanen (2014: 2834) established that corruption "is not simply grease or grit on the wheels, but perhaps more importantly . . . a risk factor for economic performance (productivity) in the development process." They refer to the proposed risk interpretation as the "gamble hypothesis" of corruption. According to this probabilistic hypothesis, corruption increases the variance of productivity and can hence be seen as a source of macro risk. The empirical work performed by the authors, based on a sample of 80 countries in two distinct periods of time (1990 and 2010), suggests that at the higher corruption levels, there are large variations in how corruption affects the productivity of countries, corroborating their "gamble" hypothesis. Notwithstanding, they also find some support for the "grit-on-the wheels" hypothesis, particularly in the latest cross-section from the year 2010, and failed to encounter evidence to support the idea that corruption is directly beneficial to economic performance—in other words, their evidence refutes the grease hypothesis.

Most of the empirical evidence is consistent with the theories that hold corruption to be purely detrimental (Ahmad *et al.* 2012). Indeed, cross-country literature summarized in Campos *et al.*'s (2010) meta-analysis finds no evidence in favor of the greasing the wheels hypothesis. Mauro (1998b), for example, investigates the impact of corruption on economic growth for separate samples of high and low red tape countries. His results show no evidence in favor of a beneficial effect of corruption. Méon and Sekkat (2005) find some evidence that corruption even sands the wheels of the system (instead of greasing them). Specifically, these latter authors show that the negative impact of corruption on economic growth becomes worse when indicators of the quality of governance deteriorate. More recently, Ugur (2014: 472) established that "[c]orruption is a symptom of weak institutional quality [with] adverse effects on economic growth." His meta-analysis exercise shows that the adverse effects of corruption are more pronounced when data refer only to low-income countries and when the original primary-study estimates relate to longer- rather than shorter-term effects.

2.3   The tribes of "economics of corruption" and "economic growth"

2.3.1   An appraisal criterion of the history and methodology of science: Hoover's "Tribe and Nation" perspective

Hoover (1991), based on Kuhn (1970), offers the so-called "Tribe and Nation" perspective, an alternative framework to the Lakatosian Methodology of Scientific Research Programmes, the criterion that dominated the debate on economic methodology until the late 1980s (Silva 2009). We draw on Hoover's approach to examine both the economics of corruption and the endogenous economic growth theory. The choice of this appraisal method was more importantly associated with the analysis of the economics of corruption, which we consider less able to be captured by the Lakatosian perspective of a research core. In fact, in the presence of relatively diffuse patterns of research (Jancsics 2014), the adoption of an appraisal methodology such as the one proposed by Hoover is more encompassing (Silva 2009). As Hoover (1991) stresses, the higher flexibility of this proposal derives from it being used as a language or a train of thought, useful to identify some patterns in certain theories, and not as a formal methodology.

The method proposed by Hoover and followed in the present chapter offers an anthropological metaphor, the "family tree." This metaphor depicts "science as a collection of tribes," with "[m]odels and theories united by ties of kinship and consanguinity" (Hoover 1991: 375). Hoover underlines the two main meanings associated to the term "paradigm" that Kuhn identifies as:

> the entire constellation of beliefs, values, techniques, and so on shared by the members of a given community . . . [or] one sort of element in that constellation, the concrete puzzle-solutions which, employed as models or examples, can replace explicit rules as a basis for the solution of the remaining puzzles of normal science.
>
> (Kuhn 1970: 175)

Resorting to the second sense of the term "paradigm," Hoover adopts a portrayal of scientific practice as specific models serving as concrete "*exemplars.*" From here, he considers that some models may appear only as elaborations or variations of the exemplars, others may borrow crucial assumptions or techniques, even if different in purpose, and some may import only the "spirit" of the exemplar. Hence, scientific practice is conceived as groups of correlated and, in some measure, overlapping models and practices (Hoover 1991).

Using what Hoover calls an anthropological metaphor, we consider scientific endeavor as a "family tree" of corruption/economic growth, represented in Figures 2.1 and 2.2, respectively. The entries correspond to studies (articles, reports or books) considered important in the development of that field. It is important to bear in mind that the goal here is not to draw up an exhaustive

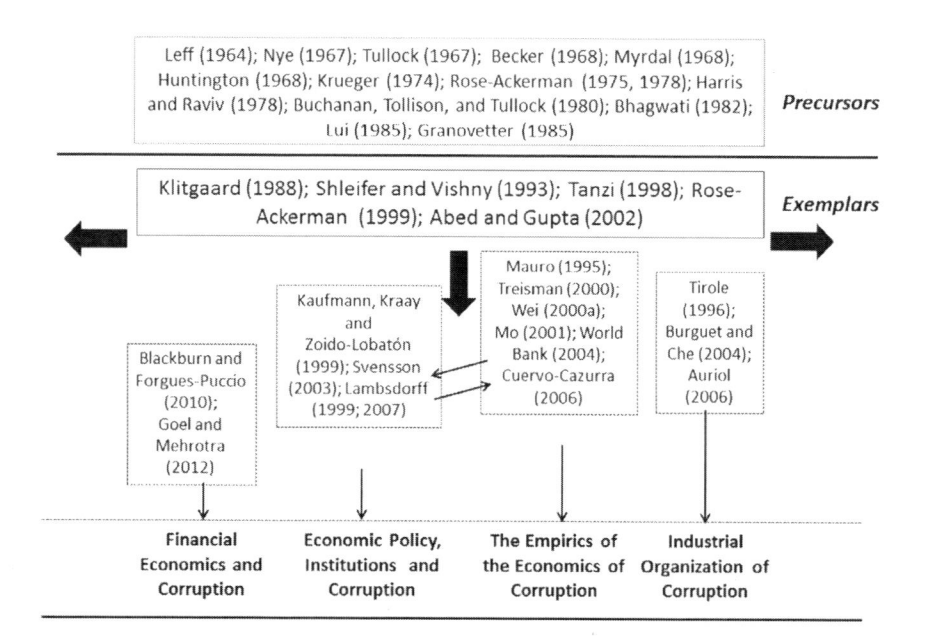

Figure 2.1 The economics of corruption tribe.

list of the literature but to use the studies as *exemplars* of the most important lines of research within the given area. The arrows provide some information about the direction of influence without reproducing the complete interrelationships between the exemplars studied. The bottom row of cells of each column shows the families of current, active research within the tribe. In the economics of corruption we have: Financial Economics and Corruption; Economic Policy, Institutions and Corruption; the Empirics of Corruption; and Industrial Organization and Corruption. In the endogenous growth theory, the families of current, active research include: Endogenous Technological Change; Growth and International Trade; Political Economy of Growth—Institutions, Human Capital, Inequality; Economic Development and Growth; and the Unified Growth Theory.

Note that the *exemplars* selected to define the *family tree* may not be the most cited studies within each family. The crucial aspect here is that they are recognized by the elements of the tribe as crucial engines for the development of a certain type of scientific approach. Other subsequent contributions may be more relevant in terms of citations.

In short, and as mentioned above, using Hoover's anthropological metaphor and following Silva (2009), we represent the scientific ventures of both the economics of corruption and the endogenous economic growth as family trees. Hence, based on Hoover's appraisal method, we define taxonomies for each research field, conducting an in-depth analysis of the related literature. The sources used to identify the main contributions in the literature are critical scientific books and articles on both the economics of corruption (e.g., Ades and Tella 1997; Abed and Gupta 2002; Jain 2001b; Aidt 2003; World Bank 2004; Jancsics 2014; Ugur 2014) and endogenous economic growth (e.g., Barro and Sala-i-Martin 2004; Acemoglu 2008; Galor 2011).

2.3.2   *The economics of corruption tribe*

Until the 1980s, scientific research on corruption was mainly restricted to the fields of sociology, political science, history, public administration, and criminal law (Abed and Gupta 2002). One of the first studies that received wide attention within economics (but not only) was Rose-Ackerman's (1975) article, "The economics of corruption" (in the *Journal of Public Economics*). Notwithstanding, other influential *"precursors"* have contributed in distinct areas of economics, most notably the economics of crime (Becker 1968; Becker and Stigler 1974), agency theory (Harris and Raviv 1978), rent-seeking (Tullock 1967; Buchanan *et al.* 1980), development economics (Myrdal 1968), and economic sociology (Granovetter 1985).

The *"precursors"* of the economics of corruption tribe tended to focus on weaknesses in public institutions and distortions in economic policies that gave rise to rent-seeking by public officials and the nurturing of corrupt practices (Rose-Ackerman 1975, 1978; Buchanan *et al.* 1980; Bhagwati 1982). In the vast majority of these studies, corruption is considered to be a behavioral phenomenon occurring between the state and the market domains. In such studies, ethical attitudes matter and the "temptation threshold" (Brytting *et al.* 2011) is subject to the individual's moral foundation. They nevertheless stress, in the line with Becker's (1968) argumentation, that people respond to incentives and, thus, changes in corrupt activities occur if the marginal returns from crime exceed the marginal returns from legal occupation by more than the expected value of the penalty. But, as the sociological concept of "embeddeness" by Granovetter (1985) magnificently exposes, in corruption the issue of individuals' incentive is just a part of an immense and much more complex narrative. The social status and kinship responsibilities and linkages are key precursors to corruption (Roman and Miller 2014). Granovetter (1985) uncovered the importance of networks and relationships for social and economic action, which are critical for a proper understanding of these issues, intimately associated with corrupt acts, such as social norms and values, as well as trust and reciprocity. As Hodgson and Jiang (2007: 1057) put it, "[c]orruption reduces levels of trust in dealing with both business and the state. . . . [it] encourages the reliance upon ethnic, religious, family and other ties, where contract enforcement relies on sanctions and reputational effects within a defined group . . . . Business life becomes fractured into clans or illegal mafias, with the loss of the benefits of wider cooperation an competition."

Regarding the impact of corruption, two opposing approaches co-existed: efficiency-enhancing ("grease the wheels") and efficiency-reducing ("sand the wheels") approaches. Earlier advocates (*"precursors"*) of the efficiency-enhancing approach, most notably, Leff (1964), Huntington (1968), or Nye (1967), argue that corruption expedites business and commerce and facilitates economic growth and investment. Another efficiency argument in favor of corruption is to look upon it as "speed money," which reduces delay in moving files in administrative offices and in getting ahead in slow-moving queues for public services (Bardhan 1997). Lui (1985), using an equilibrium queuing model, derives bribing functions where the size of the bribe is linked to the opportunity costs of time for the individual client. He shows that the bribing strategies will form a Nash equilibrium of this non-cooperative game that will minimize the waiting costs associated with the queue, thereby reducing the inefficiency in public administration. Thus, corruption would increase efficiency in an economy.

"Precursors" of the efficiency-reducing approach, such as Krueger (1974) and Myrdal (1968), claim that corruption grits the wheels of business and commerce. Consequently, it hampers economic growth and distorts the allocation of resources, causing a damaging impact on efficiency. Later, some influential authors/studies, like Shleifer and Vishny (1993), Tanzi and Davoodi (1997), and Mauro (1995), supported this line of argumentation.

By the end of the 1980s and in the 1990s, there was a clear blast of academic writing on the economics of corruption. The most fundamental pieces of research on the topic (the *"exemplars"*) were written in this period. They were intimately associated with the increasing awareness of the costs of corruption in both developed as well as developing countries (Shleifer and Vishny 1993; Rose-Ackerman 1999), the transformation of the transition economies (namely after the dismantlement of the Soviet Union) (Abed and Gupta 2002), the accelerating trend of globalization and world economic integration, which increased the pressure on countries to be more transparent and accountable in the management of their economies (Rose-Ackerman 1997b).

Among such influential contributions stand those of Klitgaard and Tanzi. Klitgaard (1998) established that corruption emerges when an organization or a public official has monopoly power over a good or service that generates rent, has the discretionary power to decide who will receive it, and is not accountable. In a connected perspective, Tanzi (1998) recognized that the roots of corruption are deeply grounded in the social and cultural history, political and economic development, bureaucratic traditions and policies of a country, and identified corruption's *direct* (regulations and authorizations, taxation, spending decisions, provision of goods and services at below market prices, and financing political parties) and *indirect* (quality of bureaucracy, level of public sector wages, penalty systems, institutional controls, and transparency of rules, laws, and processes) factors.

As in Hoover (1991), the proposed appraisal exercise must go through a diachronic analysis that can highlight the common origins of the current lines of research within the tribe—Financial Economics and Corruption; Economic Policy, Institutions and Corruption; the Empirics of Corruption; and Industrial Organization and Corruption. Such origins are multidisciplinary, ranging from the economics of crime to political science, development economics and sociology. The *exemplars*—Klitgaard (1998); Shleifer and Vishny (1993); Tanzi (1998); Rose-Ackerman (1999); Abed and Gupta (2002)—performed a defining role in the consolidation of the tribe: they highlighted the economic, political and social costs of corruption (grand and petty/political and bureaucratic) for economic growth and development. They further emphasized the need to fight corruption and recognize that corruption is an institutional phenomenon, affecting both private and public spheres.

On the other hand, a synchronic analysis can identify competition between some families encompassing micro-level (Financial Economics and Corruption) and industry-level (Industrial Organization of Corruption) perspectives where corruption is viewed as resulting from rational decisions of individual actors, and macro and relational perspectives (Economic Policy, Institutions and Corruption) that focus on social norms and the structural arrangements that facilitate corruption, and examine social interactions and networks among corrupt actors. Recognizing the interdisciplinary and multifaceted nature of corruption, the studies within the family of "Empirics of the Economics of Corruption," most notably, those by Mauro (1995) and Treisman (2000), understand that corruption is associated with particular historical and cultural traditions, levels of economic development, political institutions, and government policies. Mo (2001) explicitly frames corruption within an economic growth framework and explores the investment, human capital and political instability mechanisms to assess the impact of corruption on economic growth. The institutional setting and quality is also the focus of Wei (2000b) and Cuervo-Cazurra (2006), who analyze the impact of corruption on Foreign Direct Investment. Another type of empirical studies based on case study analysis and intimately influenced by Klitgaard's contributions is the account of the anti-corruption activities of leading international organizations such as the World Bank or the IMF. It is important to highlight that the connection between the "The Empirics of the Economics of Corruption" and "Economic Policy, Institutions and Corruption" is even more apparent given that a vast majority of the empirical studies have benefited from the methodological developments regarding data gathering and harmonization undertaken by the Transparency International, which created the Corruption Perception Index (Lambsdorff 1999) and the World Bank, which produced the Aggregating Governance Indicators (Kaufmann *et al.* 1999). Such an active line of research shares the emphasis attributed by Svensson (2003) and Lambsdorff (2007) to the role of policies, regulations and institutions in general for explaining acts of corruption and their diverse impacts.

The studies by Blackburn and Forgues-Puccio (2010) and Goel and Mehrotra (2012) related to the "Financial Economics and Corruption" family, and Tirole's (1996), Burguet and Che's (2004) and Auriol's (2006) contributions within the "Industrial Organization of Corruption" family, stand as competitive "families" to the "Economic Policy, Institutions and Corruption" (and to some extent, the "The Empirics of the Economics of Corruption") family, being more akin to the mainstream neoclassical paradigm associated with competitive, rational agents and general equilibrium models frameworks.

2.3.3 The endogenous economic growth theory tribe

Endogenous economic growth theories flourished since the mid-1980s, being highly focused on formalizing understandings about technological change and economic growth (Nelson 1998). Strongly inspired by Solow (1956, 1957) and the subsequent scientific inquiries on growth, in general, and growth accounting, in particular, these formalized theories were crucial for the appearance and consolidation of modern economic growth (e.g., Blaug 2000). The appraisal of their knowledge structure leads us to a well-defined research core, featured in the key hypotheses of mainstream neoclassical economics as the perfect rationality of economic agents, optimality and growth through balanced paths (Dequech 2007; Silva and Teixeira 2009).

Figure 2.2 represents the "endogenous economic growth" tribe. In a similar manner to the "economics of corruption" tribe, the portrayed entries are studies considered significant for the construction and development of knowledge in this research area. As stressed earlier, such a representation aims to identify the articles or books which may be understood as exemplars of lines or families of research within the area of endogenous economic growth, rather than provide a definitive and all-encompassing view of the area. Again, the cells at the bottom of the figure identify the active research families within this tribe: Endogenous Technological Change; Growth and International Trade; Political Economy of Growth; Economic Development and Growth; Unified Growth Theory.

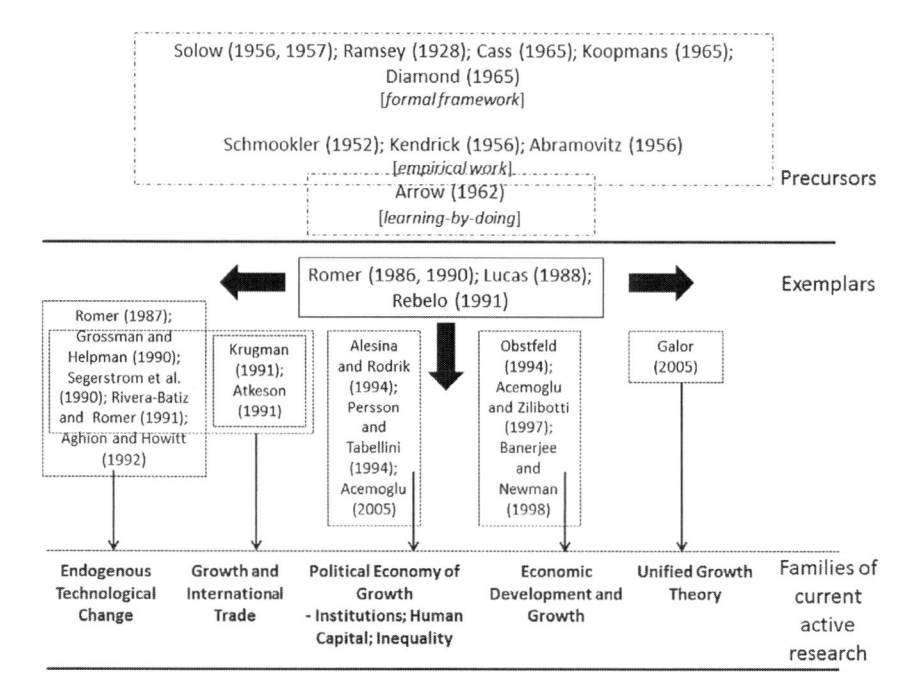

Figure 2.2 The economics of growth tribe.

As commonly recognized in this research field, the work of Solow is essential as a predecessor to the emergence of endogenous growth theories. The articles by Romer (1986) and Lucas (1988) emerge as *exemplars* responsible for the first generation of endogenous growth modeling, whereas Romer (1990) and Rebelo (1991) strongly inspired the so-called second generation of formal frameworks within this research line. These studies are clearly cornerstones and recognized as exemplars with transversal influences throughout the field.

Besides this diachronic analysis, which is responsible for stressing the most important and cross-cutting contributions to the tribe, the assessment exercise must also encompass a synchronic study (Hoover 1991). This last perspective serves to identify potential competition and/or collaboration between some families within a tribe. For example, within the tribe under analysis, the family based on the endogenous growth theory (Romer 1987; Grossman and Helpman 1990; Segerstrom *et al.* 1990; Rivera-Batiz and Romer 1991; Aghion and Howitt 1992) and the Unified Growth Theory (Galor 2005), and the family of the endogenous role of institutions, highly supported by Acemoglu's work—Political Economy of Growth—and again the recently proposed unified growth framework by Galor—Unified Growth Theory.

Modern endogenous growth theory has its origins in the work of Paul Romer (1986, 1990) added to by important subsequent contributions from Lucas (1988), Grossman and Helpman (1991), and Aghion and Howitt (1992) (see Setterfield 2010). As Afonso (2001: 14) puts it,

> [t]he models of endogenous economic growth did not come about by accident ... they are consequence of the general development of economic theory ... [the] dissatisfaction with Solow's work, [and the contribution of] the earlier studies of themes such as learning by doing (Arrow 1962), the role of human capital (Uzawa 1965), increasing returns to scale (Kaldor 1961), and even the idea of per capita growth sustained by increasing income from the investment in capital goods, which include human capital, dating back to Knight (1944).

Linking the "Endogenous Technological Change" family with that of "Growth and International Trade," the model developed by Rivera-Batiz and Romer (1991) was centered on the effects of knowledge spillovers and international trade on the R&D activities that stem within domestic economies. The international trade family departs from the traditional perspective of trade based on the comparative advantage of countries with very different characteristics to Krugman's (1991) new perspective of trade between similar countries, considering that consumers prefer a diverse choice of brands, and that production favors economies of scale and is associated with the so-called "home market effect" (i.e., the result that the country with a larger demand for a good shall, at equilibrium, produce a more than proportionate share of that good and be a net exporter of it).

The unified growth theory was developed to address the inability of endogenous growth theory to explain key empirical regularities that characterized the growth process over longer time horizons in both developed and less developed economies (Aghion 2014). Unified theories offer multi-stage interpretations of long-run economic growth which integrate the Malthusian world of stagnant output per capita with the modern era of sustained output per capita growth, where the productivity effects of technological progress are not offset by population growth (Greasley *et al.* 2013).

Although recognizing geography (i.e., exogenous differences of environment) and culture (i.e., differences in beliefs, attitudes and preferences) as potential fundamental causes of economic growth, Acemoglu (2005) highlights the role of economic and political institutions, that is, humanly devised rules shaping incentives (North 1990: 3), contributing to a separate stream of research within economic growth literature—the "political economy of growth." Economic institutions comprise, among others, property rights, and entry barriers shape economic incentives, contracting possibilities and distribution, whereas political institutions (e.g., form of government, constraints on politicians) shape political incentives and the distribution of political power.

2.3.4   Economics of corruption and economic growth: a merge between tribes?

Corruption is a problem that indicates inefficiency inherent to political institutions and cultures (Otáhal 2014), and it is most prevalent where there are other forms of institutional inefficiency, such as political instability, bureaucratic red tape, and weak legislative and judicial systems. North (1990) asserts that an efficient institution that ensures the secured property rights, which derive incentives to invest or innovate, is crucial for economic growth and development. Countries with weak institutions often do not establish the rule of law and, thus, property rights are not secured. If property rights are not secured, economic agents lack the incentive to invest or innovate because the return on investment or innovation could be plundered from investors (Li and Ferreira 2011). Government corruption and weak institutions are often interrelated. In countries with a poor-quality legal enforcement system, government corruption is often prevalent because corrupt government officials are not punished by the law if a country has a weak judicial system. In turn, government corruption often causes inefficient and weak institutions because corrupt government officials have strong incentives to establish and maintain a poor-quality law enforcement system if the gains from corruption are greater than the wages of government officials (Kunieda *et al.* 2014).

Some authors (e.g., Aidt *et al.* 2008; Méon and Weill 2010) contend that (government) corruption has regime-specific effects on growth. Admitting that corruption causes low growth, Johnson *et al.* (2011) claim that the reform of political institutions deserves, in this case, to take center stage. Thus, corruption, economic growth and institutions are intimately related. Such interconnections have become progressively visible in economics-related research. Indeed, as depicted in Figure 2.3, corruption-related studies within economics research have increasingly focused on economic growth and institutions. Out of the 1,140 articles published between 1990 and 2014 on corruption,[3] 688 referred to economic

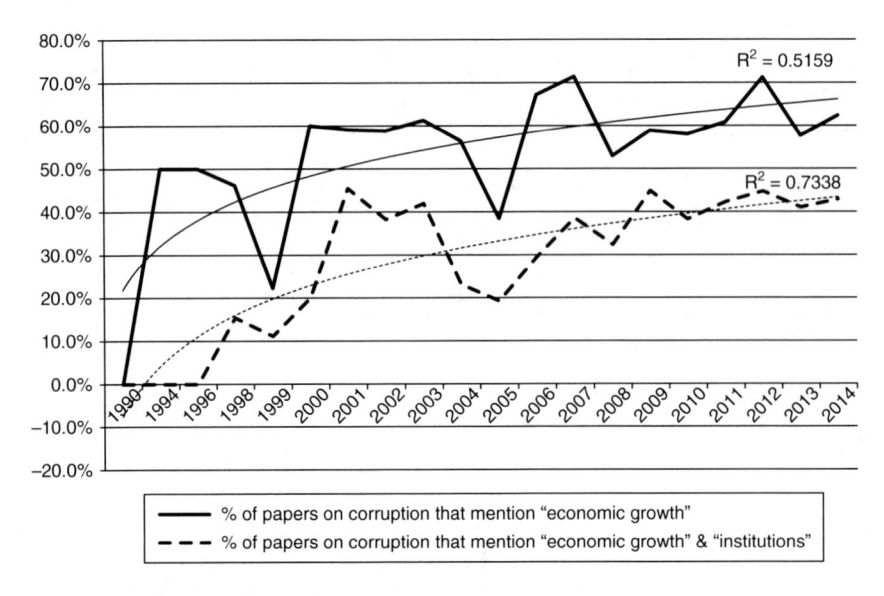

Figure 2.3 The weight of articles on economic growth and institutions within (the economics of) corruption, 1990–2014.

Note: Search performed in Scopus using "corruption" as the keyword, limited to articles and reviews within the area of "Economics, Econometrics and Finance", and then refined to economic growth-related articles and finally, out of the latter, refined to institutions-related articles.

growth and 435 dealt with issues related to economic growth and institutions. In relative and dynamic terms, the weight of corruption-related articles focusing on economic growth increased from an average share of 33.7 percent in the 1990s to 62.0 percent in the most recent period (2010–14). The corresponding figures for corruption-related articles focusing simultaneously on economic growth and institutions depict an even sharper upward trend: 5.3 percent and 42.7 percent.

When we depart from economic growth studies to identify, within this area, the relative importance of the studies focusing on institutions and on institutions and corruption jointly considered, the picture (see Figure 2.4) shows a similar albeit less visible convergence path to that depicted in Figure 2.3. Between 1990 and 2014, 6,403 articles were published on economic growth, 1,606 of which addressed institutions and 256 focused simultaneously on institutions and corruption.[4] In relative terms, the average percentage of economic growth-related articles focusing simultaneously on institutions and corruptions was 0.9 percent in the 1990s, and 4.4 percent in the most recent period (2010–14), which reflects a marked (almost a fivefold) increase.

The evidence gathered on the scientific production on (the economics of) corruption and economic growth signals a steady merge between these two research streams.

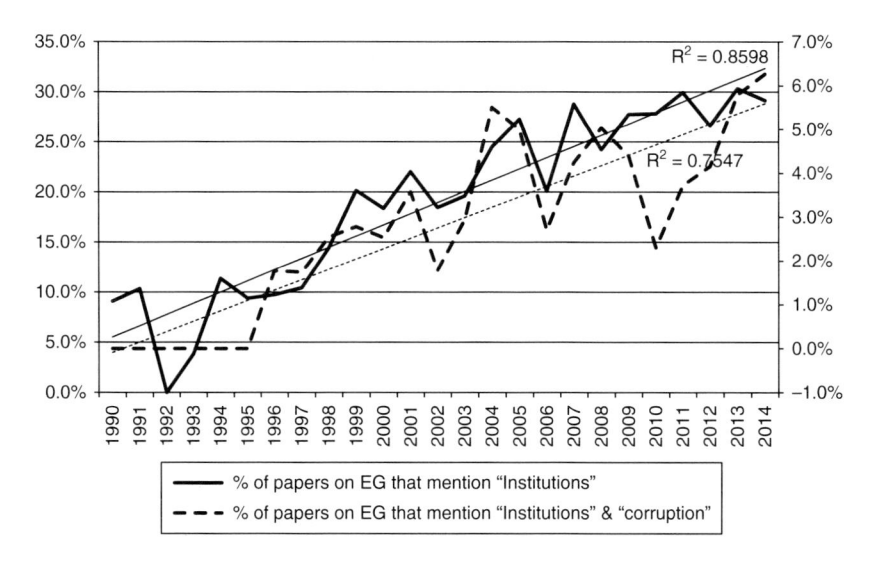

Figure 2.4 The weight of articles on corruption within economic growth and institutions, 1990–2014.

Note: Search performed in Scopus using "economic growth" as the keyword, limited to articles and reviews within the area of "Economics, Econometrics and Finance", and then refined to institutions-related articles and finally, out of the latter, refined to corruption-related articles.

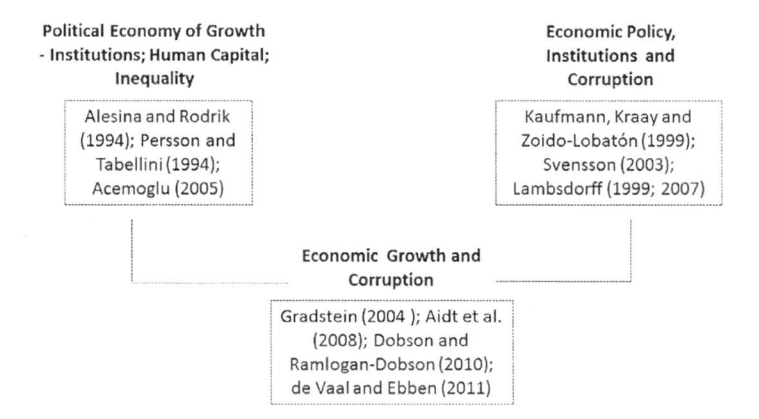

Figure 2.5 The merge between the economics of corruption and economic growth research.

The studies by Alesina and Rodrik (1994), Persson and Tabellini (1994), and Acemoglu (2005), which address the political economy of growth, including the issues of institutions, human capital, and inequality, and those by Kaufmann *et al.* (1999), Svensson (2003), and Lambsdorff (1999, 2007), related to economic policy, institutions and corruption, translate this gradual process of convergence between the economics of corruption and economic growth research. Such a merge is captured in the studies of Gradstein (2004), Aidt *et al.* (2008), Dobson and Ramlogan-Dobson (2010) or de Vaal and Ebben (2011), which analyze economic growth and corruption (see Figure 2.5).

2.4   Economics of corruption and economic growth through the lens of bibliometrics

After presenting the main scientific roots and family tribes of (the economics of) corruption and economic growth research streams, and having shown that they have, to some extent, experienced a convergence trend, it seems interesting and useful to highlight the key studies, authors and sources based on a simple bibliometric, citation-based exercise.

Bibliometrics contributes to tracing scholarly communication patterns and the evolution of knowledge on a topic (Lasda Bergman 2012). Such a method relies strongly on the bibliographic databases available, such as the Web of Science/Knowledge (former ISI), Scopus or Google Scholar. The Web of Science is the oldest and most-renowned bibliographic database; however, it tends to emphasize the "hard" sciences. As such, Harzing (2010) asserted that for the social sciences and humanities, Google Scholar would perform better in a citation count over the Web of Science (and to a lesser degree Scopus), as the journal coverage of Google Scholar is higher than both the Web of Science and Scopus. Aiming to take advantage of the strengths of these two databases, in the present section, we combine results from both.

Data gathered from the Web of Science (former ISI) shows that articles on corruption or economic growth experienced a clear upward trend over the period 1985–2013 (see Figure 2.6), presenting an annual average growth rate of, respectively, 12.6 percent and 29.5 percent. The articles focusing simultaneously on growth and corruption are much more recent, whose indexation in ISI/Web of Science started in 1995, and lower in quantity, although they do show a remarkable evolution with an annual average growth rate of almost 40 percent.

The bulk of the top-cited studies on corruption and economic growth were published between 1995 and 2005 (about 70 percent) in journals (67 percent of the total); books and book chapters represent 26 percent of the total (cf. Table 2.1). Ten journals—*Journal of Economic Growth*; *Journal of Public Economics*; *European Economic Review*; *Journal of Development Economics*; *The Quarterly Journal of Economics*; *American Economic Review*; *Economics & Politics*; *Journal of Economic Literature*; *Journal of Monetary Economics*; and *Public Choice*—encompass almost 50 percent of the top-cited articles published in such outlets.

It is interesting to note that among the top-cited studies, (the economics of) corruption "*Exemplars*"—Klitgaard (1998); Shleifer and Vishny (1993); Tanzi (1998); Rose-Ackerman (1999); Abed and Gupta (2002), cf. Figure 2.1—are not those receiving the largest citation counts. Those at the very top comprise

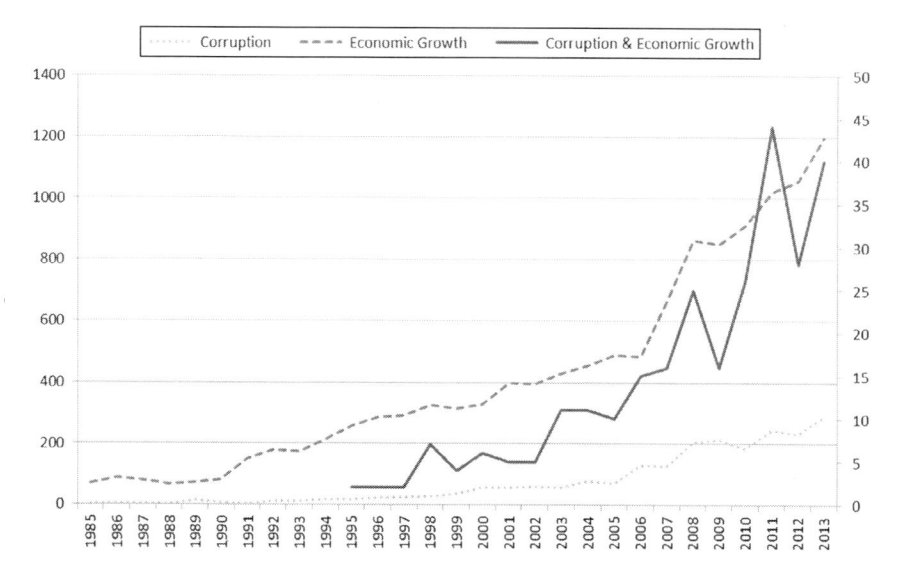

Figure 2.6 Evolution of the number of articles on corruption (left scale), economic growth (left scale), and corruption and economic growth (right scale).

Note: Data gathered from the Web of Knowledge using as the search keywords "corruption", "economic growth", or "corruption and economic growth", refined to the area of business economics. The number of articles obtained for the period 1985–2013 was 2,203 for "corruption", 12,186 for "economic growth", and 278 for "corruption and economic growth".

Source: Authors' computations based on the Web of Science, Thomson Reuters.

studies belonging to the "families" of current, active research in both (the economics of) corruption and economic growth. In concrete, regarding the former, "The Empirics of the Economics of Corruption" family, which includes the studies of Mauro (1995), Treisman (2000), Wei (2000a), and Mo (2001), shows high scientific impact. Regarding the economic growth tribe, the works of Rodrik and Acemoglu belonging, respectively to the families "Political Economy of Growth—Institutions; Human Capital; Inequality" and "Economic Development and Growth," are worth mentioning.

Considering the most-cited studies in the economics of corruption we were able to get the most cited authors in corruption studies (those with more than 1,000 citations in Google Scholar), cf. Table 2.2. The hegemony of US universities in the economics of corruption is apparent, as well as the IMF's noticeable importance in this domain.

Paolo Mauro is by far the most cited with his contributions to the empirics of the economics of corruption. He is followed, at some distance, by two "exemplars," Susan Rose-Ackerman (Yale University) and Vito Tanzi (International Monetary Fund). The other two *exemplars*, Robert Klitgaard (Claremont Graduate University) and Sanjeev K. Gupta (IMF Fiscal Affairs Department) rank below, with 2,071 and 1,652 citations, respectively.

Table 2.1 Top cited studies on corruption and economic growth

Title	Authors	Source	Type of source	Year	Cites	Cites per year
Corruption and growth	**P Mauro**	The Quarterly Journal of Economics	Journal	1995	6,684	351.8
Does social capital have an economic payoff? A cross-country investigation	S Knack, P Keefer	The Quarterly Journal of Economics	Journal	1997	5,836	343.3
Social capital and economic development: toward a theoretical synthesis and policy framework	M Woolcock	Theory and Society	Journal	1998	4,586	286.6
Trade policy and economic growth: a skeptic's guide to the cross-national evidence	F Rodriguez, **D Rodrik**	NBER Macroeconomics Annual	Working Paper	2001	3,563	274.1
Fractionalization	**A Alesina**, A Devleeschauwer, W Easterly...	Journal of Economic Growth	Journal	2003	2,966	269.6
Stock markets, banks, and economic growth	R Levine, S Zervos	American Economic Review	Journal	1998	4,230	264.4
Africa's growth tragedy: policies and ethnic divisions	W Easterly, R Levine	The Quarterly Journal of Economics	Journal	1997	4,484	263.8
Determinants of economic growth: a cross-country empirical study	RJ Barro		Working Paper	1996	4,649	258.3
Culture and institutions: economic development in the regions of Europe	G Tabellini	Journal of the European Economic Association	Journal	2010	990	247.5

Table 2.1 Continued

Title	Authors	Source	Type of source	Year	Cites	Cites per year
Do institutions cause growth?	EL Glaeser, R La Porta, F Lopez-de-Silanes...	Journal of Economic Growth	Journal	2004	2,422	242.2
One economics, many recipes: globalization, institutions, and economic growth	**D Rodrik**		Book	2008	1,446	241.0
Introduction to modern economic growth	**D Acemoglu**		Book	2008	1,445	240.8
Financial intermediation and growth: causality and causes	R Levine, N Loayza, T Beck	Journal of Monetary Economics	Journal	2000	3,318	237.0
Institutions and economic performance: cross-country tests using alternative institutional measures	S Knack, P Keefer	Economics & Politics	Journal	1995	4,315	227.1
Law, finance, and economic growth in China	F Allen, J Qian, M Qian	Journal of Financial Economics	Journal	2005	1,943	215.9
Social capital: implications for development theory, research, and policy	M Woolcock, D Narayan	The World Bank Research Observer	Journal	2000	2,875	205.4
Corruption and government: causes, consequences, and reform	**S Rose-Ackerman**		Book	1999	2,861	190.7
The causes of corruption: a cross-national study	**D Treisman**	Journal of Public Economics	Journal	2000	2,662	190.1
The curse of natural resources	JD Sachs, AM Warner	European Economic Review	Journal	2001	2,301	177.0

(Continued)

Table 2.1 Continued

Title	Authors	Source	Type of source	Year	Cites	Cites per year
Tropics, germs, and crops: how endowments influence economic development	W Easterly, R Levine	Journal of Monetary Economics	Journal	2003	1,848	168.0
Money and capital in economic development	RI McKinnon		Book	1973	6,656	162.3
Africa works: disorder as political instrument	P Chabal, JP Daloz		Book	1999	2,418	161.2
Corruption and development: a review of issues	P Bardhan	Journal of Economic Literature	Journal	1997	2,582	151.9
The mystery of economic growth	**E Helpman**		Book	2009	753	150.6
Geography and economic development	JL Gallup, JD Sachs, AD Mellinger	International Regional Science Review	Journal	1999	2,175	145.0
FDI and economic growth: the role of local financial markets	L Alfaro, A Chanda, S Kalemli-Ozcan...	Journal of International Economics	Journal	2004	1,392	139.2
How taxing is corruption on international investors?	**SJ Wei**	Review of Economics and Statistics	Journal	2000	1,927	137.6
Social capital, civil society and development	F Fukuyama	Third World Quarterly	Journal	2001	1,700	130.8
Greasing the wheels? The impact of regulations and corruption on firm entry	A Dreher, M Gassebner	Public Choice	Journal	2013	129	129.0

Table 2.1 Continued

Title	Authors	Source	Type of source	Year	Cites	Cites per year
Financial and legal constraints to growth: does firm size matter?	T Beck, A Demirgüç-Kunt...	The Journal of Finance	Journal	2005	1,095	121.7
The place of social capital in understanding social and economic outcomes	M Woolcock	Canadian Journal of Policy Research	Journal	2001	1,567	120.5
The real exchange rate and economic growth	**D Rodrik**	Brookings Papers on Economic Activity	Journal	2008	712	118.7
Goodbye Washington consensus, hello Washington confusion? A review of the World Bank's economic growth in the 1990s: learning from a decade of reform	**D Rodrik**	Journal of Economic Literature	Journal	2006	949	118.6
Using ICTs to create a culture of transparency: e-government and social media as openness and anti-corruption tools for societies	JC Bertot, PT Jaeger, JM Grimes	Government Information Quarterly	Journal	2010	464	116.0
What Washington means by policy reform	J Williamson	Latin American Adjustment: How Much Has Happened?	Book Chapter	1990	2,783	116.0
Economic development as self-discovery	R Hausmann, **D Rodrik**	Journal of Development Economics	Journal	2003	1,255	114.1
Growth and development	AP Thirlwall		Book	2006	876	109.5
The economic role of political institutions: market-preserving federalism and economic development	BR Weingast	Journal of Law, Economics, & Organization	Journal	1995	2,046	107.7

(*Continued*)

Table 2.1 Continued

Title	Authors	Source	Type of source	Year	Cites	Cites per year
Corporate governance, economic entrenchment and growth	R Morck, D Wolfenzon, B Yeung		Working Paper	2004	1,067	106.7
Rents, competition, and corruption	A Ades, R Di Tella	American Economic Review	Journal	1999	1,582	105.5
Corruption around the world: causes, consequences, scope, and cures	**V Tanzi**	IMF Staff Papers	Journal	1998	1,637	102.3
Where did all the growth go? External shocks, social conflict, and growth collapses	**D Rodrik**	Journal of Economic Growth	Journal	1999	1,533	102.2
Eight questions about corruption	**J Svensson**	The Journal of Economic Perspectives	Journal	2005	869	96.6
The new empirics of economic growth	SN Durlauf, DT Quah	Handbook of Macroeconomics	Book Chapter	1999	1,407	93.8
What have we learned about the causes of corruption from ten years of cross-national empirical research?	**D Treisman**	Annual Review of Political Science	Journal	2007	617	88.1
Natural resources, education, and economic development	T Gylfason	European Economic Review	Journal	2001	1,110	85.4

Table 2.1 Continued

Title	Authors	Source	Type of source	Year	Cites	Cites per year
The institutional environment for economic growth	WJ Henisz	Economics & Politics	Journal	2000	1,192	85.1
Disease and development: the effect of life expectancy on economic growth	**D Acemoglu**, S Johnson		Working Paper	2006	677	84.6
Controlling corruption	**R Klitgaard**		Book	1988	2,107	81.0
Economic development, legality, and the transplant effect	D Berkowitz, K Pistor, JF Richard	European Economic Review	Journal	2003	883	80.3
Culture matters: how values shape human progress	LE Harrison, SP Huntington		Book	2000	1,107	79.1
Corruption, public investment, and growth	**V Tanzi**, H Davoodi		Book	1998	1,242	77.6
Geography, demography, and economic growth in Africa	DE Bloom, JD Sachs, P Collier, C Udry	Brookings Papers on Economic ...	Journal	1998	1,201	75.1
Political instability and economic growth	**A Alesina**, S Özler, N Roubini, P Swagel	Journal of Economic Growth	Journal	1996	1,348	74.9
Modern economic growth: rate, structure, and spread	SS Kuznets, JT Murphy		Book	1966	3,532	73.6
Does corruption affect income inequality and poverty?	**S Gupta**, H Davoodi, R Alonso-Terme	Economics of Governance	Journal	2002	876	73.0
Decentralization and corruption: evidence across countries	R Fisman, R Gatti	Journal of Public Economics	Journal	2002	874	72.8

(*Continued*)

Table 2.1 Continued

Title	Authors	Source	Type of source	Year	Cites	Cites per year
Does mother nature corrupt? Natural resources, corruption, and economic growth	CA Leite, J Weidmann	IMF Working Papers	Working Paper	1999	1,068	71.2
Small and medium-size enterprises: access to finance as a growth constraint	T Beck, A Demirgüç-Kunt	Journal of Banking & Finance	Journal	2006	567	70.9
Law, finance, and economic growth	R Levine	Journal of financial Intermediation	Journal	1999	1,063	70.9
A free press is bad news for corruption	A Brunetti, B Weder	Journal of Public Economics	Journal	2003	741	67.4
The China miracle: development strategy and economic reform	JY Lin, F Cai, Z Li		Book	2003	734	66.7
Political corruption: concepts and contexts	AJ Heidenheimer, M Johnston		Book	2011	199	66.3
The moral consequences of economic growth	BM Friedman	Society	Journal	2006	529	66.1
The effect of health on economic growth: a production function approach	DE Bloom, D Canning, J Sevilla	World Development	Journal	2004	657	65.7
Do corrupt governments receive less foreign aid?	**A Alesina**, B Weder		Working Paper	1999	983	65.5
Corruption: a review	AK Jain	Journal of Economic Surveys	Journal	2001	837	64.4

Table 2.1 Continued

Title	Authors	Source	Type of source	Year	Cites	Cites per year
The varieties of resource experience: natural resource export structures and the political economy of economic growth	J Isham, M Woolcock, L Pritchett, G Busby	The World Bank Economic . . .	Book Chapter	2005	579	64.3
Economic analysis of corruption: a survey	TS Aidt	The Economic Journal	Journal	2003	703	63.9
Corruption and the composition of government expenditure	**P Mauro**	Journal of Public Economics	Journal	1998	988	61.8
Corruption and the shadow economy: an empirical analysis	A Dreher, F Schneider	Public Choice	Journal	2010	245	61.3
Power and plenty: trade, war, and the world economy in the second millennium	R Findlay, KH O'Rourke		Book	2007	424	60.6
Are corruption and taxation really harmful to growth? Firm level evidence	R Fisman, **J Svensson**	Journal of Development Economics	Journal	2007	421	60.1
The political economy of dictatorship	R Wintrobe		Book	1998	962	60.1
The legal environment, banks, and long-run economic growth	R Levine	Journal of Money, Credit and Banking	Journal	1998	956	59.8
The economic growth engine: how energy and work drive material prosperity	RU Ayres, B Warr		Book	2010	234	58.5
Electoral rules and corruption	T Persson, G Tabellini, F Trebbi	. . . of the European Economic . . .	Book Chapter	2003	618	56.2
Why is rent-seeking so costly to growth?	KM Murphy, **A Shleifer, RW Vishny**	The American Economic Review	Journal	1993	1,177	56.0

(*Continued*)

Table 2.1 Continued

Title	Authors	Source	Type of source	Year	Cites	Cites per year
Bureaucracy and growth: a cross-national analysis of the effects of "Weberian" state structures on economic growth	P Evans, JE Rauch	American Sociological Review	Journal	1999	831	55.4
Seize the state, seize the day: state capture, corruption and influence in transition	JS Hellman, G Jones, D Kaufmann	World Bank Policy Research ...	Book Chapter	2000	742	53.0
Foreign direct investment in Africa: the role of natural resources, market size, government policy, institutions and political instability	E Asiedu	The World Economy	Journal	2006	418	52.3
Corruption and foreign direct investment	M Habib, L Zurawicki	Journal of International Business Studies	Journal	2002	622	51.8
An East Asian renaissance: ideas for economic growth	IS Gill, HJ Kharas, D Bhattasali		Book	2007	362	51.7
A theory of collective reputations (with applications to the persistence of corruption and to firm quality)	**J Tirole**	The Review of Economic Studies	Journal	1996	922	51.2
Trade openness and economic growth: a cross-country empirical investigation	H Yanikkaya	Journal of Development Economics	Journal	2003	556	50.5

Note: The studies reported received, according to the Google Scholar bibliographic database, 50 or more citations per year (average citations). The grey cells indicate the studies are (co)authored by individuals (in bold) who belong to the corruption or economic growth tribes.

Source: Citations were gathered using the software "Publish or Perish" by Harzing (2007) having as keywords "corruption" and "economic growth."

Table 2.2 Top cited authors in the economics of corruption

Rank	Author	Tribe position	Affiliation organization	Country	Citations
1	Mauro, Paolo	*"The Empirics of the Economics of Corruption" Family*	Johns Hopkins University	USA	8,319
2	Rose-Ackerman, Susan	*Exemplar*	Yale University	USA	4,002
3	Tanzi, Vito	*Exemplar*	International Monetary Fund	USA	3,825
4	Wei, Shangjin	*"The Empirics of the Economics of Corruption" Family*	Columbia Business School	USA	3,640
5	Treisman, Daniel	*"The Empirics of the Economics of Corruption" Family*	University of California, Los Angeles	USA	3,311
6	Davoodi, Hamid		International Monetary Fund	USA	3,166
7	Di Tella, Rafael		Harvard Business School	USA	3,301
8	Bardhan, Pranab K.		UC Berkeley	USA	2,528
9	Ades, Alberto		Goldman Sachs Group	USA	2,474
10	Daloz, Jean Pascale		Institute of Political Studies	France	2,360
11	Chabal, Pierre		Universite du Havre	France	2,360
12	Fisman, Raymond		Columbia Business School	USA	2,294
13	Klitgaard, Robert	*Exemplar*	Claremont Graduate University	USA	2,071
14	Svensson, Jakob	*"Economic Policy, Institutions and Corruption" Family*	Stockholms Universitet	Sweden	1,775

(Continued)

Table 2.2 Continued

Rank	Author	Tribe position	Affiliation organization	Country	Citations
15	Gupta, Sanjeev K.	*Exemplar*	IMF Fiscal Affairs Department	USA	1,652
16	Gatti, Roberta		The World Bank and CEPR	USA	1,578
17	Johnston, Michael		Colgate University	USA	1,577
18	Weder Di Mauro, Beatrice		Johannes Gutenberg Universitat Mainz	Germany	1,489
19	Kaufmann, Daniel	*"Economic Policy, Institutions and Corruption" Family*	Swiss National Bank	Switzerland	1,480
20	Olken, Benjamin A.		Massachusetts Institute of Technology	USA	1,239
21	Uslaner, Eric M.		University of Maryland	USA	1,109
22	Gupta, Anil K.		University of Maryland	USA	1,098
23	Ashforth, Blake E.		Arizona State University	USA	1,082
24	Leite, Carlos		International Monetary Fund	USA	1,050
25	Weidmann, Jens		Universitat Bonn	Germany	1,050
26	Della Porta, Donatella Ella		Scuola Normale Superiore di Pisa	Italy	1,007
27	Acemoglu, Daron	*"Economic Development and Growth" Family*	Massachusetts Institute of Technology	USA	1,002
28	Verdier, Thierry		École Nationale des Ponts et Chaussées	France	1,002

Note: The grey cells indicate the exemplars of the corruption tribe.

Source: Citations were gathered using the software "Publish or Perish" by Harzing (2007) and summing up the authors' citations from the search resulting from using the keyword "corruption."

The bibliometric exercise undertaken confirms therefore the relevance of the exemplars highlighted in the economics of corruption tribe and provides quantitative information which endorses to some extent the merge that has been occurring between the economics of corruption and the economic growth tribes.

Notes

1 Corruption includes acts of bribery, embezzlement, nepotism or state capture, and it is often associated with and reinforced by other illegal practices, such as bid rigging, fraud or money laundering (OECD 2014). However, it is important to note that illegal acts such as fraud, money laundering, drug trafficking, and black market operations do not constitute corruption in and of themselves because they do not involve the use of public power (Jain 2001b). In a recent book, Buchan and Hill (2014) found that from Antiquity through to the end of the eighteenth century, corruption was not always a concept particular to the abuse of public office; instead was often applied to more nebulous fears of moral, spiritual and physical degeneration.
2 The other 13 global problems included: Human rights abuses in the world; Pollution and environmental problems in the world; The spread of human diseases; Extreme poverty in the world; Terrorism; The migration of people between countries; War and armed conflicts; The state of the global economy; Religious fundamentalism; Violation of workers' rights in the world; Climate change or global warming; The rising cost of food and energy; and The growing power of global companies. For further details, see www.globescan.com/news_archives/bbc_corruption/keyfindings.html (accessed April 15, 2015).
3 The search was performed in December 2014 in the bibliographic database Scopus Sci Verse using corruption as the keyword, limited to articles and reviews within the area of "Economics, Econometrics and Finance."
4 The search was performed in December 2014 in the bibliographic database Scopus Sci Verse using "economic growth" as the keyword, limited to articles and reviews within the area of "Economics, Econometrics and Finance."

3 Globalization and corruption

Impacts and nonlinearities

Joseph Attila

3.1 Introduction

Do developing countries benefit from globalization? The centrality of this question is evident but the mixed empirical results raise some skepticism about the benefits of globalization. Contrary to the "optimistic" studies that point to the potential gains of globalization (Dollar 2005), a significant strand of the literature considers globalization a "dangerous" phenomenon. Globalization may cause serious adverse consequences in fragile countries—that is, countries where for example the degree of internationalization is not high enough (Agenor 2004; Harrison 2006).

The present chapter focuses on the consequences of globalization with regard to a serious curse in developing countries: corruption. As the interactions between countries intensify, it seems that cases of corruption involving multinationals as well as politicians and diplomats increase (Rose-Ackerman 1999; Hawley 2000; Straub 2008). Corruption in the global economy tends to expand to the domestic economies. Yet, since the seminal work of Mauro (1995), it is well-established that corruption exerts adverse consequences in local developing economies. This study contributes to the literature in three main aspects.[1] First, the nonlinearity between globalization and corruption is thoroughly scrutinized. In this endeavor, in addition to the standard U-shape test, we perform a recent U-test developed by Lind and Mehlum (2010) based also on the Fieller interval. Second, it is likely that the different dimensions of globalization exert different impacts on corruption, depending on the intensity, nature and the types of agents involved in a specific global interaction. Hence, we investigate whether the impact of globalization on corruption differs according to each individual dimension (economic, political and social). Finally, we discuss the causality issue and develop an instrumental variables strategy suitable to address it.

The econometric analysis conducted confirms our expectations of a U-inverted relationship. In other words, globalization can contribute to reducing corruption (better governance) in developing countries only if they reach a certain level of international integration. Our research also highlights the importance of the different dimensions of globalization. The adverse consequences of globalization seem to be driven by the flows of information, people or culture that probably do not take into account the negative externalities they may induce on less developed countries.

The chapter is organized as follows. The next section describes the econometric approach and the results are then discussed. Additional tests are then provided, followed by concluding remarks.

3.2 Methodology

As we intend to test the relevance of a nonlinear relationship between corruption and globalization, we consider the following equation:

$$C_i = \beta_0 + \beta_1 G_i + \beta_2 G_i^2 + \sum_{k=3}^{l} \beta_k x_{ki} + \varepsilon_i \qquad (3.1)$$

In this equation, C, G, G^2 represent respectively the corruption and globalization (log-transformed) variables and their square. X is a set of other determinants of corruption. ε_i is the error term assumed to be independently and identically distributed among countries and following the normal distribution. i denotes countries.

The square term is introduced so as to assert the nonlinearity of the relationship. To identify the U (or inverse U)-shapes, we use two approaches:

1 *The common approach.* Equation (3.1) is estimated with the globalization variable and its square and the control variables. Then we test whether the coefficients β_1 and β_2 are individually and jointly significantly different from zero. If the coefficient of either the globalization variable or its squares is non-significant, then we re-estimate the equation omitting the square of the globalization variable.
2 *Lind and Mehlum's (2010) approach.* In this approach, the authors argue that the significance of both coefficients is not a sufficient condition for a U-shaped relationship. According to the authors, the common approach may be misleading if the true relationship is convex but monotone over relevant data values. They therefore propose to test whether the relationship is decreasing at low values within some interval of values and increasing at high values within the interval.

All in all, the quadratic model is considered as a better fit for the data than the linear model if all these tests are conclusive.

The analysis is conducted on a sample consisting of 122 developed and developing countries (see Table A3.1 in Appendix). Two different periods are considered: 1990–95 and 2005–06. Using two distinct periods makes it possible to test whether our results hold over time. Equation (3.1) is estimated on cross-sectional data using two complementary methods: the ordinary least squares (OLS) and the instrumental variables approach for each sub-period.

3.3 Data

We focus our attention on the two variables of interest, corruption and globalization.

3.3.1 Corruption data

It is difficult to measure corruption because its activities are developed secretly. On a macroeconomic level, only perception indexes are available.[2] The present work draws on the corruption data of the International Country Risk Guide (ICRG). For the ICRG, corruption is assessed in a broad sense by a panel of international experts: it includes not only corruption cases in the political sphere but also in administrative services (nepotism, patronage, favoritism, requests for special payments and bribes). For the purpose of our analysis, this variable has been rescaled so that lower values (0) correspond to low levels of corruption and higher values (10) to high levels of corruption.

3.3.2 Globalization data

The present study uses the 2007 KOF index of globalization (Dreher 2006), which computed indexes of globalization according to three dimensions: economic, social and political.[3] Table 3.1 summarizes the different components of each dimension and their respective weight in the overall index.

3.3.3 Control variables

In addition to the globalization variable, it is necessary to include other determinants of governance in order to avoid the bias of omitted variables. These variables capture the country's economic conditions, political environment, social conditions and colonial history. *Economic conditions* are captured by the natural logarithm of the gross domestic product (GDP) per capita: a higher level of income is associated with a lower corruption (Paldam 2002; Treisman 2000). In addition to this variable, a variable is used to portray endowment in natural resources. The natural resources endowment is generally considered as a source of rent extraction. Hence, the countries that export minerals and fuel are assumed to be more corrupt. *The political environment* is not only a determinant of the decision of foreign firms to locate in a host country but it can also affect corruption. Limited political liberties increase corruption. Thus, the political rights index from Freedom House is used to test this hypothesis. *Some social attributes* can generate corruption or constrain it. They are captured by ethno-linguistic fractionalization and proportion of Protestants and Muslims in 1980. *The colonial history* is captured in the legal origins: legal origin affects corruption (La Porta *et al.* 1999). Two variables are considered here, namely British and French legal origin.

Table 3.2 provides the descriptive statistics of all the variables used in the study.

Table 3.1 Indices, variables and weight of dimensions of globalization

Indices and variables	Weights
A. Economic Globalization	**(36%)**
i) Actual Flows	(50%)
Trade (percent of GDP)	(21%)
Foreign Direct Investment, stocks (percent of GDP)	(28%)
Portfolio Investment (percent of GDP)	(24%)
Income Payments to Foreign Nationals (percent of GDP)	(27%)
ii) Restrictions	(50%)
Hidden Import Barriers	(24%)
Mean Tariff Rate	(27%)
Taxes on International Trade (percent of current revenue)	(26%)
Capital Account Restrictions	(23%)
B. Social Globalization	**(37%)**
i) Data on Personal Contact	(34%)
Telephone Traffic	(25%)
Transfers (percent of GDP)	(4%)
International Tourism	(26%)
Foreign Population (percent of total population)	(21%)
International letters (per capita)	(25%)
ii) Data on Information Flows	(35%)
Internet Users (per 1,000 people)	(33%)
Television (per 1,000 people)	(36%)
Trade in Newspapers (percent of GDP)	(32%)
iii) Data on Cultural Proximity	(31%)
Number of McDonald's Restaurants (per capita)	(44%)
Number of Ikea (per capita)	(45%)
Trade in books (percent of GDP)	(11%)
C. Political Globalization	**(26%)**
Embassies in Country	(25%)
Membership in International Organizations	(28%)
Participation in UN Security Council Missions	(22%)
International Treaties	(25%)

3.4 Econometric results

3.4.1 Main findings

The findings shown in Table 3.3 confirm the existence of an inverse U-shaped relationship between globalization and corruption, in both the period 1990–95 and in 2005–06. In the first period considered, an increase in globalization leads to an increase in the corruption index until the globalization index reaches the value of 3.43, which does not fall outside the range of our data. From this threshold, the impact of globalization becomes negative: any increase in globalization reduces corruption. Most countries that are likely to suffer from globalization are developing countries and share several common characteristics: low levels of GDP, oil-rich countries, weak political environment. It is also worth noting that the significant

Table 3.2 Descriptive statistics

	Mean	Median	SD	Min	Max
1990–95					
Overall globalization	3.773	3.759	0.383	2.726	4.494
Economic globalization	3.829	3.889	0.441	2.062	4.551
Political globalization	3.729	3.839	0.615	2.286	4.552
Corruption index ICRG	3.461	3.708	1.359	1.000	7.000
Corruption index WB					
GDP per capita	7.671	7.620	1.558	4.884	10.462
Exports of fuel	1.092	1.164	2.283	−8.202	4.571
% of Protestants in 1980	14.396	3.000	22.516	0.000	97.800
% of Muslims in 1980	19.323	1.300	33.249	0.000	99.400
% of Catholics in 1980	36.799	25.500	36.924	0.000	97.300
Ethnic fractionalization	0.835	0.782	0.513	0.004	1.853
British legal origin	0.319	0.000	0.468	0.000	1.000
French legal origin	0.479	0.000	0.502	0.000	1.000
2005–06					
Overall globalization	4.016	4.018	0.307	3.109	4.523
Economic globalization	4.118	4.175	0.301	3.297	4.563
Political globalization	3.959	4.094	0.538	2.439	4.591
Corruption index ICRG	4.365	4.500	1.242	1.000	7.000
Corruption index WB	4.801	5.317	2.110	0.165	8.301
GDP per capita	7.882	7.801	1.639	4.511	10.863
Exports of fuel	1.399	1.616	2.081	−4.752	4.493
% of Protestants in 1980	14.396	3.000	22.516	0.000	97.800
% of Muslims in 1980	19.323	1.300	33.249	0.000	99.400
% of Catholics in 1980	36.799	25.500	36.924	0.000	97.300
Ethnic fractionalization	0.834	0.777	0.511	0.004	1.853
British legal origin	0.319	0.000	0.468	0.000	1.000
French legal origin	0.479	0.000	0.502	0.000	1.000

effect of globalization persists even after controlling for the GDP per capita variable. This result differs significantly from that of Lalountas *et al.* (2011), who found a non-significant impact of globalization on corruption in low-income countries.

Our results build a bridge between the studies that have established, on the one hand, a negative relationship between globalization and corruption (Bonaglia *et al.* 2001; Prakash and Hart 2000) and those, on the other, that have established a positive relationship (Williams and Beare 1999; Balestrini 2001; Johnston 1998). These results are also consistent with previous studies, which estimate the impact of globalization on poverty (Agenor 2004; Dollar 2005) or on human development (Akhter 2004).

The different dimensions of globalization do not share the same relationship pattern with corruption as overall globalization. In the 1990–95 period economic globalization does not significantly affect corruption (see Table 3.4). However, in the 2005–06 period an inverse U-shaped relationship between economic globalization and corruption is evidenced. For countries having an economic

Table 3.3 Overall impact of globalization on corruption: OLS results

	1990–95 (1)	2005–06 (2)
Globalization (log)	12.33**	29.89***
	(5.941)	(8.797)
Overall globalization squared	−1.796**	−3.847***
	(0.760)	(1.096)
Log of real GDP per capita	−0.147	−0.242*
	(0.129)	(0.128)
Exports of fuels	0.0459	0.0670
	(0.0378)	(0.0426)
Proportion of Protestants	−0.00470	−0.0231***
	(0.00435)	(0.00357)
Proportion of Muslims	0.00855**	−0.000837
	(0.00370)	(0.00316)
Proportion of Catholics	0.00765**	−0.00201
	(0.00348)	(0.00272)
Ethnic fractionalization	0.271	0.233
	(0.276)	(0.264)
British legal origin	0.410	−0.711***
	(0.290)	(0.259)
French legal origin	0.283	−0.529**
	(0.285)	(0.217)
Constant	−17.09	−50.90***
	(11.77)	(18.13)
Extremum point	3.432	3.884
Slope at X_l	2.537	8.911
Slope at X_h	−3.915	−4.913
Appropriate U test	1.37	3.13
Obs.	83	75
Adjusted R-sq	.641	.733

Notes: Robust standard errors in parentheses. *, **, *** denote significances at 1, 5, and 10% levels.
Overall test of presence of a Inverse U shape based on the Fieller Interval.
P-values in square brackets.

globalization level below 4.01, corruption increases with economic globalization (see Figure 3.1). After this value, globalization significantly reduces corruption.

As far as social globalization is concerned, the impact varies. The nonlinear relationship between corruption and globalization is supported only for the 2005–06 period. This result is in the line with that obtained for economic globalization in this period but it should be noted that the differential magnitude of the impacts are two facets of the same phenomenon. Finally, political globalization has a negative effect on corruption, a result that holds for the two periods under study. Once again, the magnitude and the significance of this effect vary when one considers the sub-periods. In the 1990–95 period, a 1 percent increase in political globalization helps to reduce corruption by 0.38 percent, an impact that is a bit smaller than the one observed in 2005–06 (0.43 percent).

Table 3.4 Different dimensions of globalization and corruption: OLS results

	1990–95 (1)	2005–06 (2)	1990–95 (3)	2005–06 (4)	1990–95 (5)	2005–06 (6)
Economic globalization (log)	−0.228 (0.348)	22.54** (10.04)				
Economic globalization squared		−2.808** (1.243)				
Political globalization (log)			−0.376** (0.184)	−0.430** (0.188)		
Social globalization (log)					−1.141*** (0.395)	14.54*** (4.168)
Social globalization squared						−2.013*** (0.547)
Proportion of Muslims	0.00604* (0.00327)	0.000980 (0.00417)	0.00979** (0.00386)	−0.000457 (0.00339)	0.00921** (0.00354)	0.00156 (0.00320)
Proportion of Catholics	0.00445 (0.00362)	−0.00254 (0.00305)	0.00598 (0.00372)	−0.00316 (0.00320)	0.00927*** (0.00345)	−0.000712 (0.00280)
Ethnic fractionalization	−0.00121 (0.241)	0.379 (0.253)	0.138 (0.275)	0.00632 (0.222)	0.220 (0.277)	0.260 (0.261)
British legal origin	0.554* (0.298)	−0.639** (0.278)	0.453 (0.319)	−0.473* (0.252)	0.495 (0.316)	−0.652*** (0.245)
French legal origin	0.572* (0.305)	−0.397* (0.237)	0.392 (0.311)	−0.329 (0.234)	0.232 (0.304)	−0.626*** (0.222)
Political globalization (log)			−0.376** (0.184)	−0.430** (0.188)		

Table 3.4 Continued

	1990–95 (1)	2005–06 (2)	1990–95 (3)	2005–06 (4)	1990–95 (5)	2005–06 (6)
Social globalization (log)					−1.141*** (0.395)	14.54*** (4.168)
Social globalization squared						−2.013*** (0.547)
Constant	7.003*** (1.031)	−37.71* (20.79)	7.134*** (1.098)	10.54*** (0.944)	7.749*** (0.920)	−19.75** (8.434)
Extremum point	–	4.012	–	–	–	3.610
X_l (slope)	–	2.062 (10.955)	–	–	–	2.055 (6.262)
X_h (slope)	–	4.563 (−3.096)	–	–	–	4.558 (−3.815)
Appropriate U test	H_0 rejected	2.15	H_0 rejected	H_0 rejected	H_0 rejected	3.23
Obs.	78	74	84	76	84	76
Adjsuted R-sq	.618	.695	.583	.691	.603	.728

Notes: Robust standard errors in parentheses. * , **, *** denote significances at 1, 5, and 10% levels.
Overall test of presence of a Inverse U shape based on the Fieller Interval.
P-values in square brackets.

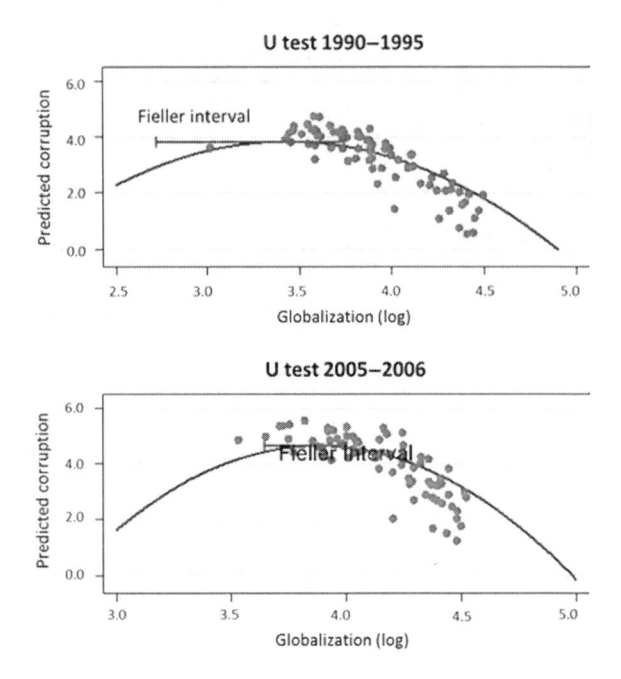

Figure 3.1 U-shape test of Lind and Mehlum (2010).

3.4.2 Robustness tests

So far, we have assumed that globalization is not endogenous to corruption, but such a hypothesis is debatable. As showed by some authors, certain dimensions of globalization, such as trade (Treisman 2000; Knack and Azfar 2003) and capital inflows (Wei 2000a) could be affected by corruption (bias of simultaneity). In addition, the corruption measure is known to be affected by measurement errors. If such errors are correlated with the unobserved factors that determine corruption, then our estimates are likely to be biased. In order to correct for the potential endogeneity problem, instrumental variables regressions are performed. More specifically, the Generalized Method of Moments (GMM) is applied, which is more efficient than the standard instrumental variables in the presence of heteroskedasticity (Baum *et al.* 2003).

The instruments are based on the distance to financial markets. Our argument is that the closer a country is to financial centers, the stronger its integration in the globalization process. Three instruments, corresponding to the biggest world financial centers, are used: the natural logarithm of the great-circle distance to the closest major financial center (London, New York, or Tokyo) and to the major bank centers (Rose and Spiegel 2009). Japan, the UK and the US are therefore dropped from our estimations.

Table 3.5 presents the results of the two-step generalized method of moments (GMM2S). The IV must satisfy two conditions to be valid: (1) relevance

Table 3.5 2SLS results

	(1) 1990–95	(2) 2005–06	(3) 1990–95	(4) 2005–06	(5) 1990–95	(6) 2005–06	(7) 1990–95	(8) 2005–06
Globalization (log)	21.48*** (7.506)	−21.39 (33.23)						
Overall globalization squared	−2.992*** (0.920)	2.042 (3.863)						
Economic globalization (log)			14.86** (5.922)	50.96** (22.16)				
Economic globalization squared			−2.052** (0.778)	−6.191** (2.693)				
Political globalization (log)					−2.387*** (0.760)	−0.653 (0.399)		
Social globalization (log)							13.73** (5.932)	23.48** (11.75)
Social globalization squared							−2.067*** (0.721)	−3.098** (1.416)
Log of real GDP per capita	−0.0959 (0.198)	0.0758 (0.222)	−0.290 (0.265)	−0.315 (0.197)	−0.194 (0.163)	−0.492*** (0.0841)	0.0105 (0.253)	−0.187 (0.172)
Exports of fuels	0.0278 (0.0414)	0.0317 (0.0433)	0.0568 (0.0411)	0.0831 (0.0542)	0.182*** (0.0618)	0.132*** (0.0468)	0.0360 (0.0360)	0.0624 (0.0556)
Proportion of Protestants	−0.00304 (0.00384)	−0.0263*** (0.00511)	−0.00342 (0.00407)	−0.0218*** (0.00328)	−0.0191** (0.00785)	−0.0248*** (0.00356)	−0.00456 (0.00422)	−0.0195*** (0.00372)
Proportion of Muslims	0.00803** (0.00373)	−0.00376 (0.00489)	0.00970** (0.00420)	0.00465 (0.00529)	0.0108* (0.00628)	−0.000612 (0.00320)	0.0101** (0.00381)	0.00197 (0.00357)
Proportion of Catholics	0.00784** (0.00360)	−0.00321 (0.00338)	0.00646 (0.00399)	−0.00279 (0.00301)	0.00201 (0.00571)	−0.00351 (0.00316)	0.0101** (0.00478)	−0.00152 (0.00315)

(Continued)

Table 3.5 Continued

	(1) 1990–95	(2) 2005–06	(3) 1990–95	(4) 2005–06	(5) 1990–95	(6) 2005–06	(7) 1990–95	(8) 2005–06
Ethno-linguistic fractionalization	0.467*	−0.128	0.103	0.514	0.315	−0.0194	0.413	0.502
	(0.268)	(0.332)	(0.384)	(0.311)	(0.355)	(0.236)	(0.308)	(0.366)
British legal origin	0.227	−0.811**	0.721**	−0.538*	−0.464	−0.463*	0.0634	−0.640**
	(0.292)	(0.311)	(0.346)	(0.312)	(0.540)	(0.274)	(0.348)	(0.267)
French legal origin	0.208	−0.700**	0.389	−0.354	−0.206	−0.318	−0.251	−0.454*
	(0.305)	(0.317)	(0.276)	(0.261)	(0.475)	(0.236)	(0.363)	(0.264)
Constant	−34.95**	58.01	−21.93*	−97.57**	14.04***	11.49***	−19.66*	−38.00
	(14.76)	(70.21)	(11.70)	(46.21)	(2.552)	(1.854)	(11.14)	(23.85)
Observations	81	73	76	72	82	74	82	74
adjusted R-squared	0.608	0.504	0.280	0.601	0.00705	0.670	0.520	0.690
Hansen J statistic	6.560	5.974	7.901	9.330	1.371	1.265	6.088	8.815
p-value of Hansen J statistic	0.363	0.426	0.245	0.156	0.712	0.738	0.413	0.184

Notes: Robust standard errors in parentheses. *, **, *** denote significances at 1, 5, and 10% levels.

(2) exogeneity ($Cov(Z, \varepsilon) = 0$). The null hypothesis of the over-identification of the Sargan–Hansen test could not be rejected in all specifications. That is, our instruments can be considered valid and the model is correctly specified (Baum *et al.* 2003). The globalization variable and its squares are considered endogenous. Most of the results (except in the 2005–06 period) confirm the inverted U-shaped relationship between globalization and corruption.

3.4.3 Using an alternative measure of corruption

A second source of corruption data is used to test whether our previous results still hold. The data is taken from the Kaufmann, Kraay and Mastruzzi (KKM) (2011) database. The variable is rescaled from 0 (lowest corruption) to 10 (highest corruption). This index is a composite one and is therefore more reliable than any individual indicator. The KKM data include continuous variables, meaning we can dispense multinomial model regressions. This corruption variable is computed for 1996–98, 2000–04 and 2005–09. The KKM corruption variable is highly correlated with the ICRG data, with correlation coefficients of 0.817 in 1990–95, 0.868 in 1995–2000 and 0.898 for the 2005–09 period.

Table 3.6 displays the instrumental variables regressions for the overall globalization index and its three dimensions as considered in this study. The instruments used are those described above. The OLS results which are also consistent with the IV results are displayed in Table A3.2 in the Appendices. Most of our previous results are confirmed.

The OLS as well as the instrumental variables approach show the nonlinear relationship between globalization and corruption as previously evidenced. As far as the dimensions of globalization are concerned, the nonlinearity holds for economic and social globalization but not for political globalization. In other words, some countries, mostly developing ones, are likely to suffer from globalization. Furthermore, the regressions confirm the time-varying nature of the relationship between globalization and corruption.

Before concluding, it is worth noting that the findings are consistent with the empirical studies on the determinants of corruption (Treisman 2000; Serra 2006; Pellegrini and Gerlagh 2004). Indeed, the factors that seem to impact most often and significantly and through many specifications are GDP per capita, exports of fuels, proportion of Protestants, Muslims and Catholics. An increase in GDP per capita reduces corruption and a higher proportion of Protestants leads to lower levels of corruption. On the contrary, the more a country exports fuels or has a greater proportion of Muslims, the higher its level of corruption. Ethno-linguistic fractionalization does not seem to affect corruption. British and French legal origins display mixed results.

3.5 Concluding remarks

This chapter aimed to reexamine the consequences of globalization on corruption, two multidimensional phenomena. An important feature of the present study is to consider that the relationship between these two phenomena might not be as

Table 3.6 Globalization and corruption: IV regressions with KKM corruption data

	(1) 1995–2000	(2) 2000–05	(3) 2005–09
Globalization	38.67***	36.12***	40.28***
	(13.04)	(11.80)	(14.31)
Globalization squared	−5.127***	−4.627***	−5.067***
	(1.583)	(1.424)	(1.647)
Log of real GDP per capita	−0.709***	−1.188***	−0.983***
	(0.184)	(0.258)	(0.270)
Political rights	0.130	0.255**	0.270**
	(0.0852)	(0.105)	(0.127)
Exports of fuels	0.133***	0.0542	0.144**
	(0.0473)	(0.0565)	(0.0606)
Proportion of Protestants	−0.00237	−0.00482	−0.0130*
	(0.00518)	(0.00499)	(0.00666)
Proportion of Muslims	0.00245	−0.00346	−0.00675
	(0.00431)	(0.00499)	(0.00425)
Proportion of Catholics	0.0112***	0.00944***	0.00362
	(0.00337)	(0.00355)	(0.00381)
Ethno-linguistic fractionalization	0.276	−0.103	−0.320
	(0.208)	(0.291)	(0.240)
British legal origin	−0.483*	−0.0876	−0.299
	(0.280)	(0.309)	(0.310)
French legal origin	−0.356	0.0135	0.0884
	(0.351)	(0.326)	(0.345)
Const.	−62.92**	−56.96**	−67.59**
	(26.23)	(23.17)	(30.54)
Obs.	104	109	79
Adjusted R2	0.836	0.759	0.831
Hansen J statistics	5.077	3.178	4.472
(p-value)	0.2795	0.5285	0.3459

Note: The dependent variable is from KKM (2011) database.
Robust standard errors in brackets: *$p < 10\%$, **$p < 5\%$, ***$p < 1\%$.

simple as suggested by the current literature. Several dimensions of globalization have been therefore taken into consideration: economic, political and social. The study has been conducted on a sample consisting of 122 countries from 1990 to 2006, divided into different sub-periods. In order to disentangle the positive and negative effects of globalization, we have assessed a quadratic functional form, using ordinary least squares as well as the instrumental variables approach.

Our study confirms the nonlinear relationship between globalization and corruption. Thus, the findings suggest that not all developing countries could gain from globalization, unless they take part more intensively in the globalization process so as to go beyond some critical threshold. Furthermore, our research suggests that each individual dimension of globalization has a different impact on corruption. As observed for overall globalization, countries need to achieve a minimum level of economic and social integration before they can take advantage of the reducing effect of globalization. In contrast, political globalization plays an important role in curtailing corruption, the only condition being that countries be open to the process. A combination of the different results suggests that the increasing effect of globalization on corruption is driven by economic and social globalization.

The results established in the present study help to gain further insight into the consequences of globalization in developing countries. In particular, it seems that globalization does not benefit most sub-Saharan countries, insofar as their participation in the process is not high enough.

Notes

1 To the best of our knowledge, Attila (2013) is the most extensive analysis of the relationship between globalization and corruption. The author documents this relationship over four different periods (1990–95, 1995–2000, 2000–05) using a sample consisting of 122 developed and developing countries. The other empirical studies (Sandholtz and Gray 2003; Akhter 2004; Lalountas *et al.* 2011) are rather limited and focus only on one period, generally a year. For instance, Das and DiRienzo (2009) used the Corruption Perception Index in 2008 and the control variables represent either 2005 or 2003.
2 For discussions on the use (abuse) and criticism of governance and corruption indicators, see Williams and Siddique (2008), Seligson (2006), Kurtz and Schrank (2007), Arndt and Oman (2006), and Kaufmann *et al.* (2007).
3 Keohane and Nye (2000) refer to military globalism as long-distance networks of interdependence in which force, and the threat or promise of force, are employed. Environmental globalism refers to the long-distance transport of materials in the atmosphere or oceans, or of biological substances such as pathogens or genetic materials that affect human health and well-being.

Appendices

Table A3.1 List of countries

Albania	Canada	Estonia	Ireland
Algeria	Central Africa Republic	Fiji	Israel
Argentina	Chad	Finland	Italy
Australia	Chile	France	Jamaica
Austria	China	Gabon	Japan
Bahamas, the	Colombia	Germany	Jordan
Bahrain	Congo, Dem. Rep.	Ghana	Kenya
Bangladesh	Congo, Rep.	Greece	Korea, Rep.
Barbados	Costa Rica	Guatemala	Kuwait
Belgium	Côte d'Ivoire	Guinea-Bissau	Latvia
Belize	Croatia	Guyana	Lithuania
Benin	Cyprus	Haiti	Luxembourg
Bolivia	Czech Republic	Honduras	Madagascar
Botswana	Denmark	Hungary	Malawi
Brazil	Dominican Republic	Iceland	Malaysia
Bulgaria	Ecuador	India	Mali
Burundi	Egypt, Arab Rep.	Indonesia	Malta
Cameroon	El Salvador	Iran, Islamic Rep.	Mauritius

(*Continued*)

Mexico	Panama	Singapore	Tunisia
Morocco	Papua New Guinea	Slovak Republic	Turkey
Myanmar	Paraguay	Slovenia	Uganda
Namibia	Peru	South Africa	Ukraine
Nepal	Philippines	Spain	United Arab Emirates
Netherlands	Poland	Sri Lanka	United Kingdom
New Zealand	Portugal	Sweden	United States
Nicaragua	Romania	Switzerland	Uruguay
Niger	Russian Federation	Syrian Arab Republic	Venezuela, RB
Nigeria	Rwanda	Tanzania	Zambia
Norway	Saudi Arabia	Thailand	Zimbabwe
Oman	Senegal	Togo	
Pakistan	Sierra Leone	Trinidad and Tobago	

Table A3.2 Globalization and corruption: OLS regressions with KKM corruption data

	(1) 1995–2000	(2) 2000–05	(3) 2005–09
Globalization	30.57***	18.53***	22.55***
	(5.575)	(3.922)	(4.431)
Overall globalization squared	−4.182***	−2.669***	−3.022***
	(0.707)	(0.515)	(0.584)
Log of real GDP per capita	−0.626***	−0.750***	−0.848***
	(0.0943)	(0.106)	(0.113)
Political rights	0.127	0.171*	0.148
	(0.0832)	(0.0936)	(0.108)
Exports of fuels	0.156***	0.142***	0.155***
	(0.0385)	(0.0464)	(0.0491)
Proportion of Protestants	−0.00415	−0.00842*	−0.0185***
	(0.00417)	(0.00432)	(0.00403)
Proportion of Muslims	0.00139	−0.00323	−0.00510
	(0.00416)	(0.00430)	(0.00421)
Proportion of Catholics	0.0106***	0.00907***	0.00188
	(0.00323)	(0.00332)	(0.00368)
Ethno-linguistic fractionalization	0.204	0.0262	−0.214
	(0.201)	(0.217)	(0.217)
British legal origin	−0.498*	−0.386	−0.412
	(0.262)	(0.263)	(0.287)
French legal origin	−0.405	−0.480*	−0.147
	(0.301)	(0.276)	(0.299)
Constant	−46.29***	−21.51***	−30.02***
	(10.95)	(7.596)	(8.502)
Observations	108	113	83
Adjusted R-squared	0.857	0.851	0.864

Note: The dependent variable is from KKM (2011) database Robust standard errors in brackets: $*p < 10\%$, $**p < 5\%$, $***p < 1\%$.

Part II

Corruption types and economic growth impacts

A globalized perspective

4 Everyday opinions on grand and petty corruption

A Portuguese study

Gabrielle Poeschl and Raquel Ribeiro

4.1 Introduction

Corruption is not a new phenomenon. Indeed, Plato and Aristotle used the concept, which they applied to whole societies, to characterize political regimes that benefited the interests of particular groups or sectors instead of applying laws and seeking the well-being of the citizens (Friedrich 2002). Much later, a well-known nineteenth century Portuguese writer, Eça de Queiroz,[1] maintained that the fate of Portugal was left to randomness, nepotism, and opportunism, and asked whether a country governed by chance, vanity and interests, speculation and corruption, privileges and crony influence would be able to preserve its independence. Without providing an answer to this question, it seems that no country is unaffected, to a greater or lesser extent, by some form of corruption (Andvig and Fjeldstad 2001). This explains why corruption is a source of concern for governments, non-governmental organizations and individuals, and why it is presently at the center of attention of authors from various disciplines. The academic debate over corruption focuses on its definition, its measurement, its extent, its causes and consequences, as well as on the role of globalization in its evolution (Blundo 2000).

Corruption is not only an object of debate among specialists, but has also invaded the media, which recurrently reveal cases—or suspected cases—of corruption. This kindles the interest of common people in the phenomenon animating their daily conversations (Tumber and Waisbord 2004). Although more absent from the media, petty corruption constitutes another facet of the phenomenon that generates divergences in the scientific community with regard to its similarity with grand corruption, its importance, the seriousness of its consequences, the concept of morality that it implies (Harrison 2007).

Thus, this study intends to understand whether the general public also has an opinion about petty corruption, whether they know how to identify its attributes, and whether, in terms of morality, they distinguish between the actors and the practices associated with grand and petty corruption. Before presenting the results of our research, we review different points of view on the definition of corruption and discuss some of the facets of corruption that have generated debate among scholars.

4.2 Corruption: an overview

To define corruption is a complex task. The most common definitions concern political corruption. Thus, corruption refers to acts in which the power of public office is used for personal gain (Jain 2001a), or to the misuse of public resources by officials for private gain (Treisman 2000). Political scientists maintain that "a public official is corrupt if he accepts money or money's worth for doing something that he is under a duty to do anyway, that he is under a duty not to do, or to exercise a legitimate discretion for improper reasons" (McMullan 1961: 183–4). Other authors note that the private benefits of corruption may be economic, when an exchange of cash or material goods occurs, or social, in the case of clientelism, nepotism or favoritism (Andvig and Fjeldstad 2001), and define corruption as "behavior that deviates from the formal rules of conduct governing the actions of someone in a position of public authority because of private-regarding motives such as wealth, power, or status" (Khan 1996: 12).

Corruption can be found at the international level, possibly fostered by globalization (Das and DiRienzo 2009), and, at the national level, in the different branches of government, often because of overlapping and conflicting authority (Andvig and Fjeldstad 2001).

Economists have questioned a definition of corruption restricted to the public sector. They maintain that there is considerable evidence that many acts of corruption occur in the private sector and that corruption is not only used for private benefit (Hodgson and Jiang 2007). Indeed, corruption exists within and between private businesses, within non-governmental organizations, trade unions and sport associations. Finally, corruption is also a moral and cultural problem and can affect interactions among individuals (Miller 2005). Private sector corruption is detrimental to the development of a society, but public corruption is more important because "controlling public sector corruption is a prerequisite for controlling private sector corruption" (Andvig and Fjeldstad 2001).

The literature on corruption covers various facets of the phenomenon, such as types of corrupt practices, forms of corruption, causes and consequences of corruption.

4.2.1 Corrupt practices

The United Nations Global Program against Corruption, which aims to implement anti-corruption measures both in the public and private sectors, describes different expressions of corrupt practices, such as bribery (offering money or favors to influence a public official), embezzlement (stealing money or other government property), extortion (coercing a person to pay money or to provide favors in exchange for acting or failing to act), influence peddling (using one's influence or connections to obtain favors) or nepotism (showing favoritism to relatives or close friends). These different expressions of corrupt practices appear under both grand and petty corruption (CICP 2001).

However, these corrupt practices can be classified into different levels of gravity, depending on the extent to which they are morally approved and accepted

(Heidenheimer 2002). Thus, some acts are almost universally condemned and people generally think that they should be punishable (so called "black corruption"). Others are frequently held to be corrupt, but opinions of the public and the decision-makers are divided ("grey corruption"). Finally, there are acts that may be generally considered as mildly or "not really" corrupt, that are widely tolerated and deemed as unworthy of punishment ("white corruption"). Even if they are not encouraged, these acts are accepted and are difficult to uproot (Gibbons 2010).

Heidenheimer (2002) argues that these categories are flexible: practices that are objectively similar come to be more severely condemned and possibly punished, as one moves from the traditional to modern communities, and from the top to the bottom of the hierarchical scale.

Consequently, citizens may view corruption differently in different societies. Moreover, in modern societies, there is some consensus about white and black corruption, but there are changing attitudes toward grey corruption due to the influence of the media, which frequently shine the spotlight on corrupt practices (Lipovetsky 1996).

4.2.2 Forms of corruption

Another distinction is related to the forms of corruption. Political or grand corruption can be distinguished from bureaucratic or petty corruption. Grand corruption involves top officials and political decision-makers, is large in scale and often involves great amounts of money. In grand corruption, highly placed individuals exploit their positions to extract bribes, embezzle large sums of money, or tailor regulations to benefit their private interests (Andvig and Fjeldstad 2001).

Petty corruption involves middle- or low-level public officials, who may be underpaid and who interact directly with the public. Petty corruption involves small sums of money but generally harms the poorest members of a society in their interactions with public services (schools, hospitals, police, tax administration, etc.). Petty corruption is thus a "street level" form of corruption (Andvig and Fjeldstad 2001). Although grand corruption is viewed as having more of a negative impact on the economy, petty corruption, with its small sums of money, represents, when aggregated, a substantial amount of public resources (Shah and Schacter 2004).

Petty corruption seems to be more frequent in less developed countries, where people must often pay a bribe to obtain the services that they should get for free (Riley 1999). Nevertheless, levels of the different types of corruption can vary within a country. For example, grand corruption may take place in a country where there is little petty corruption and petty corruption may take place in a country where the government is clean. In spite of this, grand corruption and petty corruption tend to go hand-in-hand and to be mutually reinforcing (Andvig and Fjeldstad 2001; Riley 1999).

Recently, authors have noted some types of practices in more advanced countries that can be viewed as corrupt even if they differ from the behaviors that are usually taken into consideration. These are legal acts that benefit private interests and belong to a third form of corruption: state capture (Hellman and Kaufmann 2001), defined as corruption in which "firms make private payments to public officials to influence the choice and design of laws, rules and regulations" (Hellman and Kaufmann 2001: 1). This implies the collusion by private actors with public officials or politicians for their mutual, private benefit, a kind of "capture" of the state apparatus (Shah and Schacter 2004). State capture may coexist with political corruption, in which public officials exploit the private sector for their own private ends.

4.2.3   Causes of corruption

The literature points to three types of causes for corruption, highlighting individual, structural and contextual factors. Individual factors include a predisposition for crime, lack of ethics and greed, or rational choices made by actors involved in corruption (Miller 2005). Contextual factors refer to the opportunity to engage in corrupt actions, created by important governmental projects or credit incentives, or due to the lack of measures likely to prevent corruption (Argandoña 2001).

Structural factors underline, first of all, the lack of democracy, underdevelopment and poverty (Seyf 2001). In highly corrupt countries, there is little notion that the state must defend the public interest or that the law must protect the public rather than private interest, there is no institutional control of abuse of power, and no willingness or ability to address corruption (Shah and Schacter 2004).

Thus, there is more corruption in less developed, less democratic countries with a weaker judicial system and where poverty is rife (Seyf 2001). However, the relationship between the level of development and the level of corruption is not linear (Transparency International 2009). In addition, structural factors include culture and ethics, societal norms and values (Graaf 2007).

In this respect, it may be noted that there is no consensus about the relationship between globalization and corruption (Das and DiRienzo 2009). According to some authors, the intensification of relationships among nations has contributed to revealing corruption, to the adoption of anti-corruption regulations and to decreasing corruption (Williams and Beare 1999). For other authors, corruption has, on the contrary, increased because international institutions fail to promote the fair development of nations, produce poverty and create favorable conditions for corruption, or because the reduced autonomy of the states gives them less power to fight corruption (CMI 2009). A third position maintains that when nations begin to be globalized their levels of corruption increase, but these levels decrease as they progress in the global economy. Thus, the highest levels of corruption may be observed in countries with moderate levels of globalization (Das and DiRienzo 2009).

Finally, some specialists argue that corruption is widespread in countries where not only the public administration and the legal system are weak and undeveloped, but also where the media are under state control (Chinhamo and Shumba 2007). The media are indeed crucial in making political wrongdoing public (Tumber and Waisbord 2004): they can play the role of watchdogs (checking on powerful sectors and leaders), agenda-setters (raising awareness of social problems) and gatekeepers (bringing together a plurality of viewpoints). When there are no restrictions on press freedom, no limited access to media, and when journalists do not lack professionalism, the media often have political and moral effects (Odugbemi and Norris 2010). They may, more specifically, lead governments to discuss the problems raised, trigger sanctions, or change rules or policies even though public attention is more likely to be caught by scandals involving well-known figures (Coronel 2010).

4.2.4   Consequences of corruption

The authors who focus on the economic and social consequences of corruption are reluctant to consider corruption merely as a question of morality. On the contrary, they emphasize that corruption produces victims. They also reject the opinion, once defended, that the benefits of corruption might exceed the costs (Leys 2002) and argue that corruption entails numerous negative social consequences, namely the maintenance or even escalation of poverty (Riley 1999; Seyf 2001).

For example, according to McMullan (1961), corruption triggers the following consequences: injustice, inefficiency of services, mistrust of the government, waste of public resources, discouragement of (foreign) enterprise, political instability, repressive measures (against accusations of corruption), and restrictions on government policy. These consequences are also taken into consideration by the United Nations Organization, which underlines the role of corruption in undermining democratic institutions, slowing economic development and contributing to government instability (UNODC 2012), and by the World Bank (1997), which states that corruption is the greatest obstacle to economic and social development. In addition, in all countries, it is the poorest people who suffer most from corruption because the economic benefits and national resources revert to the rich, instead of being attributed to programs and services that should make it possible to fight poverty (CMI 2009).

Finally, it should be noted that the problems caused by political and bureaucratic corruption seem much more severe than the problems caused by state capture (Bauhr *et al.* 2010). However, some authors see "legal corruption" as a major problem and, according to Kaufmann (2008), a former Director of the World Bank Institute, the current financial crisis has its roots in legal corruption.

4.2.5   The general public's views about corruption

Because of the social relevance of the phenomenon, numerous studies have attempted to capture the opinions of the general public about corruption. In addition to the surveys regularly conducted by Transparency International, the PEW Global Attitudes Project (2002) has shown, for example, in a survey conducted with 38,000 respondents from the five continents, that corruption, together with crime, is considered the biggest national problem in many countries (Pew Research Center 2002).

With regard to Portugal, the extensive media coverage of political scandals has made grand corruption highly visible in recent years. As, on average, the Portuguese watch television for three and a half hours per day,[2] and as a quarter of the time dedicated to the national channels is used to view information programs,[3] we can conclude that the Portuguese have some opinions about corruption. These opinions are revealed in the perceived level of corruption rated by Transparency International's Corruption Perceptions Index, which has recorded a consistent rise. In 2010, Portugal ranked 6.0 on a 10-point scale, where 10 represents the lowest level of corruption (Transparency International 2010) and, on the 2010/11 Global Corruption Barometer, 84 percent of the Portuguese respondents declared that corruption had increased in the country in the last three years (Transparency International 2010/11).

Furthermore, data from the European Social Survey (Round 2) of the International Social Survey Programme and results of the survey "Corruption and ethics in democracy: the case of Portugal" (Sousa and Triães 2008) suggest that corruption in Portugal is structural: on the one hand, there is a culture centered on individual success where the interests of relevant others (members of in-groups) are more important than the interests of the community at large. On the other hand, political power lacks transparency, is blind to the problems of the citizens, and permeable to private interests. Consequently, in spite of symbolically condemning corruption, the Portuguese are likely to adopt some of the condemned behaviors when they think that they are justified (Sousa and Triães 2008).

Quantitative surveys give valuable information on opinions about corruption, but they measure people's positioning on selected aspects of the phenomenon, failing to capture the way people's thought systems are organized and vary according to the situation at hand. Nevertheless, and even if Portuguese media coverage of the scandals generally fails to present an in-depth analysis of corruption, common people, like the specialists, have probably constructed theories about the causes, consequences, costs and benefits of corruption. Thus, a recent study using free association has shown, for example, that different elements of corruption emerge when people think about corruption in general, at the global level and at the national (Portuguese) level (Poeschl and Ribeiro 2010). It has also revealed that, when people think about corruption, they are likely to evoke actors, roles and sectors, but overlook the consequences of corruption.

As media coverage of corruption scandals has undoubtedly had an impact on the immediate responses about corruption obtained in this study, we decided to proceed by focusing on grand corruption and petty corruption. The objective was to obtain more information about the general public's views on corruption and identify possible theories about the phenomenon, in particular about the importance given to individual, organizational (contextual) and societal (structural) factors (Graaf 2007). We believe that it is important to uncover these theories, because they explain the general public's attitudes toward corrupt actors and practices, and account for their behaviors, which may range from following the example to getting ready to act against corrupt practices.

4.3 Method

4.3.1 Respondents

Two hundred participants answered our questionnaire but eighteen had to be removed because they did not understand the term petty corruption. Thus, our sample comprises 182 respondents, of which 87 male and 95 female respondents, 88 were aged under 35 years (minimum: 16 years, average: 23.74) and 94 over 35 (maximum: 62 years, mean: 47.27 years). Almost all the respondents (except four) were of Portuguese nationality. Among the respondents, 88 were single, and 92 were or had been married (2 did not answer this question). With regard to professional activity, 55 were independent workers, senior or junior executives, 65 employees or factory workers, 61 were not employed (among whom there were 47 students) (one person did not answer this question). In relation to educational level, 47 respondents had completed compulsory education, 41 had completed high school and 90 were attending or had completed a university degree (4 did not answer this question). Most of the respondents said they were Catholic (109), moderately observant (4.66 on a 7-point scale where 1 = not at all observant), 58 declared they had no religion, and 20 did not answer this question.

Politically, the respondents ranged from the extreme-left (11 respondents) to the extreme-right (3 respondents), and 40 declared they had no political orientation. On average, respondents were located to the center-left (3.69 on a 7-point scale where 1 = extreme-left). They stated they did not have much interest in politics (at the national level: 4.35; at the international level: 3.87, on a 7-point scale where 7 = extremely interested).

4.3.2 Questionnaire and procedure

The study was conducted by means of a questionnaire made up of open and closed items. First, respondents were asked to write ten words or expressions that come to mind when they thought about grand corruption (i.e., corruption practiced by persons in important positions) and petty corruption (i.e., corruption practiced by common citizens). The order of presentation of the stimuli was counterbalanced. Then respondents had to rate on a 7-point scale (1 = not at all; 7 = extremely) the extent to which, in their opinion, at the national and international levels, corruption affects politics, justice, economy and finance, and society in general, and the extent to which national and international institutions show the ability and willingness to address grand and petty corruption.

Respondents were also asked to rate national and international institutions (1 = very negative; 7 = very positive). Finally, socio-demographic data were gathered (gender, age, nationality, marital status, profession, level of education, religion, political orientation, and interest in politics at the national and international level).

The questionnaire was randomly administered by the students who participated in the study in April 2010. The distribution by age group and gender was controlled and respondents answered the questions individually.

4.3.3   Experimental design

The study followed a 2 (gender: male respondents *vs.* female respondents) × 2 (age group: young adults versus older adults) factorial design.

4.3.4   Data analysis

We began by analyzing the extensiveness and the nature of the information gathered from the open items. All the words were recorded in a data file, applying only the reduction rules generally used in free association tasks (Rosenberg and Jones 1972). Then, some obvious synonyms were grouped, but a content analysis was not performed. To describe the information, the following statistics were calculated (cf. Poeschl and Ribeiro 2010): fluidity (the total number of words); amplitude (the number of different words); richness (the ratio between amplitude and fluidity).

Second, we analyzed the content of the information gathered, registering the most frequent words and comparing, by means of the chi-square statistic, the frequency of their association with grand and petty corruption. According to some authors (e.g., Hampton 1979), frequency may be taken as a measure of the importance of the words for the definition of a concept.

Then, the *Alceste* program of textual data analysis was applied to uncover the structure of the information on corruption, i.e., to extract its different dimensions and identify whether they were more representative of some groups of respondents. *Alceste* executes a descending cluster analysis based on the co-occurrence of the words that constitute the corpus, using the chi-square distance (e.g., Reinert 1993).

Finally, we analyzed the extent to which respondents perceive that national and international institutions have the ability and willingness to address grand and petty corruption and looked for distinct types of opinions. We attempted to relate these opinions to the rating of national and international institutions as well as to the dimensions of grand and petty corruption.

4.4   Results

4.4.1   Information about corruption

Globally, 1993 responses were recorded, among which 244 different words with a frequency of occurrence varying from 1 (62 words) to 63 (politics). Table 4.1 presents the measures of amplitude, fluidity and richness, globally and separately for grand and petty corruption. As expected, information about grand corruption was more structured than information about petty corruption.

Table 4.2 presents the words mentioned by more than 10 percent of the respondents. The most frequent words, after politics, were money (56), power (55), greed (52) and football (51), recorded by more than one quarter of the respondents. The frequency of occurrence of money and greed did not differ when applied to grand or petty corruption and they may constitute the very core of the definition of corruption.

Table 4.1 Information about grand corruption and petty corruption

	Grand corruption	*Petty corruption*	*Total*
Amplitude	187	204	244
Fluidity	1068	925	1993
Richness	0.18	0.22	0.12

Note: Richness varies between 0 and 1, i.e., from total consensus to total divergence.

Table 4.2 Most frequent words about corruption. Significant differences between petty and grand corruption, as shown by the chi-square statistic

Word	*Total frequency*	*Petty*	*Grand*	*Chi-square*
Politics	63	12	51	24.14***
Money	56	25	31	0.64
Power	55	11	44	19.80***
Greed	52	22	30	1.23
Football	51	10	41	18.84***
Lack of principles	49	17	32	4.59*
Cheat	48	29	19	2.08
Thieves	45	20	25	0.56
Robbery	44	27	17	2.27
Lies	43	22	21	0.02
Dishonest	41	22	19	0.22
Bribery	36	20	16	0.44
Favors	32	21	11	3.13
Injustice	31	15	16	0.03
Ambition	26	18	8	3.85*
Selfishness	26	13	13	0.00
Lack of respect	24	12	12	0.00
Opportunism	23	13	10	0.39
False	23	11	12	0.04
Scandal	22	1	21	18.18***
Need	22	21	1	18.18***
Lack of personality	22	8	14	1.64
String-pulling	21	16	5	5.76*
Embezzlement	21	8	13	1.19
Abuse of power	20	2	18	12.80***

Note: ***$p < .001$; **$p < .01$; *$p < .05$.

The words presented in Table 4.2 suggest that grand corruption is associated with the sectors in which several scandals were given wide coverage by the Portuguese media (see also Poeschl and Ribeiro 2010). They also refer to the positions of power of the actors of corruption. Additionally, petty corruption is more specifically associated with needs or ambition, and suggests the common practice of pulling strings, which seems particularly well tolerated in Portugal (Sousa 2008).

4.4.2   *Structure of the information about corruption*

The *Alceste* software for textual data used to uncover specific ways of thinking about corruption included all words with a frequency of at least three occurrences and classified 88 percent of the responses. Eight classes of words were extracted: three classes are more representative of grand corruption, two more representative of petty corruption, and the other three are common to both types of corruption.

Grand corruption is positioned in the organizational context. The first class (16.30 percent of the corpus) mentions the institutions most likely to favor corruption, e.g., politics, football ($\chi^2 > 90$), local authorities ($\chi^2 > 80$), public sector, banks ($\chi^2 > 50$), government, and police ($\chi^2 > 40$). The second class (10.03 percent of the corpus) points to specific unethical practices likely to take place in these institutions. It is organized around money ($\chi^2 > 40$), and includes money laundering, embezzlement ($\chi^2 > 30$), taxes, drugs, and arms ($\chi^2 > 25$). The third most representative class of grand corruption (12.54 percent of the corpus) is made up of moral judgments about these institutions and practices. It comprises interests ($\chi^2 > 30$), mistrust, schemes, deterioration ($\chi^2 > 20$), lies, opportunism, abuse of power, and revolt ($\chi^2 > 15$).

There is only one class that is slightly more representative of a group of respondents: younger adults are more likely to mention the practices that are typical of grand corruption ($\chi^2 = 2.39$).

The first class that appears most often associated with petty corruption (13.17 percent of the corpus) positions the phenomenon in a societal context that promotes instrumental practices involving money, e.g., bribe ($\chi^2 > 80$), money ($\chi^2 > 20$), blackmail, kickback, opportunities ($\chi^2 > 15$). The second most representative class of petty corruption (5.96 percent) focuses on the importance of general economic conditions, and is organized around poverty ($\chi^2 > 166$). It also includes needs ($\chi^2 > 70$), scoundrel ($\chi^2 > 40$), and wise guy ($\chi^2 > 20$). The groups of respondents do not differ with regard to the dimensions of petty corruption.

The two classes of words associated with petty corruption are related to the three common classes. The first class (7.21 percent of the corpus) stresses Portuguese cultural specificities, namely complacency ($\chi^2 > 70$), economy ($\chi^2 > 60$), social status, mentality ($\chi^2 > 50$), ethics ($\chi^2 > 30$), influence peddling, and social norms ($\chi^2 > 20$). The second class (21.32 percent) points to different traits related to individualist values, such as selfishness ($\chi^2 > 60$), nastiness ($\chi^2 > 50$), greed ($\chi^2 > 40$), lack of respect, ambition ($\chi^2 > 30$), disloyalty, and hypocrisy ($\chi^2 > 20$). Finally, the remaining class of common responses (13.48 percent) positions corruption at the individual level and depicts the actors of corrupt practices as criminals ($\chi^2 > 120$), or also bastards ($\chi^2 > 80$), shameless ($\chi^2 > 50$), thieves ($\chi^2 > 40$), and spineless, parasites, nonsense ($\chi^2 > 30$).

Respondents agree about cultural specificities, but there are differences between groups with regard to the two other classes: the class of traits related to individualistic values is more typical of young adults ($\chi^2 = 9.58$) and of female respondents

($\chi^2 = 6.85$), whereas the "criminals" class, which associates corruption with stable personality factors, is more representative of older adults ($\chi^2 = 5.73$).

In short, the opinions about grand and petty corruption seem to have a relatively consensual organization. Only the young adults seem to be more aware of the types of practices that characterize grand corruption. Young adults, as well as female respondents, are also more likely to explain corruption in terms of personality traits acquired from current individualistic values, whereas older adults, in contrast, seem to attribute corruption to individuals whose moral character is defined by their acts (cf. Miller 2005).

4.4.3 Affected institutions

Respondents were asked to indicate to what extent they think that corruption affects politics, justice, economy and finance, and society as a whole. The data indicate that they perceive a high level of corruption in all sectors (see Table 4.3).

We performed an analysis of variance 4 (sector: politics versus justice versus economy and finance versus society) × 2 (gender: male respondents versus female respondents) × 2 (age group: young adults versus older adults) with repeated measures on the first factor, on the ratings of corruption at national level. The analysis revealed that sector has a significant effect, $F (3, 534) = 7.13$, $p < .001$. As can be seen in Table 4.3, this effect indicates that respondents perceive more corruption in the politics and economy and finance sectors than in the sphere of justice or society in general. It should be noted that, although respondents spontaneously associate corruption with the public sphere, they do not believe that the level of corruption is lower in the private sector.

There are also gender-based differences, $F (1, 178) = 14.25$, $p < .001$, showing that, generally, female respondents perceive more corruption than male respondents (male respondents: 5.83; female respondents: 6.28), as well as differences related to age group, $F (1, 178) = 5.23$, $p = .023$, showing that young adults perceive less corruption than older adults (young adults: 5.92; older adults: 6.19). There are no effects of interaction between the variables.

Finally, in the opinion of our respondents, all Portuguese sectors are more affected by corruption than the equivalent sectors at international level (Table 4.3, right column).

Table 4.3 Levels of corruption perceived to affect different sectors, at national and international levels (1 = not at all; 7 = very much)

	National	*International*	*t (181)*
Politics	6.24	5.69	7.33***
Justice	5.85	5.45	3.88***
Economy and finance	6.22	5.87	4.50***
Society	5.97	5.64	4.23***

Note: ***$p < .001$.

4.4.4   *Opinions about the institutions' ability and willingness to address corruption*

We performed a cluster analysis (K-means cluster analysis of IBM SPSS) on respondents' ratings of the ability and willingness of national and international institutions to address corruption. The analysis extracted three types of position (see Table 4.4). The first cluster groups respondents who perceive that institutions have the ability and willingness to act on corruption—with the exception of national institutions that do not seem to be likely to address grand corruption; the second cluster groups respondents who believe that institutions have the ability but not the will to address corruption and the last cluster groups respondents who think that institutions have neither the ability nor the will to act on corruption.

Table 4.4 shows that respondents are equally divided into the three clusters. This is also the case of respondents of both genders, χ^2 (2) = 2.77, *ns*. However, there are significant differences with regard to the distribution by age group, χ^2 (2) = 7.54, $p = .023$. These differences are due to the fact that there are more

Table 4.4 National and international institutions' capability and will to address corruption (1 = no, not at all; 7 = yes, very much)

	Capability and will (n = 61)	*Capability but no will (n = 59)*	*No capability and no will (n = 62)*	*F (2, 179)*
National institutions have the capability to address grand corruption	3.74b	5.47a	2.47c	53.09***
National institutions have the capability to address petty corruption	5.41a	4.99a	3.10b	40.43***
International institutions have the capability to address grand corruption	5.04b	5.68a	2.66c	88.31***
International institutions have the capability to address petty corruption	5.33a	4.83a	2.85b	48.01***
National institutions have the will to address grand corruption	3.72a	3.00b	1.87c	22.97***
National institutions have the will to address petty corruption	5.34a	3.41b	2.31c	67.81***
International institutions have the will to address grand corruption	5.18a	3.93b	2.55c	47.46***
International institutions have the will to address petty corruption	5.51a	3.71b	2.55c	76.80***

Note: ***$p < .001$.

young adults than older adults who believe that institutions have the ability and willingness to address corruption (respectively 37 versus 24), whereas there are more older adults than young adults who believe that institutions have more ability than willingness to fight corruption (respectively 38 versus 21). In the third cluster, grouping people who think that institutions neither have the ability nor willingness to address corruption, young and older adults are equally represented (respectively 30 versus 32).

It thus seems that young adults, who in earlier questions indicated that they perceive less corruption in the different national sectors, are somewhat more optimistic in relation to the fight against corruption than older adults. An analysis of the remaining socio-demographic variables indicates that there are no differences in opinions due to religion, political orientation, level of education, or whether or not the respondents were employed.

4.4.5 Correlates of opinions about the institutions' ability and willingness to address corruption

Different analyses of variance were performed in order to identify whether differences in opinions about the institutions' ability and willingness to address corruption were associated with differences in opinions on the variables under scrutiny and, particularly, on the ratings of national and international institutions (see Table 4.5). Results show that respondents generally have a rather negative opinion about institutions, and an even more negative opinion in relation to national than international institutions (national institutions: 3.27; international institutions: 3.84), $F(1, 179) = 36.24$, $p < .001$. Moreover, respondents who believe that institutions have no ability and no will to fight corruption express a significantly more negative opinion about national and international institutions, $F(2, 179) = 9.30$, $p < .001$.

Furthermore, differences in opinions about the institutions' ability and willingness to address corruption are not associated with differences in the ratings of corruption in the different sectors (politics, justice, economy and finance, society), neither at the national, $F(2, 179) = 2.20$, *ns*, nor at the international level, $F(2, 179) = 1.54$, *ns*.

Finally, differences in opinions about the institutions' ability and willingness to address corruption are related to three dimensions of the structure of the information about corruption. Thus, respondents who think that institutions have

Table 4.5 Opinions about national and international institutions (1 = very negative; 7 = very positive)

	National institutions	International institutions
Capability and will	3.51	4.21
Capability but no will	3.53	3.98
No capability and no will	2.79	3.32

the ability but not the will to fight corruption are more likely to list practices of petty corruption, $\chi^2 = 3.89$, and to mention the personality of corrupt actors, $\chi^2 = 3.37$. The lack of motivation of the institutions to address corruption appears, therefore, to be linked to the opinion that petty practices are known but tolerated by institutions and, for older adults more specifically, that it is a problem caused by a group of shameless criminals.

For their part, respondents who think that institutions have the will to fight corruption and the ability to deal with petty corruption are more likely to mention the Portuguese complacent culture, $\chi^2 = 4.99$. For these respondents, corruption appears as a type of mentality that is difficult to uproot and which is resistant to the efforts of the institutions.

4.5 Conclusions

The information gathered from the free association task suggests that, for our respondents, corruption is above all a question of money and greed. It is less associated with practices such as nepotism or influence-peddling, for example, which is in line with the findings of Sousa (2008). Nevertheless, corruption appears as a familiar concept to most respondents, although the concept of grand corruption seems more structured than that of petty corruption. In the opinion of our respondents, corruption is widespread. Grand corruption takes place in organizational contexts, with specific practices that originate negative judgments. Petty corruption also has its specific behaviors but they are associated with a societal context of poverty. This does not prevent people from viewing corruption as a phenomenon related to a criminal personality, to traits developed by current individualistic values, or to a particular cultural context of complacency. Institutions are not viewed as very motivated to address corruption, especially grand corruption, and are not positively rated.

Thus, our results suggest that corruption and corrupt people are severely condemned by the general public, who focus on factors likely to favor corruption, such as socio-cultural and organizational contexts, or personality traits. However, as already observed in a more general perspective (cf. CICP 2001), people generally seem rather unaware of the social consequences of corrupt practices. This fact might explain why Portuguese citizens disapprove of corrupt practices and reluctantly accept lenient verdicts in the cases of grand corruption, but do not show much motivation to participate in organized actions against corruption. The results thus highlight the need for better information on the social costs of corruption if we want the fight against the phenomenon to become, in the words of the United Nations, "a shared responsibility" (UNODC 2008).

Notes

1 *O Distrito de Évora*. Weekly magazine. 1867.
2 Marktest. www.aqui.com.pt/tvnews/2012/01/13/portugueses-em-media-viram-3h38m-diarias-de-televisao-em-2011/ (accessed April 15, 2015).
3 Marktest. www.marktest.com/wap/a/n/id~18ff.aspx (accessed April 15, 2015).

5 Corruption in China through the lens of Finnish firms

Päivi Karkuhnen and Riitta Kosonen

5.1 Introduction

Host-country corruption is a feature that firms investing abroad increasingly need to take into account. This is due to the growing importance of China and other emerging economies, many of which are high-corruption countries, as foreign investment locations. In addition, corruption control in developed economies has become stricter in recent years (Karhunen and Ledyaeva 2012). Hence, a firm investing abroad will increasingly run the risk of encountering corruption in the host country, being at the same time subject to corruption control from its home country.

Moreover, firms from low-corruption countries investing in high-corruption ones face situations in which local players may gain competitive advantage through illicit payments in business transactions or bribery of public sector officials for preferential treatment. Consequently, a foreign firm pursuing an anti-corruption policy needs to build a different basis for its competitiveness.

International business research on corruption has mainly focused on its impact on entry mode choice. The primary question has been whether high host-country corruption—often measured in terms of corruption distance—drives a foreign entrant to ally with a local partner or to keep full control over its foreign operations. The corruption distance construct was coined by Habib and Zurawicki (2002) to conceptualize differences in the level of corruption in the investor's home country and the host country.

Interestingly, although most empirical studies in other countries (Demirbag *et al.* 2007, on Turkey; Driffield *et al.* 2010, on Eastern European countries; Karhunen and Ledyaeva 2012, on Russia) have shown that high corruption distance can lead to shared ownership, research conducted on China (Duanmu 2011) has yielded opposite results. This could mean that firms from low-corruption countries do not consider corruption in China a serious obstacle as they would, for example, in Russia (Karhunen and Ledyaeva 2012; see also Karhunen and Kosonen 2013). This finding also supports the "East Asian paradox" (Wedeman 2002), which illustrates that although corruption is generally perceived as harmful for economic growth, countries such as China have grown remarkably well in spite of high levels of corruption (Wang and You 2012).

Here, an explanation may be the predictability of corruption, i.e., when corruption is organized and surrounded with less uncertainty, it may have a less negative impact on investment (Campos *et al.* 1999). Hence, foreign firms feel confident about entering such an environment on their own, without needing a local partner to cope with corruption.

Nevertheless, the "East Asian paradox" does not imply that foreign firms entering China do not need to take corruption into account at all. Luo (2011) shows that a multinational enterprise (MNE) is less likely to commit resources to Chinese subunits in which it perceives that corruption is high. In addition, high perceived corruption can lead the investor to prefer exports to local sales in the subunit (Luo 2011). These findings indicate that high corruption may decrease the interest of a MNE to join local business networks.

Furthermore, Millington *et al.* (2005) analyze the challenges that UK companies operating in China face with corruption in terms of illicit payments in buyer–supplier relations. They show that under-the-table activities in purchasing operations are a serious problem for the studied firms in China. In addition, drawing the line between gift-giving and corruption was found to be challenging (Millington *et al.* 2005).

The present chapter contributes to the existing literature on foreign business strategies and corruption in China by showing how corruption influences business operations of Finnish firms in China. Finland has been repeatedly ranked among the world's least corrupt countries, sharing the first place in Transparency International's ranking of 176 countries in 2012 (Transparency International 2012). Hence, operating in a high-corruption country such as China can be expected to be particularly challenging for Finnish firms, not accustomed to dealing with corrupt stakeholders.

Our theoretical perspective is the neo-institutional organization theory, which we use to identify strategic responses that Finnish firms take in their Chinese subunits to cope with corruption as a feature of the local institutional environment. Our empirical data consists of 60 qualitative interviews with executives of Finnish firms operating in China. Based on this dataset we analyze, first, how strongly the interviewees perceive the influence of corruption in China on their business and, second, how does this reflect on the strategies the firms take to cope with corruption.

We show that firms can take different responses, which vary according to the emphasis on home versus host country institutional demands. The scale of responses ranges from strict compliance with home country institutional demands to acquiescence with host country pressures. At these extremes, the firm may completely ignore the demands from corrupt institutional constituents in the host country, or acknowledge host-country corruption as an institutional feature, dealing with what needs to be taken into account in firm strategy.

This chapter is structured as follows. We start with an overview of corruption in China, and then present the theoretical background and conceptual framework for our empirical analysis. The section following describes the data and methods employed and continues the empirical analysis. The chapter concludes with the discussion of our results, conclusions and practical implications.

5.2 Overview of business-related corruption in China

Corruption is one of the negative consequences of the socio-economic transformation in China from a planned economy to a socialist market economy (Deng *et al.* 2010). In 2012, China ranked 80th with two other countries (Serbia and Trinidad and Tobago) in Transparency International's Corruption Perceptions Index (Transparency International 2012) among 176 countries. This index aims to measure public sector corruption and applies a scale from 0 to 100, where 0 means a country is perceived as highly corrupt and 100 is perceived as very clean. China's 2012 score in this rating was 39. According to some estimates the value of corruption could be 3–5 percent of China's gross domestic product (Pei 2007).

Corruption has been acknowledged as a serious problem by the Chinese government as well, and it has taken measures to fight it. This includes the establishment of institutional arrangements to control corruption, such as state agencies that handle complaints of corruption and anti-corruption guidelines for state institutions (Deng *et al.* 2010). In addition, the sanctions for corruption in China are severe including the death penalty. Nevertheless, the efficacy of the government's efforts is frequently questioned. It has been emphasized that public corruption cases are just the tip of the iceberg, and that corruption campaigns are not able to deter the causes of corruption, which are deeply rooted in the society.

Corruption can be broadly defined as an illegitimate exchange of resources involving the use or abuse of public or collective responsibility for private ends (Rose-Ackerman 1999). In this chapter, we focus on business-related corruption, which we define as those corrupt transactions in which at least one party is a firm. Such corruption includes illicit payments related to buyer–supplier relations, and bribery of public sector representatives with the aim of preferential treatment.

Public sector corruption in contemporary China started to increase after the economic reforms towards a socialist market economy were launched in 1978 (Deng *et al.* 2010). One of the reasons was the introduction of a dual track system, where products could have a state-controlled price or a market price. The authority granted to state officials to stipulate which products were sold at what prices provided an opportunity for rent-seeking (Wu 2003). Businesses and individuals that wanted to maximize their profits were often motivated to bribe public officials to obtain products at the lowest possible cost (Deng *et al.* 2010). The corruption enabled by the dual price policy first concentrated on consumer goods, but soon the focus shifted to state-controlled commodities such as coal, steel, timber and cement (Hu 1989). This lasted until the early 1990s, when the dual price policy was gradually abolished (Deng *et al.* 2010).

Nevertheless, public sector corruption did not disappear but took new forms, enabled by new stages of economic reforms. The decentralization of the financial system, which gave local governments more discretionary power on issues such as budget allocation, land allocation and construction, opened doors for rent-seeking behavior (Deng *et al.* 2010). The new forms of corruption included embezzlement, illegal approval of land sales, large-scale smuggling, and leaks in construction bidding information (Deng *et al.* 2010).

Currently, two major areas particularly plagued by public sector corruption in China are land and transportation. Corruption related to land includes schemes by officials to purchase land at low prices from the state and then let relatives or associates act as land brokers to transfer it to developers. Corruption related to transportation is fuelled by the officials' control over infrastructure construction funds, responsible for allocating projects to contractors who, in turn, need to use every possible means to win the contract (Deng *et al.* 2010).

From the foreign firms' point of view, they may believe they are relatively protected from large-scale public sector corruption, as long as they are not involved in the real estate business or infrastructure construction projects. However, there are other sectors in which public sector corruption has been recently recognized as a frequent phenomenon. For example, it has been proposed that corruption in the Chinese court system may be more institutionalized and systematic than previously thought (Li 2012). Therefore, a foreign investor should be aware that dealing with the public sector in China will most likely include the risk of encountering corruption.

The second form of business-related corruption is illicit payments related to business transactions between private firms. The most frequent form is illicit payments in buyer–supplier relationships, where the person making the purchasing decision on behalf of the firm gets a bribe from the supplier for their favorable decision. Such "under-the-table," "back-door" or "red-envelope" practices are often characterized as a part of the Chinese business culture (Millington *et al.* 2005; Luo 2011). In other words, making private money in purchasing is not considered as unacceptable as in many developed countries.

Moreover, what makes this kind of corruption even more challenging for foreign firms in China is the difficulty of drawing the line between gift-giving and bribery. *Guanxi*—a system of personal connections that carry long-term social obligations—are held as playing a significant role in business relationships in China (e.g., Park and Luo 2001). From the foreign business perspective, the emphasis of *guanxi* on reciprocal favors and gift-giving (Steidlmeier 1999) and on the level of individual rather than the organization (Chen 1995) is in part identifiable with corruption (Millington *et al.* 2005). In principle, there is a clear distinction between gift-giving within *guanxi*, which is related with building relationships, and bribery which is targeted at illicit transactions (Steidlmeier 1999). Nevertheless, the culture of gift-giving provides the context in which bribery can be undertaken under the umbrella of *guanxi* (Lovett *et al.* 1999).

Given the multifaceted nature of corruption in China described above, it is worth studying how a foreign firm from a low-corruption country investing in China adjusts to the challenges associated with corruption. The following section presents the conceptual framework which we apply to analyze this question.

5.3 Theoretical background

The theoretical perspective of our analysis on the ways in which Finnish firms cope with corruption in China is the neo-institutional organization theory, which centers on the relationship between organizations and their institutional environments. The basic assumptions of this theory are that organizations seek to attain legitimacy with their institutional environment, and that such legitimacy results from conformity to demands from institutional constituents (DiMaggio and Powell 1983). At the early stages of theory development, such conformity was conceptualized with the construct of institutional isomorphism, which means acquiescence to pressures from the institutional environment (DiMaggio and Powell 1983). The analysis of the origin and forms of these pressures was based on Scott's (1995) conceptualization of institutional environments as consisting of regulative, normative and cognitive pillars.

Furthermore, the process of attaining conformity with regulative, normative and cognitive institutional pressures was identified as occurring through different mechanisms. These include being subject to coercion of state regulation, mimicry of others, successful organizations, and normative isomorphism carried out by professional organizations and individuals (DiMaggio and Powell 1983). As a result of this process, organizations subject to the same set of institutional pressures would adopt similar structures and practices, labeled as "templates of organizing" (DiMaggio and Powell 1991).

In this chapter, we view corruption as a source for institutional demands. Corruption is a multifaceted construct which is associated with each of Scott's (1995) three pillars. Corruption control by the government, such as anti-corruption legislation, represents the regulatory pillar, whereas corruption as a feature of business and administrative culture is associated with the normative and cognitive pillars. Correspondingly, the organizational "templates" for conforming to institutional pressures in terms of corruption depend on the efficacy of corruption control, policies on corruption from other organizations perceived as successful and prevalent norms regarding corruption in professional communities and educational organizations.

Later, however, neo-institutional organization theorists started to criticize the idea of institutional isomorphism for its strong environmental determinism with little room for organizational action. It was suggested that although organizations are subject to institutional pressures, they may comply with them to varying degrees (see, e.g., Oliver 1991). In other words, organizations were recognized as exerting strategic choice. This led to the development of different typologies of strategic responses to institutional pressures varying in terms of active action and degree of resistance to institutional pressures (Oliver 1991; Kraatz and Block 2008).

This idea of strategic responses is central to our study. We acknowledge the criticism of blind conformity to institutional pressures and assume that Finnish firms with different organizational determinants may take different strategic responses to corruption in China instead of applying a shared "template" response.

Furthermore, after recognizing that organizational responses may vary, neo-institutional organization theorists broadened the scope of their attention to the variety of institutional environments that organizations operate in. Inspiration for this was provided by international business strategy research, where one of the instrumental questions is how MNEs can achieve a balance between global integration and local responsiveness (Porter 1986; Bartlett 1986). From the institutional point of view, foreign subsidiaries of MNEs face a dual set of institutional pressures: the pressure to be isomorphic with the local environment and pressures to comply with the institutional demands derived from the MNE's structure and practices (Rosenzweig and Singh 1991: 346–7), rooted in its home country institutional environment (Kostova 1999). Correspondingly, the MNE subsidiaries are perceived as seeking external and internal legitimacy, respectively (Hillman and Wan 2005). According to the theory, it is the relative strength of the two sets of institutional pressures and their degree of conformity that defines the actual response. In institutionally distant home and host countries the dissonance between the internal and external pressures are large, which entails that the firm is not able to conform to them simultaneously.

Finally, the most recent contributions from international business and management scholars to the neo-institutional organization theory argue that, due to their foreign roots, MNEs would often lie beyond the reach of isomorphic pressures from the host country environment (Kostova *et al.* 2008; Karhunen 2008). To conceptualize this situation, the construct of institutional deviance was introduced by Shi and Hoskisson (2012). To support their argument, these authors resorted to the social comparison theory (see, e.g., Suls and Wheeler 2000), maintaining that foreign firms are less likely to be compared with local firms by local stakeholders and therefore be less subject to social obligations and cultural expectations.

Our theoretical approach can be summarized as follows. The core of our argumentation is that the strategic responses of Finnish firms to institutional pressures from the high-corruption environment in China depend on two aspects. First, how strongly they perceive corruption as influencing their business operations in China and, second, how strong is the internal pressure to stay non-corrupt. Our review of the theory leads us to assume that the pressures for internal legitimacy would be strongest in subsidiaries of large MNEs because as public companies they are subject to close monitoring by stakeholders. In addition, they face the need for global integration within the MNE, which reflects in control mechanisms.

To sum up, we apply the theoretical concepts presented above to empirically address three aspects. First, we analyze the existence of a corporate anti-corruption policy and its implementation at the Chinese subsidiary as a source of pressure for internal legitimacy. Second, we examine the external pressures on legitimacy within the corrupt Chinese environment. Taken the unrecorded and illegal nature of corruption, which makes its objective measurement virtually impossible, we analyze these pressures against subjective perceptions from interviewees regarding the significance of corruption for their business strategy in China. Finally, we identify the actual responses that Finnish firms have taken to deal with corruption in China, and potentially conflicting internal and external pressures.

5.4 Data and methodology

The source for our empirical data is an interview database from the Center for Markets in Transition, hosted by the Aalto University School of Business. This database includes approximately 100 transcripts of interviews with executives from Finnish firms operating in China. The interviewees represent both Finnish executives and the local (Chinese) managers of their subsidiaries. The share of Finnish informants is approximately two thirds of the total. The interview data has been regularly collected since 2003 in various research projects that address Finnish business operations in China. These projects share an emphasis on the interaction of the firm with its institutional environment, such as interactions with the state, and their implications for business strategy and practices. Therefore, the database is a rich source for empirical data on the Chinese business environment from the perspective of foreign firms. The interview transcripts were coded with the NVivo qualitative data analysis software, which enables different classifications and searches in data analysis.

For the purposes of this chapter, we retrieved data from those interviews in which corruption was explicitly discussed. The first basic terms used to search the interview database were "corruption" and "bribery," resulting in 60 interview transcripts. These interviews were conducted between 2003 and 2011 and comprise the first phase of empirical analysis. The interviewees are mainly expatriate or local firm managers in China. The firms they represent range from small firms to large MNEs, and operate in different industries ranging from manufacturing to business services. The industry structure of our data generally matches the presence of Finnish firms in China, where fields such as electronics and component manufacturing are well represented.

The data analysis was conducted in two phases. The first phase was mainly focused on obtaining a general picture of corruption in China from the perspective of Finnish firms, and aimed to identify patterns in the data that would require a more detailed analysis. One of the most striking features in the data was that practically all the interviewees acknowledged corruption as prevalent in Chinese society and economy, but did not however consider that corruption affected their business in China. This paradox led us to ask: how are Finnish firms able to operate beyond the reach of institutional pressures regarding corruption? Therefore, the second phase of the analysis focused on structuring and examining the interview material more deeply against the study's theoretical framework. The interview data were organized under the categories outlined in Table 5.1.

The following sections of the chapter present our empirical findings, which we structure according to the main headings of Table 5.1. Since corruption as a research topic is very sensitive, the data was handled in a strictly confidential manner. Therefore, we present the findings anonymously. Moreover, we had to take into account that the number of Finnish firms operating in China, particularly large MNEs, is relatively limited. Consequently, characteristics of the interviewees' firms (such as industry) are omitted when presenting direct quotations from interviews.

Table 5.1 Components of Finnish firms' responses to corruption in China

---

INSTITUTIONAL PRESSURES FOR CONSISTENCY WITHIN THE COMPANY
- The existence and nature of a formalized anti-corruption policy in the company
- The existence of anti-corrupt demands from home country constituents (e.g., legislation, shareholders)

PRESSURE FOR ISOMORPHISM WITH THE CORRUPT CHINESE ENVIRONMENT
- The perception of corruption as affecting one's own business
- The actual experiences from encountering corruption in China

STRATEGIC RESPONSES TO CORRUPTION
- The existence of anti-corruption policy and its enforcement at the Chinese subunit
- The organization of relationships with potentially corrupt stakeholders
- The responses to actual corruption requests

5.5   Institutional pressures for consistency within the company

The analysis focuses first on the internal pressures that the Chinese subunits of Finnish firms face in terms of corruption. Our interview data shows that such pressures include corporate anti-corruption policy, and pressures from home country (or international) constituents that are channeled to the subsidiary through the headquarters. Few interviewees, however, explicitly referred to the home country's regulatory institutions as preventing corruption abroad: "You must not engage in corrupt acts, because they are punishable in Finland irrespective of where they may occur." Other external stakeholders mentioned as exerting pressure for transparency were the Finnish state-owned investment agencies that provided funding to the firm, and international auditing firms: "We have our ethical principles and we are audited by [international auditing firms]. So our capability to operate on that ground is zero." Moreover, the demands from shareholders were perceived as strong: "The local [corruption] incidents may have surprisingly large consequences, if they are reported in the international media. We cannot take any risks in terms of corruption, because the risk of damaging our reputation is too high. Even the smallest incident can negatively influence our share value."

When analyzing the nature and existence of anti-corruption policies in the firms analyzed, there is a clear difference between large MNEs and small firms. Those interviewees who represented Chinese subsidiaries of MNEs often referred to the corporate anti-corruption policy as governing their actions in China: "Our code of conduct clearly defines our policy on corruption and fraud, including the sanctions." In contrast, small firms in our data seldom had an explicit corporate anti-corruption policy, which would apply to operations in China as well. Rather, some informants referred to the Finnish business culture on a more general level as a guiding principle of their operations: "Getting involved in corruption is completely excluded from our business culture."

5.6 Pressure for isomorphism with the corrupt Chinese environment

After analyzing the internal anti-corruption pressures, we then examined the external pressures for isomorphism with the corrupt Chinese environment. Here, we present our findings concerning the interviewees' perceptions on whether corruption directly affects their business in China, and their personal experiences of encountering corruption in China.

The prevailing opinion among the informants was that corruption is strongly present in Chinese society and economy, but it does not directly affect their business. As one informant summarized: "Corruption is an integral part of Chinese business culture, but it takes place among Chinese firms or between the public sector and Chinese firms." The status as a foreign firm was perceived as protecting the company to some degree from corrupt requests related to business transactions: "Perhaps the Chinese buyers have accepted that it does not make sense to ask for extra money from foreign suppliers, as they know we will not pay." On the other hand, it was pointed out that in some industries the competition is often among global suppliers, which are less likely to make illicit payments than Chinese firms. Hence, the pressure from corrupt competitors was not considered strong enough to push transparent firms out of the market.

The existence of public sector corruption in China was recognized as well, but it was associated with large state orders such as infrastructure projects and being "something between the Chinese companies and the Chinese authorities." In addition, a few respondents referred to the corruptness of the court and law enforcement system: "If you have a case against a powerful local player, the investigation is likely not to lead anywhere." Moreover, few interviewees referred to the cumbersome bureaucracy related to licenses and customs documents, which may tempt some players to take shortcuts with illicit payments: "You can take the official route which takes longer, or pay to make things happen faster." When interpreting the data, it should however be noted that the majority of the interviews were conducted in large cities (Shanghai and Beijing), where corruption control is perceived as working better than in the province: "The further you go from Beijing the more uncontrolled the situation is. In the countryside the local authorities continue collecting bribes as usual."

Those interviewees who perceived corruption as influencing their business in China were relatively unanimous about the ways in which this happens. The practice of illicit payments in buyer–supplier relations was mentioned most often: "We lost a considerable part of our sales to one of our largest customers because of a competing supplier who paid bribes. The change was noticeable and we really felt its financial influence." In addition to competitors, the practice of "red envelopes" had influenced some firms through their local purchasing staff, who had been caught engaged in such practices. The deep-rootedness of illicit payments related to purchases in China therefore influences foreign firm operations through increased monitoring costs of staff.

Interestingly, two respondents referred to the anti-corruption measures of the Chinese government as negatively influencing their business. In both cases, the firm had participated in governmental tenders, the procedures of which had become more complex and decision-making slower. With regard to the influence of anti-corruption measures, one respondent cynically commented: "Those who decide the purchases postpone them, because they are searching for new ways to get their share of the deal."

When analyzing the interview data in terms of the interviewees' actual encounters with corruption in China, most reported they had not actually dealt with it directly, and they do not want have anything to do with it. The few informants who mentioned incidents related with corruption referred to both public sector corruption and illicit payments related to buyer–seller relations. Two respondents had been in situations where a public sector representative had hinted they could speed up the administrative procedure with some extra payment. The refusal to pay did not however have any major consequences: "Perhaps some parts of the process could have been faster but in the end they were handled in the official way as well." Another two informants, who represented large firms, had detected that their Chinese purchasers took illicit payments from suppliers. In both cases the result was immediate dismissal. The informants, however, emphasized that such cases are more of an exception than the rule.

5.7   Strategic responses to corruption

The final part of our empirical analysis of corruption as affecting the firm's business in China focuses on the question presented earlier: how are Finnish firms able to operate beyond the reach of institutional pressures regarding corruption? The analysis of our interview data reveals different strategies, which are analyzed in terms of three dimensions: how tightly are the subsidiary's practices integrated with the potential anti-corruption policy of the parent company, how closely do they interact with potentially corrupt stakeholders, and how are potential corruption requests handled.

The strategic responses that the Chinese business units of Finnish firms have taken can be classified according to the dimensions of global integration and local responsiveness. At one extreme there are large multinationals in our sample that ignore external pressures from the Chinese business environment and firmly stick to their corporate practices. In doing so, the firm follows a principle of 100 percent transparency and acknowledges that being non-corrupt may result in extra costs or deals lost to competitors. In relation to the public sector this means that the firm accepts the risk that refusing "speed up" payments may result in delays in obtaining permits and other processes when dealing with authorities, Similarly, illicit payments in buyer–supplier relations are not accepted at the Chinese sub-unit: "You need to start from the fact that corruption is part of the Asian way of doing business and constantly monitor that it does not take place within your own company." The ways in which the situation is controlled include proactive measures, such as training and clear rules defining the maximum value for business gifts given and received, and reactive measures such as immediate dismissal of employees caught for corruption.

It is, however, noteworthy to mention that strict compliance with corporate anti-corruption policies in large firms does not imply that pressures from the institutional environment can be completely ignored. The informants generally acknowledged the importance of personal relations in the Chinese business culture (see, for example, Michailova and Worm 2003; Millington *et al.* 2005). In particular, having close contacts in public administration was viewed as helpful in navigating the bureaucratic maze. In a way, such relations can be used instead of extra payments to speed up different procedures. "If the Communist party representatives in the local administration decide that it wants your firm to invest in the locality, everyone will give you favorable treatment." In large investment projects, the maintenance of such relations often involves cooperation with Finnish public sector organizations in China, which have their own local networks.

When discussing the maintenance of personal relations with authorities, respondents often refer to the culture of gift-giving and emphasize that it is clearly distinguishable from corruption: "If needed, we can invite authorities to have lunch and give small gifts, it is normal hospitality. It is completely different from corruption where you pay a certain sum to someone's account." Similarly, in business-to-business relations most informants draw the line between the maintenance of *guanxi* relations and corruption as follows: "The maintenance of business relations requires joint lunches and tea drinking, it cannot be avoided. Paying someone's expenses is not corruption as long as you do not transfer money directly to that person."

Finally, our analysis reveals that the small firms in our data respond to corruption in China differently from the large multinationals. There are small firms in our sample which do not pursue any active anti-corruption policies in their Chinese subunits. Rather, they feel unequipped to deal with certain features of the Chinese business culture and hence delegate the dealings with local stakeholders to their Chinese employees. Their approach to payments related to business transactions is pragmatic: "What is from the European perspective corruption in Chinese business is for the Chinese commissions. If such commissions are paid, they need to be paid in such a way that they are transparent in the bookkeeping. Then it is not corruption." Similarly, contacts with the public sector are delegated to Chinese employees: "It is better that when you need permits from the authorities, you let the Chinese handle the issue among themselves."

5.8 Discussion and conclusions

This chapter focused on the implications of host-country corruption and corruption distance between home and host country as a hot topic in current international business research. From a managerial point of view, firms from low-corruption countries entering high-corruption ones need to ensure that the foreign subunit complies with the parent's internal policy regarding corruption. Our empirical analysis focused on a pair of countries with a large corruption distance, Finland as the home country and China as the host. The empirical data consisted of 60 interviews with the management of Chinese subsidiaries of Finnish firms, collected between 2003 and 2011. The firms in the data represent large multinationals and small firms alike, as well as different industries.

The theoretical framework for our study was constructed on the basis of the neo-institutional organization theory. This theory provides tools for analyzing the strategic responses of organizations to two sets of potentially conflicting institutional pressures, internal and external. Correspondingly, we took two perspectives to analyze the interview data. First, we identified internal and external institutional pressures regarding corruption, originating from corporate anti-corruption policies rooted in the home country institutions, and from the corrupt Chinese business environment, respectively. Second, we identified strategic responses that the Chinese subunits of Finnish firms in our data have taken to these conflicting pressures.

The empirical findings can be summarized as follows. First, our data shows that although corruption is recognized as a common feature of Chinese society and economy, its influence on foreign firms is not as significant as could be expected. Large-scale public sector corruption seems to be concentrated in certain sectors, such as the real estate industry and infrastructure projects, and foreign firms operating, for example, in consumer goods manufacturing do not necessarily encounter it. In addition, smaller-scale public sector corruption associated with dealing with state bureaucracy does not seem to be a major issue for the firms in our data. Furthermore, corruption in business transactions between firms is acknowledged as an integral part of Chinese business culture, but according to our informants it is mostly related to transactions between Chinese firms. However, it is encountered sometimes through the malpractice of their Chinese employees, or as deals lost to local competitors. In contrast, firms operating in sectors dominated by global firms feel more protected from such forms of corruption.

Our second finding is that the size of the firm is a key determinant of the strategic responses towards corruption. In particular, we identified strong internal anti-corruption pressures in subsidiaries of large MNEs, whereas Chinese subunits of small firms are not subject to similar pressures. Large MNEs as publicly listed companies are under the scrutiny of multiple stakeholders, and therefore need to have explicit anti-corruption policies and codes of conduct that apply to all subsidiaries. In high-corruption host countries, however, such strict compliance with internal anti-corruption pressures can often become costly. Refusal to engage in bribery and kickbacks may result in losing deals to competitors or in delays in investment projects due to slow administrative procedures.

Therefore, few firms can afford to completely ignore the external pressures from the corrupted institutional environment. Importantly, this does not mean engaging in corrupt practices, but rather substituting corruption with reliance on personal networks. In network-based societies such as China, good personal relations with high-level public sector officials can be used to shortcut the bureaucracy as an alternative to speed-up payments.

Third, we found that although small firms do not face strict internal pressures against corruption, they do not blindly conform to the external pressures favoring corrupt practices and ignore the anti-corruption pressures rooted in the Finnish home country environment either. Instead, our data analysis revealed a pattern showing how small firms are balancing between conflicting internal and external pressures. A central element of such a response strategy is that interactions with potentially corrupt Chinese stakeholders, such as authorities and business partners, are delegated to the local staff. In other words, situations in which encountering corruption is most likely occur purely among the locals. This strategy helps Finnish firms and their potential expatriate management in China to simultaneously conform to the home country's anti-corruption institutional pressures and the external pressures from the host environment to do business "in the local way."

Our study contributes to the neo-institutional organization theory by identifying the ways in which corruption as an institutional pressure influences the firms' strategic responses. In particular, we illustrate how firms operating in a foreign country need to take into account a dual set of institutional pressures. Moreover, our findings support the recent notion of institutional deviance (Shi and Hoskisson 2012), which proposes that due to their foreign origin, firms would not be subject to the same institutional pressures as local firms. The frequent notion in our data that corruption in China is taking place between the Chinese actors indicates that foreign firms would not be expected to play according to the same rules as the local ones.

Our study also has managerial implications, which include illustrating the different dimensions through which host-country corruption may affect foreign business operations in high-corruption countries. We show that in such business environments, where corruption is considered a "normal" business practice, foreign firms sticking to their non-corrupt principles may need to prepare for extra costs and competitive disadvantage towards local competitors. At the same time, the adaptation to the local business environment in terms of adopting corrupt practices is a risky option. From the economic point of view, it may bring short-term benefits but in the long-term cause serious legal consequences and damaged reputation. However, what is encouraging in our data is that the deviance of the local institutional norms, in this case operating transparently in a high-corruption environment, seems to not always prevent operating profitably. One way of doing business in high-corruption countries might therefore be to opt for other foreign firms as partners and therefore minimize the risks of encountering corruption.

Acknowledgments

The authors are grateful for financial support for the study from the Finnish Funding Agency for Technology and Innovation TEKES (project "Business Security in Russia and in China"). The first author acknowledges the financial support from the Academy of Finland (Grant No. 264948).

6 Corruption and network relationships
Theory and evidence from Thailand

Sirilaksana Khoman

6.1 Introduction

Network relationships have formed the cornerstone of human interaction since time immemorial. Worldwide social networking, loose or tight, has indeed exploded within the last decade. Network relationships foster trust which in turn facilitates efficient interaction by reducing the three components of transaction costs: information and search costs, negotiating and contracting costs, and policing and enforcement costs. Whether in business, politics, or any other area of interaction, network relationships play an important role and help to create efficiency. Indeed, investing in creating trust, brand loyalty, recognition and reputation, whether in personal or business relationships, can be seen as networking. Trust implies confidence that some person or institution will behave in an expected way (Rose-Ackerman 2001).[1] However, there are also dangers inherent to maintaining the status quo and creating situations of bilateral monopoly, as well as facilitating transactions with corrupt intent.

This chapter focuses on public procurement as fertile ground for both petty corruption and "grand state capture," and examines the role of network relationships in facilitating corrupt activity. The characteristics of network relationships are examined to ascertain which aspects of group or network relationships are conducive to corrupt activity. Case studies are then used to determine the pattern of patron–client networks that affect procurement. The institutional and legal framework in Thailand is also briefly explored, and possible measures to alleviate current problems are advanced. We argue that although procurement regulations are clear and seemingly strict, loopholes can be found that allow patron–client networks to engage in wrongdoing with impunity, to the detriment of Thailand's development.

6.2 The nature of network relationships

A network may be regarded as a set of contracts, which can be loose or tight, formal or informal, that establishes rules of exchange and cooperation internally. In some cases, the set of contracts gives the group a collective identity vis-à-vis others and thus replaces individual identity. An organization, or clan, is thus a set of contracts and rules that define their roles and establish their relationships within the network, in which individuals play or leave the roles that have been defined. Investment in identity takes place in the selection for roles and in the process by which individuals select the organization/clan that they join. This network may start out as an innocuous social network where members assist each other and some kind of reciprocity is the norm. However, it can be transformed into a patron–client relationship, paving the way for the formation of more pernicious networks whereby the patron provides resources and protection to the clients who, in return, provide services, rent collection, and other forms of support to the patron, including facilitating corrupt acts.

Since there are many competing networks of patrons and clients, each patron needs to accumulate a large amount of resources to feed the needs of the clan. Corruption then becomes a method to accomplish this task and allows the network to accumulate sufficient funds and attract large numbers to compete successfully against other clans. Members recruited into the corruption ring may actually not be aware of the ring at first. But the cost of leaving the network becomes prohibitive and the option of moving to another network is not available due to the mutual distrust and possible hostility between clans/networks.

In its broadest sense, a transaction consists of activities or transfers of property rights by or between at least two individuals or groups. All individuals engage in two kinds of transaction: personal (where identity dominates) and impersonal (where identity is subsumed). In petty corruption, such as traffic police extorting money from motorists, or queue-jumping by bribery, identity is not important, and suppression of identity may even be desirable. But in certain forms of illegal transactions, especially corrupt ones that take on the nature of conspiracies, the identity of the people engaged in them is vital. Some transactions can take place only between mutually or unilaterally identified parties, and many corrupt practices of significance fall into this category. Parties in an identified relationship invest resources that are specific to that relationship in order to save transaction costs. And there are economies of scale related to these "set-up" costs. This facilitates activity between them and leads to a concentration of exchange between the same parties. Ben-Porath (1980) calls this "specialization by identity," and patron–client relationships are repeated relationships of exchange between specific patrons and their clients (Khan 1998).

In certain corrupt transactions, the network or clan has an advantage over other institutional forms for the following reasons:

a   Being part of a clan usually involves a lengthy time period, but the duration is often not specified in advance. The expectation of continuing exchange has a favorable effect on the behavior of the members. Abstention from "cheating" is an investment that could reap gains in the future. Even in a corruption ring, there is some honor among thieves, but no hesitation in cheating or inflicting harm on others outside the clan.[2] Anthropologists call this "contextual morality." In some primitive societies, ethical codes forbid internal cheating within a tribe but allow the cheating of others (Sahlins 1965). It is thus important not to regard all existence of social capital as necessarily advantageous to society. Social capital without ethical capital can have deleterious or disastrous consequences, if manipulated by unscrupulous leaders.

b   While the scope and importance of various activities change, the connection generally encompasses a large variety of activities.

c   Not all terms of membership are specified explicitly, and most activities are contingent on events and are decided sequentially; the response to contingencies remains unspecified, guided by custom or implicit rules of behavior.

d   The highly interdependent elements of the contract between network members exist as a package and prices cannot be used as weights for adding up the various elements of the contract.

e   There is generally no explicit balancing of the exchange in terms of a unit of account, although certain money payments can be interpreted as approximations to the *ex ante* differences in the expected value of the packages being exchanged. The individual components need not be balanced at any particular point in time, and there may be no obvious quid pro quo. Instead, large outstanding balances may be tolerated, often because of the unspecified nature of the contract; when and how these balances are liquidated may remain open. This tolerance of outstanding balances reflects the presence of trust or implicit threats.

f   Enforcement is mostly internal, although the contract may be supported to some extent by the origin of the relationship or the sub-faction head.

g   To varying degrees, the clan/network creates a collective identity that affects each member's interaction with people outside the network, but members may have unequal benefits based on some hierarchical structure, as well as different exit opportunities.

h   The most important characteristic of the network is that any implicit or explicit "contracts" are embedded in the identity of the partners. Otherwise the contracts would lose their meaning. It is thus usually specific and non-negotiable or nontransferable, and so most of the characteristics of a corrupt clan are connected with the issue of identity. Identity is important because of imperfect or asymmetric information, that is, there is uncertainty about the quality of the object of exchange or the terms of the transaction. Identity reduces this uncertainty, if personal traits are not completely observable. In addition, in transactions that are not consummated instantly and involve obligations or consequences that extend over time, the quality of promises to pay or deliver depends on the identity of the promise giver. In general, if a transaction is contracted between strangers over time, the contract would have to be specified in a manner that allows a third party to adjudicate in case of disagreement. This, of course, cannot be done in the case of corrupt practices because of the secret and illegal nature of the transaction. Thus, identity is important, or the third-party adjudicator has to be from within the clan.

In order to set up a successful corruption ring, several aspects related to the members' characteristics are important. Where do the network members come from?

There is an inherent bias in favor of homogeneity for some aspects, but heterogeneity for others. Family and close friends may be the first choice for recruitment because of existing ties. This first ring of relationships will then recruit others. Routine actions that do not require a great deal of expertise, such as falsifying land deeds, or engaging in protest rallies, favor homogeneity—working with the same people. However, when purchasing sophisticated equipment, trust in friends or relatives cannot compete with the technical know-how of a specialist. It then becomes necessary to recruit technical expertise as well. With differences in the importance of identity in various transactions and in the specificity of investment of identity to certain activities, people will be organized in small clusters for some purposes and large ones for others, and these groupings may intersect for different purposes (Ben-Porath 1980).[3] Parties who have already invested specifically in each other are in a short-run position of bilateral monopoly. If the self-enforcement mechanism is imperfect, trust, or fear, or violence and intimidation, or the threat thereof, becomes more important.

The role of network affiliation, particularly the family network, is clearly evident during the early stages of economic development. Families played an important part in employment placement both in nineteenth-century England (Anderson 1971) and in Japan at the onset of the migration to towns (Vogel 1967). And family affiliation also played an important part in the capital market by reducing the transaction costs for individuals in both Europe and part of the developing world (Benedict 1968). Family relationships indeed played an important part in the struggle over the establishment of property rights and their physical protection in America's early pioneering moves to the west. Business cooperation between members of rich families continues in highly developed economies. Long-term partnerships with non-relatives simulate some of the properties of the family type contract, again with mutual investment in identity in order to save transaction costs and reap the benefits of joint action. The need to invest in identity to operate efficiently even in developed markets is an element in the high salaries of top executives.

In present-day Thailand it can be seen that political networks are defined by their head. The head of the network serves as the director for communication, trust, and redistribution, and reduces the transaction costs within the network by reducing the need for bilateral relationships. The pairwise investment of each member with the center links him to all the others. In his theory of social interaction, Becker (1974) shows why a central figure that cares, or appears to care, can generate optimal behavior in the others, even if the head is an egoist. When the head is absent, miscommunication often occurs, or miscommunication can be blamed for unpopular deeds by the network. The difficulty is to distinguish between the truly benevolent head and the self-serving one.

A corruption ring can be represented in Figure 6.1, where layers of patrons and clients direct the flow of resources.

From Figure 6.1, Patron A is the ultimate power of the clan. Below Patron A are the clients, shown by nodes connected to Patron A with dashed lines. For simplicity, this patron is shown to have two clients at level 1, labeled A1 and A2.

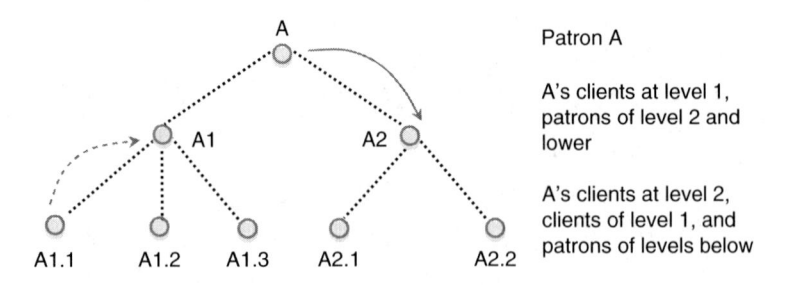

Figure 6.1 Typical patron–client structure.

Source: Khoman *et al.* (2009).

Below each level-1 client there may be many layers of clients that propagate downward. The patron in this clan could also serve as a client of yet another larger patron–client structure located higher up.

Members in the same clan relate to each other in two ways, vertically and horizontally, the former in cooperative exchange and the latter sometimes in the form of rivalry. The patron is expected to provide vital resources that the client needs. In Thailand, the patron may provide land to the client for cultivation, give loans for emergency use, settle conflicts with other clients within the clan, provide protection against threats from other clans, promote the client to a higher position in the clan, and/or ensure that clients receive government procurement contracts. The solid arrow in Figure 6.1 represents the flow of resources or protection provided by the patron.

In return for the patron's support, the client has a duty to serve the immediate patron and those in higher positions, in whatever tasks the patron may assign. If procurement contracts are obtained, usually at inflated prices, then kickbacks are paid up the hierarchy. The dashed arrow in Figure 6.1 shows the flow of returns from the client to the patron. The returns could take the form of carrying out simple tasks (such as pouring drinks, carrying suitcases), or being bodyguards. Or it could be a supporting role against other clans, beating up the patron's enemies, rallying people to support the patron's political ambitions, and extracting economic rent from contracts awarded to the patron. The resources could consist of monetary support or adding members. Thai political parties always consist of many factions, or sub-clans, in which the leader of the particular faction acts as the patron. If the leader of the faction manages to bring in sufficiently large numbers of elected MPs under his wing, he is entitled to become a minister in a grade A ministry, such as the Ministry of Communications, which commands a large government budget. He would also have the right to nominate members under his wing to be appointed as ministers in grade B or C ministries, or as deputy ministers in grade A ministries.

Because of this quid pro quo, members of the group evaluate actions or policies as being beneficial or detrimental to the group or subgroup's interests, and to a large extent, political loyalties are not directed towards ideas, but towards the identity of the leader. Therefore, for the most part, it is not ideological persuasion, but the identity of individual politicians that determine political structures.

Although members of a clan tend to cooperate with one another in the vertical hierarchy, there is often rivalry when they deal with members at the same client level. Many examples can be found in Thai political parties where leaders of factions try to outperform each other in terms of getting more members of parliament under their wing. The leader of that faction is then entitled to a Cabinet position. And there is of course rivalry between clans, which accounts for why some long-running projects do not get implemented. The plans for a new international airport, for example, were on the table 30 years before construction finally commenced. And a large number of procurement cases connected with the new international airport are currently being investigated.

The patron–client network in Thailand is shown in Figure 6.2. The bureaucracy (B) is represented on the left, while the network of politicians (P) is depicted on the right. The capitalists (C) refer to big businesses, while the non-politicians (N) include small businesses as well as non-governmental organizations (NGOs), and other social or lobbying groups. Solid arrows show the flows of the benefits from C1 to B1 and C2 to B2. The capitalists who act as the patrons of the sub-clans kick back some of their corrupt benefits to the bureaucracy who originally facilitated the special licenses, concessions, and procurement projects. The patrons of the sub-clan and the non-politician capitalists also need to provide the political and financial support to the highest patron who is either a politician or a capitalist turned politician. Thus, government procurement is a vehicle for corrupt enrichment.

A large number of businessmen made fortunes by receiving favored subsidies, licenses, and concessions from the patron–client network three-way interaction between politicians, the bureaucracy and business, shown by the solid arrows pointing from B1 and B2 to C3 and C4.

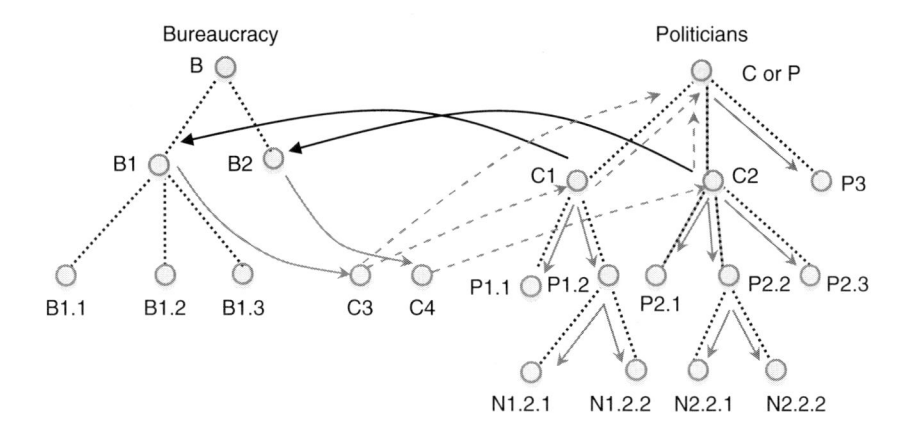

Figure 6.2 Flows within patron–client networks in Thailand.

Notes: B = bureaucracy, C = capitalists, P = politicians, N = non-politicians.

One unique point about the patron–client network in Thailand is that capitalists often place themselves in the politician's network. In fact, the number of businessmen in Thailand's parliament is the highest in the region (Sidel 1996). A recent trend has been the movement of many capitalists, formerly at high client levels, to become the highest patrons of the political party or the faction leader. Many leaders of Thai political parties are businessmen and tycoons.[4]

The business–politics nexus can be clearly seen from the concessions received by former Prime Minister Thaksin Shinawatra before he became a politician. Indeed, he is the most successful businessman turned politician, a former Lieutenant-Colonel in the Police Department. He built his business career by concentrating on government telecommunication concessions as shown in Table 6.1. The ministers who approved the concessions subsequently became staunch political allies after Thaksin entered politics. They received important political appointments after he became prime minister.

In this framework of connected relationships, it can be seen that economic policies can be adopted not to eliminate market failures but because they create opportunities for corruption (Aidt 2003), and procurement offers a lucrative means to take advantage of these opportunities. Tanzi and Davoodi (1997: 284–5) lament that "experience with public sector projects, especially in developing countries, is full

Table 6.1 Thaksin Shinawatra's concessions

Year	Thaksin's companies	Concessions	Concessions value (million Bht)/ number of years	Government/ Minister of Transportation
1989	Digital Paging Service	Pager service	200/15	Chatichai government/Montree Pongpanit
1989	IBC	Cable television	NA/20	Chatichai government/Chalerm Yoobumrung*
1989	Shinawatra DataCom	Data networking service	400/10	Chatichai government/Montree Pongpanit
1990	Advanced Info Service (AIS)	Public Telephone (card phone)	3,000/20	Chatichai government/Montree Pongpanit
1990	Advanced Info Service (AIS)	Analog 900 MHz mobile phone	3,000/20	Chatichai government/Montree Pongpanit
1991	Shinawatra Satellite	Communications satellites	6,500/30	Chatichai government/Samak Sundaravej
1992	Advanced Info Service (AIS)	Card Phone	NA/10	Anand government/Nukul Prachuabmoh

Notes: *PM's Office Minister.
Source: Pathmanand (2008).

of stories about roads that need to be repaired a short time after completion, power plants that worked at much lower capacity . . . because projects are chosen for their bribe-generating capacity and not for their productivity. The productivity of the projects becomes almost irrelevant." Networks designed to serve corrupt activity not only rely on bribes, but also siphon resources and funds to members of the clan.

6.3 Corruption and networks: cases from Thailand

Various interviews with foreign companies have shown that corruption is often considered a major impediment to doing business in Thailand, along with hidden costs related to red tape, government and policy instability and inefficient government bureaucracy.[5]

A survey of Thai businesses also echoes the prevalence of corruption. Looking only at procurement, Table 6.2 shows that in 2009, about 34 percent of the survey respondents felt that government procurement is not conducted in a transparent and efficient way. Those who felt that government procurement is often conducted in a transparent and efficient way decreased from more than 90 percent in 2003 to only about 66 percent. Of course these are subjective responses and could reflect the fact that there has been greater exposure of corrupt practices and more prosecutions in later years.

A more objective question whose answer is presented in Table 6.3 is asked of those who actually paid kickbacks to government officials to acquire contracts, how much they had to pay, and what percent of the value of the contract was paid. Table 6.3 shows that more than half the respondents said they had to pay bribes, with the largest number of businesses (34 percent) claiming they had to pay less than 6 percent of the contract value to obtain the contract, and less than 4 percent said they did not have to pay at all.

Interviews with contractors who asked to remain anonymous indicate that bid collusion is the norm rather than the exception. Collusion can take several forms. First, there could be the formation of a bidding ring, whether ad hoc or long-standing, between the private contractors themselves. Bid-rigging occurs when members of the bidding ring offer prices within a narrow (inflated) range.

Table 6.2 Opinions of Thai businesses regarding transparency in government procurement contracts

How often do you think government procurement contracts are conducted in a transparent and efficient way?	*Year (percent of respondents)*	
	2003	*2009*
Never	0.4	4.8
Hardly ever	0.6	15.8
Not frequently	7.9	13.1
Quite frequently	47.0	28.1
Very frequently	42.7	34.0
Every time	1.5	4.2

Source: Adapted from Thairungroj *et al.* (2010).

Table 6.3 "Special payment" as percentage of value of government contract

"Special Payment" (% of value of contract)	Year (percent of respondents)		
	2001	2003	2009
0%	3.8	0.4	3.9
Less than 6%	18.0	27.9	34.3
6–10%	11.0	36.1	16.7
11–15%	4.8	10.1	0.9
16–20%	2.8	0.4	0.9
More than 20%	2.3	0.2	0.3
Don't know	57.5	25.1	43.0

Source: Adapted from Thairungroj *et al.* (2010).

Bid rotation often occurs, whereby suppliers take turns offering the lowest bid and therefore getting the contract. This is also called complementary bidding. In some cases, bid suppression occurs, where competitive suppliers are coerced into withdrawing from the bidding process or suppliers in the bidding ring abstain. Any of these practices could be coupled with sub-contracting, whereby members of the bidding ring receive sub-contracts from the winning bidder.

Table 6.4 presents the range of possible points where corruption can occur in the process of procurement. We can only look at a few points of corruption risk in this chapter. Corruption risks in procurement are examined by means of six case studies, selected to highlight the connection between corruption and network relationships. These are cases of alleged corruption as well as completed cases in Thailand. Only corruption that involves networks of connected persons is examined, in the form of either "political corruption" where projects are designed and initiated to benefit specific suppliers within connected networks, possibly identified prior to project initiation, or collusion among networks of private-sector suppliers. Even simple kickbacks from suppliers to government officials can involve a network of players and brokers to reduce the possibility of detection.

Thailand is a country of contradictions. Religious piety and affection for the monarchy predisposes government officials to honesty. But a culture of kinship and caring for friends and relatives reinforces the tendency towards "prebendalism," whereby state offices are regarded as "prebends that can be appropriated by officeholders, who use them to generate material benefits for themselves and their constituents and kin groups" (Joseph 1996). The cases examined here explore these influences.

6.3.1   Case 1: Intervention in the longan fruit market: strategic (corrupt) partners

Thailand has a range of market intervention schemes to assist agricultural producers. One of the most widely used schemes is what is called the "pledging scheme" that was intended to mitigate the effects on agricultural producers of the

Table 6.4 Possible points of procurement corruption and cases in Thailand

Project initiation	Cases in Thailand
1. Initiating projects with certain connected contractors in mind	Longan*
Feasibility study	
2. Overstatement of benefits	NGV buses
3. Connected consultants	King Power
Project design	
4. Manipulation of design	Many cases
5. Manipulation of specifications	NGV buses
6. Inflation of resources and time requirements	
7. Specification of overly sophisticated design	
8. Manipulation of size to circumvent PPP law	King Power
9. Manipulation of size to favor certain suppliers	NGV buses
10. Specifying source of supply	Pharmaceuticals
Pre-qualification	
11. Manipulation of pre-qualification, e.g., Inappropriate supplier qualifications	Many cases
12. Requiring supplier history with specific agencies	Irrigation projects
13. Bribery to obtain certification	
Tender – agency	
14. Intimidation from superiors/politicians	Pharmaceuticals, Thai Oil
15. Obtaining a quotation only for price comparison	
16. Using "special methods" beyond necessity	Many Ministries
17. Corruptly negotiated contract	King Power
18. Violation of regulations	Longan*
19. Manipulation of bid price	Thai Oil
Tender – supplier	
20. Bribery to obtain contract	BKK Film Festival, CTX
21. Intimidation of competitors	Highway construction*
22. Submission of false quotation	
23. Loser's fee	
24. Price fixing	
25. Collusion, bid rigging and rotation	Road construction*
26. Concealment of financial status	
27. Falsely obtaining credit insurance	
28. Planned bankruptcy	
Project execution	
29. False invoicing: supply of inferior materials	
30. False invoicing: supply of less equipment	
31. False work certificates	
32. Excessive repair work	
33. Non-existing work	Rural roads
34. Overstating man-day requirements	

(*Continued*)

Table 6.4 Continued

Project initiation	Cases in Thailand
35. Inflated claim for variation	
36. False variation claim	
37. Issue of false delay certificate	
38. False extension of time application	
39. False assurance that payment will be made	
40. Delayed issue of payment certificates	
41. Concealing defects	
42. False rectification costs	
43. Refusal to issue final certificate	
44. Requirement to accept lower payment than is due	
45. Extortion by client's representative	
46. Facilitation payments	
47. Overstating/understating of profits	
48. False job application	
49. Transfer pricing	King Power
50. Inappropriate project modification or location	Klong Dan*
Project inspection and acceptance	
51. Delayed issue of payment certificates	
52. Refusal to issue final acceptance, citing minor flaws	
53. Requirement to accept lower payment than is due	
54. Extortion by agency representative	
55. Facilitation payments	
Dispute resolution	
56. Submission of incorrect contract claims	
57. Concealment of documents	
58. Submission of false supporting documents	
59. Supply of false witness evidence	
60. Supply of false expert evidence	
61. Bribery of witness	
62. Blackmail of witness	
63. False information regarding financial status	
64. False statement regarding settlement sum	
65. Over-manning by law firm	
66. Excessive billing by lawyer	
67. Complicity by lawyer	

Note: *Cases examined in this chapter.

Source: Expanded and adapted from OECD (2007).

seasonal variation in prices. The example of intervention in the longan fruit market is presented here.[6]

The intervention scheme used in the longan market (as well as previously used in the rice market) is called the "pledging" scheme. Simply put, a government agency operates like a pawn shop so that just after harvesting when prices are low producers need not be at the mercy of the market and can "pledge" or pawn their crop at the government agency, to redeem their produce after prices improve.

For longan, the scheme was started in the year 2000. Initially, the buying price was set at 70 percent of the market price. However, in 2002–3, this scheme was hijacked by politicians and turned into a populist scheme, and the buying price was jacked up to be higher than market price, which encouraged excessive expansion of production. The successive intervention prices are summarized in Table 6.5. As a result of the jacked-up price, the level of intervention (defined as the quantity purchased divided by total production) increased from 4.4 percent in 2000 to 62.2 percent in 2002 (Singhapreecha and Boonyasiri 2010).

The corruption ring involved in the 2002–03 intervention scheme is presented in Figure 6.3. It can be seen that wrongdoing occurred at every stage of the process. The "pledge" prices of 72 baht per kilogram for grade AA, 54 baht per kilogram for grade A, and 36 baht per kilogram for grade B were well above market prices, and attracted wrongdoers to extract undue benefits from the scheme. Starting from the producers and cooperatives, estimates of production were inflated to take advantage of the high prices offered by the scheme. At this stage, "substitution of rights" also occurred, whereby legitimate longan producers were asked/coerced/recruited to sign documents falsifying production figures. These documents were subsequently used by non-producers to obtain payment for non-existent stock.

Next, at the level of the government agencies (the Public Warehouse Organization: PWO and the Marketing Organization for Farmers: MFO), an illegal queue-jumping fee was charged at the "acceptance point," where supposed longan producers submitted their pledge. At the quality verification stage and for the leasing of private-sector silos and warehouses, the same company was awarded the contract both for quality verification and warehousing, so there was no check or balance. Investigation by the National Anti-Corruption Commission uncovered fraud in the grading process, sub-standard packaging that allowed the produce to deteriorate, the siphoning off of produce from the warehouse, and produce stock that never existed in the first place.

Table 6.5 Intervention in the longan market

Year	Intervention measure
2000	– Bank of Agriculture and Agricultural Co-operatives (BAAC) accepts pledging documents to dry longan – Pays 70% of target price – Receives target of 30,000 tons of longan
2002–03	– Pays a price higher than market price – Huge increases in size of scheme
2004	– Longan market management, through such schemes as output distribution outside production location, further processing such as canning, promotion of fresh longan export, domestic consumption, and purchase of fresh longan for processing into dried longan.
2005–present	– Limited intervention and greater reliance on market mechanism and consumption boosting measures.

Source: Adapted from Singhapreecha and Boonyasiri (2010).

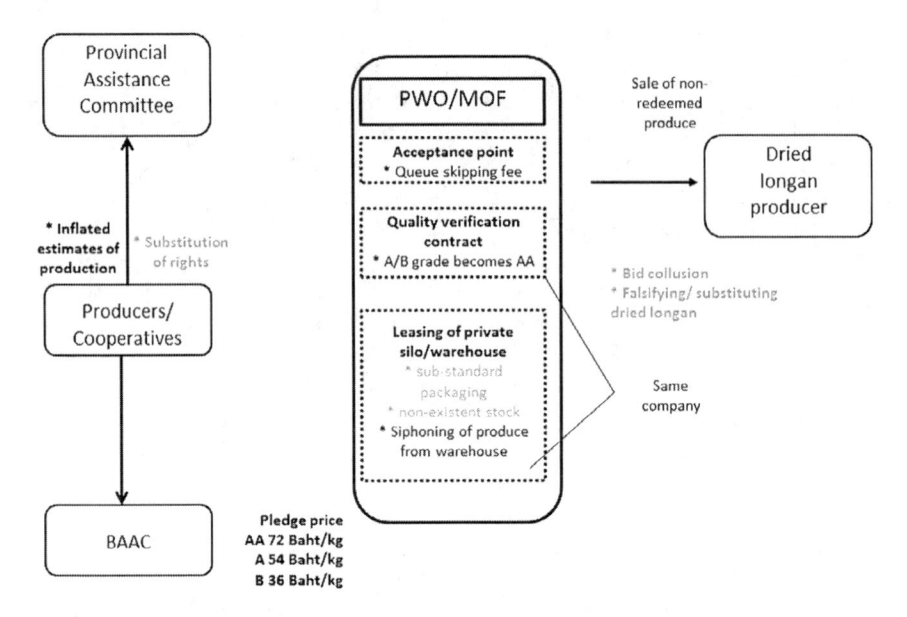

Figure 6.3 Corruption ring in 2002–03 longan pledging.

Source: Adapted from Singhapreecha and Boonyasiri (2010).

The high purchase price also led to low redemption rates as there was no incentive to redeem the pledged produce. The stock in the warehouse therefore deteriorated and was sold at a loss to dried longan producers, a process that again involved bid collusion and fraud.

Consequently, in 2004 the intervention scheme was adapted to focus more on market management, output distribution outside the production location, promotion of domestic consumption and fresh longan export, further processing in the form of canning, and the purchase of fresh longan for processing into dried longan. This led to another systemic pattern of procurement corruption. Figure 6.4 shows that the inflated production estimates and the substitution of rights continued at the producer level. Krungthai Bank was brought in to replace the Bank of Agriculture and Agricultural Cooperatives (BAAC), and Chiangmai University (CMU) was recruited for quality inspection and grading. However, grading fraud continued, and the Por Heng Inter Trade Company was awarded the contract for drying the fresh longan even though the company did not even possess any drying facilities and had no experience in agricultural processing. The fact that Por Heng did not have the qualifications, but obtained the contract in any case, shows the collaboration of the network members: procurement officers, politicians, and private business. The scandalous failure to deliver 49,000 tons of dried longan led to exposure of the corruption ring. The poor quality of dried longan produced as a result of the corrupt practices further damaged the export market.

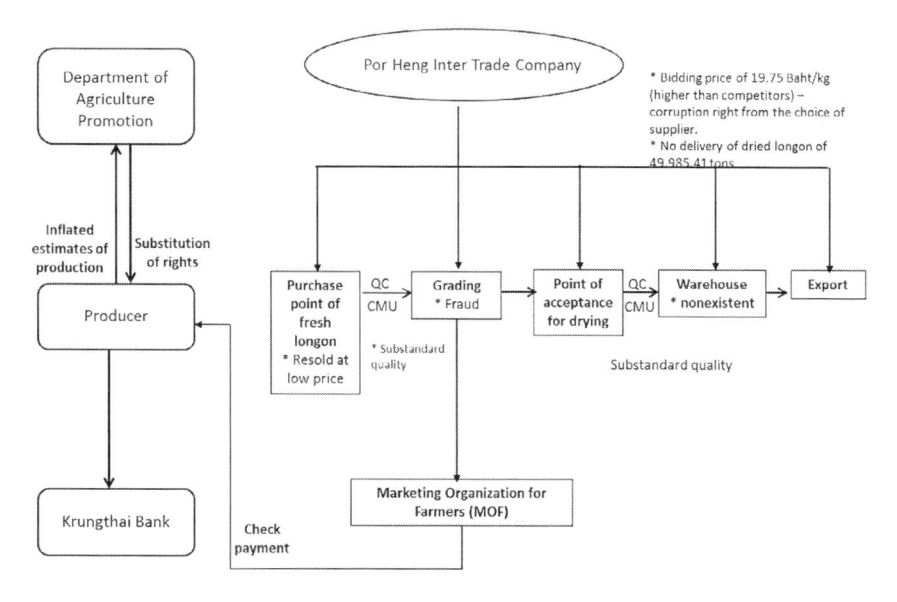

Figure 6.4 Corruption ring in 2004.

Source: Adapted from Singhapreecha and Boonyasiri (2010).

6.3.2 Case 2: Intervention in rice market: insider information about policy

Intervention in the rice market is similar to the longan market above and in fact preceded it, and is not discussed here. Only one phenomenon is examined here. Just as in the case of the longan market, the "pledging" scheme for rice, introduced in 1995, was intended to operate like a pawn shop to advance loans to rice farmers to tide them over during the harvest season until market prices subsequently increased. The pledging price is thus, in principle, always lower than the market price so that farmers would redeem their produce after market prices increase. This had been the norm until the 2001–02 season when the Thaksin government unprecedentedly announced a pledge price above market prices, as seen in Figure 6.5. This led to the falsification of documents, substitution of rights to take advantage of the high government price, non-redemption of pledged output leading to enormous stockpiles that cost hundreds of millions of baht per month to store. In addition, only the wealthy farmers were able to take advantage of the government's high price.

What is more significant is that in early 2004 President Agri Trading (PAT) Company, a newcomer to rice exporting, inexplicably made a bid to buy 1.68 million tons of rice from the government *at prices above market price*, thereby knocking out all the competition and subsequently possessing the largest amount of rice of all the exporters: 2.2 million tons. A few months later, the government announced the pledging price for the new season paddy at 10,000 baht *(higher than the market price and higher than PAT's purchase price)*. Consequently, the

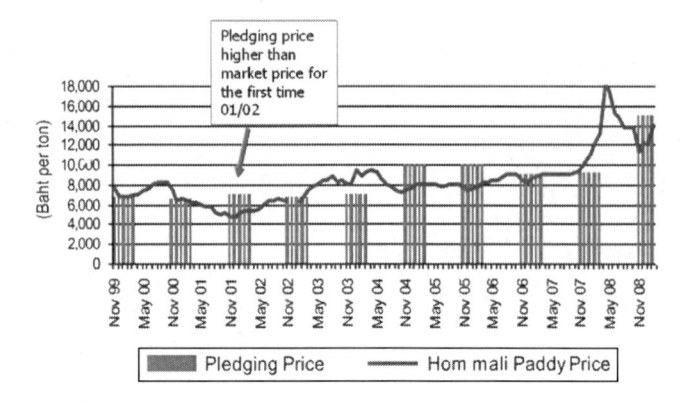

Figure 6.5 Comparison of pledging price and market price of jasmine (Hom mali) rice.

Source: Adapted from Poapongsakorn (2011).

market price shot up, other exporters could not compete with PAT and many had to resort to buying rice from PAT. PAT was subsequently backlisted for other reasons by the Ministry of Commerce, but was reinstated when a "friendly" government was in power.

This strongly suggests a connection between this company and policy makers in certain governments.

6.3.3 Case 3: Highway Department—collusion and bid rotation

The close ties between political parties and road projects have long been known in Thailand. In fact, many of the key politicians made their fortunes by owning construction companies the bulk of whose business was undertaken with government agencies.

Table 6.6 provides a glimpse of the close connection. All of the top ten road projects during fiscal years 2007–11 went to companies known to have political affiliation with or to have made large overt campaign contributions to political candidates and parties.

The Office of the Attorney-General has found that there are various ways in which collusion and favoritism can occur in the award of highway contracts. Risks are present at each stage of procurement, i.e., at project initiation or site of construction, technical specifications and reference prices, canvassing of suppliers, the tendering process, contract design and management, and verification and acceptance of work.

Interviews with contractors who asked to remain anonymous indicate that bid collusion is the rule rather than the exception. Collusion can take several forms. First, there could be the formation of a bidding ring, whether ad hoc or long-standing, between the private contractors themselves. Bid-rigging occurs when members of the bidding ring offer prices within a narrow (inflated) range.

Table 6.6 Top ten contracts of the Highway Department and political affiliation, fiscal years 2007–11 (Highway Department contracts from October 1, 2006 to September 30, 2011)

	Contract No.	Project	Value of contract (THB)	Contractor	Political affiliation
1	SRN 27/2551 LW 23 Sept 2008	Rehabilitation of asphalt surface, number 2081 CS 0100 at intersection of Highway 214 (Taha) – and Highway 219 (Stuk)	19,657,158,361	Yingcharoen Construction Buriram Limited Partnership	Bhumjaithai Party
2	SKM 2/2552 LW 6 May 2009	Construction of bridge across Mekong River at Nakorn Panom	1,723,234,000	Italthai PLC	Pueathai Party + contributes to Democrat Party
3	SPB 6/2551 LW 23 Sept. 2008	Construction of overpass at Sukapiban intersection 2–3	913,988,982	Prayoonwit Company Limited	Chart Thai Pattana Party
4	SPB 6/2551 LW 30 Sept 2008	Construction of overpass at Sukapiban intersection 2 and 3 (West Bridge and East Bridge), casting and installing of Precast Segment Box Girder, 3,235 meters in length	913,988,982	Prayoonwit Company Limited	Chart Thai Pattana Party
5	STI 1/5/2551 LW 23 Sept 2008	Widening of road from 4 lanes to 8 lanes, and rehabilitation of surface, Highway 9 Bang-pa-in to Bangplee (section 9)	800,038,725	Chainan Construction Supplies Company Limited (2524)	Pueathai Party
6	STI 1/1/2552 LW 11 Dec 2008	Rehabilitation of highway 3256 intersection of highway 3 (Bangpu) Ban Klong Krabue section 1 between km. 2+200.00 – kilometers. 5+209.329 (west) 3,009 kilometers	776,442,243	See-sang Yotha Company Limited	Chart Thai Party

(*Continued*)

Table 6.6 Continued

	Contract No.	Project	Value of contract (THB)	Contractor	Political affiliation
7	STI 1/2/2551 LW 22 Sept 2008	Widening of road from 4 lanes to 8 lanes, rehabilitation of surface, Highway 9 Bang-pa-in to Bangplee (section 2)	766,881,047	Roj-sin Construction Company Limited	
8	SPB 5/2551 LW 23 Sept 2008	Construction of Highway 9 Bang-pa-in to Bangplee (section 8)	712,899,338	Krungthon Engineer Company Limited	Chart Thai
9	SPB 4/2551 LW 23 Oct 2008	Construction of Highway 9 Bang-pa-in to Bangplee (section 6)	683,946,431	Prayoonwit Company Limited	Chart Thai Pattana Party
10	STI 1/4/2551 LW 23 Sept 2008	Widening of road from 4 lanes to 8 lanes, rehabilitation of surface, Highway 9 Bang-pa-in to Bangplee (section 4)	680,209,428	Kampaengpet Wiwat Construction Company Limited	Bhumjaithai Party
11	STI 1/1/2551 LW 22 Sept 2008	Widening of road from 4 lanes to 8 lanes, rehabilitation of surface, Highway 9 Bang-pa-in to Bangplee	658,338,675	M.C. Construction Company Limited (1979)	Democrat

Sources: Contracts selected from http://procurement-oag.in.th; Public procurement of supplies and services, accessed on June 1, 2012. Political affiliation from various news; party contributions from www.ect.go.th. THB30 = USD 1 approximately.

Bid rotation, whereby suppliers take turns offering the lowest bid and therefore getting the contract, often occurs. This is also called complementary bidding. In some cases, bid suppression occurs, where competitive suppliers are coerced into withdrawing from the bidding process, or suppliers in the bidding ring abstain. Any of these practices could be coupled with sub-contracting, whereby members of the bidding ring receive sub-contracts from the winning bidder. Quite often, the procurement officer is complicit and can exclude non-favored potential bidders (who are not part of the network) in various ways, such as hiding the project announcement and sending it only to select groups. Network relationships are built up over time and often succeed in eliminating competition. Many cases are currently being investigated by the NACC.

6.3.4 Case 4: "Simple" (alleged) kickback: alleged bribery of the Thailand Tobacco Monopoly (TTM) officials

This case involves both domestic and international players. In August 2010, the US Securities and Exchange Commission charged two tobacco companies based in Richmond, Virginia, USA, with violations of the Foreign Corrupt Practices Act (FCPA) by paying bribes to government officials in Thailand and other countries to illicitly obtain tobacco sales contracts. The SEC alleges that Richmond, VA-based Universal Corporation Inc. and two competitors who have since merged to form Alliance One International Inc. engaged in a coordinated bribery scheme in Thailand. Universal allegedly paid approximately $800,000 in bribes to officials within the government-owned Thailand Tobacco Monopoly (TTM) in exchange for securing approximately $11.5 million worth of tobacco sales contracts for its subsidiaries in Brazil and Europe. The companies that became Alliance One—Dimon Inc. and Standard Commercial Corporation—allegedly paid more than $1.2 million in bribes to TTM officials to obtain more than $18.3 million in sales contracts. To settle the SEC's charges against them, Universal agreed to pay disgorgement of more than $4.5 million and Morrisville, NC-based Alliance One agreed to pay $10 million in disgorgement. Universal agreed to pay a criminal fine of $4.4 million and Alliance One agreed to pay a criminal fine of $9.45 million in separate criminal proceedings brought by the US Department of Justice.[7]

It is likely that the Thai officials had networks of politicians and businessmen that brokered these deals.

The problem for Thailand is that, once the US offender agrees to pay the criminal fine, the investigation in the US does not proceed further. In many cases, such as the CTX explosives-detecting device for the new international airport,[8] the Department of Justice responds to enquiries for details and identities involved on the Thai side, the US Department of Justice responds by saying they had "no evidence of bribes being received, or agreed to [be] receive[d]" by Thai officials. This response tipped the scale in favor of the charges being dropped by the Thai Office of the Attorney-General. Network relationships also play a role here. In some cases, it is merely a loose affiliation that motivates action or non-action, with no personal gain appearing to be at stake.

6.3.5   Case 5: Klong Dan wastewater treatment plants: strategic (corrupt) partners and meaningful anti-corruption people's participation

Strategically-placed parties allow systematic wrongdoing to occur with impunity. The Klong Dan wastewater treatment project illustrates this situation.

In November 1995, the Asian Development Bank (ADB) approved a USD 150 million loan to support the Thai government's Pollution Control Department (PCD) in establishing systems to manage wastewater discharged by factories and residents in the Bangkok metropolitan area, including Samut Prakarn. The initial plan was to build two separate treatment plants close to the main pollution sources, which consisted of about 5,000 factories. However, by the time the ADB approved an additional loan of USD 80 million, the project site had been relocated some 20 kilometers away to Klong Dan, towards the eastern border of Samut Prakarn Province. A new plan was proposed to build one of the largest, most centralized wastewater treatment plants in Southeast Asia, capable of treating 525,000 cm^3 of wastewater with heavy metals and hazardous waste every day. The rationale offered to the Cabinet was that a single plant would be more economical than two separate plants. It turned out, however, that even though the rationale for re-siting would save money the Cabinet approved an increase in the budget for the project. Japan's International Cooperation Agency (JICA) co-financed the project with an additional USD 50 million loan. After the site change, the total cost of the project more than doubled to USD 687 million.

Klong Dan villagers only learned about the project after construction had started. In late 1998, they saw a sign put up by a joint venture (JV) construction company in front of the wastewater management facility. They were surprised to learn that a huge wastewater treatment plant was already under construction in their neighborhood. Apart from the total lack of information disclosed to and meaningful participation of the local community, stakeholders pointed out the following major flaws with the project:

1   the plant was not equipped to properly treat heavy metals and hazardous waste. These would be discharged into the sea and would destroy local fishing activities;
2   the plant was built on soft soil along the coast and would be impacted by flooding and erosion;
3   no environmental impact assessment (EIA) was conducted in Klong Dan; and,
4   the project site included public land such as canals, which was not for sale. The land for the plant, approximately 1,900 *rai* (1 *rai* equals 1,600 m^2), was sold at a much higher price than the official price.

The land for this new site belonged to a local politician, and suspicions were raised about whether this could account for the sudden change in the project site. In addition, the transport of waste from the source or pollution, through a long and winding pipeline for some 20 kilometers, was not technically sound.

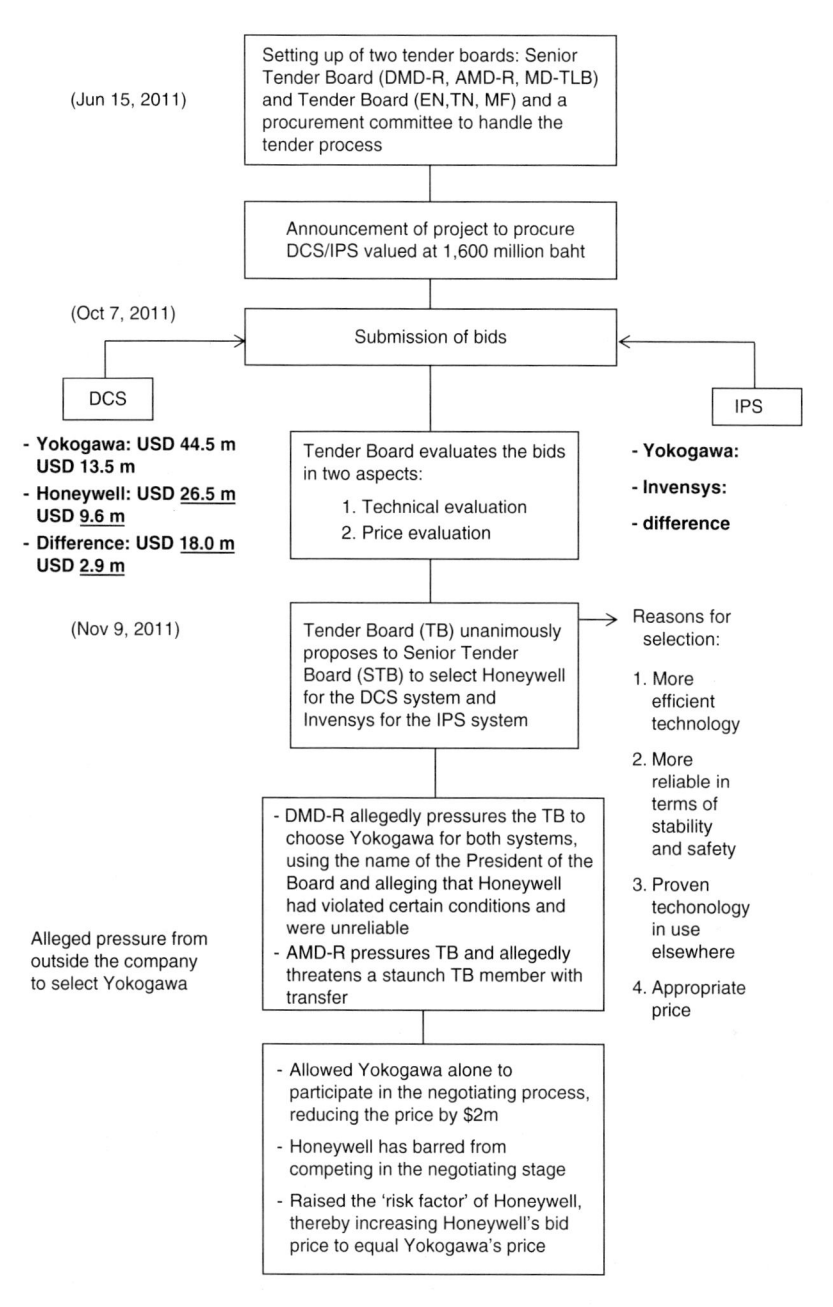

Figure 6.6 Thai Oil Public Company: Procurement process of computerized DCS/IPS.

Sources: Anonymous interviews and tender reports.

Table 6.7 Related companies and board members

Company name	Mr. Somkhit Theeraboonchaikul	Mr. Takeshi Aoyama	Mr. Wichai Suwannavasit	Mr. Somchart	Mr. Thee	Mr. Masatochi Nakahara
Yokogawa (Thailand) Ltd.	✓	✓	✓	✓	✓	
E&I Solution Co., Ltd.	✓		✓	✓		
Advance Computer Machinery Co., Ltd.			✓			
Bilonker Company Limited			✓			
Boonkij Development Ltd., Part.			✓			
Computer and Communication Dynamic Co., Ltd.			✓			
Direction of Technology Co., Ltd.			✓			
Dynamic Computer Co., Ltd			✓			
Dynamic Engineering System Co., Ltd.			✓			
Dynamicsupply Engineering Registeredordinary Partnership			✓			
Edynamic Co., Ltd.			✓			
River Process Engineering Co., Ltd.			✓			
Thai International Foam Co., Ltd.			✓			
Wood Talk Co., Ltd.			✓			

Source: Search of database of Department of Business Development, Ministry of Commerce.

On January 13, 2004, PCD filed charges against 19 private firms and individuals in the Thai criminal court, including Vatana Asavahame, a former Deputy Minister of the Interior for having illegally obtained title deeds to the project site land and selling it to PCD at an inflated price. In March 2004 the Land Department revoked the deeds to an area of land of 1,358 *rais*. This invalidated the government's contract with the JV. On June 14, 2007 the NACC concluded that nine government officials, including Vatana, had been involved in illegal land deed acquisition and sent the case to the Supreme Court's Criminal Division for Holders of Political Positions. By that time Vatana had fled Thailand, but the court ruled that he was guilty of bribing officials in the land grab connected with the project and sentenced him in absentia to ten years in prison.[9] This case shows the connection between the minister and collaborators in the Land Department who were involved in falsifying the land deeds.

6.3.6 Case 6: Outside interference and intimidation: Thai Oil Public Company (TOP)

The case of the Thai Oil Public Company (TOP) involves the project to purchase a distributed control system (DCS) which controls the production processes of the refinery, and an instrumented protection system (IPS) which is the emergency shutdown system for the refinery.

The procurement irregularities are summarized in Figure 6.6.

A search of business registration records and board members finds the following cross-membership, depicted in Table 6.7. It remains to be determined whether there was bid-rigging and collusion. If so, then the companies can be indicted for collusion.

6.4 What can be done to improve procurement in Thailand?

To counter corruption networks, it is important to note that certain types of social action, even if effective, may change the types of connections created but do not necessarily reduce their number or importance. The threat of punitive social action for certain transactions induces connections of mutual dependence at different stages within the network. High penalties for crimes tend to increase the mutual dependence of the criminals but not necessarily their number, if the network is strong.

The difficulty with network relationships and social capital is that it can both benefit and harm society. Close-knit, trusting criminal groups may create networks based on a mixture of empathy, threats, and shared goals that negate law enforcement efforts (Gambetta 1988, 1993). And trust between law enforcers facilitates the processing of cases. But trust motivated by moral values such as respect can militate against effective law enforcement, even when extended altruistically. Both kinds of organization can exhibit interpersonal solidarity, reinforced as though in repeats of the prisoners' dilemma game, can create benefit or harm, and a critical mass of desirable networks needs to be created because people are affected by their perception of what others are doing (Fehr and Gächter 2000).

What is perhaps alarming in Thailand is that harmful networks are being created and perpetuated. The massive proceeds of corruption can be used to mobilize supporters to protest court verdicts, indictments, and anti-corruption efforts. Network members show solidarity with the group or network leader, whatever the issue, by their readiness to protest, block roads, put up barricades, and even openly threaten the lives of judges and their families.

The creation of networks is grafted onto the "democratic" machinery and right and wrong becomes a popularity contest.

What complicates the situation further is that sometimes in helping particular persons or failing to act against certain persons does not have any corrupt intent or even expectation of reciprocity. A person's good reputation, or affiliation, or being a son or a daughter of a respected person can cause people to act in their favor without any personal gain. Deference to an institution can become a priority. For example, Thais often advise children to respect "the monk's cloth" and ignore the individual monk's behavior.

Accusations of "double standards" float around every day. The question on many people's minds, though, is whether "good" people should allow their children to be punished, knowing that the "bad" people would get off scot free because of their connections. There are a few examples of "good people" resigning when faced with corruption charges; the really corrupt however cling on to their positions tenaciously. Both good and bad people have connections. "Everybody knows everybody" and is related to everybody, and this is the key to Thailand's political turmoil. Even among non-corrupt academics, when suspicions arise concerning "someone known for a long time" they would refuse cooperation even when they know the facts. The Thai word *khon gun eng* and Chinese word *kaki nung* are both often evoked. It can be seen that interpersonal relationships play an important role in every aspect of life, including securing procurement contracts.

The returns on corrupt acts depend on how widespread corruption is in society, that is, how much corruption is inherited from the past. The larger the share of corrupt agents the higher the returns on corruption for several reasons. First, with widespread corruption in society the task of auditing corrupt officials is not easy. Second, the expected profitability of corruption from an individual point of view is a positive function of the degree to which society as a whole is corrupt (Andvig and Moene 1990). Third, corrupt officials have an incentive to establish communications or networking between themselves and will fuel the corruption ring (Sah 1988). In addition, in societies where rent-seeking and bribery abound, the return on rent-seeking relative to entrepreneurship is high (Murphy *et al.* 1991, 1993; Acemoglu 1995). Finally, when corruption is widespread individuals may be discouraged from trying to fight it, even if everybody would be better off if corruption were eliminated.

If corruption in procurement is to be tackled, reform or measures are needed in the following areas: (1) legal infrastructure, (2) corrupt-friendly economic policies, (3) upgrading of the database, (4) social mobilization for enhanced transparency.

We also argue that membership of international conventions such as the World Trade Organization's Government Procurement Agreement (WTO-GPA) could be a tool to help alleviate current problems.

6.4.1   Improving the legal infrastructure

The legal infrastructure needs to be reformed in many ways and only a few key points are made here.

First, even though Thai procurement regulations emphasize openness and transparency as the main principles, many improvements can be made. For openness and transparency, announcements and dissemination of information must be made through the Public Relations Department, Mass Communication Organization of Thailand, the G-Procurement website, etc. Procurement committees have to be formed, often with citizen participation. Contracts worth more than one million baht have to be sent to the Office of the Auditor-General and Revenue Department within 30 days of signing. Regulations for e-procurement include these additional criteria: value for money, transparency, efficiency and effectiveness, and accountability and responsibility for completion. At least three tenderers (for a standard license or to meet quality control systems) are required. However, Cabinet decisions are only placed on the OPM website in very succinct form. Many cases that have led to corruption proceedings were approved by Cabinet decisions, and more detailed disclosure should be required.

Second, the technical specifications allow what is called "locking of specifications," in order to favor certain suppliers. The dilemma is how to specify enough detail so as to verify suitability and at the same time avoid such specificity that includes/excludes suppliers, particularly for complex, sophisticated procurement that need customized designs. Often the suppliers themselves are consulted for the expert knowledge. Under WTO-GPA Article X Technical Specifications and Tender Documentation, it is required that:

> A procuring entity shall not seek or accept, in a manner that would have the effect of precluding competition, advice that may be used in the preparation or adoption of any technical specification for a specific procurement from a person that may have a commercial interest in the procurement.

There are similar provisions in Thailand, but enforcement is a problem, especially with projects involving very advanced technology, where the suppliers themselves are often informally invited to write the specifications.

GPA's Article X is particularly interesting in stating that: "In prescribing the technical specifications for the goods or services being procured, a procuring entity shall, where appropriate: (a) specify the technical specification in terms of performance and functional requirements, rather than design or descriptive characteristics."

The *functional requirements* are not specified in Thai regulations, and technical specifications are invariably related to physical characteristics. This is an area that could be the focus of reform in Thailand, and would require the nationwide training of procurement officers.

In terms of the legal infrastructure, it is also necessary to coordinate various law-proposing channels. The Cleansing Act of 2007, for example, allowed criminal proceedings against defendants indicted for procurement corruption to be dropped.

The National Anti-Corruption Commission (NACC) recently amended the Anti-Corruption Law that allows it to closely monitor major procurement projects, and requires procuring agencies to publish and explain how the reference prices are calculated. Protection for whistle-blowers has also been introduced. In addition a new Integrity Index has been constructed to assess all government agencies at the departmental level. The index features a procurement component that rates proper procedure and transparency in procurement.

6.4.2 Targeting corruption-friendly economic policies

The NACC is now playing an increasingly pro-active role in scrutinizing economic policies and measures that open up opportunities for corruption. Several pre-emptive interventions have been implemented such as the scheme to procure 4,000 natural-gas operated city buses and the auction of 3-G telecommunications licenses, and this has had the effect of subjecting the projects to greater scrutiny. For example, when the project was submitted for Cabinet approval in 2009 and 2010, the Cabinet asked the proposers of the bus scheme to withdraw the project so that further studies could be conducted in the areas indicated by the NACC technical committee.

Reform is also needed in areas such as intervention schemes in the agricultural sector. Reform in this area had been beginning at the behest of the NACC, but the new government that took office in 2011 seems to be bringing back some of the old risky policies.

6.4.3 Upgrading of the database

Pro-active approaches to countering corrupt networks require knowing the identity of the network members. Efforts are currently underway to improvethe anti-corruption database, with links to information from financial institutions, the Land Department, the vehicle registration office, business ownership records, and tax returns.

Non-government groups are also collecting information and analyzing the behavior of elected officials. For the 2011 election, a civil society group collected information on members of parliament who were absent from parliamentary meetings, and distributed copies of each member's "report card." However, in spite of the dismal scores given to the MPs that failed to attend any parliamentary sessions or were absent more than 50 percent of the time, they were all re-elected.

6.4.4 Increased social mobilization for enhanced transparency

Transparency of procurement information is vital to prevent wrongdoing. The Thai Office of the Prime Minister (OPM) regulations actually do require publication of information. For complaint and appeal procedures, the OPM regulations state that aggrieved suppliers or contractors may lodge complaints directly with the procuring agency, the Procurement Management Office Committee, or the Petition Council. In the case of the Petition Council, the petitioner must lodge the complaint within 90 days of knowledge of wrongdoing. The Council will then consider the petition "without delay," and remedial measure(s) (if any) will be recommended to the prime minister within seven days. Remedies might include overturning the act that is inconsistent with the law or that cannot be supported by "justifiable reason." It is also possible for an interim remedy to be issued by the Council itself, when appropriate.

However, transparency remains a problem, and efforts are needed to mobilize stakeholders in society. This sounds like a broken record, but the very means of mobilization have to be overhauled so that some benefit can be obtained from citizen involvement that would make it worth their while. The Klong Dan case of citizen involvement is a rare success story. With network connections and the possibility of retaliation, Thailand is still grappling with the means to mobilize and incentivize citizens to fight against procurement corruption.

Khoman *et al.* (2009) and Tangkitvanich *et al.* (2009) propose that the Government Procurement Agreement (GPA) could be a tool to increase transparency in Thailand's government procurement. Membership might even lead to greater transparency, more efficient use of government budget (as it would stimulate fair competition), help honest and efficient suppliers, and could foster industrial growth and development. Greater foreign involvement and competition can thus help to uncover wrongdoing. However, there is some apprehension about becoming a member of the GPA. First, the opportunities for Thai suppliers to access GPA member procurement markets are still limited, while domestic suppliers will face stiffer competition. Furthermore, foreign competition may result in difficulties for domestic suppliers in certain sectors. This is the familiar "infant industry" argument that has both pros and cons. If long-run efficiency is the goal, then gradual expansion of competition may help to attain that objective. Second, there is some concern as to whether opening up will lead to greater competition and efficiency or not, if it leads to international collusion. Finally, if foreign governments subsidize their service sectors, particularly construction, the GPA does not have any provision for countervailing action or remedy, unlike the case of subsidies under the World Trade Organization's General Agreement on Tariffs and Trade (Khoman *et al.* 2009).

6.5 Conclusion

In a society dominated by interpersonal relationships for social, business, and other activities, understanding these relationships is the key to understanding corrupt activity. Networks cut across the usual socio-economic characteristics because members with different skills and characteristics are required for a corrupt network to be effective. There are also various difficulties involved in designing a procurement system. First, government procurement usually involves multiple objectives, with efficiency being just one of them. Often procurement is used to effect a geographical redistribution of income or to favor underprivileged groups such as the disabled. It is also difficult to design a system that aligns personal incentives with public benefit, as the same observed behavior could be motivated by opposite motives. Strict conformity to rules sometimes results in less efficiency: the "special method" could reflect a sinister motive or a desire to be efficient, the lowest price may involve the sacrifice of quality and detailed specifications could limit competition.

At the societal level, social enforcement of private contracts, ready access to the award of contracts, morality, and religious pressure for generalized honesty (in contrast to "contextual morality") cannot be overlooked. These elements all tend to reduce the importance of identity, to facilitate transactions between strangers, and to reduce the need for specific mutual investment by connected parties. But procurement also needs to be accompanied by effective monitoring systems (e.g., corruption report, witness protection, etc.) and sufficiently stringent penalties for the wrongdoers and conspirators. The larger the network of corruption rings, the larger the returns on corrupt acts. The creation of networks of clean officials up to a certain critical mass is absolutely vital to counter the corrupt networks.

Notes

1 "Trust implies confidence, but not certainty" (Rose-Ackerman 2001: 1).
2 The expectation of continued contact can be analyzed in terms of strategic advantage in a repeated game. In a single, non-cooperative game, parties may fail to achieve a mutually beneficial solution because each party recognizes the opportunities to cheat or to reap a short-term advantage, a typical "prisoner's dilemma" situation. However, infinite repetition of the transaction can induce the parties to give up short-term benefits in order to realize future gains. Even unscrupulous members, whether patrons or clients, can appear to act altruistically because of this expectation.
3 In Thailand there is a common saying that defines six different groups of people that comprise a network (especially a corrupt network): family members, school friends or disciples, financial contributors, obsequious followers, marriage ties, and competent specialists. These clan or group members therefore cut across the usual socio-economic areas such as income class or occupation. Understanding group membership allows us to see that not all conflict situations are "class struggles." References to the "Arab Spring" and inequalities (that exist and persist in most societies) completely miss the mark when analyzing Thailand's current political situation.
4 For example, Thaksin Shinawatra, former leader of the dissolved Thai Rak Thai Party is a telecommunications tycoon. Banharn Silapa-Archa, leader of Chart Thai Party built himself up from government construction contracts. Suwit Khunkitti, leader of Pua Paendin Party owns SK Intergroup 2005 Co., Ltd. the sole distributer of Tupperware in Thailand.
5 www.business-anti-corruption.com/country-profiles/east-asia-the-pacific/thailand/snapshot/ (accessed July 16, 2010).
6 Adapted from Singhapreecha and Boonyasiri (2010).
7 www.sec.gov/news/press/2010/2010-144.htm (accessed April 15, 2015).
8 In 2004 it was alleged that a deal to purchase bomb-detection devices (the CTX 9000 DSi machine) for Bangkok's new international airport may have provided Thai officials

with more than US$10 million in bribes, kickbacks or inflated contracts. The US Justice Department's fraud section found that InVision's deal included "criminal liability associated with potential violations of the Foreign Corrupt Practices Act" (FCPA) and fined InVision a total of $800,000. The US Securities Exchange Commission then fined InVision an additional $1.1 million "for violations" of the FCPA.

9 www.mekongwatch.org/english/country/thailand/MW_SMBrief(2010.02.27).pdf (accessed April 15, 2015). Another case involving land is that of Somchai Khunpleum, a Chon Buri godfather with powerful political connections, wanted in a local land dispute case.

7 Quasi-corruption in public procurement

The case of the Russian Federation

Andrey Ivanov

7.1 Introduction

The origins of applying electronic auctions in public procurement can be determined fairly precisely. In 1994, Article 18 ("Procurement Methods") of the Model Law on Procurement of Goods, Construction and Services (hereafter "Model Law"), developed by the United Nations Commission on International Trade Law (UNCITRAL), did not provide for auctions as a valid method of procurement. E-auctions became a mode of public procurement at the beginning of the 2000s, when modern information and communication technologies were developed and disseminated. Brazil was an early adopter, introducing electronic auctions at the end of 2000 (Joya and Zamot 2002). The "classical" EU directive (Directive 2004/18/EC, Art. 54) provides legal certainty and specific rules and guidance for their application at European level since 2004 and they were finally introduced into the list of procurement methods in the new version of the Model Law in 2011 (UNCITRAL Model Law, 2011, Art. 27).

In the Russian Federation (hereafter "RF"), the "Law on Placement of Orders for Supplying Goods, Executing Works, and Providing Services for State and Municipal Needs" (Federal Law #94-FL, hereafter, "Federal Law" or "PPL"), which came into force on January 1, 2006, considered the open outcry auction as the primary procurement method and permitted e-auctions for small contracts only. Public bodies were prohibited from applying for tenders in the procurement of goods, works, and services included in "The list of goods (works, services), placing orders for supplies (performance rendering) which is carried out through an auction" as stipulated by the RF government.

Of the four basic types of auction (English auction, Dutch auction, Vickrey auction, and requests for quotations (McAfee and McMillan 1987)), the PPL required the use of the English auction in open outcry and electronic form, as well as requests for quotes for small-volume purchases. Faced with many cases of the suppliers' mala fide behavior at open outcry auctions, Russian lawmakers were forced to replace them completely with e-auctions in 2010 for federal public bodies, and then in 2011 for other public procurement bodies. The government was convinced that applying e-auctions would help suppliers to become involved in the procurement process, to reduce corruption, and to hinder the possibility of collusion by suppliers, which would subsequently lead to improved competition in auctions and to larger price reductions (Shalev and Asbjornsen 2010).

Before the introduction of e-auctions, the dynamics of competition and price reduction at outcry auctions was as follow.[1]

In 2010, the first year when å-auctions were applied on a large scale, 142,450 auctions were announced and carried out on three Electronic Trade Platforms (hereafter ETP) specifically established in the RF: ETP of the Republic of Tatarstan, the Moscow ETP, and Sberbank-AST ETP (hereafter, T-ETP, M-ETP, S-ETP, respectively).

To assess e-auction performance, we will review large-scale studies on this type of auction conducted by researchers from the Higher School of Economics (Moscow) in 2011. Below we will use the statistics presented at the XII April International Academic Conference on Economic and Social Development (April 6, 2011).[2] The researchers took a random sample of 32,283 auctions in total from each of the three platforms (see Table 7.2).

The data analysis yielded very similar results on all the ETPs.

Comparing the data from Tables 7.1 and 7.3, it is clear that competition declined and correspondingly the price reduction decreased.

There is also the problem of auctions that did not take place. There are more than a dozen cases in which the PPL recognizes that auctions did not go through, but practice shows that the main reasons in this case were the lack of bids or only a single bid had been placed. In particular, in 2011 the total number of auctions which did not take place due to a lack of bids or receiving a single bid was 90 percent in January, 86 percent in February, 87 percent in March, and 85 percent in April.

As a rule, there are no bids at an auction if the public body[3] is incompetent (i.e., unable to set properly the initial price and/or to specify the subject of procurement), but the number of such cases should decrease as the public body's experience in procurement improves. Thus, without losing generality, we can consider that auctions did not take place because only one bid was made.

The data in Table 7.3 were so contrary to the expectations associated with the transition to e-auctions that they were met with distrust by the Federal Antimonopoly Service (hereafter "FAS"[4]). However, some data from the FAS itself, related to the application of auctions in 2011–12, confirmed that at least 60 percent of auctions in that period did not take place.

Thus, the question arises as to why substituting outcry auctions with e-auctions resulted in such significant negative changes in the level of competition. Without

Table 7.1 Performance of open-outcry auctions

	2006	2007	2008	2009 (Q1)
Competition in the auction (bids/auction)	2.78	9.05	2.88	3.64
Average price reduction (%)	44.89	15.02	12.19	10.5

Table 7.2 Sampling size

	M-ETP	S-ETP	T-ETP	Total
Number of auctions	39,885	84,328	18,237	142,450
Sampling size	10,916	11,732	9,635	32,283
	(27.37%)	(13.91%)	(52.83%)	(22.66%)

Table 7.3 E-auctions performance

	M-ETP	S-ETP	T-ETP	Total
Competition in the auction (second parts of bids[a]/auction)	1.5	1.6	1.8	1.6
The auction hasn't taken place[b] (%)	75	69	71	72
Average price reduction (%)	6.0	4.0	4.0	4.7

Notes

a   There are two parts of every bid: first part describing the supplied goods, work or service (hereafter "goods") and second part describing the supplier. The second parts are considered just after the auctioning is over.

b   There are many cases when RF legislation states that auction didn't take place. But in the any such case there was no competition in the auction. In contrast to Model Law, PPL doesn't demand from public entity to designate "The minimum number of suppliers or contractors whose registration for the auction is necessary for the auction to be held" (Model Law, 2011, Art. 53-j).

losing generality, we can assume that during the transition to e-auctions, the collusion problem did not sharpen. Thus, we can conclude that the decline in auction competitiveness from 3.64 in 2009 (Table 7.1) to 1.6 in 2010 (Table 7.3) had little to do with conspiracies among suppliers, but was rather caused by corrupt behavior by contracting authorities.

Below, unless otherwise stated, in corrupt behavior the contracting authority has understood its interaction with a supplier as related to giving and receiving bribes. As a rule, bribes during public procurement are obtained as so-called kickbacks: the order is placed at a higher price, whereupon the supplier returns a portion of his surplus to the public buyer.

This said, it is not easy to explain the observed data on the basis of corruption alone. There are no clear reasons for corruption to increase in the course of a transition from open outcry auctions to e-auctions. On the other hand, data in Table 7.3 do not fit other data on corruption in the RF.

Let us consider some empirical data from the Business Environment and Enterprise Performance Survey (BEEPS), a joint initiative of the European Bank for Reconstruction and Development (EBRD) and the World Bank (Table 7.4). The Enterprise Survey is answered by business owners and top managers. The manufacturing and services sectors are primary business sectors of interest (construction, retail, wholesale, hotels, restaurants, transport, storage, communications, and IT). Formal (registered) companies with five or more employees are targeted for interview.[5]

Table 7.4 Corruption in public procurement in Russia in 2008–11

	2008	2011
Percentage of firms that attempted to secure government contract (%)	36.4	26.9
Those among them that indicated that an unofficial payment was made in the process (%)	39.9	22.9

Source: World Bank (2013), Russian economic report: recovery and beyond, p. 31.

Table 7.5 Distribution of responses by enterprise managers in the manufacturing industry to the question, "How often do enterprises of your industry have to give bribes or 'kickbacks' to receive public or municipal orders?"

	2005		2009	
	Number of firms	*Sample share (%)*	*Number of firms*	*Sample share (%)*
Practically always	87	8.7	60	6.3
Often	117	11.7	104	10.9
Sometimes	142	14.2	215	22.5
Never	366	36.5	338	35.3
Hard to respond	290	28.9	240	25.1
Total	1,002	100	957	100

Source: Yakovlev *et al.* (2010: 11).

Thus, about 40 percent of the companies surveyed in 2008 and less than 23 percent in 2011 paid bribes for the right to receive a contract.[6] These figures are indirectly confirmed by the following data.

Since it is assumed that the most typical corruption practices occur in the manufacturing sector (Anderson and Gray 2006), these figures (Table 7.5) may be considered as the upper boundaries of the level of corruption in Russian public procurement.

Thus, the sharp decline in competition at auctions and the significant number of failed auctions (exceeding 60 percent) cannot be explained by anything other than unscrupulous actions by public buyers restricting competition in favor of a pre-selected "favorite."

One possible hypothesis for explaining the inconsistencies identified involves assuming the existence of "quasi-corrupt" behavior by the contracting authority. In this hypothesis, competition may be limited by both the mala fide and bona fide public buyer. The first seeks to obtain bribes, the second tries to achieve other goals.

7.2 Methods

The natural starting point for modeling corruption in public procurement is a principal–agent model.

This model was developed to describe processes in the private sector and aims to understand the agency relationship as "a contract under which one or more persons (the principal(s)) engage another person (the agent) to perform some service on their behalf which involves delegating some decision-making authority to the agent" (Jensen and Meckling 1976: 308). Accordingly, the principal faces the task of shaping a system of incentives for the agent, in which the agent's preference order, defined by a corresponding set of alternatives, coincides with preferences of the principal. In turn, the starting point for modeling public sector processes is the assumption that to meet public needs, the political elite (principal) delegates some decision-making authority to government agencies or other public entities (agents).

Following Jain (2001a), for the purposes of this study, the political elite is understood as the totality of government, as well as the legislative and administrative bodies responsible for the corresponding regulatory rules. The necessary conditions in which the agent's corrupt behavior is possible are as follows (Aidt 2003: F633):

1   Discretionary power: the relevant public official must possess the authority to design or administer regulations and policies in a discretionary manner.
2   Economic rents: the discretionary power must allow extraction of (existing) rents or creations of rents that can be extracted.
3   Weak institutions: incentives embodied in political, administrative, and legal institutions must be such that officials are left with an incentive to exploit their discretionary power to extract or create rents.

In the case of public procurement, for example, the agent is endowed with a discretionary power and a certain budget to carry out procurement. In this situation two of three conditions of corrupt behavior arise.

Imagine a situation in which a private individual attempts to corrupt a bureaucrat in order to obtain a government contract (Rose-Ackerman 1975). In this case, the agent is considered a potential "bribee," and the actual level of corruption is determined by how well the institutions governing the (corruptible) bureaucracy are designed (Aidt 2003).

Unlike in the private sector, applying the principal–agent model to the public sector has its own specifics related to the fact that in a democracy, the political elite is also an agent elected to achieve social goals. Thus, the ideal preference order in this case takes society as a whole, which we call below the basic principal.

Assume that the basic principal, the principal, and the agent equally identify a set of corresponding alternatives $\breve{A}$, and their preference orders $\succeq_{BP}$, $\succeq_P$, $\succeq_A$, respectively, are defined on this set.

DEFINITION 7.1 We call that the principal (agent) mala fide if their preference order is different from the basic principal's preference order: $\succeq_P \neq \succeq_{BP}$ ($\succeq_A \neq \succeq_{BP}$),[7] and bona fide if otherwise.

From Definition 7.1, the basic principal, the bona fide principal and the bona fide agent seek to maximize social welfare.[8]

In the above-mentioned model (Rose-Ackerman 1975), and likewise in models that describe processes in the private sector, the basic assumptions are about the principal's bona fides and agent's mala fides. Below, such models ($\succeq_P \equiv \succeq_{BP}$, $\succeq_A \neq \succeq_{BP}$) will be called classical ones.

The classical "principal–agent" model implicitly assumes that the political elite has developed regulatory rules relying solely on the interests of its principal, i.e., society. At the same time, considering the political elite as an agent hired by society naturally leads us to view politicians as "maximizing agents who pursue their own selfish interest rather than as benevolent agents seeking to maximize aggregate welfare" (Grossman and Helpman 1994: 48). Corruption, directly related to activities of the political elite, is called "grand corruption" (Rose-Ackerman 1996), unlike petty corruption, which is treated in the classical model.

Grand corruption is identified in societies with different forms of government, ranging from kleptocracy (Rose-Ackerman and Truex 2013) to a modern democratic society in which it is manifested as vertical corruption (Jain 2001a; Roncarati 2010) or is caused by the principal's bounded rationality (Simon 1961).

However, if we abandon the assumption about the principal's bona fides, we cannot presume the agent's mala fides. Accordingly, depending on the agent's goal-setting, three types of "principal–agent" models can be constructed.

In the "queue model" (Lui 1985) and the "auction model" (Beck and Maher 1986) corrupt bureaucrats try to correct pre-existing government failures. The initial hypotheses of the models are assumptions about the mala fides of both: a principal and an agent. These models form the class of "efficient corruption" models ($\succeq_P \neq \succeq_{BP}$, $\succeq_A \neq \succeq_{BP}$) (Aidt 2003: F633). Joseph Nye views the corruption of certain factory managers in the Soviet Union as an example of this kind of corruption, which gives some flexibility to a centralized planning system (Nye 1967).

In models of efficient corruption, an agent's actions violate accepted rules of regulation that allow us to identify differences in preferences of the principal and agent: $\succeq_A \neq \succeq_P$. Nevertheless, the principal can create a system of incentives for the agent, which will warn the latter against taking any action in opposition to existing institutions. This kind of model ($\succeq_P \neq \succeq_{BP}$, $\succeq_A \equiv \succeq_P$) can be called a totalitarian model.

Nathaniel Leff notes how bureaucracies in two countries, Brazil and Chile, responded differently to the policy of price regulation aimed at reducing high inflation (Leff 1964). In Chile, bona fide bureaucrats attempted to suppress price increases for food, hampering development of the market for a significant period of time, unlike Brazil, where such policy was sabotaged.

Samuel P. Huntington also believed that in the interest of society's economic development, effective corruption is preferable: "In terms of economic growth, the only thing worse than a society with a rigid, over-centralized, dishonest bureaucracy is one with a rigid, over-centralized and honest bureaucracy" (Huntington 1968: 386).

In this chapter, we intend to complete the typology of principal–agent models, by introduced the model of "quasi-corruption" based on assumptions of mala fides of the principal and bona fides of the agent ($\succeq_P \neq \succeq_{BP}$, $\succeq_A \equiv \succeq_{BP}$).

Table 7.6 The typology of the "principal–agent" models

Principal agent	Mala fide	Bona fide
Mala fide	Efficient corruption Totalitarian model	Classical model
Bona fide	Quasi-corruption	Conflict-free model

DEFINITION 7.2 The behavior of a bona fide agent in institutional conditions created by a mala fide principal will be called quasi-corrupt behavior. The model that addresses this is the quasi-corruption model.

Thus, the proposed typology of "principal–agent" models is as follows in Table 7.6.[9]

The proposed typology serves to apply the following algorithm in the modeling of corrupt/quasi-corrupt behavior:

- to identify the principal and the agent,
- to model the basic principal's preference order,
- to use rules of regulation to model the principal's preference order and prove that it coincides with or differs from the basic principal's preference order,
- to identify the existence of bona fide and/or mala fide agents,
- to propose amendments to regulatory rules and to forecast the agents' responses to the proposed changes.

The rest of the chapter considers the application of this algorithm to public procurement in the Russian Federation (RF).

7.3   The principal and the agent in the Russian Federation public procurement system

The process of establishing a public procurement system in the RF can be divided into three stages: 1992–97, 1997–2006, and 2006–13.

In the first stage (1992–97), many documents designed to provide the legal framework for public procurement were enacted. The first was Presidential Decree #826, "On arrangements for the formation of the Federal Contract System," and the government resolution on its implementation. However, at this stage, tenders for public contracts were not mandatory, which is why corruption was widespread and improving the legal framework was required.

In the second stage (1997–2006), legal documents for the basis of a regulatory system for public procurement were enacted: Presidential Decree #826, "On urgent arrangements to prevent corruption and budget cuts in the organization of purchasing goods for public needs," and Federal Law #97-FL, "On the organization of tenders for the procurement of goods, works and services for public needs." It should be noted that substantive provisions of these documents (first of all, Presidential Decree #305) were based on customary international practice, the Model

Law. In particular, open tendering was considered to be the primary procurement method, open and restricted, one- and two-stage tenders, and first-price sealed-bid tender (requests for quotations) were permitted.

However, in contrast to recommendations from the Model Law, legislative acts did not provide for any kind of negotiation in public procurement. Moreover, the above-mentioned legal documents left a significant legal void in the public procurement system, as their provisions hampered the creation of an appropriate monitoring system.

In the third stage (2006–13), the development of a national public procurement system was associated with enacting the "Law on Placement of Orders for Supplying Goods, Executing Works, and Providing Services for State and Municipal Needs."

We will focus on the major changes in the RF's regulatory framework of public procurement, related to the adoption of Federal Law, in terms of their role in hindering the development of conditions for corrupt behavior (Aidt 2003).

In order to limit the discretionary power of contracting authorities and to prevent them from rent-seeking:

- extremely low price thresholds were established;[10]
- restricted tenders (except involving information regarded as state secrets) and two-stage tenders were prohibited;
- negotiation procedures had not been provided for;
- qualification/reputation criteria were prohibited (and later limited);
- there were no mechanisms to reject abnormally low bids;
- reverse price auctions were selected as the preferred procurement method,[11] mandatory for goods and services included in the special auction list (hereafter "Auction List").

Among the measures aimed at strengthening institutions, the following were offered:

- a uniform procurement law was introduced for all government levels (federal, regional, municipal);
- the Ministry of Economic Development (Coordinator) was authorized to develop policy in public procurement, and the Federal Antimonopoly Service was commissioned as a monitor of public procurement;
- a powerful information system was created and developed;
- severe penalties for violations in public procurement were introduced;
- a temporary "embargo" on the signing of contracts based on the results of the tenders was introduced.

As a result, the Russian Federation developed a system of public procurement regulation with the aggregate principal consisting of the political and legal elite, coordinator and monitor, and the aggregate agent consisting of regional public procurement authorities and bodies governed by public law.

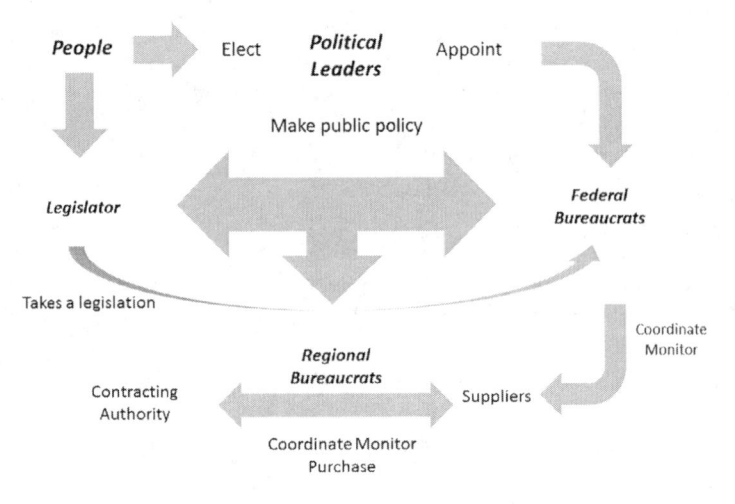

Figure 7.1 Basic principal, principal and agent in a simplified model of the Russian Federation public procurement system.

To understand the mechanism of the RF public procurement system, we consider its simplified model:

- based on public discontent with corruption, the political elite demands anti-corruption regulations,
- based on public discontent with corruption and established public policy, the legislator takes appropriate legislative measures,
- the political elite appoints federal bureaucrats to implement the legislation,
- federal bureaucrats coordinate and monitor regional bureaucrats (there are 83 regions in the RF including its two largest cities: Moscow and St. Petersburg),
- the latter coordinate and control the relationships between contracting authorities and suppliers.

Figure 7.1 illustrates the above-stated mechanism.

7.4   Mathematical modeling of the principal's preference order

Let us consider a contracting authority seeking to procure an indivisible good. Suppose that there are no reasons for single-source procurement. In this case, in accordance with Russian public procurement legislation, a contract can be awarded through auction (open English e-auction—always, requests for quotations—for relatively small contracts) or through open tender.

To formalize the subject of procurement, we apply Lancaster's hypothesis (Lancaster 1966), according to which the buyer, in the decision to acquire goods, evaluates not so much the utility of the goods but rather a finite number of their individual characteristics.

HYPOTHESIS 7.1 The buyer is assumed to be able to formalize the supplied good as a bundle of its specifications (for the sake of simplicity only, the bundle may include the time of delivery, volume and duration of the warranty, operation and, perhaps, utilization costs, and so on).

$$x = (x_1, x_2, \ldots, x_n), x_i \in D_i, \quad i = 1, 2, \ldots, n, \quad x \in D \subseteq D_1 \times D_2 \times \cdots \times D_n,$$

and to point out the feasible sets $\tilde{D}_i$ for every specification:

$$x_i \in \tilde{D}_i \subseteq D_i, \quad i = 1, 2, \ldots, n, \quad x \in \tilde{D} \subseteq \tilde{D}_1 \times \tilde{D}_2 \times \cdots \times \tilde{D}_n,$$

where the Cartesian product $A \times B$ of sets A and B is the set of all ordered pairs (a, b), where $a \in A$ and $b \in B$.

In industries with a short technology lifecycle, the adequacy of hypothesis 7.1 is provided by carrying out multi-stage (possibly, negotiated) procurement procedures. Such procedures are provided by international procurement legislation (Model Law, Art. 27, 1, e–h) and not provided by the PPL.

Consider the set of outcomes of the procurement procedure

$$A = \{(x, \ p) | \ x \in D, \ p \in [0, +\infty)\},$$

where x is a formalized description of the supplied good and p is the price at which a contract is awarded.[12] Below we will call the elements of set A "contracts."

If the selection stage of an auction or tender gives the only bidder (hereafter, the terms supplier, producer, seller, and bidder are synonymous) $x \in \tilde{D}$, he/she must be awarded the contract. Hence, set $\tilde{D}$ can be called the set of "quality goods" or simply quality set.

The initial (maximum) contract price is denoted by p_0 which should be included in the procurement notice according to Russian legislation. The set $\tilde{A} = \tilde{D} \times [0, \ p_0]$ is then introduced, each point of which is $(x, \ p)$—the basic principal's feasible contract.

Suppose that the Basic Principal's Preference Order (BPPO) is defined on this set of contracts. The same preference order according to Definition 7.1 has a bona fide agent.

We put forward the following assumptions about its properties.

1 BPPO is reflexive: a customer is indifferent between every two identical contracts.[13]

Since hypothesis 7.1 suggests that the bundle of the good's specifications contains all specifications essential to the buyer, it is natural to assume that, when comparing the two contracts that match the content, terms and cost of delivery, the buyer considers them indifferent.

2   BPPO is complete and transitive.

Given assumptions 1–2, we have:

- from any finite number of contracts, the public buyer is able to choose the best (Roberts 1976),
- each feasible contract belongs to the definite set of indifferent contracts (indifference set of the contract), and indifference sets of contracts, which are not indifferent to each other, do not intersect.

For simplicity and using visual geometric interpretations, we assume that the subject and conditions of purchase can be expressed by a single numerical characteristic q which stands for the quality of the supplier's bid, and varies in the set $(q_0, +\infty)$.[14] In this case, each indifference set does not contain internal points because the contracts that differ in price characteristic (*ceteris paribus*) cannot be indifferent to each other. Hence, we can replace the term "indifference set" with the term "indifference curve."

Thus, given these assumptions, the preferences of the basic principal with regard to the set of contracts can be represented by its indifference map.[15]

Consider the problem of procurement of homogeneous goods. In this case, contracts which differ only in the value of the qualitative characteristic, varying over a range of $(q_0, +\infty)$, are considered to be indifferent to each other and result in the following indifference map (Figure 7.2).

Consider a bid for the purchase of a differentiated product. Generally speaking, we can assume that the contract, which corresponds to the high-value qualitative characteristic introduced above, is strictly more preferable

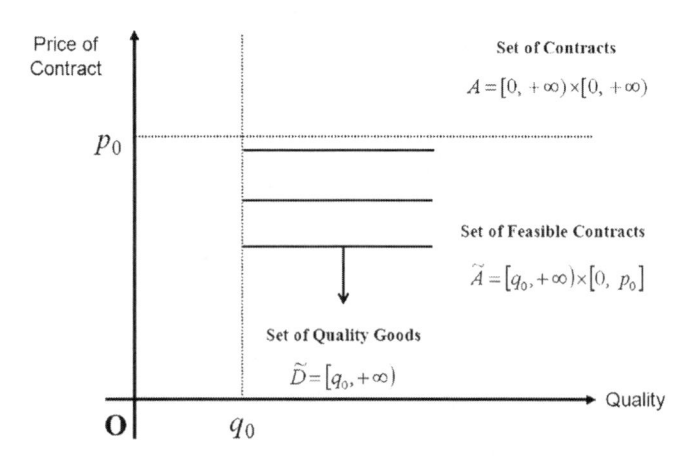

Figure 7.2 The basic principal's indifference map: the case of homogeneous goods.

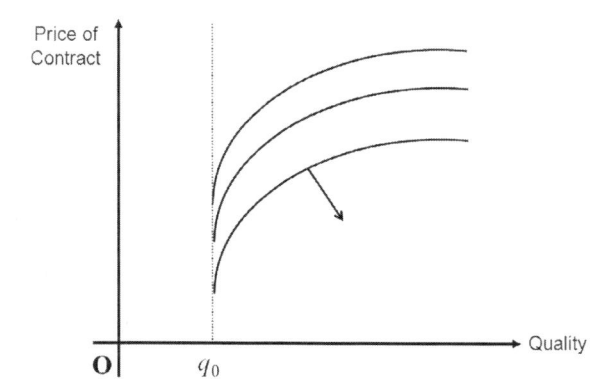

Figure 7.3 The basic principal's indifference map: the case of differentiated goods.

for the buyer (*ceteris paribus*). Given this assumption, since the more expensive contracts are strictly less preferred by the buyer (*ceteris paribus*), his indifference curves are graphs of strictly increasing functions.

3   BPPO is concave.

Indeed, it is natural to assume that

- if the basic principal considers two contracts that are not indifferent, then small changes in price and/or quality in the first contract do not change his preference relative to the other one;
- if the value of the qualitative characteristic is gradually increasing following a uniform pattern (along the indifference curve), the corresponding price changes are non-increasing.

Thus, given these assumptions, the basic principal's indifference curves are the graphs of strictly monotonically increasing, continuous, concave functions and his indifference map is as follows (Figure 7.3).

It should be noted that the BPPO's smoothness and strong convexity, generally speaking, are not assumed. Indeed, the market consists of a finite number of different groups of differentiated goods, and quality is considered to be the same within each group, thus the BPPO is modeled by family of piecewise constant non-decreasing indifference curves.

7.5   Procurement by English auction: the identification of principal bona fides

7.5.1   Base model: the case of symmetric suppliers

We assume that purchasing goods are included in the auction list, which excludes the possibility of their acquisition by open tender, and the order quantity is so large that the goods cannot be purchased by request for quotation.

Given these assumptions, the principal authorizes the agent to purchase goods by English auction. We now consistently take some hypotheses and determine the choice of the public buyer (agent) under the given regulatory rules.

HYPOTHESIS 7.2 The public buyer defines the set of feasible product offerings as $\tilde{D}$.

Suppose that there are N suppliers who can deliver the goods from this set:

$$x^i \in \tilde{D}, \quad i = 1, 2, \ldots, N, \quad N \geq 1.$$

HYPOTHESIS 7.3 Each supplier knows what their own production and delivery costs will be if they win a contract and this information is only available to them.

Hereafter, c_i denotes the i-th supplier's economic costs of production (purchase price when buying from a producer) and delivery costs of the procured items (there is no participation cost):

$$c_i = C_i(x^i), \quad x^i \in \tilde{D}, \quad i = 1, \ldots, N.$$

In this subsection, for the sake of simplicity, we assume that the numbers of suppliers are ordered according to the size of their costs: $c_1 \leq c_2 \leq \cdots \leq c_N$.

HYPOTHESIS 7.4 The suppliers are symmetric: all the bidders appear to be the same to the buyer and to each other. We assume that there is a famous probability distribution $F(\mu, \sigma)$ and suppliers independently draw their costs from it.

The constructed model is the independent private-values model (McAfee and McMillan 1987), traditionally used in the modeling of procurement by auction.

HYPOTHESIS 7.5 The public buyer sets the initial (maximum) contract price p_0 in such a way that the following inequality is satisfied:

$$\max_{i \in I} c_i \leq p_0, \quad I = \{1, 2, \ldots, N\}.$$

The last assumption implies that all contracts $(x^i, c_i), i \in I$, are available to the public buyer:

$$\tilde{A} = \{(x, p) | x \in \tilde{D}, \ p \in [0, p_0]\}.$$

HYPOTHESIS 7.6 All suppliers are supposed to be rational and risk-neutral.

HYPOTHESIS 7.7 There is no collusion among suppliers.

HYPOTHESIS 7.8 There are no dumping suppliers (nobody bids lower than their costs).

We will call the suppliers, for whom hypotheses 7.7 and 7.8 take place, bona fide suppliers.

PROPOSITION 7.1 *(McAfee and McMillan 1987). If there is a contracting authority seeking to procure an indivisible good by English auction and hypotheses 7.1–7.8 take place, then the lowest-cost supplier will win the bidding, and the price of the contract will be equal to the costs of their last remaining rival.*

Consider the problem of procurement of homogeneous goods. In this case, as $N > 1$, σ is sufficiently small, the basic principal's preference order (BPPO) can be represented by the indifference map depicted in Figure 7.4 and hypotheses 7.1–7.7 are usually performed.

For the sake of simplicity, assume $c_1 < c_2$.

Given these assumptions (Proposition 7.1), the contract (x^1, c_2) is obtained by means of an English auction. This means that:

$$(x^1, c_2) \succeq_P (x^i, c_i) \forall i \geq 1. \tag{7.1}$$

It should be noted that the contracts in the right-hand side of (7.1) are affordable to the buyer as they can be obtained by means of an open tender or, if legislation changes, first-price auction.[16]

The contract (x^1, c_2) and contracts (x^i, c_i) $(i = 1, 2, \ldots, N)$ in the coordinate system are labeled "Quality" and "Price of Contract (Costs)" and, to identify which one is preferable to the basic principal, we use the indifference map depicted in Figure 7.4.

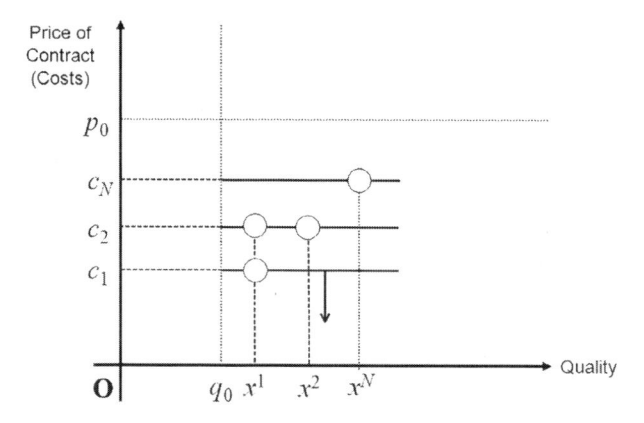

Figure 7.4 Optimal contracts for the basic principal and the principal: the case of homogeneous goods.

It is clear to the basic principal that the contract (x^1, c_2) awarded by means of an English auction is dominated:

$$(x^1, c_1) \succ_{\text{BP}} (x^1, c_2).$$ (7.2)

From (7.1) to (7.2) we have $\succeq_P \neq \succeq_{\text{BP}}$. Hence (Definition 7.1), the principal can be considered mala fide.

7.5.2 Modified model: the case of asymmetric suppliers

To describe the procurement of differentiated goods, we modify the model constructed in the previous subsection by taking the following assumptions.

HYPOTHESIS 7.9 The set of suppliers S is a union M $(1 \leq M \leq N)$ of disjoint sets (classes of suppliers):[17]

$$S = S_1 \cup S_2 \cup \ldots \cup S_M, \quad S_i \cap S_j = \emptyset \, (i \neq j), \quad |S_i| = n_i,$$

and all the bidders of each class appear to be the same to the buyer and to each other. We assume that there are famous probability distributions $F_i(\mu_i, \sigma_i)$, $i = 1, 2, \ldots, M$, and the suppliers of each class independently draw their costs from the corresponding probability distribution.

If $M = 1$, we have the independent private-values model. Below, we assume $M > 1$.

I_k stands for the set of the k-th class suppliers' numbers: $I_k = \{i_1, i_2, \ldots, i_{n_k}\}$, $1 \leq k \leq M$. It is clear that:

$$I = I_1 \cup I_2 \cup \ldots \cup I_M, \quad I_i \cap I_j = \emptyset \, (1 \leq i, j \leq M, i \neq j).$$

HYPOTHESIS 7.10 For every integer $k, l \in [1, M]$: $k < l$, the following inequalities are true:

$$c_i < c_j \quad \forall i \in I_k, j \in I_l.$$

The latter assumption is necessary for the modeling of procurement in the markets, where producers offer goods that are not indifferent to each other from the buyers' point of view. Such products can be goods or services (vehicles, medical equipment, drugs, health-care or educational services, among others) supplied by sellers of different types (public and private organizations, international and domestic firms, etc.).

Since it is assumed that higher-quality goods imply higher production costs, hypothesis 7.10 suggests that higher-quality goods supply the producers of classes with larger numbers.

HYPOTHESIS 7.11 The auction is designed in such a way that each supplier has no information on the participation/non-participation of other suppliers at the auction.

PROPOSITION 7.2 *(McAfee and McMillan 1987). If there is a contracting authority seeking to procure an indivisible good by English auction and hypotheses 7.1–7.3, 7.5–7.11 are true, then the worst-quality supplier wins the bidding, and the contract price will be equal to the costs of their last remaining rival or to the initial price of the contract.*

Consider the problem of procurement of differentiated goods. In this case, since $N > 1$ (so as $M > 1$), σ_i are sufficiently small, the basic principal's preference order (BPPO) can be represented by the indifference map depicted in Figure 7.5.

Below, for the sake of simplicity, we have assumed that $|S_i| = 1$, $i \in I$, and, correspondingly, $M = N$. In this case in particular, $c_1 < c_2$ (7.10).

Given these assumptions (Proposition 7.2), the contract (x^1, c_2) will be obtained by means of an English auction. This means that:

$$(x^1, c_2) \succeq_P (x^i, c_i) \forall i \geq 1. \tag{7.3}$$

The contract (x^1, c_2) and contracts (x^i, c_i) $(i = 1, 2, \ldots, N)$ in the coordinate system are labeled "Quality" and "Price of Contract (Costs)" and, in order to identify which one is the most preferable to basic principal, we use their indifference map.

It is clear that for the basic principal the contract (x^1, c_2) awarded by means of the English auction is dominated:

$$(x^1, c_1) \succ_{BP} (x^1, c_2). \tag{7.4}$$

It is worth noting that for the basic principal the contract (x^1, c_2) is also dominated by contract (x^2, c_2). Moreover, in terms of specific preferences as depicted in Figure 7.5, the contract (x^1, c_2) obtained according to regulatory rules is the worst one in the basic principals' Pareto set $A_{BP} = \{(x^i, c_i), i \in I\}$.

From (7.3) to (7.4) we have $\succeq_P \neq \succeq_{BP}$. Hence (Definition 7.1), the principal can be considered mala fide.

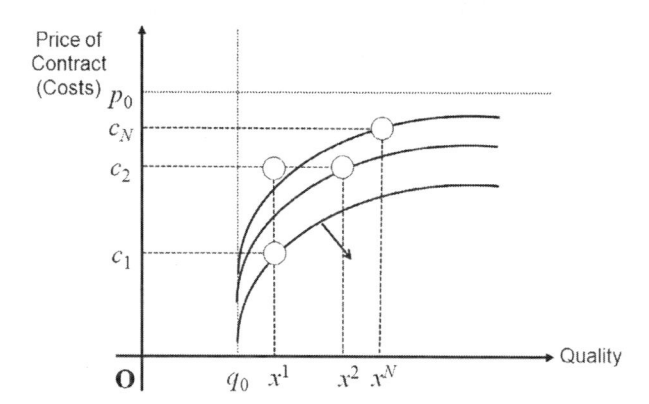

Figure 7.5 Optimal contracts for the basic principal and the principal: the case of differentiated goods.

7.6 Bona fide agent: the identification of incentives for quasi-corruption

In this section, we will consider a bona fide agent who procures under regulatory rules created by a mala fide principal.

It is clear that given the assumptions of the previous section, the set of contracts that is available to the buyer has the form $\{(x^i, p), \ p \geq c_i, \ i \in I\}$, and the agent's Pareto set $-A_A = A_{BP} = \{(x^i, c_i), \ i \in I\}$.

Given the finiteness of the Pareto set and the completeness and transitivity of the bona fide agent's preference order, the most preferred contract exists.

We assume that the contract (x^j, c_j) $(1 \leq j \leq N)$, corresponding to the bid of supplier j, and we will consistently consider a number of obstacles to obtaining the contract.

7.6.1 The second-price risk

We assume that $N > 1$ and $j > 1$. As noted above $((7.1)$ to $(7.4))$, given the existing regulatory rules, the buyer's most preferred contract cannot be obtained.

However, when purchasing homogeneous goods, the costs of suppliers are very similar to each other, and we can consider the value of the second-price risk $(c_2 - c_1)$ as sufficiently small. In this case, we can substitute the hypothesis of the basic principal's rationality with a suitably constructed hypothesis of his bounded rationality, and ascertain the acceptability of the English auction for the purchase of homogeneous goods.

Moreover, the cost of open tender to procure homogeneous goods, which can allow the contracting authority to obtain the most preferred contract (x^j, c_j), could surpass the cost of the relevant auction at an amount greater than $(c_2 - c_1)$.

When purchasing differentiated goods, such a risk evaluation is not possible. Indeed, in this case we cannot assume that $N > 1$ (Table 7.3), and we have to assess risk by the value of $(p_0 - c_1)$. This gives us grounds to speak of the "curse," rather than the risk, of the second price.

7.6.2 The risk of suppliers' mala fides

When purchasing homogeneous goods, the risk of the suppliers' mala fides connected with their collusion (7.7 is violated) is restricted due to the limited size of the supplier-favorite surplus $(p_0 - c_{\text{favor}})$. Besides this, the bona fide contracting authority is able to manage this risk through careful monitoring of prices and setting the corresponding initial contract price p_0.

When there is only one dumping supplier, for example, with the number of k $(k > 1)$ (7.8 is violated), the auction gives the contract (x^k, c_1) to the public buyer which jeopardizes its implementation: $p = c_1 < c_k$.

Nevertheless, the difference between the supplier's costs c_k and the contract price c_1, generally speaking, may be less than the difference between its economic and accounting costs, which enables the contracting authority to achieve proper performance of the contract at the relevant transaction costs.

If there are several suppliers bidding below their costs, *ex ante* estimation of the difference between the costs of the winning supplier and the contract price is not possible. In this case, the auction winner, generally speaking, is not able to satisfy the needs of the public buyer, even when homogeneous goods are purchased.

In turn, when differentiated goods are purchased, the suppliers' mala fides increase the price of the contract by an amount up to $(p_0 - c_{winner})$ in the case of collusion or $(c_{winner} - p_{final})$ in the case of dumping, or jeopardizes buyer satisfaction.

7.6.3 *The risk of transparency*

When differentiated goods are purchased, the violation of the informational opacity hypothesis 7.11 leads the j-th supplier to leave the market with other suppliers of high-quality goods.

In the case of repeated purchasing, the auction triggers the formation of a specific market of lemons (Ivanov 2012), which is characterized by the low quality of supplied goods, but is not characterized by the low cost of their purchase due to extremely low competition in the procurement.

7.7 Conclusion

Risks in the procurement of differentiated goods by means of the English auction, discussed in the previous section, prevent the bona fide buyer from obtaining the most preferred contract and create strong incentives that restrict competition in the procurement process, thereby manipulating the description of the procurement subject, the terms of the contract, abusing information, etc.

It seems that the scale of such quasi-corrupt behavior can be significantly reduced by taking the following measures as proposed in the Model Law.

1   To establish a required minimum number of suppliers in the call for tenders in order for the auction to be held (Model Law, Art. 53-j).
2   To eliminate the contradictions in the Russian public procurement legislation that hinder the implementation of scoring auctions and handicap auctions, which give the possibility of compensating a higher contract price with the higher quality of the purchased goods (Model Law, Art. 53-g).
3   If the procuring party uses an auction, it should state the reasons and circumstances that justify the use of that method (Model Law, Art. 28-3).

And finally, the scope for quasi-corruption behavior can be reduced by means of an essential increase in the price thresholds.

Notes

1 The data were presented at the XI International Academic Conference on Economic and Social Development (Moscow, Higher School of Economics (HSE), April 2010, http://conf.hse.ru/en/2010/programme, accessed April 14, 2015) and published in the journal *Public Procurement* (HSE) in Russian.

2 The findings of the survey have been published in the journal *Public Procurement* in Russian (http://conf.hse.ru/en/2011/, accessed April 14, 2015).
3 In this Chapter, the term "public body," "contracting authority," "public buyer" and even "buyer" are synonymous.
4 The government authorized the FAS to exercise control in the field of public procurement.
5 www.enterprisesurveys.org/Methodology (accessed April 14, 2015).
6 Companies with 100% state participation are not included in the BEEPS.
7 To simplify, the symbol $\neq$ is used instead of $\not\equiv$.
8 If the corresponding preference orders can be represented by the utility functions.
9 The model based on assumptions of bona fides of both (principal and agent) is called the "conflict-free model" ($\succeq_P \equiv \succeq_A \equiv \succeq_{BP}$).
10 On January 1, 2006 Russia's price threshold was 78 times below the price threshold established by the EU for government bodies (€137,000); at present (December 1, 2013) the threshold is 60 times below.
11 Initially outcry auctions could be applied to any contracts, while e-auctions were applicable to small contracts only.
12 The specific innovation of the Russian legislation, providing for the possibility of achieving negative prices at auction (the transition to auction for the right to deliver the goods free of charge) is not included in the model.
13 The firm that supplied a bid first is the winner.
14 The basic principal considers that a drop in the quality of goods below q_0 cannot be compensated by a decrease in their prices: $MRS_{qp}(q_0) = \lim_{\Delta q \to 0^+} \frac{\Delta p}{\Delta q} = +\infty$.
15 An indifference map is a symbolized set of indifference curves of the subject in which the arrow indicates the direction of the strictly most preferred alternative.
16 First-price auctions: Dutch auction and request for quotations.
17 Here |X| stands for the number of elements in finite set X. It is clear that $\sum_{i=1}^{M} n_i = N$.

8 Corruption and political party financing

The case of Serbia

Vanja Bajović and Savo Manojlović

8.1 Introduction

The European Parliament recently asked Serbia to examine twenty-four controversial privatizations that took place in the last few years. It is difficult to examine them critically and scientifically since all the relevant documentation is classed as an "official secret." However, it did raise the question of money in politics and political corruption. Monetary support and funds are a basic precondition for the proper functioning of all political matters. Political parties want to win elections and they need significant financial sources for political campaigning and marketing. Money invested in the election campaign is one of the crucial factors for success. However, it raises the question of whether political actors will represent the interests of their voters and citizens or the private interests of their wealthy donors. The connections between financial and political powers have always been strong but the problems arise when such connections start to endanger principles of free competition in politics and in the market. The political stage actually becomes a market of mutual favors and secret agreements. There is no country in the world that is immune to such diseases. Numerous scandals involving high-level government officials are reported the world over (the Helmut Kohl scandal in Germany, Sarkozy scandal in France, Lockheed in Italy, and so on). The atmosphere in post-transition countries is even more suitable for them to flourish, bearing in mind the developing free market processes, independent judiciary, and the weak and underdeveloped political and economic institutions that are unable to control their rulers. There is belief that the political system in Serbia actually encourages political corruption. According to statistics, over 80 percent of Serbian citizens believe the domain of political parties and public services is the most corrupt aspect of life (UNDP Serbia 2011).

For the purpose of this chapter political corruption is defined as "any transaction between private and public sector actors through which collective goods are illegitimately converted into private-regarding payoffs" (Heidenheimer *et al.* 1993). A fundamental criterion for defining corruption is violation of the impartiality principle that implies objective and fair decision-making, independent of financial, family or other relations between the decision-maker and any third party. Regarding this, Kurer (2005) was right in stating that "corruption involves a holder of public office violating the impartiality principle in order to achieve private gain."

The area of political party funding is particularly vulnerable to political corruption. According to a concept developed by Pareto (1935), there are three motives for providing political funds: (1) idealistic or ideological; (2) social, aiming at social honors or access, and (3) financial, striving for material benefits. Unfortunately, Serbian practice demonstrates that the last one prevails.

The purpose of this research is to examine the connection between political party funding and corruption, with particular focus on Serbia. There is belief that the political system in Serbia fosters political corruption. Election campaigns are costly and there is no political party in Serbia that can provide necessary finances solely from legal sources that are, under the law, very limited. Thus, to bridge the gap the party has to "sell something" to earn money for its operations. The consideration in the transaction is the promise that the party will, if it wins the elections, give certain benefits to its wealthy donors. Financial magnates are more than interested in such deals, bearing in mind their privileged positions in future economic transactions (public procurements, privatizations, taxes, etc.). The free market and political decisions therefore actually become the subjects of transactions. The other noticeable forms of political corruption in party funding, like party taxation, misuse of public resources for private purposes and so forth, are discussed in the first part of the chapter. The most important anti-corruption mechanisms and their implementation in Serbian practice are analyzed afterwards.

8.2   Statement of the problems

According to some sources, corruption in the financing of political parties and election campaigns may take three main forms: quid pro quo contributions to the party and candidates by individuals, groups or companies in return for benefits; the misuse of public resources by incumbent parties or politicians for electoral purposes; and the buying of votes (Open Society Justice Initiative 2004). The first and second forms are directly related to political party funding, while in the case of voter bribery instead of the money being given to the party, the party gives money for votes. Thus, bribing voters cannot be related directly or indirectly to political party funding and so this form of political corruption, although it occurs in Serbia,[1] is beyond the scope of this chapter.

The first issue concerns the most commonly recognized form of corruption in political funding, which is the provision of financial resources by private donors to the party, in return for favorable treatment. According to Philp (2002), this type of corruption has four key components: (1) a public official (A), who, acting for personal gain, (2) violates the norms of public office, and (3) harms the interests of the public (B), and (4) to benefit a third party (C) who rewards A for access to goods or services that C would not otherwise obtain. The party that wins the election is able to return the favors to its donors, allocating licenses, state contracts, tenders and other economically advantageous arrangements. As it is widely acknowledged, and following the popular quote, just as "there ain't no such thing as a free lunch" in the economy, there are no free donations in political party funding. This type of political corruption is a common feature of all systems that allow private donations, but in the post-transition countries of South East Europe it has a particular dimension, given the historical legacy of a state-managed economy, lack of a strong private sector, scarcity of resources, and bureaucratic mismanagement. The disproportionately large role of individual donors in these countries provides them in turn with a large political influence on decision-makers. It is widely speculated that politicians reward their donors with the benefits of state contracts or beneficial position in privatization. A good example is the criticism by the Serbian public provoked by the law on urban planning and construction passed in 2009 that was adopted urgently, without public discussion. In practice, this law enabled controversial businessmen who are believed to be close to the government, to purchase bankrupt public companies and public land at extremely low prices.

A particular problem of post-transition countries with a historical legacy of a one-party system is favoritism or cronyism whereby offices or benefits are granted to friends, relatives or members of a political party, regardless of merit. Fraud-ridden employment competitions or political appointments to directorships and oversight boards in public companies are an illustration of this phenomenon. The principle of impartiality is broken, since the jobs are not obtained based on expertise and qualities, but on party membership. A phenomenon often known as "corrupt mentality" and seen in people's values, attitudes and behavior is a common feature of all post-transition East European countries. In a one-party system that ruled for nearly half of the century (1945–91), membership of the Communist Party was an essential condition for professional promotion. The introduction of political pluralism at the beginning of 1990s did not mean the end of this heritage. According to Walecki (2003), "People did not change their attitudes during 1989–1991; they only modified old patron–client relations." The possibility of a job in public institutions and state-owned enterprises is a very powerful and potentially corrupt mechanism to ensure loyalty to a political party, considering that in 2007 it was estimated that the government controlled nearly 40,000 appointments at all levels of executive authority in Serbia (Pešić 2007). According to UNODC research (2011), recruitment procedures in the Serbian public sector still suffer from a lack of transparency, at least in the opinion of applicants who were not hired. Two thirds of those who did not get a job thought that somebody else was employed due to nepotism or party membership, while an additional 14 percent believed that somebody else was hired due to bribery. Only 8 percent believed that somebody else fit the job requirements better!

Another phenomenon is "party taxation" by which party members appointed to managerial positions in state-owned enterprises, public companies or other profitable positions, donate part of their high salaries to a political party. Party taxation is usually stated as a problem of the CEE (Walecki 2003), as one of the tools for compensation for the generally low income from party membership. According to a study (Mair and van Biezen 2001) conducted on four CEE countries, only 2.8 percent of citizens are party members, which is half the 5.5 percent in 16 countries of Western Europe that were analyzed. In Serbia, 6 percent of citizens are party members (Stojiljković 2008), which is more than in Western Europe, but at the same time party taxation is an additional source of funding. Available data shows that donations are sometimes even higher. An Internet search easily found that nine of the fifteen individual private donors of one of the ruling political parties in Serbia (SPS),[2] whose names are published on this party's web-page, are in leading managerial positions in state-owned enterprises or institutions. The total amount of their donations makes up 66 percent of all private donations to this party.

Donations by public officials are explained by the fact that they were appointed thanks to the political party, which "morally obliged" them to donate to that party in return. Only one fact is ignored: in a democratic society, party membership cannot be a crucial condition for employment or appointment to expert positions.

The last issue concerns the linkage between political, administrative and financial power. Leading officials of political parties provide very profitable jobs for their private companies, or companies owned by their relatives, friends or other related persons. These companies usually get very profitable jobs in dealings with the state and a privileged position in the market. Part of the profit is usually "reinvested" in the political party, or it is provided by other, not necessarily financial, services. Serbia's political stage is full of illustrative examples.

The Protekta group security company, owned by the husband of one of the highest officials of the Democratic Party, secures numerous public institutions like the Treasury, the Zvezdara Municipality, the Agency for licensing of liquidators, the National Employment Service, Tax Administration, etc. (B92, 2012, July 23). This company donated RSD 2.000,000 (around EUR 20,000) to the Democratic Party in 2011, and one year later, it donated the same amount for parliamentary elections.

Public relations agencies, marketing and production companies owned by the ruling politicians or persons related to them have a special place in media financing. The Anti-Corruption Council (2011) analyzed the examples of the McCann Erickson Agency, which is owned by Democratic Party member Srdjan Saper and the Multikom Group's Direct Media, owned by Dragan Djilas, mayor of Belgrade and the Democratic Party deputy president. These agencies have a significant role in the advertising market and numerous contracts with state institutions and other state bodies (ministries, state-owned enterprises, public companies and institutions, etc.).

The leader of the Liberal Democratic Party is the owner of a company that had a profit of RSD 3.2 million (about EUR 40,000) in 2009, although this company was registered on December 14, 2009 (Press Online 2010, May 8).

Therefore, political parties that should be the key factor in combating political corruption are actually its biggest generator. However, all formally proclaimed anti-corruption efforts are useless without the political will to fight corruption on the highest level. Given that the law can sometimes be evaded through loopholes, true reform can only be achieved when parties voluntarily adopt reforms (Shari and Baer 2005). The next sections deal with fundamental anti-corruption mechanisms, focusing on their implementation in Serbia. The question that arises is whether these mechanisms are the result of a strong political will to fight corruption or the outcome of international pressure and aspirations to EU membership.

8.3 Legislative framework

After the introduction of a multiparty system in Serbia in 1990 (before that, the Communist Party was the sole political party in former Yugoslavia), there were three legislative periods regarding political party funding:

- 1990–2003: Funding of political parties was partially regulated by several laws (Law on Political Organization from 1990, Law on Republic Participation in Political Party financing from 1991, Law on financing of Political Organization from 1992). This period was characterized by: abuse of public resources and state-owned enterprises by the ruling party; foreign donations as the main source of non-ruling party funding; uncontrolled donations by controversial donors.
- 2003–11: The first Serbian Law on the Financing of Political Parties was adopted in 2003 and entered into force in January 2004 (hereinafter Law/2003). Despite initial enthusiasm, this period was marked by completely inadequate monitoring mechanisms and a number of unclear, illogical and unenforceable provisions that ruined the entire legislative concept (see Transparency Serbia 2004). Examples include the obligation to publish financial declarations but without deadlines to do so, obligation to disclose donors of "regular" party operations but not for campaign financing, too-low limitations on campaign spending, insufficient even to cover a media campaign, provisions that could not be applied equally to all participants in an electoral campaign, and so on.[3]
- A new Law on Financing of Political Activities entered into force in 2011. Crucial anti-corruption mechanisms prescribed by this law are: more effective monitoring mechanisms, limitations on private donations and membership fees, prohibition of political party participation in lucrative activities, prohibition of prima facie corrupt donation and criminal and administrative punishments.

Public versus private funding: The new law encourages a mixture of public and private funding. Public donations are not high, but they are enough to provide proper daily functioning of political matters. The biggest advantage of public funding is financial independence from the donors. A financially independent political party is more inclined to operate in the interest of the public instead of the interest of wealthy donors. But the risks of public funding should be considered as well. According to Nassmacher (2003b), the independence of parties can be undermined by financial reliance on the public purse, which is a major problem in countries during transformation, where dominant parties are in power. Furthermore, decisions about the amount and allocation of public funds may be unfair to opposition parties. Finally, opinion polls have shown that financial subsidies for parties are extremely unpopular with citizens. Nassmacher's list could be extended by the risk of preservation of political life. Since public funds are typically shared according to electoral results, it is more difficult for new political parties that were not involved in an election to emerge and participate equally in political life. Private funding is beneficial for cultivating new political entities but opens the doors to their misuse by encouraging "godfathers" to establish their own political party or exert dominant influence on the existing ones through big donations (phenomenon known in South America as *partitudo de aluguel*). In spite of this, exclusive reliance on public funding is a dangerous concept in developing democracies whose political groundings are not yet stable. The political arena in Serbia is constantly fluctuating and new political parties emerge frequently (Table 8.1).

Despite the quite restrictive regulation of the creation of political parties (10,000 signatures), in Serbia, there are currently 85 political parties registered! New parties often emerge from the existing ones (NS emerged from SPO, DSS, DC and LDP from DS, SNS from SRS, etc.), which demonstrates the as yet unconsolidated political framework. Annulment of private donations would be an extreme and bad solution because it would mean the enforced preservation of the current political framework.

Limitations on individual private donations: Limitations on individual private donations are common in legal practice (Reginald and Tjernström 2003) and are introduced to parcel out financial influence on parties. According to Panebianco (1998), "A plurality of financial sources safeguards the party from external control." Instead of counting on one or a few wealthy donors, parties are forced to collect donations from many different individuals and companies. Donors are numerous and exchangeable, which minimizes their influence on political decisions. The Law/2003 also limited individual donations but the limitation was connected with the political party (Manojlović 2011a). Donors were allowed to donate to many political parties in a political coalition, up to the certain amount. Therefore, in practice a political coalition received much more money than it was allowed by the legal limit. As a result, the Law/2011 limits the amount of donations, which means that one donor is allowed to donate to more than one party, but the total sum of all donations cannot exceed the legal limit. Another more

Table 8.1 Fluctuations on Serbian political stage*

	1990	1992	1993	1997	2000	2003	2007	2008	2012
SPS	46.1	28.8	36.7	34.2	13.5	7.6	5.6	7.6	14.6
SPO	15.8	16.9	16.6	19.1	3.7	7.7	1.2	–	–
DS*	7.4	4.2	11.6	–	64.4	12.6	22.7	38.4	22.1
DSS*	–		5.1	–	64.4	17.7	18.8	11.6	7
SRS	1.5	22.6	13.8	28.2	8.5	27.6	32.4	29.5	4.6

Notes: *DS, DSS and other democratic parties made coalition (DOS) for 2000 election. Cited result is result of electoral coalition. The same parties boycotted elections in 1997. In 1992 DSS was small coalition party in DEPOS leaded by SPO. In 2008 and 2012, SPO was smaller partner in coalitions with DS, but according to researches, from 2007 SPO was supported by 1% to 2% of voters.

contradictory provision of Law/2003 established that the total amount from private sources (donations, membership fees, income) cannot exceed the total amount of public donations (Article 5(7)). It undermined the plurality of private sources and potential donors and also prevented the creation of new political issues. Given that private sources are limited by the amount of public donation, any emerging political entity that did not participate in the last election is automatically disqualified. Finally, this provision only motivated political entities to hide their real finances and donors.

Limitations on membership fees: Although the income from membership subscriptions in Serbia is usually low, the purpose of this limitation is to try to prevent different types of abuse. Limiting individual private donations could be avoided through an unlimited membership fee. The old law only provided that a membership fee that exceeded the limit set by the political party's bylaws would be treated as a donation (Article 5(1)). Law/2003, however, did not oblige political parties to define a membership fee, nor did political parties have to set one under their bylaws. Thus, this provision was not applicable and this legislative loophole was used to avoid limiting individual donations. In practice, contributions from individual donors doubled—donation plus a membership fee that often exceed the amount of donations! Law/2011 established a maximum contribution that combines membership fees and donations. It also contributes to the repression of "party taxation" of the party officials, appointed to leading managerial position in public companies and institutions.

Prohibition of lucrative activities: Political parties are not commercial enterprises; they perform a public function with the objective of expressing the political will of citizens. Otherwise, the ruling party would be privileged in commercial transactions and public goods could be easily abused. A problematic aspect in Serbia is that the companies owned by people closely linked to political parties and their officials have a privileged position in the market. Lucrative promotional activities like selling T-shirts, lighters, badges and similar items with the party's symbols are an important source of political funding in many countries. The popularity of American President Barack Obama during his presidential campaign, for example, could be compared with that of the biggest American movie stars. Selling items with his picture was a significant financial source for his campaign. But Serbs mostly have a negative perception of politicians and political parties. Selling items with a party's symbols has never proved a significant source of funds, but it has rather opened the door for certain abuses. Public institutions, for example, purchased books published by the ruling party,[4] which led to the creation of secret funds. Weighing the minor financial resources that parties regularly gain by selling their symbols and the possibility of different abuses, Serbia's Law/2011 prohibited lucrative promotional activities by political parties.

Prohibition of prima facie corrupting donations: Law/2011 explicitly prohibits the following sources of income:

1   Donors whose contributions imply covert danger to the sovereignty of the state (foreign states, foreign citizens or companies, anonymous donors).

2   Donations that mean exhaustion of state resources (public institutions and public companies, companies and entrepreneurs engaged in services of public interest, institutions and companies in which the state has a stake, other administrative organizations).
3   Donations by entities whose privileged positions in the market could be a cover for money laundering (trade unions, associations and other non-profit organizations, churches and religious communities).
4   Prima facie corrupting donations that result from the donor's dependence on governmental decisions (gambling industry, importers, exporters and manufacturers of taxable goods, legal entities and entrepreneurs with due and unsettled public revenue obligations).

Sanctions: Effective enforcement of legal provisions requires imposition of sanctions so as to deter violations. To be effective, the rules have to be backed by genuine sanctions. The law on financing political activities regulates different offences and provides a range of possible penalties. These are deemed criminal offenses:

- giving or providing funds to finance the political entity, contrary to the provision of the law, with the intention of concealing the source of financing or the amount of funds collected;
- committing violence or threatening violence places a person or entity at a disadvantage or denies them a right, because of a donation given to a political entity.

Breach of other provisions is treated as a misdemeanor, such as failure to publish the list of donors and amount of donations, opening multiple accounts contrary to the law, failure to open a separate account for financing electoral campaigns, failure to submit the report on electoral campaign costs, and so on. A lawsuit could be filed against a political entity and its members, as well as against the donor who breaks the law.

Law/2011 broadened the list of possible sanctions (imprisonment and fining) with the loss of public funding. Experience showed that this sanction had proved an important tool in preventing and sanctioning political finance violations, especially in countries where parties mostly depend on public funds (Ohman 2009).

However, the effectiveness of the sanctions depends on their practical implementation. The sanction will be "effective, proportionate and dissuasive" only when it is applied in practice, forcing the actors to change their behavior to avoid the punishment. Punitive behaviors and measures in Serbia are properly prescribed, but not applied effectively. In 2010 and 2011 the Anti-Corruption Agency submitted eight misdemeanor reports for irregularities in political party financing. Up to now, no sanctions have been enforced, seven procedures are still ongoing and one has lapsed! Various empirical studies suggest that the situation is no better regarding criminal procedures for criminal corruption offenses (van Duyine *et al.* 2010). It is not surprising, therefore, that according to the GRECO Report (2010), the biggest weakness of political funding in Serbia is that "not a single sanction has ever been applied in practice for violations of the rules of political financing."

8.4 Institutional mechanisms

It is believed that "Unenforced limits are worse than no limits because some day they will produce a scandal which will damage people's trust in democracy, as a form of government and in democratically elected leaders who do not live up to their own laws" (Nassmacher 2003d: 140). Legislative efforts are futile without adequate institutional mechanisms to enforce them. Regarding political party funding, crucial anti-corruption institutional factors are an independent monitoring agency, transparency in political funding, and an independent judiciary.

8.4.1 Independent control agency

Regarding political funding, the theory distinguishes four models or options (Nassmacher 2003a). The first is the autonomy option (Sweden) that treats parties as voluntary associations entitled to the unregulated privacy of their internal organization and financial transactions. This option is thus against state agencies interfering in party funding. A high level of political culture, a developed social conscience and an organized society are essential for it to function. The second is the transparency option (Germany). The focus is on the right of the people to know all aspects of party behavior, including fund-raising and spending. The purpose of the rules is to provide as much transparency in party funding as possible. The third is the advocacy option (USA) that emphasizes the need to create a public agency responsible for monitoring and controlling the flow of political funds on behalf of the general public. The fourth is the diversified regulation option (Canada) that is focused on the even stronger control and authority of the monitoring agency, with independent officials entitled to investigate failure to comply with the rules. Like the majority of emerging democracies, Serbia cannot be strictly classified according to these models, but legislative efforts have been directed toward stronger control of party funding by an independent agency.

The monitoring function in Serbia was initially given to the Republican Electoral Commission and parliamentary Finance Committee, mostly composed of political representatives. The Commission and Committee did not have the power to conduct any analyses of financial declarations submitted by political parties, and were not obliged to initiate proceedings against parties that violated the rules.[5] In addition, mutual interest forced them to respect the "law of silence," and although political parties mutually accused each other in newspapers and TV shows, not one administrative or legal proceeding has been filed.

The Anti-Corruption Agency was established in 2009 as an impartial monitoring body, independent of government and parliament. The agency has nine members, nominated by different institutions[6] and ultimately elected by the National Assembly for a four-year term. The President of the Agency is appointed by the members in a public competition procedure for a five-year term. The procedure for appointing members and the fixing of their term of office do to some extent safeguard its independence. Serbian legislation could be improved in this regard by a more stringent appointment procedure and a longer term of office. Involving more political actors in the election of public officials is one of the basic presumptions of their future impartiality and independence. Therefore, instead of Agency members being elected by a majority of representatives present in parliament when the vote is held it would be better if they were elected by the general majority of all national representatives. Four-year terms of office of Agency members overlaps the four-year term of office of the government and representatives in the National Assembly, which basically means that every new ruling majority elects new members. Therefore, the principle of impartiality requires an extension of their mandate.

The Anti-Corruption Agency is authorized to monitor party funding. Here, it is important to distinguish the financing of parties' activities in the election and in the non-election periods. Non-election spending is more noticeable (rent, bills, etc.), but spending on an election campaign (television, newspaper and billboard advertisements, promotional material, public meetings, etc.) is much higher and more ambiguous. The Agency needs far more staff at election time to monitor the campaign in the field and consequently needs much more money to engage them. The budget of an enforcement agency should preserve its impartiality and independence. The Agency recommends its annual budget but more resources are required for an election campaign. The economic situation in Serbia is characterized by very low GDP and a constant struggle with budget deficits, so it is not surprising that politicians are not willing to allocate extra money from the budget to the Agency that is meant to supervise their spending. Independence would be jeopardized in the situation when the independent control body has to beg and bargain with parliament for extra money at election time. To preserve its financial independence, a new law provides that extra resources are allocated to the Agency at election time in proportion to the funds that political parties receive for their campaign.

The State Audit Institution was established in 2005, as the highest authority for auditing public funds in the Republic of Serbia. SAI audits the lawful execution of the annual budget, local government institutions, and individuals. Irrational transactions by companies that are linked to party officials or donors are clear indicators of corruption. The property and assets of a party's officials are controlled in order to check whether they increased during their period of public office. There is reason for concern, for example, if the profit of the company owned by a public official or a relative is significantly higher during their mandate, or if any extra profit is the result of transactions with the state or public companies.

The Anti-Corruption Council was established in 2001 as an expert advisory body tasked to advise the government on preventive and repressive measures in the fight against corruption and to oversee the implementation of these measures. The Council analyzes the problem of corruption and the activities implemented to fight it. It also proposes measures the government should take to strengthen the fight against corruption, and monitors their implementation. The difference between the

Anti-Corruption Council and the Anti-Corruption Agency lies in the fact that the Council is merely an advisory body, while the Agency has much stronger powers of control, enforcement and punishment. Furthermore, the Agency is responsible for curbing conflicts of interest and controlling the funding of political parties.

In addition to the bodies noted above, the Public Procurement Office, Republic Commission for Protection of Rights in the Public Procurement Procedures, Administration for the Prevention of Money Laundering, Tax Administration and other Serbian institutions also deal with corruption. As there are so many of them, the uninformed foreign observer might get the impression that Serbia makes great efforts to fight corruption. However, the multiplication of bodies with similar functions can be counterproductive and dangerous. This overlapping of authorities often leads to situations where nobody wants to deal with the problems and responsibility is transferred to another institution. The entire anti-corruption concept could be jeopardized if only one of the responsible institutions fails to perform its function properly. For example, the director of the State Audit Institution was strongly opposed restrictions imposed on its scope of action by the new law, believing that as an independent body the State Audit Institution is not obliged to comply with the orders of the Anti-Corruption Agency. Probably the best solution would be to have just one independent anti-corruption body with stronger powers.

8.4.2 *Financial transparency*

Financial transparency plays a crucial role in the effective monitoring of political funding. The cash payment culture that traditionally prevails in Serbia, in addition to weak control of tax and property, impede this requirement. However, Law/2011 tried to make political funding more transparent by obliging political parties to open a special bank account for election campaigns and to submit annual financial reports and special election reports to the Agency, etc. Reality shows that financial transparency is not very popular with politicians. In a public discussion about Law/2011 working group members suggested that all payments and donations to political parties should be made via a bank account to improve identification of contributors (Manojlović 2011b), but MPs strongly opposed this provision. Finally, it was agreed that cash payments could be made up to certain amount, with the issuance of vouchers. However, cash payments remain a threat to financial transparency, since real donors and donations can be concealed by issuing fictional vouchers.

Financial transparency is the purpose of exercising financial control over political parties, their donations and spending. A cost analysis of the 2007 election campaign by Transparency Serbia found that parties allegedly covered the majority of costs through public sources, which is contrary to all economic calculations of such costs. A comparison of reported election campaign spending in 2007 and 2010 (Table 8.2) shows a significant increase[7] after enforcement of Law/2011, which gives more monitoring power to the Anti-Corruption Agency.

In addition to the election campaign being more expensive and the fact that only local elections were held in 2007 while local and presidential elections took

Table 8.2 Spending for electoral campaigns

	2007	2012
DS	133,391,053 (1,688,494 EUR)	563,289,835 (4,773,642 EUR)
G17+	65,632,867 (830,795 EUR)	437,077,608 (3,704,047 EUR)
LDP	74,489,380 (942,903 EUR)	214,693,053 (1,819,432 EUR)
SRS/SNS*	119,474,109 (1,518,035 EUR)	343,859,454 (2,914,063 EUR)
DSS	112,924,820 (1,439,428 EUR)	68,356,879 (579,295 EUR)
SPS	43,779,197 (554,167 EUR)	152,770,491 (1,284,665 EUR)

Notes: *Part of the leading SRS officials of SRS created in 2008 new political party (SNS) and took over majority of SRS voters.

Source: Transparency Serbia, unpublished survey.

place in 2012, the enormous rise reported in spending is certainly down to more effective monitoring. However, there are still certain omissions and a tendency of the parties to conceal real costs. The SNS, for example, reported only one public event (a media conference), even though it is general knowledge that it organized numerous public meetings and a convention during its campaign. The DS reported more public meetings, but there are still some events covered by the media and still advertised on the Internet that are not included in the submitted report.

Regarding non-electoral spending, it seems to be a common practice of political parties in Serbia to reduce this item in the reports they submit (Table 8.3). The significant disproportion in the reported spending of political parties with similar organizational structures is evident (DS and SNS). The reported spending on advertising by the G17 and LDP is lower than that reported by the DSS, although at the end of March 2011, the G17 and LDP had much stronger media campaigns than the DSS. According to CESID's calculations (Vuković 2008), based on market prices for advertising, the basic annual costs of a political campaign are about EUR 7,900,000, so it seems that no political party reports real costs. The cost analysis of the 2007 election campaign by Transparency Serbia (unpublished analysis) found that the parties covered most of their costs from public sources, which is contrary to all economic calculations of election campaign costs.

The financial reports submitted by parties contain only limited information about donors and private donations. Some parties claimed that they did not have any individual donors and that state funding covered all their needs. This raises suspicion that a great deal is not being disclosed. In spite of it being generally known that big financial magnates are usually the main donors of political parties, not one such donation was reported.

Most of the biggest political parties reported donations from companies that are not registered with Serbian Registry Agency. The only explanation for this is that such companies were temporarily established in order to make donations to a certain political party and conceal the real donors. Also noticeable are the unreasonably large donations from certain companies relative to their annual profit (Milenkovic *et al.* 2009, May 6). The profit of a company named Vinaduct,

Table 8.3 Annual spending of biggest political parties in Serbia in 2011

	Overhead costs	Advertising material	Public happenings	Salaries of employees	Different trainings	Other costs
DS	109,950,142,20 (1,057,212 EUR)	736,351,36 (7,080 EUR)	0	361,444 (3,472 EUR)	8,717,216 (83,819 EUR)	64,046,079,04 (615,827 EUR)
SNS	10,244,371 (98,503 EUR)	114,899 (1,104 EUR)	1,677,030 (16,125 EUR)	7,019,776 (67,497 EUR)	385,390 (3,705 EUR)	2,207,929 (21,230 EUR)
LDP	20,048,415 (192,773 EUR)	2,086,415 (20,061 EUR)	5,761,291 (55,391 EUR)	1,150,827 (11,065 EUR)	534,989 (5,144 EUR)	444,472,04 (4,273 EUR)
SPS	38,509,721 (370,285 EUR)	1,372,541 (13,197 EUR)	8,227,287 (79,100 EUR)	42,285,525 (406,562 EUR)	1,182,436 (11,369 EUR)	47,184,332 (453,695 EUR)
DSS	26,148,599 (251,428 EUR)	2,847,220 (27,377 EUR)	1,377,035 (13,240 EUR)	23,750,988 (228,337 EUR)	743,145 (7,145 EUR)	8,928,181 (85,847 EUR)
G17+	29,414,035 (282,827 EUR)	2,995,244 (28,800 EUR)	6,146,676.20 (59,902 EUR)	22,657,393 (217,859 EUR)	313,821,54 (3,017 EUR)	0

for example, was RSD 3,200,000 (EUR 27,000) in 2011 and it gave RSD 2,800,000 (EUR 24,000) to a political party (NS). This is 87.5 percent of its total annual profit! Outsourcing Management Solution, whose bank account was blocked from January 2011, gave RSD 7,000,000 (EUR 59,000) to the LDP for its election campaign. The question arises whether this marketing company whose bank account is blocked and does not even have a basic website was a real donor, or whether the name of this company was just mentioned in the report to hide something else.

8.4.3 Independent judiciary

Court proceedings and enforcement of sanctions are key indicators that breach of the law will not be tolerated. As it noted above, the biggest weakness of political funding in Serbia is that not a single sanction has ever been enforced for violation of the political funding rules. No proceedings against the persons who break the law during an election campaign has ever been concluded, which shows either that court procedures are not effective or that there is no political will to prosecute. According to a European Commission report from 2006, the most critical problem is the poor protection of judges and prosecutors from political influence. Judges are subject to a three-year probationary period before permanent appointment, a period when they would be particularly vulnerable to such influence. One year later, the Venice Commission (2007) drew attention to the problem of the excessive role of parliament in the process of selecting and approving the appointment of judges.

The judicial system was completely reformed in 2009, but it did not fulfill expectations. On the contrary, after the reform, the judiciary is regarded as more dependent and corrupt than before. According to research by the World Economic Forum for 2008/2009 regarding judiciary independence, Serbia ranked 106th in a total of 142 countries. According to its latest report for 2011–12, three years after the judicial reform, the perception of its independence has worsened, and Serbia ranked in 128th place! Citizens' perception of the level of corruption in Serbia also worsened after the reform.[8] According to UNDP research, 79 percent of respondents in October 2009 were of the opinion that the judiciary is too corrupt to deal with corruption; in March 2010 the figure was 81 percent, while in November 2011 the number of respondents who shared that opinion stood at 83 percent. All this time, the judiciary remained firmly third in the ranking of the most corruptive institutions, just behind political parties and the health services.

8.5 Social conditions

The free flow of information, which implies media freedom, public criticism, a certain level of political culture, trust in public institutions and an adequate economic environment form the desirable social framework for the effective fight against corruption.

The basic philosophy behind the reporting of party income and expenditure is that party accounts should be the subject of public debate (Nassmacher 2003b, c).

It is essential that voters are informed about contributions to political parties so that they can assess their policies. In another words, if the main donor is a weapons manufacturing company, they should not be surprised if a war starts tomorrow! Voters have to be informed in order to make rational decisions and crucial to being informed is the free flow of information and a free media. Serbia does not have a soundly established tradition of rule of law and free press. As in other post-communist countries, the culture of non-tolerance for differences of opinion that prevailed for more than 50 years obstructed the development of critical thinking. According to recent research, the Serbian media are still exposed to political pressure that is primarily the result of:

- lack of transparency in media ownership;
- economic influence of state institutions on the work of the media through various types of budget payments;
- the problem of RTS (Radio Television of Serbia), which, instead of being a public service, is basically the servant of political parties and ruling elites.

Numerous offshore companies are involved in media ownership, which means that the real owners are concealed. The Anti-Corruption Council found out that up to 18 of the 30 most significant media outlets in Serbia (12 daily newspapers, 7 weekly magazines, 6 TV and 5 radio stations) suffer from lack of transparency in terms of ownership—their real owners are not formally known. The owners of *TV Prva*, *TV B92*, *Radio B92*, *Radio Index* and *Radio Roadstar*, all of which have national coverage, and print media *Vecernje novosti* and *Press* are registered in Cyprus, while the owners of *TV Avala* and the weekly *Standard* are unknown, but from Austria. The significant group of media with non-transparent ownership has formal owners while the informal real owners are domestic businessmen or politicians (*Happy TV*, *Happy Kids*, *Radio S*, *Pecat* and *Akter*) (Anti-Corruption Council 2011). The European Parliament (2011) has also expressed concern, remarking on the government's efforts to control the media, lack of transparency and concentration of media ownership. The result of all this is a selective and non-objective flow of information. Legislative changes are needed to regulate media ownership by limiting media ownership concentration and removing the possibility of hidden ownership are the first priorities.

Critical voters are the final judges of political parties, given that parties depend on their votes to win elections. The main ambition of legislative concepts is to make political processes more transparent and open to citizens to enable them to follow key political and economic decisions (public procurement, privatizations, donations to the parties, etc.) and form their own opinion about the transparency and honesty of political decision-makers. The voting public has a right to know who supports which candidates and parties. It is widely acknowledged that "Sunlight is the best disinfectant" (US Supreme Court Justice Louis Brandeis). In an ideal political situation, voters would make decisions according to their rational economic interests (rational voter theory), and they could punish dubious political transactions at the next election. Therefore, corrupt transactions would not be good for political parties because of the negative effects they could have on voters. However, the real situation is far from ideal. B. Caplan (2007) showed that the rational voter is just a myth, and the average voter is partly informed, mostly uneducated, prone to populism and mostly votes emotionally. Despite all the advantages of critical public opinion, the voice of the majority is not necessarily the most reasonable voice, since the majority is prone to judge too quickly and impulsively, and even without reliable evidence. There is a very fine and ambiguous line between corrupt and legal political behavior and people sometimes react too severely, when they have no basic understanding of political circumstances. Public criticism is justified if a donating company or individual has the privilege of being granted a license or contract, if the donor posts weak economic results but still keeps a top position in the company, if donors have high-ranking positions in state-owned enterprises, etc. But unjustified criticism can have negative effects, too. Giving to a political party does not automatically mean that donors expect something in return. Lobbying is a legal political activity, although the public often views it suspiciously. A good example is when the President of Serbia Tomislav Nikolic disclosed during the election campaign that some controversial Serbian businessmen paid for his TV broadcast. It provoked strong negative reaction in the public, even though it is an open secret that many controversial businessmen are the biggest donors to political parties (Politika 2012, July 28). The only lesson that political parties learned from this incident was that they should not reveal the identity of their donors!

Another problem in Serbia is the general lack of public trust in institutions and their decisions. The opinion prevails that public institutions are corrupt or politically colored. Politicians also inflame such suspicions by frequently attacking institutional decisions as partial and politicized. Former NY Mayor Rudolf Giuliani, for example, in a visit to Belgrade during the last election campaign of the SNS political party, openly stated on a very popular Serbian TV show that his visit had been paid for. Performing its monitoring function, the Anti-Corruption Agency asked the SNS to report the details of this payment, since it was treated as a donation. The SNS refused, claiming that Giuliani "was on a private visit to his friends in Belgrade," and accused the Anti-Corruption Agency of deliberately "politicizing everything" and working in the interest of their political opponents!

Regarding the economic climate, the main generators of corruption are the long and complicated administrative procedures involved in getting different licenses (work permits, building licenses, etc.) and the broad discretion of administrative bodies. In addition, post-transition countries are faced with the privatization of former public companies and an underdeveloped market. Especially vulnerable is the sector of public procurement, which purchases goods and services with public money. Around 15 percent—approximately USD 6 billion—of Serbia's gross domestic product is spent in public procurement every year. A decline in the number of participants submitting tenders is an indicator of declining trust that the tendering procedure is impartial and objective. The State Audit Institution and the

European Parliament (2011) found many irregularities in public procurements. Some improvement might reasonably be expected if the new government fulfilled its election promise and regulated public procurement according to EU standards.

8.6 Conclusion

Essential conditions are a clear set of rules and strict control over political funds, especially in countries that go through political and economic transformation. An adequate legislative framework for political party financing is necessary to restrain corruption and provide fair political competition. In the words of Keith Ewing (1992), political competition under unregulated political financing would be like "inviting two people to participate in the race, with one participant turning up with a bicycle, and the other with a sports car."

Instead of being the result of social needs, it seems that Serbia's laws are more the result of international pressure, motivated by aspirations to European Union membership. Therefore, despite many warnings about the extremely high level of political corruption, an effective and applicable law on the financing of political parties was only adopted after more than two decades of a multiparty system.

The 2011 law on financing political activities made certain progress in this area by providing more effective control mechanisms and a more appropriate combination of public and private funding. In addition, it prohibits political party participation in for-profit, commercial activities, and certain prima facie suspicious donations, and also granted the Anti-Corruption Agency more powers, providing for its financial independence. The first practical results are visible when we compare the financial reports. Increased spending on elections is not only the result of more expensive campaigns; it also indicates more effective Agency monitoring.

However, there are still certain shortcomings. Financial reports are still incomplete or inaccurate. There is disparity in reported expenditure for political parties with similar organizational structure, raising doubts about false reports. In spite of it being generally known that big financial magnates are usually the main donors to political parties, not a single political party reported such donations! Never-ending judicial proceedings are a big concern, particularly because not a single major issue about privatization or public procurement abuse has been concluded by judicial verdict.

Regarding legislation, we strongly support the introduction of these mechanisms:

- total elimination of cash payments and donations to political parties through bank accounts so as to improve identification of contributors,
- establishment of one monitoring agency with strong powers instead of a multiplicity of bodies,
- media law reform designed to eliminate concentration of the ownership and secret media ownership,

- elimination of unnecessary administrative obstacles and discretionary decision-making,
- regulation of public procurement according to European standards.

In addition to legislative reforms, depoliticization of the judicial system, departization of public companies, institutions and state-owned enterprises should be promoted, together with the impartial appointment of public officials, a transparent recruitment process and a selection of employees according to competence and experience. It is also necessary to keep a delicate balance between corrupt and legal political behavior, public interest and media publicity, impartiality and partisanship, facts and rumors. Achieving such balance requires a certain level of political culture that cannot be reached overnight or imposed by international pressure. Fighting corruption requires the combined efforts of legislative, institutional and social mechanisms, otherwise, even the best law is only a decoration without real impact. Corruption flourishes as long as it is economically more profitable to pay a bribe than to conduct business legally. It is certainly not realistic to expect that the finalization of economic transition in Serbia will automatically mean the end of corruption, but the end of privatizations and consolidation of the market will probably lead to its decline. The reality is, however, that even in the most developed countries, no monitoring effort or legal mechanism can totally eliminate the grey areas and shady dealings, but they can be reduced to a more reasonable level. It seems that politicians usually forget what the most important thing in politics (after money) is: fighting corruption reminds them that this is the interest of the citizens!

Notes

1 Data show that an average of 7 percent of citizens at the last local elections and another 7 percent at the last parliamentary and presidential elections were asked to vote for a certain candidate or political party in exchange for a concrete offer of money, goods or a favor (UNODC 2012).

2 Serbian abbreviations for the names of political parties are used in the chapter. Socialist Party of Serbia (SPS), Serbian Progressive Party (SNS), Democratic Party (DS), Liberal-Democratic Party (LDP), Democratic Party of Serbia (DSS) New Serbia (NS), Serbian Revival Movement (SPO) and Radical Party of Serbia (SRS).

3 The law, for example required the parties to channel all financial transactions relating to campaigns through a specially designated bank account. However, entities like citizens groups, which also had a right to participate in elections, are not recognized as legal persons and therefore were not able to open bank accounts.

4 When the Serbian Radical Party (SRS) was in the government, the Ministry of Finance purchased the books published by a company named Velika Srbija that was owned by the SRS, and the profit was used to fund the party (Transparency Serbia 2006, June 14).

5 The European Commission noted the lack of enforcement of sanctions in its 2006 Progress Report (European Commission 2006).

6 Members are nominated by: (1) Administrative board of the National Assembly; (2) President of the Republic; (3) Government; (4) Supreme Constitutional Court; (5) State Audit Institution; (6) Ombudsman and Commissioner for Information of Public Importance and Personal Data Protection; (7) Social-Economic Council; (8) Serbian Bar Association; and (9) Association of Journalists.

7 The DSS is the only exception. The reason could be that in 2007, the DSS was the strongest party in the governing coalition, and its president was the prime minister of Serbia. The DSS influence was significantly lower in 2012.

8 Differences between two forms of corruption within law enforcement institutions are noted in Serbia: The first is so-called "petty" corruption or the acceptance of (or asking for) bribes for personal material gain in order to selectively carry out law enforcement duties. The second is political influence, which results in the same selective application of the law to individuals that are under the protection of, or alternatively out of favor with, a powerful political figure that could jeopardize or improve a law enforcement official's status or livelihood (CMI 2007).

9 Corruption in public management in Brazil

A hidden, regional perspective

Rodrigo Fontanelle Miranda, César Silva and Fátima de Souza Freire

9.1 Introduction

From the second half of the twentieth century onwards, different approaches and contexts have been discussed by economists and political scientists about the reasons for public agents to divert resources for private purposes, such as Nye (1967), Rose-Ackerman (1999), among others. In these studies, the reasons are often attributed to cultural and historical factors, the level of economic development or the characteristics of public institutions in different countries.

Everett *et al.* (2007) argue that in recent decades various institutional actors such as the World Bank, the International Monetary Fund (IMF), the Organisation for Economic Cooperation and Development (OECD), and non-governmental organizations such as Transparency International (TI), among others, are actively involved in combating corruption.

For the OECD (2005), corruption has become a matter of great political and economic significance and the need to take measures against it has become evident. (Transparency International 2005) considers corruption the main cause of poverty as well as a barrier to its eradication. In the attempt to eliminate, or at least to alleviate, the dire conditions of these families, various initiatives have been implemented, such as Conditional Cash Transfers (CCT). According to the International Policy Centre for Inclusive Growth (2011), this type of program currently operates in over 50 countries, including Asia, Africa, Latin America and the Caribbean. However, as a public policy, it is necessary not only to consider the good planning and careful design of such programs, but also to provide for the tight control of expenses on the part of the government.

In Brazil, control issues have become more relevant after the promulgation of the Constitution of the Federative Republic of Brazil (CF) in 1988. Several CF articles (1988) emphasize the importance given by congressmen to internal and external controls that must be performed in pursuit of efficiency, effectiveness and the economy of public programs and initiatives. For example, Article 70 of the CF (1988) provides that the accounting, financial, budgetary, operational and patrimonial supervision of the Union and of the direct and indirect branches of the federal administration shall be exercised by the external control function of the National Congress and by the internal control system of each power (CF 1988).

Established in 2003, the Random Audits Program is among the various control actions performed by the National Congress aimed at fulfilling these goals. The program intends to check, randomly and periodically, the actual use of federal government resources transferred to federal states and municipalities.

One of the programs that are subject to auditing by the Office of the Comptroller General (CGU), since its inception in 2004, is the *Bolsa Família Program* (BFP) [in English, Family Allowance Program]. The Office of the Comptroller General is responsible for controlling the federal government's direct spending and for increasing transparency in the management of government resources in Brazil. The BFP is a program created by Law 10.836 (2004), which unified several existing federal government cash transfer actions in Brazil (Brasil 2004b). Given its relevance, materiality and capillarity, it became the federal government's main social program. In 2010, the BFP benefited over 12 million households and the Union budget for 2011 assigned nearly R$14 billion (about US$8 billion) to execute the program (Brasil 2011).

Using the inspection reports issued from the control actions carried out by the CGU when verifying the implementation of BFP spending in municipalities, this chapter aims to analyze the major nonconformities found in the audit reports of those cities by comparing the quantitative and qualitative findings with the social and geo-economic key indicators of each municipality.

It is important to highlight that not all irregularities found should be deemed as corruption, that is, deliberate acts of fraud or embezzlement. However, irregularities indicate lack of control over municipal resources, and it is this negligence or inefficiency in management that cloaks corruption, hinders accountability and facilitates the actions of corrupt officials.

According to the Economic Commission for Latin America (CEPAL) (2010), the BPF is one of the largest national programs currently in course worldwide, whose surprising success stems from the increasing number of individuals assisted.

Likewise, the CGU's Random Audits Program applied in the inspection of municipalities has been recognized as an extremely effective action to control public spending for its randomness, scope and capacity to promote social control, one of the most effective weapons to combat corruption in the country.

As the theoretical framework will show, none of the various studies on the BFP has attempted to identify a relationship between the nonconformities found in CGU audits and the social and geo-economic indicators of audited municipalities.

The data used in this study was primarily collected from the municipal auditing reports issued by the CGU's Random Audits Program. The initial sample was based on the reports covering the 20th to the 32nd casting of lots. Besides providing the raw material for a qualitative and quantitative analysis of the irregularities found in each municipality, these reports also evidenced the volume of funds transferred and monitored in each case.

The analysis of the reports is focused on the BFP, thus our study only accounts for irregularities in this program. Also, for the purposes of this study, the words "irregular," "non-compliant" and "finding" are considered synonymous.

The classifications used are major and medium irregularities to differentiate the severity of these nonconformities.

The social and geo-economic indicators used in the study were collected from the Atlas of Human Development in Brazil[1] (UNDP 2010) and from the site of the Brazilian Institute of Geography and Statistics (IBGE)[2] (2010). When available, the databases used were from 2008, the median of the years used for the CGU's Random Audits Program reports, from 2006 to 2010. Regarding the Human Development Index (HDI) and the Gini Index of municipalities, we used the latest information available until the end of the data collection, namely, 2000.

9.2   Theoretical framework

9.2.1   Corruption and public management

Modernization Theory relates corruption to processes of social change and dysfunction of political institutions. This theory also analyzes the cost–benefit relation of corruption, which, as pointed out by Nye (1967), may be beneficial to political development if used to overcome bureaucratic obstacles, achieve private capital formation and the integration of political elites, among others.

Choice Theory is related to a new approach that emphasizes the need for political and economic reform following the guidelines that are derived from democracy and the market. According to Rose-Ackerman (1999), the forerunner of this new approach, corruption is related to the rent-seeking behavior of politicians, who strive to maximize their private income, inside or outside the accepted rules of conduct.

The concept of corruption is so widespread that, in an attempt to not restrict its scope, the United Nations chose to compile a list of examples of various acts of corruption, instead of defining it at the aforementioned convention against corruption. It can be said that there is corruption when using public property for private purposes (Power and González 2003), or when there is a violation of standards or expectations associated with public management (Johnston 2005).

As Morris (2004) points out, empirical studies have shown that corruption undermines not only economic growth but also social welfare policies. Following the same line of thought, Power and González (2003) believe that corrupt practices are generally more rooted in developing countries than in industrialized countries, which gives rise to some questions. The first is that corruption may be more endemic in poor, non-democratic or politically volatile countries. Another question is whether, in fact, cultural attributes could explain the level of corruption featured in various world regions. Finally, this generalization leads to speculation on the relationship between corruption and social, economic and political factors, which may or may not be linked to culture.

Johnston (2005) believes that corruption can be found in affluent market democracies as well as in societies with more rapid changes. In fact, some of the corruption problems of poorer, less democratic countries originate in the most developed parts of the world.

In Brazil, Claudio Ferraz was a pioneer in analyzing corruption by means of the indicators drawn from the CGU's inspection reports in an attempt to measure the phenomenon (Ferraz and Finan 2005; Ferraz 2008; Ferraz *et al.* 2012). Ferraz and Finan (2005), in a study intended to test whether the possibility of re-election significantly affected the level of corruption in a municipality, used the breaches found by CGU auditors as an indicator of corruption, classifying irregularities into several categories. Surprisingly, the authors did not find any relationship between corruption and GDP per capita in their study.

9.2.2 *Conditional Cash Transfer Programs (CCTs) worldwide*

The eradication of poverty is one of mankind's greatest challenges and a major obstacle to development. Innumerous initiatives and policies have been implemented in an effort to find a solution to this problem. Among the various alternatives developed, the Conditional Cash Transfer Programs (CCTs) are today considered one of the most powerful tools for achieving this goal. However, as pointed out by Santos (2010), in spite of being a powerful tool, this type of program is not the solution to all problems related to poverty.

Some European countries introduced a Conditional Cash Transfers (CCTs) system after the Second World War, as a means to respond to the lack of resources stemming from professional activities or even from social exclusion processes. In 1948, the UK introduced the National Assistance Act, a minimum income program for families which guaranteed the maintenance of a certain level of subsistence with no time limit, supplementing the social security system. Other countries established certain conditions for beneficiaries, such as checking whether they really had an insufficient income or were able to work, for example, or the beneficiaries' family status, among others.

Following the programs implemented in the post-war period, as noted by Ferro and Nicolella (2007), one of the first Conditional Cash Transfer Programs was Food for Education (FFE), implemented in 1994 in Bangladesh. The government provided food to poor rural households on a monthly basis. However, families had to send their children to school in exchange. Families could freely negotiate the food received through the program for other goods. Ravallion and Wodon (2000) evaluated the impact of FFE on child labor and education, finding a positive effect on school attendance and a negative effect on child labor. However, they noted that the decrease in working time corresponded to a small part of the increase in schooling, indicating that the time dedicated to school was mainly subtracted from leisure and not from working time.

In Latin America, CCTs began in the 1990s and, in general, demanded compensation from families in health, education and food agreements. The focus on poor people was intended to restore effective access to the universal rights this social group was systematically denied. Such programs serve to complement universal public policies such as health and basic education.

Among the many CCTs implemented in Latin America are: Plan Oportunidades (Mexico); Programa Bolsa Família (Brazil); Familias en Acción

(Colombia); Bono de Desarrollo Humano (Ecuador); Chile Solidario (Chile); Ingreso Ciudadano (Uruguay); Juntos (Peru); and Jefes de Hogares (Argentina).

In Mexico, Progresa (Programa de Educación, Salud y Alimentación), a health, education and food program, began in 1997 and is now called Plan Oportunidades (Opportunities Plan). The program grants monthly money transfers to poor families who are required to have their children enrolled and attending school, and to visit health facilities to prevent and treat diseases. Chile Solidario, created in May 2002, is a social protection program with a focus on the estimated 225,000 extremely poor families in that country. The program is based on family support provided by social workers, as well as various monetary allowances and the granting of priority access to other social protection programs (Soares *et al.* 2007).

Soares *et al.* (2007) analyzed the impact of CCTs on income inequality in Brazil, Mexico and Chile, as measured by the Gini Index, noting that in the first two countries these programs accounted for 21 percent of the of 2.7-point decrease in the index.

According to the ECLAC (2010), in a study on CCTs in Latin America, these programs are an important mechanism in social policies to combat poverty. They are non-contributory initiatives that strive to increase levels of consumer spending by means of cash transfers and thus reduce poverty in the short term and strengthen their beneficiaries' human development.

ECLAC has also found that in this region the programs with the largest number of beneficiaries in absolute terms are the Brazilian Bolsa Família (52 million), the Mexican Plan Opportunities (27 million) and the Colombian Familias en Accion, (12 million). In its turn, Ecuador's Bono de Desarrollo Humano is the CCT that covers the largest percentage of the population (44 percent), in comparison with the other countries.

As noted by Ferro and Nicolella (2007), CCTs became common in developing and underdeveloped countries as a means to alleviate poverty and to provide investments in human capital, ultimately leading families to better living conditions in the long run. The first goal is achieved whenever poor families receive money from the government each month as a source of supplementary income. The second objective is achieved by conditioning the transfer of income to certain actions, such as school attendance and health monitoring.

Rawlings and Rubio (2003) evaluated the results achieved by CCTs in Colombia, Honduras, Jamaica, Mexico, Nicaragua and Turkey and evidenced the success these programs have had in solving many social problems, such as school attendance, access to preventive health programs and an increase in domestic consumption.

Handa and Davis (2006) compared six CCT programs in Latin America and the Caribbean: BFP (Brazil), Oportunidades (Mexico), Programa de Asignación Familiar II (Honduras), Red de Protección Social (Nicaragua), Programme for Advancement Through Health and Education (Jamaica) and Familias en Accion (Colombia). The authors concluded that it is unclear whether this type of program is the solution that offers these countries the best cost–benefit ratio or whether it is a sustainable solution to low-income countries. Moreover, despite the remodeling of the paradigm of social protection in Latin America, the political future of these programs in countries where they are being implemented is not ensured, according to the authors.

Finally, in relation to the BFP, the program has been embraced by the Brazilian government within an agenda which prioritizes social programs focused on cash transfers and is tailored to its specific needs. So as to address the effectiveness of social spending, the BFP was implemented combining intersectoral coordination at three levels of governance, since CCTs alone reduce mobility and social change, the main objectives of social policies.

9.2.3   The Brazilian Bolsa Família Program (BFP)

The BFP was created in January 2004, through Law 10,836/2004, and unified actions from existing income transfers granted by the Brazilian federal government, namely: the National Minimum Income for Education, known as Bolsa Escola (School Grant), the National Access to Food (NPAA), the National Minimum Income for Health (Food Grant), the Cooking Gas Supply Grant Program and the Federal Government Single Registry. It should be noted that the program was piloted in the city of Campinas, in 1994, and in the Federal District, in 1995, before being implemented nationwide by the Brazilian federal government.

One of the main features of the BFP is the relationship developed between the federal government and the other authorities of the Federation. The program is based on the constitutional premise that decentralization facilitates the universalization of social services but at the same time, leads to the need for a complex relationship between each level of government. Although the program is decentralized, the executive branch of the federal government maintains high centralized control over its operation, by defining who is entitled to the program's benefits.

Coordinated by the Ministry of Social Development and Fight against Hunger (MSD), the BFP's primary goals in relation to its beneficiaries are (Decree 5,209/2004, see Brasil 2004a): the promotion of access to the network of public services, especially health, education and social assistance; the fight against hunger and the promotion of food security and nutrition; the sustained empowerment of poor and extremely poor families, as a means to combat poverty; and the promotion of public social actions which are intersectoral, complementary and synergic. Zimmerman (2006: 155), however, considered the compensations demanded from beneficiaries and estimates of the number of needy persons by the competent governmental agencies as limitations to the program.

As Figure 9.1 shows, the number of families supported by BFP has risen since its implementation. It is also clear that most beneficiaries of the program are concentrated in the North and Northeast regions, those with the highest rates of poverty and extreme poverty in the country.

Since its launch in 2004, the BFP has become the government's main social program, a fact confirmed by the growth of the program's budget, which has gone from R$3.7 billion to almost R$14 billion in eight years (Figure 9.2). This

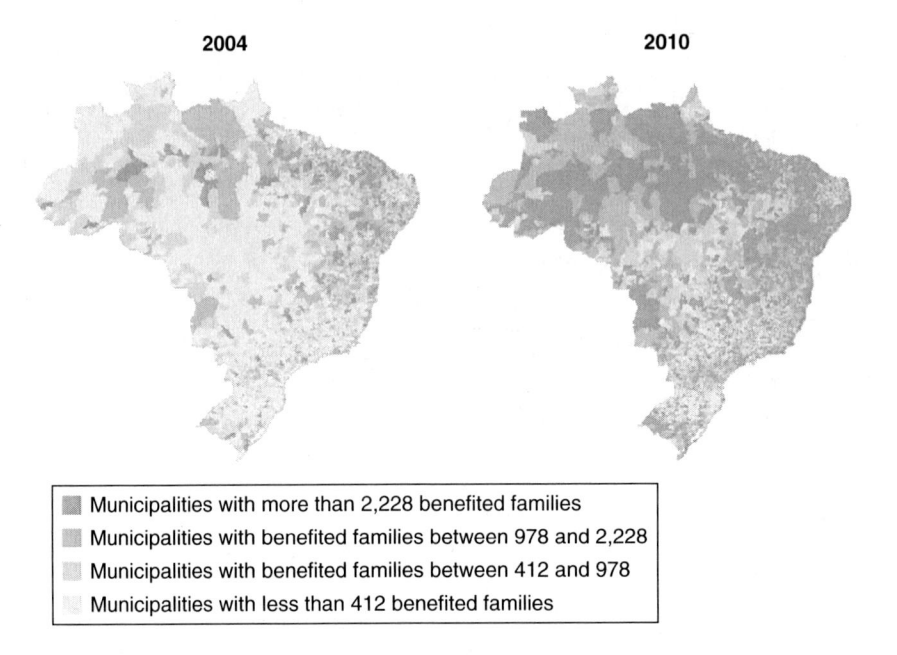

2004 **2010**

Municipalities with more than 2,228 benefited families
Municipalities with benefited families between 978 and 2,228
Municipalities with benefited families between 412 and 978
Municipalities with less than 412 benefited families

Figure 9.1 Families benefited by BFP: comparative figures 2004–10.

Source: Social Information Matrix, Ministry of Social Development and Fight against Hunger (MSD).

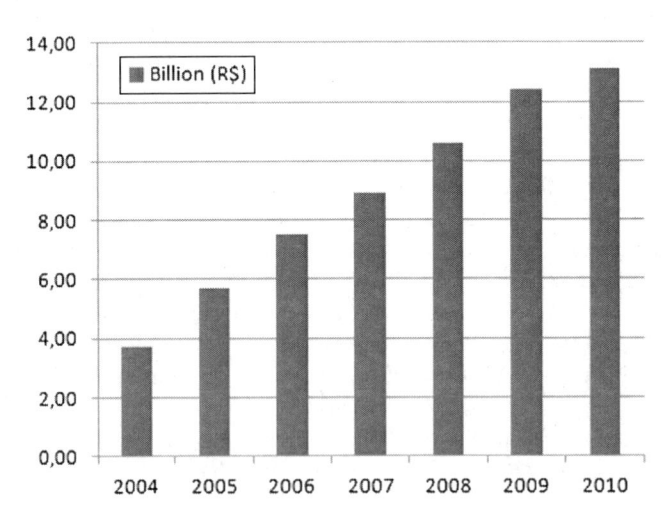

Figure 9.2 Evolution of money invested in the Brazilian Bolsa Família Program (BFP).

Source: MDS (Brasil 2010d), adapted by the authors.

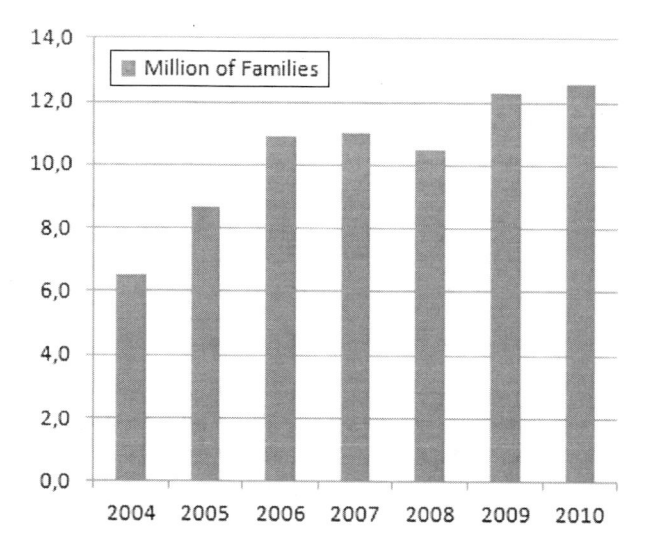

Figure 9.3 Evolution of the number of families supported by the Brazilian Bolsa Família Program (BFP).

Source: MDS (Brasil 2010d), adapted by the authors.

significant increase is due mainly to the program's importance and the results it has obtained in achieving the policy's main goal, reducing the percentage of families living in poverty or extreme poverty.

Similarly, the number of families benefiting from the program has also grown (Figure 9.3). In 2004, just over 6.5 million families benefited from the BFP. In 2010, that number almost doubled to 12.7 million, which corresponds to 42.4 million people, if we use the average of 3.34 people per household calculated by the IBGE Census (IBGE 2010).

9.2.4 *Random Audits Program to select units for auditing by the CGU*

The Random Audits Program—a mechanism based on random sampling (castings of lots) used by the CGU to define the municipalities that will be subject to inspection—was established by Administrative Rule 247/2003 (Brasil 2003), but it did not set a specific number of municipalities. After the 10th casting of lots in 2004, a limit was established at 60 cities.

Before creating the casting of lots mechanism, monitoring of municipalities only focused on the production of management information in order to evaluate governmental programs. With the new monitoring methodology, the management of federal funds came to be scrutinized on the basis of the total federal programs executed by each municipality, providing greater transparency to government management, ensuring the correct application of public resources, inhibiting and combating corruption and promoting social control.

The casting of lots is conducted by Caixa Economica Federal (CEF), a financial institution linked to the Brazilian federal government, based on the same technology used to run Brazilian federal lotteries. These events are public, which means that representatives from the mass media, political parties and civil society organizations are invited to join and attest to the randomness and fairness in defining the areas to be audited.

Considering the universe of 5,565 Brazilian municipalities, CEF excludes the capitals of each federate state and also localities with more than 500,000 inhabitants from the casting, since they are already subject to permanent supervision. Moreover, the cities selected in the three previous casting of lots are also excluded.

In those municipalities selected by the Random Audits Program, the application of federal public resources under the responsibility of federal, state, municipal, or legally authorized bodies are subject to inspection by CGU inspectors. Thus, before moving to a particular selected municipality, inspectors gather all the information related to transfers of federal funds, as well as information about possible agreements signed and complaints received regarding that municipality.

The data collected by the CGU indicate trends in the implementation of government programs in those municipalities. This allows for an analysis of how resources are spent, and also for the identification of where relevant problems are located.

For towns with up to 20,000 inhabitants, all federal funds received during the period set for review are checked. For cities whose population exceeds that number, the CGU selects drawn groups of expenditure for monitoring.

9.3   Methodology

9.3.1   Selection of samples

The study analyzed the municipal auditing reports in the period between 2006 and 2010, comprising the 20th to the 32nd casting of lots.

The initial year of reference is 2006 because, in each casting of lots, monitoring of the selected municipalities' resources covers the previous two financial years in most cases. As the BFP was established in early 2004, auditing since 2006 is related to this program and not to the social programs that it unified. Furthermore, reports previous to the 20th casting of lots employed a different methodology.

As mentioned previously, each casting of lots selects 60 municipalities for inspection. Thus, considering that 13 casting of lots were performed during the period considered, this study's sample consists of 780 reports. However, the following cities were removed from the sample: (a) those whose BFP grants were subject to inspection (13 cases); (b) those where BFP resources were not detailed in the inspection reports (22 cases); (c) cities selected more than once, in which case the most recent lot/report was considered (25 cases); and (d) the ones that lacked any of the social indicators used as independent variables (3 cases).

After this process of exclusion, 717 cities comprised the final sample of reports divided according to the country's regions, as shown in Figure 9.4.

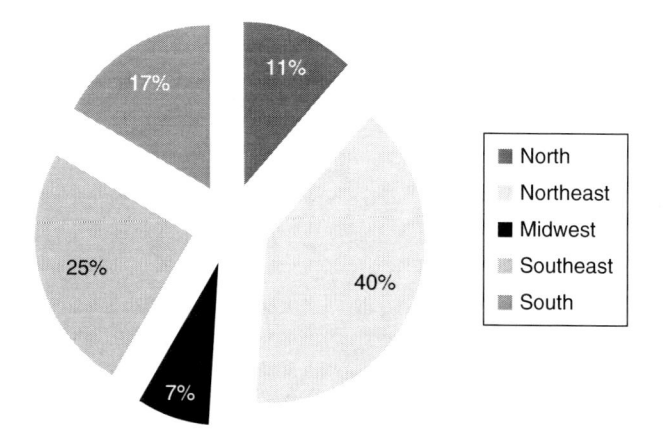

Figure 9.4 Percentage of municipalities relating to each sample of Brazilian region.
Source: The authors.

9.3.2 Classification of irregularities

Upon completion of the supervisory work, CGU auditors classified the findings from the evidence gathered in the field into:

a   *serious irregularities*: those that significantly impact program performance and result from situations such as failure in accountability, the practice of illegal, illegitimate or wasteful acts, misappropriation or embezzlement of public assets or securities, among other actions that harm the Treasury.
b   *medium irregularities*: undesirable situations that, while impacting the program's performance, do not fit into the definition of serious irregularities. They result from acts or omissions not in conformity with established parameters of legality, efficiency, economy, effectiveness or quality.
c   *form-related irregularities*: those that do not impact the program's management, are isolated and have low materiality and relevance.

In view of their relevance, serious and medium irregularities are necessarily part of inspection reports. Despite the concept presented for each failure, there is a degree of subjectivity in the analyst/inspector's classification. However, this limitation tends to be of marginal importance since the classification is the same for similar irregularities in different cities.

According to Brasil (2010a) the BFP's monitoring is mainly targeted at determining whether the beneficiaries' records are updated, the per capita income of families is in conformity with the program's regulations, the appropriate compensations are allocated in the areas of education and health, and whether complementary municipal actions to the BFP have been instituted.

9.3.3   Variables of the model

9.3.3.1   Dependent variables

To build the models, the serious and medium irregularities in CGU audit reports were used as explained variables. They were quantified and qualified so as to obtain the dependent variable for each of the models built. These variables were also used by Ferraz and Finan (2005), Zamboni (2007), and Sodré and Alves (2010).

9.3.3.2   Independent variables

The Brazilian Institute of Geography and Statistics (IBGE) publishes consolidated social indicators for each region annually. Since the objective of this study is to assess the relationship between the social indicators of certain municipalities and the level of irregularities found in the execution of the BFP, indicators that reflect the income, social inequality and poverty of the cities monitored were selected to define the model's explanatory variables.

In addition to these variables, the following were introduced as explanatory variables: (1) the population, to check whether the municipality's size influences the quantitative and qualitative monitoring of irregularities found in the reports; and (2) the amount of resources audited by the CGU, to analyze whether there is a relationship between the amount of funding received and the level of its reported nonconformities.

a   *Income*:
   The municipal GDP was used as an indicator for income. Data from 2008 were used in the regression, as it represents the sample's median year (2006–10).

HYPOTHESIS 9.1 The higher the municipal GDP, the lower the number of irregularities found. A negative coefficient for this variable would therefore be expected.

b   *Social inequality*:
   The Gini coefficient was used to measure social inequality in each municipality, given its ease of understanding, recurrence in the literature and diversity of use in previous studies. The data refer to the year 2000 (last publication).

HYPOTHESIS 9.2 The higher the Gini coefficient, i.e., inequality, the greater the number of irregularities found. A positive coefficient would therefore be expected for this variable.

c   *Poverty*:
   The Municipal Human Development Index (HDI-M) was used as an indicator of poverty, to measure the degree of economic development and quality of life offered to the population. The HDI, created by the UN in the early 1990s, is calculated taking into account economic and social data, and is also used to assess the development of cities, states and regions. The HDI based on

Brazil's 2010 population census was still unavailable when we completed the data collection phase of our study.

HYPOTHESIS 9.3 The higher the HDI-M, the lower the number of irregularities. A negative coefficient is therefore expected for this variable.

d   *Population*:

Population estimates for each municipality conducted by the IBGE in 2008 were taken as a geographical variable in this study. It aims to identify a possible correlation and/or causality between the size of the local population and the number of irregularities found.

HYPOTHESIS 9.4 The larger the city's population, the lower the number of irregularities found. Thus, a negative coefficient would be expected for this variable.

e   *Transferred and audited resources*:

The BFP funds transferred to municipalities, subject to CGU supervision, are presented in detail in the audit reports. Thus, they were the source of data for this variable.

HYPOTHESIS 9.5 The greater the amount of resources transferred, the greater the number of irregularities found. Therefore, we expected a positive coefficient for this variable.

9.3.4   *Econometric models*

To search for possible causal relationships between the analyzed variables, the following regressions were estimated, using the total sample (717 municipalities):

$$SERIOUS = \beta_1 HDI + \beta_2 GINI + \beta_3 GDP + \beta_4 POP + \beta_5 RES + \varepsilon \qquad (9.1)$$

$$MEDIUM = \beta_1 HDI + \beta_2 GINI + \beta_3 GDP + \beta_4 POP + \beta_5 RES + \varepsilon \qquad (9.2)$$

Where:

SERIOUS = Number of serious irregularities found in the municipality
MEDIUM = Number of medium irregularities found in the municipality
β_n = Coefficients of variable n
HDIM = Municipal Human Development Index
GINI = Gini coefficient
GDP = Municipal Gross Domestic Product
POP = Municipal population
RES = Transferred and audited resources
ε = Error.

At first, we used a constant for the estimation of the equations. From the practically irrelevant results obtained for that term, we selected equations (9.1) and (9.2), called regression through the origin. According to Theil (1971: 176, cited in Eisenhauer

2003: 76), "from an economic standpoint, a constant term usually has little or no explanatory virtues." Eisenhauer (2003) points out that, although this statement may be being slightly overstated, there are many cases in which the constant can be removed. One such case is when $Y = 0$ if variables X are equal to 0. In the model developed in this study, if POP equals zero, there is no municipality, so the other independent variables will also be zero, as will serious and medium irregularities.

After estimating these two regressions, we classified the municipalities in the sample according to Brazil's five geographic regions (North, Northeast, Southeast, South and Midwest) in order to examine whether the relationships between variables differ when target areas are segmented. Thus, the two regressions were re-estimated for each region. The South Region sample had 121 municipalities, the Southeast, 177, the Midwest, 53, the Northeast, 284, and the North, 82.

The estimation of the previous models was performed using the SPSS 18.0 software. We opted for the Backward method to select the variables in the analyzed models.

Finally, also using SPSS, some tests were performed in order to assess the models' robustness, such as t-tests of significance, Variance Inflation Factor analysis (VIF),[3] standardized Beta coefficient analysis and the F Statistics.[4]

9.4   Results and analysis

This section presents the results of the study from the data collected and from the regressions identified in the previous section. For the sake of clarity, this section is divided into three parts: Descriptive Statistics, Correlations and Statistical Inferences. The last part presents the results for the full sample and the country's targeted regions.

9.4.1   Descriptive statistics

Table 9.1 shows that each city had, on average, five deficiencies in the implementation of the BFP, and the diversity among the monitored cities is also clear. The audit sample ranged from municipalities that have a GDP just over R\$6,000 to those whose GDP is more than R\$8 million. Similarly, this variation is evidenced in terms of population, ranging from just over 800 inhabitants to more than half a million. The same is true of the amount of funds received by municipalities and subject to auditing, which ranged from just over R\$2,000 to more than R\$29 million.

In Figure 9.5, showing a histogram of serious and medium irregularities, there are 539 municipalities (75.2 percent) with 0 to 3 medium irregularities, 171 (23.9 percent) with 4 to 6, and only 7 (0.98 percent) have 7 or more medium irregularities. Likewise, most municipalities (465 or 64.9 percent) yielded 0 to 3 irregularities, 227 (31.7 percent), 4 to 6, and 25 had 7 or more.

Still in relation to the descriptive analysis, we found that, of the 717 municipalities investigated, 665 (92.8 percent) had at least one serious irregularity, 646 (90.1 percent) had at least one medium irregularity, and only 23 (3.2 percent) showed no serious or medium irregularities. These high rates of nonconformities corroborate the statistics released by the CGU following the 30th casting of lots,

Table 9.1 Descriptive statistics

	Mean	Median	Standard deviation	Minimum	Maximum
Audit Reports					
Serious irregularities	2.95	3.00	1.75	0.00	8.00
Medium irregularities	2.46	2.00	1.59	0.00	8.00
Audited resources (in R$)	2,348,072.65	1,264,442.00	3,365,032.18	2,015.00	29,675,794.00
Variables Sociodemographic					
HDI-M	0.68	0.69	0.08	0.48	0.85
Gini coefficient	0.57	0.56	0.06	0.40	0.79
Municipal GDP (in R$)	263,312.42	67,046.30	773,246.31	6,823.11	8,033,460.98
Population	25,125	11,847	50,849	834	536,785

Source: SPSS, from a spreadsheet prepared by the authors.

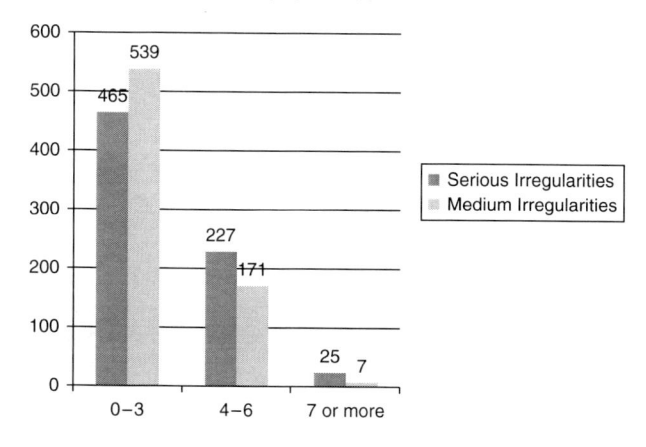

Figure 9.5 Histogram.

Source: The authors.

which found irregularities in 57 of the 60 municipalities surveyed (95 percent) (Brasil 2010b). Kadri (2009), in a study covering 850 CGU inspection reports in the period from 2004 to 2007, obtained similar results, finding at least one nonconformity in 90.7 percent of the audited municipalities.

Finally, Figure 9.6 shows the most frequently repeated irregularities in municipalities. For more than half of the inspected locations, the main problems were outdated registry information (medium irregularity) and beneficiaries with a higher per capita income than that established in the BFP.

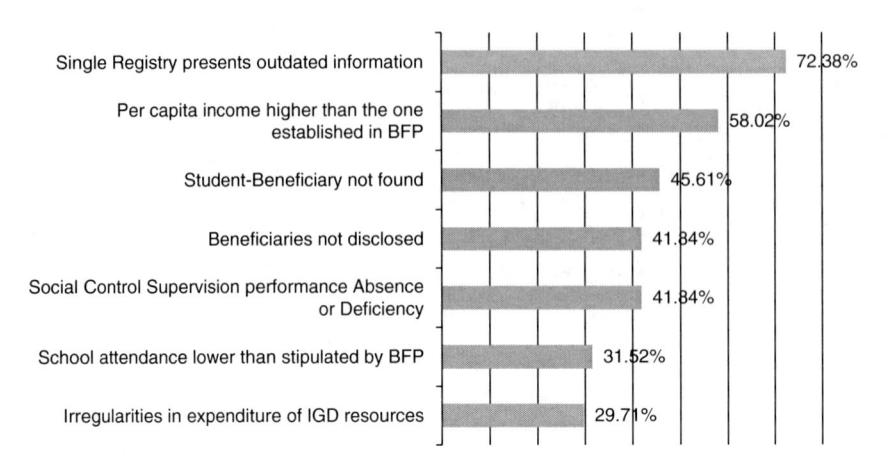

Figure 9.6 Principal irregularities found in municipalities.

Source: The authors.

9.4.2   *Correlations*

Following the data analysis based on the descriptive statistics, we proceeded by examining the correlation between the variables of the two regressions. For this purpose, the Pearson correlation coefficient, which measures the linear correlation between two variables, was employed.

9.4.2.1   *Correlations between serious irregularities and the independent variables of equation (9.1)*

Table 9.2 shows a strong correlation between the Gini coefficient and the number of irregularities (0.857). The HDI for municipalities also strongly correlates with the dependent variable (0.852). The amount of funds audited (0.524), the size of the local population (0.358), and GDP (0.245) had lower correlations in regard to serious irregularities.

Besides the correlation between the dependent variable and the independent variables, Table 9.2 reveals strong collinearity between the HDI and the Gini coefficient (0.983). This relationship means that, as we will discuss, the model had high multicollinearity, which led to the performance of corrective actions.

9.4.2.2   *Correlation between medium irregularities and the independent variables of equation (9.2)*

Replacing the dependent variable "serious irregularities" with the variable "medium irregularities" caused little change in the observed correlations. The HDI (0.835) and the Gini coefficient (0.834) continued to show strong correlation with respect to the irregularities found in audits and audited resources (0.461), and the local population (0.335) and municipal GDP (0.245) revealed lower collinearity

Table 9.2 Correlation: serious irregularities

		Serious	Gini	POP	Resources	HDI	GDP
Std. Cross-product	Serious	1.000	0.857	0.358	0.524	0.852	0.245
	Gini	0.857	1.000	0.449	0.592	0.983	0.324
	POP	0.358	0.449	1.000	0.711	0.464	0.882
	Resources	0.524	0.592	0.711	1.000	0.552	0.494
	HDI	0.852	0.983	0.464	0.552	1.000	0.359
	PIB	0.245	0.324	0.882	0.494	0.359	1.000
Sig. (1-tailed)	Serious	·	0.000	0.000	0.000	0.000	0.000
	Gini	0.000	·	0.000	0.000	0.000	0.000
	POP	0.000	0.000	·	0.000	0.000	0.000
	Resources	0.000	0.000	0.000	·	0.000	0.000
	HDI	0.000	0.000	0.000	0.000	·	0.000
	GDP	0.000	0.000	0.000	0.000	0.000	·

Source: SPSS, from a spreadsheet prepared by authors. N = 717 in all cases.

Table 9.3 Correlation: medium irregularities

		Serious	Gini	POP	Resources	HDI	GDP
Std. Cross-product	Resources	1.000	0.834	0.335	0.461	0.835	0.245
	Gini	0.834	1.000	0.449	0.592	0.983	0.324
	POP	0.335	0.449	1.000	0.711	0.464	0.882
	Resources	0.461	0.592	0.711	1.000	0.552	0.494
	HDI	0.835	0.983	0.464	0.552	1.000	0.359
	GDP	0.245	0.324	0.882	0.494	0.359	1.000
Sig. (1-tailed)	Resources	·	0.000	0.000	0.000	0.000	0.000
	Gini	0.000	·	0.000	0.000	0.000	0.000
	POP	0.000	0.000	·	0.000	0.000	0.000
	Resources	0.000	0.000	0.000	·	0.000	0.000
	HDI	0.000	0.000	0.000	0.000	·	0.000
	GDP	0.000	0.000	0.000	0.000	0.000	·

Source: SPSS, from a spreadsheet prepared by authors. N = 717 in all cases.

with the dependent variable. Since the independent variables in equation (9.2) are the same as in equation (9.1), the correlations between these variables are identical to those shown in Table 9.3.

After the existing correlations had been found, and in order to understand the causality between the variables, we estimated the following regressions, which are then analyzed.

9.4.3 Statistical inferences

After the presentation of the descriptive statistics and the correlation tests, this section will examine the results of the estimated regressions for the full sample (717 municipalities) and also those produced in the regional samples.

Brooks (2008: 164) states that "for sufficiently large sample sizes, the violation of the normality assumption is almost irrelevant."

As described in the methodology, two regressions were estimated for the complete data of the sample. The first sought to investigate the relationship between social and geo-economic indicators and the serious irregularities found by CGU auditors. The second regression sought to investigate the relationship between these indicators and the medium irregularities in CGU audit reports. The results are shown and discussed below.

9.4.3.1   Relationship between serious irregularities and social and geo-economic indicators

The estimation of equation (9.1), explained in the methodology section above, yielded the results listed in Table 9.4. From the explanatory variables, only the GDP did not emerge as significant (t-test significance was greater than 0.05). However, when checking the multicollinearity of the variables, the HDI and the Gini coefficient showed a Variance Inflation Factor higher[5] than 10, indicating the presence of high multicollinearity.

Hair *et al.* (2009) and Heij *et al.* (2004) suggest that a variable in the model can be deleted in order to fix the problem detected; this exclusion should be carried out randomly. Following this reasoning, the variable "HDI" was then removed, because its composition included some elements that were already captured by other model variables such as income, for example. Thus, the following equation was estimated:

$$SERIOUS = \beta_1 GINI + \beta_2 GDP + \beta_3 POP + \beta_4 RES + \varepsilon \qquad (9.3)$$

Using the Backward Method regression in (9.3) produced the results listed in Table 9.5. The model presented an explanatory power (adjusted R^2) of 0.736, which means that the independent variables explain 73.6 percent of the dependent variable "serious irregularities."

The *t-test*, used to test individual hypotheses (Brooks 2008), was used to check the statistical significance of each independent variable. Only the variable GDP

Table 9.4 Result of the estimation of equation (9.1)

Explanatory variables	β Standard	t Test	VIF
HDI	0.484	4.38*	33.933
GINI	0.358	3.157*	35.858
GDP	−0.018	−0.406	5.473
POP	−0.118	−4.131*	2.278
RES	0.129	4.01*	2.858
Adjusted R^2	0.742		
F Statistics	517.55**		
Númber of observations	717		

Note: *Signification level at 5%, **Signification level at 1%.

Table 9.5 Result of the estimation of equation (9.3)

Explanatory variables	β Standard	t Test	VIF
GINI	0.845	35.427*	1.543
GDP	0.006	0.139	5.388
POP	−0.077	−2.800*	2.026
RES	0.078	2.579*	2.489
Adjusted R²	0.736		
F Statistics	666.694**		
Number of Observations	717		

Note: *Signification level at 5%, **Signification level at 1%.

was not statistically significant (sig. *t* > 5 percent). The other three variables, GINI (0.000), POP (0.005) and RES (0.010) were statistically significant and remained in the model. These three variables were VIF lower than 10, which eliminated concern regarding the model's high multicollinearity.

The analysis of the regression coefficients reveals that RES showed a positive coefficient and POP a negative one. These signals also corroborate the research hypotheses and mean that the greater the amount of funds audited and the smaller the population of the municipality, the more serious the irregularities found.

Following the analysis of the significance of individual independent variables, the F-test serves to verify the general model's significance which, according to the above-mentioned author, should be applied to regressions with more than one coefficient. The regression had an F value of 666.69 and a significance of 0.000, indicating that the coefficients used in the model can be considered jointly significant.

Finally, we used a standard Beta (β) as a regression coefficient because this standardization allows for direct comparison between two or more coefficients, as highlighted by Hair *et al.* (2009). Thus, the Gini coefficient has a positive β of 0.84, and, compared with other variables, it is the variable that most impacts on the dependent variable. The coefficient of the "GINI" variable was expected to be positive, since it means that the greater the social inequality in municipalities, the more serious their irregularities.

9.4.3.2 Relationship between medium irregularities and social and geo-economic indicators

Bearing the problems in estimating equation (9.1) in mind, we estimated regression (9.2) described in the previous section, which showed the same inconsistencies (high multicollinearity). Thus, the following equation was estimated to determine the relationship between social variables and geo-economic and medium irregularities found in the municipalities audited by the CGU:

$$MEDIUM = \beta_1 GINI + \beta_2 GDP + \beta_3 POP + \beta_4 RES + \varepsilon \qquad (9.4)$$

Table 9.6 Result of the estimation of equation (9.4)

Explanatory variables	β Standard	t Test	VIF
GINI	0.856	37.171*	1.253
GDP	−0.050	1.251	4.655
POP	−0.101	−2.154*	1.253
RES	−0.013	−0.375	2.881
Adjusted R²	0.696		
F Statistics	823.222**		
Number of observations	717		

Note: *Signification level at 5%, **Signification level at 1%.

The results from this regression are shown in Table 9.6. As in the previous model, the Gini coefficient (0.000) and population (0.032) were statistically significant. Additionally, the GDP was significant (0.211). However, the volume of audited resources, unlike the estimation of equation (9.3), did not turn out to be significant (0.708).

The model showed good explanatory power (adjusted $R^2 = 0.696$) and low multicollinearity. Furthermore, the F value showed 823.222, with 0.000 significance, confirming the significance of the model's independent variables.

Regarding regression coefficients, the GINI coefficient was positive and POP was negative as expected, which confirmed the model's results for serious irregularities. Again, the Gini coefficient is the one that most impacts on the dependent variable ($\beta = 0.856$).

To examine whether the results for Brazil are reproduced when municipalities are segmented by geographic regions, equations (9.3) and (9.4) were estimated for the country's five regions.

In relation to the models estimated to examine the variables that influence the behavior of the medium irregularities found in the audited municipalities, only the Gini coefficient turned out to be statistically significant in all five geographical macro-regions in the country, always with high explanatory power and presenting a positive correlation with the dependent variable. In the model estimated for the 717 municipalities of the full sample, we found that, in addition to this coefficient, the population variable is also statistically significant, being negatively correlated to medium irregularities. This means that the greater the inequality and the lower the population, the more likely it is to find medium irregularities in the municipality.

The estimation of the models used to determine the relationship between serious irregularities found by CGU auditors and the municipalities' social and geo-economic indicators yielded more robust results. For the full sample, the Gini coefficient, the volume of funds received and the population were considered statistically significant, the first two presenting a positive correlation, and the last one a negative one, in connection with the explanatory variable. The same result was found in the Northeast and South samples. As for the Midwest and Southeast regions, only the Gini coefficient was statistically significant. In the North, besides the Gini coefficient, the population variable was also found to be statistically significant.

9.5 Concluding remarks

There as several studies on the BFP but they have mostly focused on the effectiveness of the program's public spending. There are also some studies that have used the number of irregularities found by the CGU as a measure of corruption, although they do not address the BFP. However, to date, no study had examined the relationship between the nonconformities found by the CGU and the social and geo-economic indicators of the audited municipalities.

Based on the Random Audits Program's inspection reports issued by the Office of the Comptroller General (CGU), this study aimed to determine the relationship between the major nonconformities found in those municipalities in the financial execution of the BFP by comparing the quantitative and qualitative results of those findings with the key social and geo-economic indicators of each municipality.

In relation to serious irregularities, we found that there is statistical significance between these nonconformities and the variables "Gini coefficient," "Audited Resources" and "Population." The first two are positively correlated with the dependent variable and the third has a negative correlation. This indicates that the greater the social inequality and the amount of funds transferred to the municipality, and the smaller the town, the greater the likelihood of irregularities in the management of BFP resources.

In the regression model that estimated the medium irregularities regression for failures, the Gini index and population proved to be significant variables, with the same correlation observed in the previous model. For both regressions, GDP showed no statistically significant relationship with serious and medium irregularities, a result in line with Ferraz and Finan (2005), who found no relationship between corruption and GDP.

These same models were estimated for Brazil's five geographical macro-regions, in order to determine whether the results would be similar to those found in the analysis of the full sample. In relation to serious irregularities, the same result was found in the Northeast and South samples. With regard to the Midwest and Southeast regions, only the Gini coefficient was the statistically significant variable and, in the North, besides the coefficient, the population variable was also statistically significant.

With the exception of the GDP variable, the results confirm all of the study's hypotheses listed initially, thus showing the relevance of the identified social and geo-economic indicators. They proved to be related and influence the expansion of corruption in each municipality, here measured with reference to the irregularities identified by the CGU auditors. We believe that the findings presented here can contribute to the discussion on the control of public policies executed by both the CGU and the Ministry of Social Development and Fight against Hunger (MDS) (Brasil 2005, 2010c), as well as serve as a basis for at least three specific actions that should be implemented, namely:

a assist the MDS, responsible for the BFP, in the improvement of public policies executed by means of the program, improve primary control in the municipalities where there is a greater probability of nonconformities, as well as invest in the training of public officials responsible for the municipal management of the BFP, since nonconformities are often due to unpreparedness and lack of knowledge of the relevant legislation.

b   enable the CGU to focus its systematic control actions on municipalities where statistical irregularities tend to be greater, increasing the efficiency of its audits. As an example, in this study we found that there is a strong correlation between the Gini coefficient and the number of irregularities. Thus, given the limited resources to inspect all of the country's municipalities, priority could be given to those revealing higher rates of social inequality.

c   Serve as a basis for new studies using the methodology shown here, allowing for other government programs to be evaluated in this way, and from then on, investigating whether the results found here are repeated in programs run by other ministries.

Finally, one should be cautious when extrapolating the conclusions obtained here, since, as noted earlier, there are limitations to the methodology due to the subjectivity of the classification of nonconformities found in the BFP. However, the study has shown the importance of improving the program's control mechanisms and financial execution, which will help to fight corruption and improve the administrative structure of municipalities, enabling a more efficient and effective implementation of this type of public policy.

Notes

1 Project prepared by the João Pinheiro Foundation (FJP), in partnership with the United Nations Development Program (UNDP) and the Institute for Applied Economic Research (IPEA).

2 The Brazilian Institute of Geography and Statistics (IBGE) is the main provider of data and information in the country and it fulfills the demands of several different segments of civil society, as well of other governmental institutions at federal, state and municipal level.

3 Indicator of the effect that the other independent variables have on the standard error of a regression coefficient. VIF values indicate a high degree of collinearity or multicollinearity between independent variables (Hair *et al.* 2009).

4 The F value provides the additional contribution of each variable over all the others in an equation (Hair *et al.* 2009).

5 According to Hair *et al.* (2009), a common cutting reference is a value of $VIF = 10$. However, according to Field (2000), there is divergence about the limit of acceptance of the VIF value for indicating multicollinearity.

Part III

Corruption prevention and control

Towards a sustainable growth trajectory

10 Opportunity as a factor in public sector fraud and corruption[1]

António Maia

> Whenever a public official has discretionary power over distribution to the private sector of a benefit or cost, incentives for bribery are created.
>
> (Susan Rose-Ackerman 1997a: 31)

10.1 Introduction: the problem of corruption

The topic of corruption took a central place in the social and political discourse of Portuguese society, following similar processes taking place in many Western societies.

According to Maia (2008), the importance of the topic in Portuguese society has been heightened by the media, in particular by frequently reporting on suspicions about unclear practices involving some important leaders of political, economic and business groups. Indeed, authors such as Gigiioli (1996), Brunetti and Weder (2001), and Pujas (2003) also focused on similar trends in other countries.

There are many different scientific approaches to the problem of corruption. First, it is recognized as a matter of culture (Rose-Ackerman 1999), but it is also a problem that can be analyzed from the perspective of the economy (Leff 1964), as an ethical problem associated with low-quality political leadership and elites (Huntington 1968; Porta and Mény 1995), or even as a societal problem (Tanzi and Davoodi 1997). In practice, we can consider it a problem of public administration. In fact, corrupt practices often correspond to a distortion of expectations about the functioning of public administration services (Johnston 1997; Osborne and Gaebler 1993; Osborne 2002).

In any one of those approaches, the question of corruption can also be addressed on the basis of the factors that explain the problem, the effects that derive from it, as well as the contexts that characterize the corresponding practices.

Based on some of the findings of ongoing research we are developing, this chapter focuses on the contexts that characterize practices of corruption in public services, especially the opportunity factor and its characteristics.

Finally, authors such as Grilo (2005) or Maia (2004) assume that there are most certainly a high number of unreported cases, resulting from the strong pacts of silence these practices often imply (see Figure 10.1). As such, it is important to

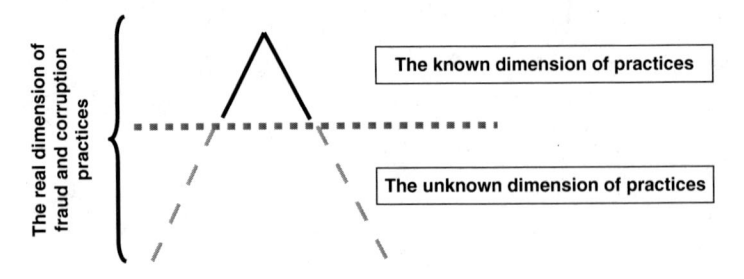

Figure 10.1 The known dimension of fraud and corruption is only a part of the entire problem.

Source: Maia (2004) and Grilo (2005).

Table 10.1 Official statistic dimension of corruption crime in Portugal (1993–2010)

Year	Number of cases			Number of suspects		
	Started cases	Cases with decision of accusation	Medium ratio value between trialed and filed cases	Accused	Sentenced	Medium ratio between sentenced value and accused suspects
1993	149	35		47	28	
1994	144	38		70	49	
1995	173	40		47	32	
1996	173	27		41	26	
1997	152	52		67	46	
1998	416	40		50	33	
1999	353	32		43	24	
2000	90	46		62	43	
2001	102	49		68	38	
2002	121	45		82	57	
2003	115	53		63	55	
2004	72	48		69	49	
2005	105	47		89	60	
2006	106	29		147	71	
2007	122	51		79	48	
2008	103	58		112	59	
2009	62	44		106	69	
2010	51	64		164	70	
Average values	145	44	30,6%	78	48	61,0%

Source: Portuguese official statistics of Justice, www.dgpj.mj.pt/sections/estatisticas-da-justica/ (accessed April 15, 2015).

note that some specific contexts of corruption are very difficult to study because they will probably never be known.

Table 10.1 shows the known dimension of corruption crimes in Portugal between 1993 and 2010.[2]

As can be seen in Table 10.1, in almost one-third of all corruption cases, there is sufficient evidence to accuse someone of a suspected act of corruption (active or passive). About two-thirds of the accused suspects were found guilty of acts of corruption. In our opinion, these numbers show that the judicial system seems to be effective in dealing with this crime. However, these numbers correspond only to the known dimensions of corruption, and there are strong indicators that most cases will remain unknown, as previously suggested (Maia 2004).

10.2   Public administration and corruption

Corruption occurs within the state, in both the process of definition of public policies (political level), and in public services in the process of implementing those public policies (administrative level). It always results in a failure of social expectations regarding the performance of a public function (see Figure 10.2). It is a problem that coexists within the state and public administration services in their relationship with citizens and society. That is why, in our opinion, it is very important to study and to understand how public services create opportunities for corruption practices.

10.2.1   Corruption in public services – a model of analysis

The model of analysis used to investigate the opportunity factor in public services[3] is based on Cressey's (1953) fraud triangle theory.

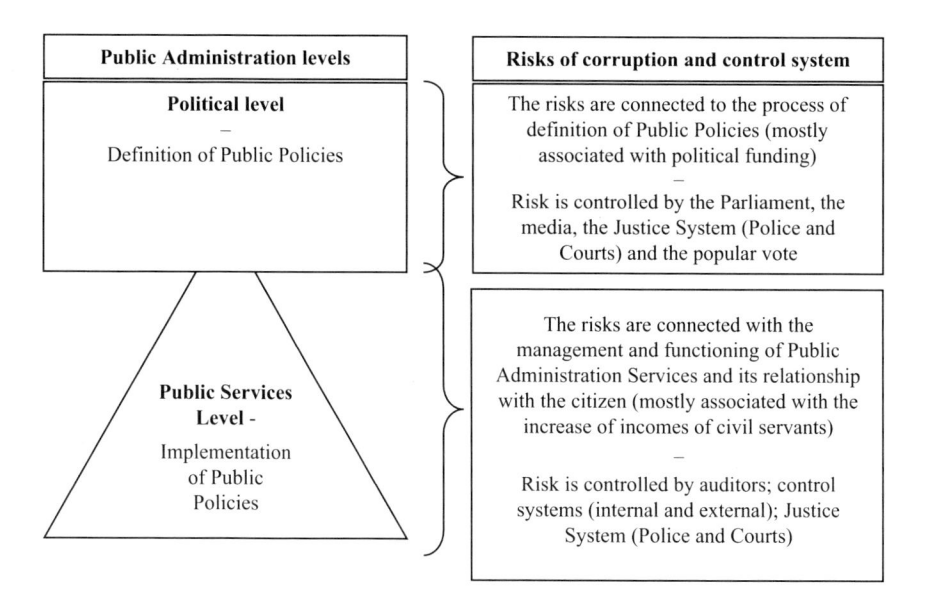

Figure 10.2 The two levels of state and public administration where corruption may occur.

According to this theory (see Figure 10.3), based on the study of practices of occupational fraud in different kind of organizations, fraudulent and corrupt acts result from the combination of three factors:

- *Rationalization*, or the capacity of subjects to rationalize all the decisions and actions of their daily life including, of course, the option to undertake acts of fraud and corruption, the capacity to perceive, and the determination and ability to explore opportunities for the practice of illegal acts.[4] In our opinion, this rationalization factor should also be considered along with other theories that will help develop a better understanding of it. There are at least two theories that we believe are relevant in this case. First, the economic theory of limited rationality by Simon (1947), which argues that decisions are based on information and perceptions about reality. However, as information is always more or less incomplete, decisions tend to be at least as limited as the natural limitations of the information that was considered to produce them. Second, Becker's (1968) rational choice theory applied to criminal actions is also relevant. Before deciding to commit a crime, the individual ponders and rationalizes the gains and possible losses, including the chance of being caught and punished. On this specific point, it is important to mention that the Portuguese generally believe the judicial system is highly inefficient at detecting and punishing the perpetrators of corruption crimes, as discussed in Maia (2008), and Sousa and Triães (2007, 2008).
- *Pressure*, which results from the specific context of each individual's private life, including their economic situation, the need to solve financial problems arising, for example, from debts or drug or alcohol addiction, and even the

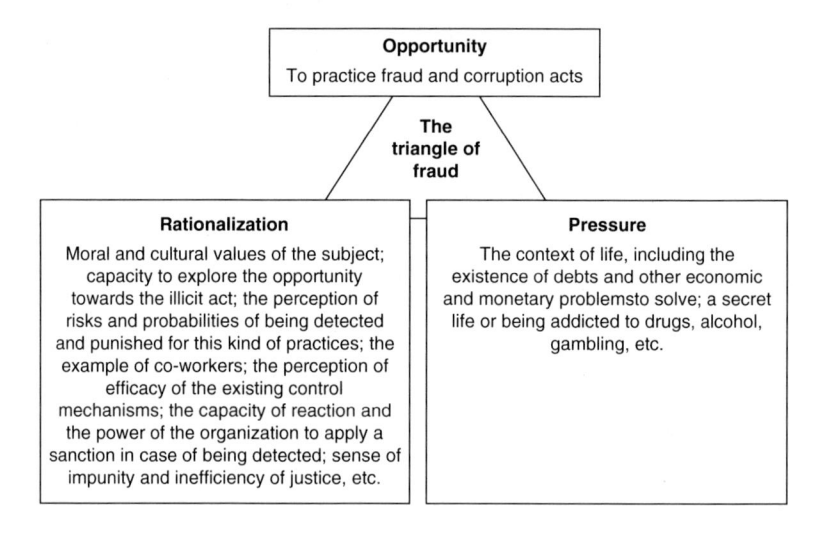

Figure 10.3 Model of triangle of fraud by Cressey.

Source: Adapted from Donald Cressey (1953).

need to have (or show) a high social status by having a certain type of vehicle or wearing certain brands. On this point we are reminded of Merton's (1938) social anomie theory, according to which individuals have several alternative means (some of them unexpected and illegal) to solve a problem when they are under social and cultural pressure and cannot perceive any expected (normal, legal) ways to do so, for instance, the need to own a certain vehicle but lacking the necessary income to fulfil this desire. Opting for corrupt practices may be a possible alternative (unexpected, illegal) to make more money and to buy that vehicle. This theory explains social deviance options and the social process of changing values, rules and laws.

- *Opportunity* for committing fraud and corruption actions. Opportunity arises in the context of the administrative duties of each public servant, and opting for these practices is always in contradiction with existing social expectations of administrative function. Opportunity is a factor that has been incorporated in every criminological theory to explain crime practices. The criminal act is made possible only if there in an opportunity for it, as argued by Cusson (1998). In fact, according to this author, focusing on this factor has been decisive in defining preventive strategies over criminal practices. It is interesting to revisit the theory of differential association (Sutherland 1924), which considers the existence of a natural tendency for the practice of illicit acts when the subjects are exposed to a cultural, social and organizational context where illegal practices are the norm, where there is a large number of opportunities for those actions, and the perception of impunity over those practices is present. Some years later, the same author (Sutherland 1945) presented for the first time the concept of white-collar crime, corresponding to the criminal acts committed by influential people in organizational contexts (public or private).

Finally, our model is also informed by the theory developed by Cloward and Ohlin (1960) concerning the existence of a structure of opportunities for illegal and criminal practices. According to the authors, this structure truly exists and depends on factors such as the perception of opportunity by the potential perpetrator of the fraudulent act; the context of the moment and its evaluation; the technical knowledge, the skills and the capacities of potential perpetrators to practice the acts.

Based on these two theories, it is possible to assume that the structure and organization of public services creates a framework of opportunities for the practice of fraudulent and illegal acts, including corruption.

Taking this as our starting point, our study was based on the hypothesis that:

Models of structure, organization and operating procedures of public services have the potential to create opportunities that public servants can explore and take advantage of to commit acts of fraud or corruption.

Many authors of public administration studies, including Bilhim (2004) in Portugal, feel that it is possible to define a basic universal model of how organizations are structured, namely the public administration services. Through this model it is possible to view the structure of an organization (any organization) on two levels and in two dimensions:

- The formal and informal levels, and;
- The group and individual dimensions.

It is important to consider the distinction between the formal and informal levels, as it corresponds to a kind of a gap between the normative and bureaucratic side of organizations (laws and norms created to conduct administrative procedures) and the way the administrative procedures are effectively conducted (the real side of it). Crozier (1963), and Crozier and Friedberg (1977) studied the bureaucratic phenomena and found that the gap between the formal and informal levels is the basis for the development of strategies and lines of power among the members of the organization.

Furthermore, it is important to consider the separation between the individual and group dimensions, because any organization is always a group of individuals organized around a common project (the project of their organization), but, at the same time, each one of those individuals has their own context, their expectations, their own life projects, which are probably are not related to the objectives of the organization.

Starting from these segmentations, it is possible to identify four different areas in any organization. As Figure 10.2 shows (and it is not difficult to imagine), these four areas are always part of the daily life of organizations, and mutually influence each other.

This interpretative model of public organizations is important for understanding fraud and corruption acts, because they are the result of wrongdoing by public servants (alone or aggregated in small or big groups). This means that fraud and corruption always correspond to informal practices by public servants, against the law and norms of the organization (against social and organizational expectations).

As Figure 10.4 shows, based on the two levels and two of the dimensions mentioned, it is possible to identify the existence of the following four areas within an organization:

- *Individual/Formal*—This area comprises all the existing rules and standards formally defining the specific role of each public servant in order to perform their duties adequately, according to the purpose and objectives of the public service where they work;
- *Individual/Informal*—Corresponds to the area of how each public servant truly carries out their duties within the organization. These actions may be more or less in keeping with the laws and regulations provided at the formal level. It is expected that some explanations for individual practices of corruption may be found here;

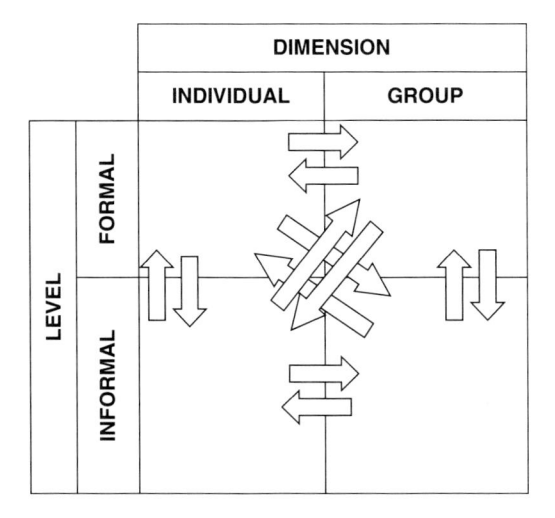

Figure 10.4 The basic universal model of how organizations are structured.

- *Group/Formal*—This area consists of all existing rules and standards defining the strategy, objectives and functions of each department and the entire organization (Public Service);
- *Group/Informal*—Area pertaining to how each department and the entire organization (public service) perform their functions. These actions (conducting administrative procedures) may be more or less according to the laws and regulations provided at the formal level. It is expected that some explanations for practices of corruption by public servants organized in groups may be found here.

10.3 Methodology and results

In this study, we take what is commonly referred to as the sociological concept of corruption, described for example in Maia (2008), Sousa and Triães (2007), Grilo (2005), Sautu (2004), Morgado and Vegar (2003), Rose-Ackerman (1999), Tanzi (1998), and Johnston (1997). In practice, we are considering not only what criminal law defines as corruption, but all other deliberate practices by public servants that may cause damage to the public services where they work and that criminal law defines as different crimes. According to Portuguese Criminal Law, the main crimes included in this concept are *Abuse of Trust* (Art. 205); *Fraud* (Art. 218); *Passive Corruption* (Art. 372); *Active Corruption* (Art. 374); *Embezzlement* (Art. 375); *Economic Participation in Business* (Art. 377); *Crime of Concussion* (Art. 379); and *Misuse of Public Power* (Art. 382). The legal definition of some of these crimes is presented in the Appendix.

The methodology used in this study consisted of the content analysis of over 60 judicial sentences for this type of crimes, supplemented with information collected through interviews with qualified informants. It was considered important for this study to collect information from auditors, inspectors, magistrates, judges, and other public servants with monitoring powers over public services mandated to curb illicit practices. The use of two different but complementary strategies to obtain information has been strongly encouraged by most authors, for example, Amaro (2006), Hill and Hill (2005), Carmo and Ferreira (1998), Moreira (1994), Foddy (1993), Quivy and Van Campenhoudt (1988), Bardin (1977), and Goode and Hatt (1952).

10.3.1　Results of the content analysis of judicial sentences

Table 10.2 shows some collated results from the content analysis of over 60 judicial sentences served to public servants for crimes against public administration services at their place of work. These 60 judicial sentences correspond to the total collected by DCIAP between 2002 and 2010.[5]

As can be seen in Table 10.2, most crimes (91.7 percent, corresponding to 55 cases) consisted of actions of isolated public servants within their functions. The results suggest that this is probably the easiest solution, or even that individuals prefer to act alone because this gives them dominance and control over the act.

10.3.1.1　Analysis of individual practices

The following tables present the results of the analysis of the 55 individual practices.

Table 10.3 shows that embezzlement was clearly the most frequent crime inside public services (79.1 percent), and passive corruption ranked second (12.7 percent).

Table 10.4 shows a tendency for multiple instances (76.4 percent) of the same crime over time, as confirmed in the next table (Table 10.5). Only 23.6 percent (1 in 4 cases) correspond to single acts, which means situations that were detected the moment the act occurred.

These results suggest that for most of the criminal acts (3 in 4), the control mechanisms over administrative action were not as effective as they were supposed to be.

According to the figures in Table 10.5, most of the situations of multiple acts of the same crime occurred over an 18-month period until the moment of detection (about 67 percent of this type of cases).

Table 10.2 Typology of action

Typology of act	*Number of cases*	*%*
Practices from isolated public servants	55	91.7
Practices from public servants organized in group	5	8.3
TOTAL	60	100.0

Table 10.3 Main type of crime

Typology of crime	Number of cases	%	Gender			
			Male	%	Female	%
Embezzlement	44	79.1	26	47.2	18	32.7
Passive corruption	7	12.7	6	10.9	1	1.8
Abuse of trust	1	1.8	0	0.0	1	1.8
Concussion	1	1.8	0	0.0	1	1.8
Fraud	1	1.8	0	0.0	1	1.8
Misuse of public power	1	1.8	1	1.8	0	0.0
TOTAL	55	100.0	33	60.0	22	40.0

Table 10.4 Typology of act

Typology of act	Number of cases	%	Gender			
			Male	%	Female	%
Multiple acts (several practices of the same crime before being detected)	42	76.4	24	43.6	18	32.7
Single act (only one practice of the crime)	13	23.6	9	16.4	4	7.3
TOTAL	55	100.0	33	60.0	22	40.0

Table 10.5 Temporal duration in situations of multiple criminal acts before the detection

Time between the moment of first practice of crime and detection	Number of cases	%	Gender			
			Male	%	Female	%
No reference	1	2.4	1	2.4	0	0.0
Less than 1 month	4	9.5	2	4.8	2	4.8
1 to 6 months	11	26.2	6	14.3	5	11.9
6 to 12 months	9	21.4	5	11.9	4	9.5
12 to 18 months	4	9.5	3	7.0	1	2.4
18 to 24 months	3	7.1	1	2.4	2	4.8
2 to 3 years	1	2.4	0	0.0	1	2.4
3 to 4 years	4	9.5	2	4.8	2	4.8
4 to 5 years	2	4.8	2	4.8	0	0.0
More than 5 years	3	7.1	2	4.8	1	2.4
TOTAL	42	100.0	24	57.1	18	42.9

First, Table 10.6 shows that it was not possible to get information about this topic from a significant number of cases (almost half of them, 45.6 percent).

However, information gathered from the other cases (30 from a total of 55) suggests that public servants tend to commit criminal acts only after at least one year of service. This fact is probably because, during the first months, new public servants are not familiar with how the services are organized and how they work. In addition, in many services the first year corresponds to a kind of a probation period, when new workers are more supervised.

These figures do not reveal much, but this table suggests that public servants take the option of committing criminal acts between 1 and 10 years of active duty in public services or after 20 years.

Table 10.7 shows that public servants from all hierarchical sectors have committed criminal acts in their public functions, which means that there are opportunities for criminal acts at all hierarchical levels.

Table 10.8 clearly emphasizes the main objective of public servants who decide to commit a criminal act. Obtaining money was the most frequent objective of the criminal act (83.6 percent).

This fact suggests that public services that deal directly with money or that may facilitate access to it (for example, services related with administrative

Table 10.6 Time in public functions

Time in public functions	Number of cases	%	Gender			
			Male	%	Female	%
No reference	25	45.5	17	30.9	8	14.5
Less than 1 year	0	0.0	0	0.0	0	0.0
1 to 5 years	8	14.5	5	9.1	3	5.5
5 to 10 years	8	14.5	1	1.8	7	12.7
10 to 15 years	3	5.5	2	3.6	1	1.8
15 to 20 years	3	5.5	3	5.5	0	0.0
More than 20 years	8	14.5	5	9.1	3	5.5
TOTAL	55	100.0	33	60.0	22	40.0

Table 10.7 Hierarchical position of authors of crimes

Hierarchical position	Number of cases	%	Gender			
			Male	%	Female	%
Director or Head of Public Service	7	12.7	6	10.9	1	1.8
Chief of Department or Team	18	32.7	13	23.6	5	9.1
Frontline	30	54.6	14	25.2	16	29.1
TOTAL	55	100.0	33	60.0	22	40.0

Table 10.8 Typology of goods associated to the criminal acts

Type of goods	Number of cases	%	Gender Male	%	Female	%
Money	46	83.6	25	45.5	21	38.2
Money and objects	4	7.3	3	5.5	1	1.8
Objects	3	5.5	3	5.5	0	0.0
No injury to the public service	2	3.6	2	3.6	0	0.0
TOTAL	55	100.0	33	60.0	22	40.0

Table 10.9 Value of the damage associated to the criminal acts

Value of the damage	Number of cases	%	Gender Male	%	Female	%
No reference	1	1.8	1	1.8	0	0.0
No value	2	3.6	2	3.6	0	0.0
Less than 100€	4	7.3	3	5.5	1	1.8
100€ to 500€	10	18.2	7	12.7	3	5.5
500€ to 2,000€	5	9.1	2	3.6	3	5.5
2,000€ to 3,000€	6	10.9	0	0.0	6	10.9
3,000€ to 5,000€	7	12.7	4	7.3	3	5.5
5,000€ to 10,000€	3	5.5	2	3.6	1	1.8
10,000€ to 20,000€	5	9.1	3	5.5	2	3.6
20,000€ to 50,000€	5	9.1	3	5.5	2	3.6
50,000€ to 1,00,000€	4	7.3	3	5.5	1	1.8
More than 1,00,000€	3	5.5	3	5.5	0	0.0
TOTAL	55	100.0	33	60.0	22	40.0

decision-making that affect private interests, where corruption may occur) are probably areas and services with a high level of risk for criminal acts.

Table 10.9 gives an idea of the values that were associated with the analyzed criminal acts. In our opinion, the numbers show that after the decision to commit the criminal act, public servants tend to take as much money as possible or necessary. However, as seen previously (Tables 10.4 and 10.5), in most situations the money is not obtained in one go, but through several acts over time.

10.3.1.2   Analysis of group practices

The following tables present information about the five cases of group practices (cf. Table 10.10).

Once again, it is possible to see that embezzlement was the most frequently committed criminal act in public services.

Table 10.11 shows that all five situations correspond to multiple acts (several instances of the same crime before detection).

As we had already seen in Table 10.6, Table 10.12 confirms that public servants tend to commit criminal acts only after being in service for at least one year.

Likewise (see Table 10.7), Table 10.13 shows that public servants from all hierarchical levels have committed criminal acts in their public functions. In these five

Table 10.10 Number of individuals of each group

Case	Main crime	Number of individuals of the group	%	Gender			
				Male	%	Female	%
A	Embezzlement	2	13.3	2	13.3	0	0.0
B	Passive corruption	5	33.3	4	26.7	1	6.7
C	Embezzlement	3	20.0	3	20.0	0	0.0
D	Embezzlement	2	13.3	1	6.7	1	6.7
E	Embezzlement	3	20.0	2	13.3	1	6.7
TOTAL		15	100.0	12	80.0	3	20.0

Table 10.11 Temporal duration in situations criminal acts before detection

Time between the moment of first practice of crime and detection	Number of cases	%
1 year	1 – (E)	20.0
2 years	1 – (C)	20.0
4 years	1 – (B)	20.0
4 years	1 – (D)	20.0
5 years	1 – (A)	20.0
TOTAL	5	100.0

Table 10.12 Time in public functions

Time in public functions	Number of authors	%	Gender			
			Male	%	Female	%
No reference	5	33.3	4	26.7	1	6.7
Less than 1 year	0	0.0	0	0.0	0	0.0
1 to 5 years	1	6.7	1	6.7	0	0.0
5 to 10 years	7	46.7	5	33.3	2	13.3
More than 10 years	2	13.3	2	13.3	0	0.0
TOTAL	15	100.0	12	80.0	3	20.0

Table 10.13 Hierarchical position of authors of crimes

Hierarchical position	Number of cases	%	Gender			
			Male	%	Female	%
Director or Head of Public Service	3	20.0	3	20.0	0	0.0
Chief of Department or Team	9	60.0	7	46.7	2	13.3
Frontline	3	20.0	2	13.3	1	6.7
TOTAL	15	100.0	12	80.0	3	20.0

Table 10.14 Typology and value of the damage associated to the criminal acts

Type of goods	Value (€)
Objects (D)	11,29
Money (E)	400,00
Money (A)	22.228,68
Money (C)	66.290,72
Money (B)	2.000.000,00

cases it was possible to see that the group of individuals that committed the criminal acts included public servants from at least two hierarchical positions, working together in the same department.

Again, as seen in Tables 10.8 and 10.9, Table 10.14 shows that money seems to be the main objective of the criminal acts committed by groups of public servants.

10.3.2 Findings from the interviews

To complement the elements from the content analysis of the judicial sentences, it was important and necessary to obtain additional information from qualified informants. In this case, we elected public servants mandated with the monitoring of public services, as well as oversight and prevention departments. It was important to record their perceptions of these criminal practices, especially of the opportunity factor, because of their professional experience in dealing with the problem on a daily basis (auditing and controlling public services, detecting and investigating illicit practices, including criminal acts, punishing the perpetrators of those crimes, etc.).

Information was collected from more than 30 individuals from auditing and control departments of several ministries and government departments, including magistrates and judges.

The main perceptions, explanations and ideas that were taken from these interviews are as follows:

- Corruption is a problem that finds its deepest roots in the cultural matrix of the Portuguese people. However, there are signs that things are getting better.

Slowly, the public sector is fostering a new culture of how to develop public service, showing more consideration for public and social interests and citizens, and also having new models of control systems over administrative procedures;

- Corruption is a problem that exists in Portuguese public administration, like in any other country. However, the scale of the problem is not as serious as the existing social perception of it assumes;
- The problem was worse a few years ago. It has improved as a result of the efforts to change the organizational culture of the services, as mentioned previously;
- All departments and hierarchical levels of the public sector services have natural risks for this kind of acts. However, the risk is not equal, not even similar, in all departments, areas, hierarchical levels or functions. It is bigger and more likely in areas of public procurement, where the public functions include dealing with and managing money, managing public assets, and also where there are public powers to decide over private interests;
- Embezzlement was the most frequently discovered criminal act, and it was often committed to obtain money that was available in the services;
- At times, the control systems over administrative procedures are not as effective as they are supposed to be. But it is not a problem of the model itself. In fact, the model often seems to be good, but there are still difficulties in implementing it effectively. For financial reasons, it is sometimes difficult to have the best computer systems to more efficiently control administrative procedures. Other times, owing to a lack of human resources, it is not possible to meet the real needs of the departments. Finally, it is necessary to consider that there is still some cultural resistance. For example hierarchical situations that hinder effective control over the actions of public servants in their departments, because they do not want to have problems with them, or because they simply do not care about it;
- High levels of trust in some public servants, in particular older ones or those who have been in the same department and position for many years, is also a problem. In these situations there is a tendency to reduce the effectiveness of control procedures over the actions of these public servants, precisely based on the effect of trust and, frequently, on friendship;
- The lack of codes of conduct and values for the public services, or, when these documents exist, the need to explain their importance and objectives for the integrity and image of the institution and their public servants;
- The lack of best practices manuals for all roles within each public service, or, when they exist, the need to explain them through appropriate training plans for all public servants.

10.4   Conclusion

Considering the data obtained from the cases under study and from the informants, it is possible to present some conclusions about this kind of crime, namely about the opportunity factor in public services.

First, it was possible to confirm the proposed model and hypothesis. Thus, in the context of Cressey's (1953) fraud triangle model, these results confirm the existence of opportunity as a factor to explain corruption practices in Portuguese public administration services.

It is even possible to outline a structure of opportunities, according to Cloward and Ohlin's (1960) model. In fact, the information gathered shows the existence of criminal acts committed by public servants (mainly individuals) at all hierarchical levels of service and the informants acknowledge the existence of risks in all departments and hierarchical levels. Yet it seems the risks are not equal in all departments, hierarchical levels or positions. They are more significant in some areas than in others. The analyzed cases and the informants' perceptions show that the departments and services that deal with money, or where it is possible to obtain money, seem to be particularly exposed to risk, namely for the practices of embezzlement.

Therefore, in our opinion, it is likely that there is a kind of grid of opportunities, which has a vertical dimension, i.e., the hierarchical structure, a horizontal segmentation, i.e., the departmental structure, and some areas where the risks are more considerable than others.

Another particularity that is apparent from this study is that the dimension of the problem is not as significant as the general public's perception of it. Nevertheless, there are indicators of the existence of a considerable number of unknown cases. Either way, this problem does exist and it is important to obtain more information about it, to continue the development of strategies to control it.

Finally and according to the informants, in order to reduce the opportunities for corruption practices, strategies need to be developed to create codes of conduct in each public service. These documents should include the values of the public service and, more importantly, should lead to the creation and dissemination, within the organization, of best practices manuals for all positions and for all administrative procedures. This could be a good way to transform best practices into a more formal framework, according to our model, and contribute to reducing the margins of opportunity for criminal acts in administrative procedures.

Notes

1 The author would like to thank the DCIAP (Central Department for Criminal Investigation and Prosecution), in particular its directors, Cândida Almeida, Amadeu Guerra and Antonieta Borges, for their collaboration in this study, namely by authorizing access to and use of the judicial sentences that were the object of the content analysis.
2 The data in Table 10.1 include only judicial cases and suspects of passive and active corruption crimes.
3 It is important to clarify that this study is only about opportunity as a factor for public services fraud and corruption practices. There are of course opportunity factors for fraud and corruption also on the political level, but they lie beyond the purpose of this study.
4 Wolfe and Hermanson (2004) argue that the capacity, ability and determination of the perpetrator to explore opportunities for illegal practices comprise a fourth vector of Cressey's model, and they rename it the fraud diamond model. We believe that ability and determination are very important—even determinant for the success or avoidance of the practice—but they are in fact part of the rationalization process.

5 According to its director, Cândida Almeida, the number of all judicial sentences for this type of crime is probably greater than the 60 that were analyzed. However, these are all the judicial decisions that the Courts sent to the DCIAP (Central Department for Criminal Investigation and Prosecution) from 2002 to 2010. It is may be possible that for unknown reasons some Courts did not send their judicial decisions to the DCIAP.

Appendix

Main economic crimes in Portugal: Legal definitions

Table A10.1 Portuguese criminal law

Article 205 – Abuse of Trust

1 – Anyone who illegally takes ownership of moving thing it has not been delivered by title of transfer of property is punishable with imprisonment up to three years or with a fine.

2 – The attempt is punishable.

3 – The criminal prosecution depends on a complaint.

4 – If the thing referred to in no. 1 is: (a) high value, the agent is punished with imprisonment up to five years or a fine of up to 600 days; (b) a considerably high value, the agent is punished with imprisonment from one to eight years.

5 – If the agent has received something on deposit imposed by law on grounds of occupation, employment or profession, or acting as guardian, legal custodian or trustee, is punished with imprisonment from one to eight years.

Article 218 – Fraud

1 – Anyone, with intent to obtain for himself, or for a third person, unlawful enrichment, through error or mistake on the facts that led astutely determine others to acts which cause, or causes to another person, economic loss is punished with imprisonment up to three years or with a fine.

2 – The penalty is imprisonment of between two and eight years if the economic loss of value is considerably high.

Article 375 – Embezzlement

1 – The officer who illegitimately appropriates, in own benefit or for the benefit of another, of money or any movable property, public or private, which has been handed to him, is in his possession or is accessible to him by virtue of his duties, is punished with sentence of imprisonment from one to eight years, if a more serious sentence is not applicable to him by virtue of another legal provision.

2 – If the objects or values mentioned in the previous number are of slight value, pursuant to paragraph (c) of Article 202, the agent is punished with sentence of imprisonment for not more than three years or with fine penalty.

3 – If the officer grants as loan, pledges or otherwise encumbers values or objects mentioned in no. 1, is punished with sentence of imprisonment for not more than three years or with fine penalty, if a more serious sentence is not applicable to him by virtue of another legal provision

Article 372 – Passive Corruption

1 – The public official who by himself, or through another person, with his consent or ratification, demands or accepts, for himself or a third party, any undue advantage whether of economic nature or not, or its promise, for any act or omission contrary to the duties of his position, even if prior to such demand or acceptance, is punished with imprisonment from one to eight years.

(Continued)

2 – If the act or omission is not contrary to the duties of his position and if the advantage is undue the offender is punished with imprisonment from one to five years.

Article 379 – Crime of Concussion

1 – An official in the exercise of its functions or powers arising by itself or through an intermediary with the consent or ratification, receiving for himself, for the State or to a third party through or use misleading error the victim's pecuniary advantage which is not due, that is higher than due, including contribution, fee, emolument, fine or penalty, is punished with imprisonment up to two years or a fine of up to 240 days, where a heavier penalty is not applicable by virtue of other statutory provision.

2 – If the act is committed through violence or threat to harm important, the agent is punished with imprisonment from one to eight years, where a heavier penalty is not applicable by virtue of other statutory provision.

Article 382 – Misuse of Public Power

The officer who, outside the cases foreseen in the previous articles, abuses of powers or breaches obligations inherent to his duties, with the intent to obtain, for himself or for a third party, an unlawful benefit or cause harm to another person, is punished with sentence of imprisonment for not more than three years or with fine penalty, if a more serious sentence is not applicable to him by virtue of another legal provision.

Source: United Nations on Drug and Crime www.unodc.org/documents/treaties/UNCAC/SA-Report/PO_ UNCAC_ 2011.pdf (accessed April 15, 2015).

11 Results-based management

An effort to prevent corruption in the Thai public sector

Orapin Sopchokchai

11.1 Introduction

Governments around the globe face the growing concern of their citizens or taxpayers with the quality and cost of public services. Citizens' voice and pressure are intense as they learn more about frauds and scandals in the public sector. Citizens and societal organizations demand that government be more open, transparent, and accountable for results. Governments, on the other hand, also want to show their voters some tangible results they had promised. Elected governments initiate public policy; but to get things done right, they rely on civil servants to produce the overall results of government performance from which they can publicly announce annual performance results at the end of each fiscal year. Can anything be done to improve government performance?

Scholars and administrators have discussed and considered this issue for more than three decades. Since the 1980s, the New Public Management movement introduced several approaches to improve government performance and public service. The idea is to put efforts into and focus on the results of government performance that satisfy users or citizens rather than on the traditional administrative process.

Results-based management (RBM) has been widely discussed and has been an important key concept in public sector reform for many decades. Results-based or results-oriented management is a tool for governments to initiate public sector improvement, particularly efficiency, effectiveness and economy of public service delivery. RBM is not a new concept; it has been called different names and is similar in meaning and concept to "scientific management," "social indicators," "management by objectives," "performance management," "performance measurement," "logical framework approach" and the latest "evidence-based policy." To effectively implement RBM in public organizations, at least four management tools must be included, namely strategic planning, benchmarking, performance measurement, and a performance information system to help government make better policy decisions, determine and plan the best use of resources including public money, enhance public service quality, and improve communication with citizens. Across the board, the emphasis is on accountability for results—measuring whether or not public programs are successfully addressing the real needs of the individuals, families, communities, and societies they seek to serve. Currently, governments want to prove that their strategies are working and producing the expected results; that they are spending money efficiently and economically. Moreover, modern governments are pressured to focus on openness, transparency, accountability, and to give priority to fiscal management.

Accountability for results involves setting measurable goals and responsibilities, planning what needs to be done, doing the work, monitoring progress, reporting on the results, then evaluating results and providing feedback. The existing accountability framework has undergone significant change as the government focuses on results. Effective accountability means that those managing public resources depend on sound information, not speculation, to determine the effectiveness of government programs. In developed countries such as New Zealand, Australia, and the UK, it is noted that public managers and elected officials realize the benefits of results-based management and communication with the public. They are increasingly accepting of accountability, strategic planning, performance management, and development of performance measurement systems. And yet, it is still possible that managing results could become just one more exercise in other countries, part of the latest trend. Thailand has followed this administrative development in order to do better in public management and, after the economic and financial crisis in 1997, the Thai government implemented RBM not only to improve government performance, but also to enhance good governance in Thai public organizations.

Thailand, located in Southeast Asia, is a beautiful and developing country in the globalized world. The population is about 66.72 million and the average population growth rate is 0.57 percent (2011). Domestically, life expectancy continues to increase (73.6 years for the total population in 2011) and infant mortality to decrease (about 11.2 per 1,000 live births in 2010). All Thai children, ensured by the Constitution, have equal access to education and the adult literacy rate is increasing (93.5 percent in 2005). An increasing number of people have sustainable access to improve sanitation and fewer people are undernourished. With a well-developed infrastructure, a free-enterprise economy, generally pro-investment policies, and strong export industries, Thailand enjoyed solid growth from 2000 to 2007—averaging more than 4 percent per year—as it recovered from the Asian economic and financial crisis of 1997–98. Thai exports—mostly machinery and electronic components, agricultural commodities, and jewelry—continue to drive the economy, accounting for more than half of the GDP. The global financial crisis of 2008?09 severely cut Thailand's exports, with most sectors experiencing double-digit drops. In 2009, the economy contracted 2.2 percent. In 2010, Thailand's economy expanded 7.6 percent, its fastest pace since 1995, as exports rebounded from their depressed 2009 level. GDP per capita (PPP) was about $8,700 (2010), and the unemployment rate in 2010 was about 1 percent. Based on 2008 statistics, 42.4 percent of the labor force was in the agriculture sector; 19.7 percent in the industrial sector; and 37.9 percent in the service sector (Indexmundi 2012).

While the data indicate progress, the path to developing the nation has not been easy and has, from time to time, been interrupted by financial and political crises as well as the flood in 2011. While Thailand has a long history of effective and strong public administration that could drive such past progresses, the country has faced many problems (political crises, social and economic problems, etc.) and, among them, corruption in the public sector. Transparency International has conducted annual corruption perception surveys since 1995 and reports that Thailand's Corruption Perceptions Index (CPI), in 2011, was 3.4 on a 10-point scale, and that Thailand ranked 80th among 183 countries. The CPI in 2012 was slightly lower but it has not improved much since 1995. (See details in the Appendix.)

Apart from these problems and pressures from both internal and external institutions, the Thai government faces a number of challenging issues, including how to improve the quality of life for Thai citizens, how to reduce corruption problems, and how to develop the nation to meet all the challenges of the twenty-first century. Additionally, after the Thai economic and financial crisis in 1997, the government had to borrow money from the International Monetary Fund (IMF), and one of the requirements was reforming the public sector. By 2003, the Thai government had initiated a public sector reform program and implemented results-based management across the board in order improve government performance. As expected, resistance to change has occurred, especially with regard to adopting complex new ideas that must be painstakingly implemented over time, across ministries, departments, provinces and public organizations.

This chapter intends to discuss the Thai public sector reform, focusing particularly on how strategic planning and results-based management has been introduced and implemented in Thai public organizations. The chapter explores how the Thai government uses RBM not only to improve government performance, but also to enhance the transparency and accountability of public organizations. It will examine the efforts made to use RBM as a tool to curb and reduce corruption as part of the reform program. The final part of this chapter will describe what have we learned from this difficult exercise.

11.2 Results-based management in the public sector

Results derived from government performance have been a main focus as long-standing as the existence of the government itself. In the past, autocratic governments sought to explain their performance and justify their rule by showing their citizens how much they could benefit from it. In modern democratic societies, this idea is elaborated by politicians and political parties who promise voters that their policies will deliver their version of quality of life (better health care, economic growth, safer community, better welfare system, lower taxes, etc.) (Talbot 2000). Governments implement results-based management in an attempt to deliver what they have promised. In real situations, however, there is often a big gap between policies promised and results delivered. Challenging questions are how to bridge this gap, what should be done to achieve the desirable results, and how to deal with the complexity of public organizations. As a result, the most central feature of public sector reforms has been the emphasis on improving performance and ensuring that government activities achieve the desired results.

Conceptually, managing for results is a management practice dating back to the early twentieth century. Van Dooren *et al.* (2010) conclude that there are eight similar results-based management movements that can be clustered into three time segments: (1) pre-World War II (social survey movement, scientific management, and cost accounting); (2) the 1950–1970s (performance budgeting, and social indicators); (3) 1980s–present (new public management, and evident-based policy).

Today, performance management is a widely used management option geared to achieving specific results. Several factors have contributed to the growing focus on managing for results which is at the heart of the "New Public Management" (NPM) movement. NPM emphasizes strategic planning, focused implementation, monitoring and evaluation of operations, re-engineering operations to optimize results, customer-oriented, and the values of service provision and quality. Public sector reforms using the NPM concept experimented in many developed countries such as New Zealand, Australia, and the UK aimed to respond to the following pressures. In the early 1980s, it was widely recognized that resources were finite and had to be used properly and strategically, therefore, savings and value for money were the main focus. Additional factors included, but were not necessarily limited to: pressure for improvements in service delivery brought by citizens; growing demand to participate in public policy decision-making processes; and growing regional and global competition so that only productive countries could thrive, build strong economies, and provide high living standards for all citizens. Strategic planning and RBM become the heart of the NPM.

Implementing RBM is not easy when used in the public domain; this issue has been widely debated among public administrators and academics for many decades. Results in the public sector and government performance are ambiguous. Results mean different things to different people, depending on individual interpretation and situations. The meaning of performance in the public sector, however, can be defined as the intentional behavior of government actors to generate more and better quality output from activity most of the time. When performance is about the quality of achievement rather than about the quality of actions, performance equals results (Van Dooren *et al.* 2010). In this case, government performance is closely associated with quality or desirable results that go beyond outputs. It refers to outcomes from government actions. For many public policies, measuring and defining outcomes can be difficult.

The OECD (2000) reviewed that results-based management, also referred to as performance management, can be defined as a broad management strategy aimed at achieving important changes in the way government agencies operate, with improving performance (achieving better results) as the central orientation. In short, RBM is a management approach that integrates strategy, human factors, resources, processes, and measurement to improve decision-making, transparency, and accountability (CIDA 2009). The approach focuses on achieving outcomes, implementing performance measurement, learning and adapting, as well as reporting performance. Its primary purpose is to improve efficiency and effectiveness through organizational learning, second, to fulfil accountability obligations through performance reporting and third, to institutionalize transparency in implementation. Therefore, a key to its success is the involvement of stakeholders, both internal and external, throughout the management processes. Participatory governance from which related stakeholders or citizens are allowed to participate and participative management approaches from which employees at all levels are allowed to engage in management processes (Creighton 2005).

RBM aims to achieve the expected results; clearly defining realistic results with valid indicators, performance measurement, and accurate performance information are also important to implement RBM. The best way to understand RBM is to consider it as a production process described on the basis of a logic model. Originally, the basic model, used by private sector organizations, simply focuses on inputs, activities or processes, and outputs. For the public sector where contexts and situations are more complex politically, it is also necessary to assess the outcomes and impacts of a public policy or program. The difficulty is an attempt to define outputs and outcomes in the public sector. Results or outputs from the production process of public organizations often have no immediate impact on the level of consumption, such as national security programs, scientific research programs, etc. To further explain the RBM model in public organizations, public administration researchers added and redefined the model by including important elements, such as socio-economic issues, government policy agenda, outcomes and effectiveness of the performance.

To formulate a policy or program, analyses of socio-economic situations and issues on how to improve the quality of life for people are, but not necessary limited to, the starting point of the production process (No. 1 in Figure 11.1). Policy formulators and decision-makers (politicians and public officials) define the societal problems and needs (2), design the public policy or program in which it is expected to clearly identify objectives and expected results (3). There are four keys questions that help to clarify objectives, actions, inputs, management processes, and expected outputs and outcomes of such programs. These questions are:

a   How should this program be implemented? Elected government and related stakeholders set a policy agenda and civil servants translate and integrate the policy agenda into the organizational objectives or programs and determine how many inputs, such as human resources, budget, time, and equipment (4), are needed to successfully implement these programs. Necessary activities and management process (5) are designed to achieve expected results economically (9) and efficiently (10).

b   What should be produced? To justify policy decision, it is necessary to identify outputs (6) and outcomes (7) from the program. Outputs are direct products or services as a result of processes or activities of the policy or program implemented. Outputs include a number of categories in both quantity of service (number of students in schools, vaccination provided, etc.) and service

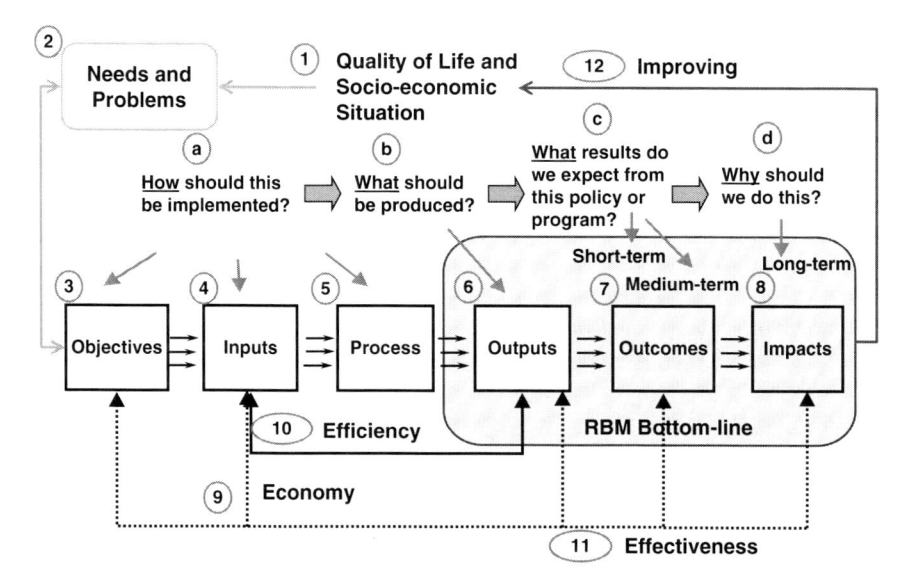

Figure 11.1 Results-based management logic.

Note: Adapted and based on the Logic Model by Carol Weiss, Joseph Wholey and others (Wei *et al.* 1972) and the Production Model of Performance (Van Dooren *et al.* 2010).

quality (speed of service delivery, availability and accessibility of provision, etc.). The ratio of outputs to inputs is one way to define efficiency.

c   What results do we expected from this policy or program? This question should be answered in terms of expected outcomes that respond to the identified needs of the intended beneficiaries. They are three levels of outcomes: short-term, medium-term, and long-term. The short term or immediate outcome is a change directly attributed to actions and outputs of the policy or program initiative, such as training programs which can increase level of skills. The medium-term or intermediate outcomes can occur after one or more immediate outcomes have been achieved, for example, the beneficiary can get a job after learning new skills. The long-term outcome is an answer to the last question.

d   Why should we do this? The ultimate or long-term outcomes are the highest level of change which usually provides the reasons for the policy or program implemented. They take the form of sustainable change among beneficiaries, such as improving quality of life.

Considering the management concept of RBM, researchers have usually paid more attention on the 3Es model centered on the economy, efficiency, and effectiveness of the public sector. Economy is the cost of procuring specific inputs (human resources, facilities, time, equipment, and budget) of a given quality and quantity. This is typically equated with the level of spending on a service or activity.

Efficiency is defined in two ways: (1) technical efficiency refers to the cost per unit of output, and (2) allocative efficiency refers to the responsiveness of service to public preferences. Effectiveness is the actual achievement of the formal objectives of services (Walker 2010).

11.3 Results-based management and corruption prevention

On the other hand, RBM can be used as a tool to combat corruption. The key principle for employing RBM in the public sector needs to consider building partnerships, and establishing accountability and transparency (Figure 11.2). Public participation in government decision-making and performance measurement is best viewed as a continuous process to provide information to the public so people understand what program or policy will be implemented, to listen to citizens expressing their needs, problems, and concerns, to engage in problem-solving with people or stakeholder groups and, together, to develop agreements based on consensus among all related stakeholders (Creighton 2005). The relationships between government and citizens shift the emphasis of modern public sector management towards a fundamental need to re-conceptualize public sector governance. It cannot merely include a focus on the importance of structures and processes in decision-making, but also get to the heart of governance: the importance of individual citizens or stakeholders and public organizations in the process of making public decisions (Edwards 2008). Therefore, participatory governance is an important institutional strategy of public agencies to develop good governance through the implementation of a new management approach which engages

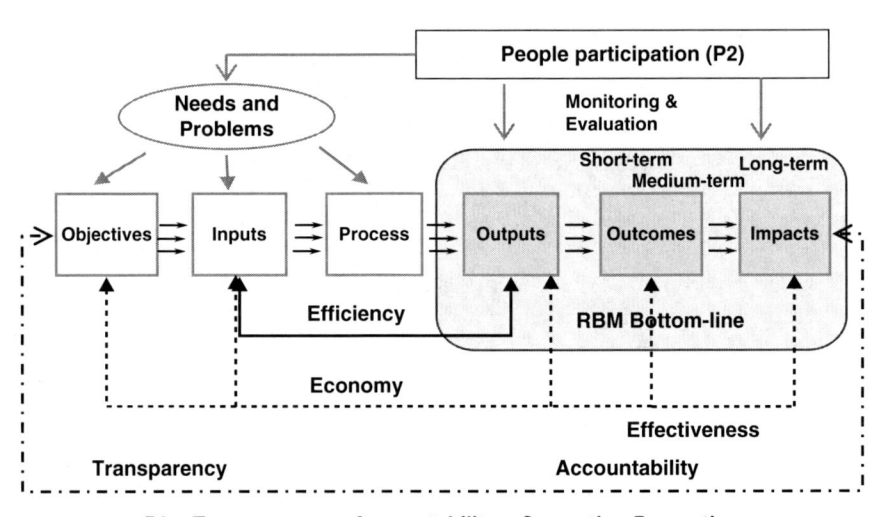

P2 + Transparency + Accountability = Corruption Prevention

Figure 11.2 RBM with participatory governance to prevent corruption.

citizens by not only informing them, but bringing them in as a part of policymaking, decision-making, and implementation processes (United Nations, Economic and Social Council 2007). The desirable end of participatory governance is public participation.

RBM needs to determine accountability among stakeholders by sharing performance expectations. The process must continue with shared management decision-making and ultimately lead to shared accountability. Under these ideal circumstances, public officials and stakeholders could assume shared accountability for policy or program results when reporting to their respective constituencies. Other key factors include the number of the partners involved, the extent of their participation in the design and planning of the policy or program and the degree of management decision-making authority they can exercise over implementation decisions. Establishing the appropriate level of accountability vis-à-vis the results chain is thus context dependent. As a general principle, the more control and ownership the public officials, or the related stakeholders, have over the policy or program, the greater the potential for demonstrating attribution and thus assuming accountability for results, i.e., outcomes and impacts.

Transparency is necessary to ensure that the benefits of the above-mentioned RBM principles are fully realized. Clarity is needed in defining the respective roles and responsibilities of all parties involved in government actions, and specifically the implementation of the RBM approach. Appropriate disclosure of the methodologies used to collect valid and reliable performance indicator data is critical in fulfilling public officials' accountability and obligations for reporting to their respective constituencies. Broad dissemination and active discussion of performance information, including progress made toward the achievement of outcomes, lessons learned and proposed adjustments, will enhance and improve performance as well as provide information for organizational learning. The RBM approach is significantly weakened in an environment that lacks transparency.

If the government provides opportunities for citizens to engage and get involved, the activities and processes of public organizations will be transparent. Public officials will be more accountable for results as it is clear for them what to deliver and how they can respond to the citizen's needs. Civic participation, transparent processes and public officials who are accountable create a check and balance system and prevent corruption.

11.4   Thai public sector reform: introducing RBM

Thai citizens in a modern democratic society demand and expect more from their elected government, but unfortunately most Thai citizens have not realized that waste and leaks in the public sector are partly derived from corruption. People are increasingly aware of their rights, granted by the 1997 and 2007 Constitution to get access to all public information and to participate in public decision-making processes. Additionally, government institutions have been heavily dominated by traditional bureaucratic concepts and values. In this case, we can say that Thailand's public administrative system is very unique in many ways. The traditional bureaucratic system had a highly pervasive influence since 1932 when the country changed from a traditional to a democratic monarchy. Before 1932, the public administration system was at the service of the King and the palace, serving the people through their commands.

Although the public sector management system became more open after the adoption of the democratic system in 1932, in its early period, the system was dominated by educated elite groups who shaped the nation's policy and direction. The most notable feature of the Thai public sector management is that it is highly centralized and control-oriented. While many previous Thai governments realized an urgent need to reform the public sector, very few achievements were recorded. Although the system was not adequate for the emerging requirements of the country's economic and political development, and public servants still placed them above the citizen, the Thai public sector did, however, coexist with a very high rate of economic growth and managed the previous crises well.

Reviewing Thailand's past reform experiences, the previous incremental reform efforts were only a drop in the ocean. Evidently, the reform efforts were unable to introduce real changes to the Thai public sector because: government was frequently changed and the reforms initiated were always canceled or revised; strong bureaucrats quietly found ways to resist change; many pilot initiatives and studies often ended up on the shelf; and outsiders—private sector, civil society, and mass media—had limited opportunities to participate.

Public sector reform is a difficult and complex task and it is not easy to implement. Many public institutions have not changed materially since their establishment and unstable coalition governments and limited coordination among public agencies weakened the government's ability to formulate and implement its reform policies. However, when it is the right time and place, a public sector reform policy can be initiated and successfully implemented, as in the case of New Zealand in the 1980s. At that time in Thailand, due to rapid changes in the global environment, modern information and communication technology, and the need to develop the country as well as to complete with other countries, there were some signs that the Thai public sector also tried to adjust but at a very slow pace. The private sector took the lead in rapidly adapting to the modern world. The private sector and civil society have heavily criticized the Thai public sector for its rigid regulations and inability to facilitate private sector development. During the 1990s, there were three key factors stimulating changes in Thai public sector organizations:

- Political uprising in 1992 followed by the promulgation of the new Constitution in 1997;
- Citizen demands for good governance due to increasing corruption in the public sector; and
- Economic and financial crisis in 1997.

The 1997 Constitution clearly established, for the first time, new governance concepts: enhancing transparency and accountability, increasing citizen participation (especially citizens' right to public information, right to express opinions, right to participate in public decision-making processes), and decentralization. The Constitution emphasized that it is the government's duty to improve public sector efficiency and effectiveness and it clearly provided a mandate to all elected governments to reform the public sector. In particular, it mandated the establishment of accountability institutions ("independent organizations") such as the Administrative Courts, Office of the Ombudsman, Office of the Auditor-General, and National Counter Corruption Commission, and promulgated new standards for transparency and guidelines for decentralizing authority and resources to local administrations. In addition, the 1997 Official Information Act provided greater public access to official information. With this new mechanism and governance concept, the Thai public sector had to be reformed.

Over the past few decades, corruption spread in Thailand and became a motive for military groups to seize power, usually followed by political crises. With the new Constitution, the Thai people gained more confidence to demand a more transparent and cleaner government, better public services and their right to participate in public decision-making processes.

The 1997 economic and financial crisis gave Thailand a bitter lesson with regard to having a weak public sector. The crisis revealed critical weaknesses in the public sector's ability to response to a changed environment, aside from other classic problems such as inefficiency and mismanagement of public resources, waste, low quality and inadequate public services, lack of coordination and unclear public policy, especially on monetary and fiscal policy. After the crisis, people claimed that it was time to reform the implemented policies, but, at the time, political will was not strong enough to get it off the ground. However, a public sector development strategy and master plan were prepared and approved by the Cabinet in May 1999. The master plan consisted of five major reform areas: structural reform, administrative processes and procedural reform, financial and budgetary reform, public personnel reform, and public servants' value and cultural reform. In the master plan, the idea of initiating a results-based management system was still unclear.

Section 75 of the 1997 Constitution of the Kingdom of Thailand clearly specified that the public sector was required to effectively organize public services and other related functions in order to respond to the needs of the people. In 1997, the Office of the Civil Service Commission (OCSC) initiated a "results-based management" (RBM) project within several pilot departments and in a number of pilot districts. These departments and districts experimented with a range of re-engineering efforts directed at improving service delivery through the RBM system. The objectives for using the RBM system in public organizations were to: (1) set up a performance measurement system that focused on the outcomes by using key performance indicators (KPIs) with clear targets, (2) obtain the performance data for management planning, organizational development, and resource allocation, (3) compare the performance results of different offices with a benchmark, and (4) allow public personnel to participate and know how well they were doing their work and how to achieve the targets set.

Some experiments resulted in changes in government management. For instance, a pilot department in the Ministry of Commerce introduced an operation that improved the way in which Thai companies could rapidly register their business domain. By improving services to businesses, the government created a better investment atmosphere and helped companies to become more competitive in global markets. The Ministry of Labor's Social Security Office learned how to analyze customer satisfaction and used such information to set performance targets and re-engineer the service delivery system. At the district level, one pilot district established on-site provision of citizen identification cards by organizing a data link with its headquarters in Bangkok, thereby providing citizens with more convenient access to services.

Because participation in the RBM project was voluntary, the participating departments and districts were led by enthusiastic supporters of RBM, who were committed to experiment to achieve success. This experience indicates that successful RBM is possible, but that its success will depend on strong leadership, structured monitoring and effective incentives. Even though by 2003 the OCSC had introduced RBM in 48 public organizations, many pilot departments did not continue after the project ended or policy was changed.

A window of opportunity to improve the performance of Thai public sector management opened after the General Election in 2001. The elected government faced an urgent need to bring the country out of the 1997 economic and financial crisis and, in an attempt to gain popular support, announced a public sector improvement policy. The proposed measures showed a strong commitment to reform the country in order to solve economic and social problems. The government policy included: optimizing the size of the public sector to serve actual needs and respond to the nation; changing the role of the public sector from controller to facilitator; using modern tools and technology to improve public service delivery and management; developing staff and public servants' capacity to serve the public; and reforming the budgetary and administrative processes.

In 2002, Parliament passed the Public Administrative Act (Number 5) (or B.E. 2545) (Thailand 2002) which led to several changes. First, the Law, particularly Section 3/1, laid out the blueprint for new public management and good governance in Thailand, emphasizing that public administration must address the following:

- benefits that accrue to the Thai people;
- results-oriented administration;
- responsiveness to the needs of the people;
- effective administration;
- worthiness of government functions;
- de-layering of work processes (streamlining);
- abolishment of unnecessary agencies and functions;
- decentralization of missions and resources to local administrative units;
- empowerment in decision-making;

- participatory governance; and
- accountability for endorsements.

Public agencies were expected to function under the principles of good governance, in particular, focus on accountability for endorsements, promote public participation, disclose information, as well as monitor and evaluate performance. The specific focus of different agencies varied according to the functional nature of each agency.

Second, in accordance with Section 71/9 of the 2002 Public Administration Act, a new reform mechanism was created, the Public Sector Development Commission (PDC), chaired by the prime minister and assisted by its Secretariat (Office of the Public Sector Development Commission (OPDC)). The OPDC, under the Office of the Prime Minister, is responsible for performing the tasks assigned by the PDC and all tasks pertaining to the principles and directions specified in Section 3/1 of the 2002 Public Administration Act and the 2003 Royal Decree on Good Governance, including monitoring and evaluating the performance of all agencies under the executive branch. The PDC and OPDC have become important actors in driving the change, implementing the RBM system, and in monitoring and reporting the annual performance of all public organizations.

Third, the 2002 Public Administration Act required the government to promulgate a Royal Decree that established principles and practices for new directions in public administration. Known as the 2003 Royal Decree on Good Governance, it requires all public organizations to operate on the basis of "good governance," i.e., accountability, public participation, transparency, monitoring and evaluation of performance. It also requires that budget and personnel administration take these principles into account. The Decree consists of 10 sections, each providing directions for the performance of government agencies in accordance with the overarching principles indicated in Section 3/1 mentioned above.

11.5 Implementing RBM in the Thai public sector

Evidently, several reform initiatives in Thailand were directed at creating capacity to measure outputs and results. As a result of an earlier pilot project on the Ministry of Public Health's Planning, Programming and Budgeting System (PPBS) in the 1980s, the Bureau of the Budget reoriented the budget process towards a greater emphasis on results. It asked departments and ministries to supplement their line-item budget requests with performance-oriented budget plans. In the 1990s, the OCSC experimented with RBM in 48 governmental departments and agencies.

In accordance with the 2002 Public Administrative Act (Number 5) (Section 3/1) and the 2003 Royal Decree on Good Governance, OPDC proposed to the Cabinet the use of the strategic management system to drive national and governmental development agenda and, through the strategic management system, the OPDC also implemented the results-based management (RBM) approach in order to comply with the Laws that require the OPDC to measure and improve Thai public sector performance. The implementation of the strategic and results-based management model encompasses vision and mission and requires the formulation of strategic plans, the identification of key performance indicators along with targets and reporting mechanisms. The government adopted an annual twelve-month cycle process (starting on October 1 to September 30 in the following year), with intermediate reporting requirements at three, six and nine month intervals. All government ministries, departments and provinces participated in Thailand's strategic and results-based program. To launch the system, pilot tests were carried out in the 2003 fiscal year in order to ease resistance and reduce confusion. A total of 238 agencies joined the programs, mainly voluntarily. They were clustered into three groups: Group I included agencies that volunteered to participate in the learning scheme and implement the whole system with supervision from the OPDC technical team; Group II consisted of 23 agencies that wanted to implement the program but preferred to challenge; and Group III encompassed the remaining agencies, which were asked to preliminarily implement RBM in order to prepare for the following fiscal year (see Table 11.1). Since the 2005 fiscal year, all government agencies in Thailand are required by the Cabinet to join the performance agreement system.

The strategic and results-based management system implemented in the Thai public sector is quite simple. In fact, increasing regional and rural development has been a main point of all development plans, up to the current Eleventh National Economic and Social Development Plan (2012–17). The issue is how to translate the goal of nationwide development into strategies and actions in all areas.

Table 11.1 Number of departments, provinces and public agencies volunteer to implement RBM from 2003 to 2005

2003	*2004*	*2005*
Group I Action Learning Scheme		
– Pilot group (147)	• 142 Ministries/ Departments	• 142 Ministries/ Departments
• 10 Pilot Ministries (72 Departments)	• 62 Academic institutes	• 72 Academic institutes
• 75 Provinces		
Group II Challenge Scheme (23)	• 75 Provinces	• 75 Provinces
• 14 Departments		
• 9 Universities		• 30 Public organizations and public agencies
Group III Across the Board Scheme (68)	• 57 Departments	
• 11 Universities		
238 agencies	**279 agencies**	**319 agencies**

Source: The Office of Public Sector Development Commission.

Thailand has considerable experience in dealing with these and similar issues in moving towards managing for results. For more than 50 years, strategic planning in Thailand has been led by the National Economic and Social Development Board (NESDB), whose five-year cycles have provided a framework from which departments select their goals. The Bureau of the Budget (BOB) has also played an important role in disciplined allocation of resources to the various elements of the departmental budgets based on perspectives of the national plans.

How has the Thai public sector managed for results and how can this system be used to prevent corruption and increase transparency and accountability? In general, the results-based management approach aims to improve the efficiency and effectiveness of government performance. In the case of the Thai public sector, transparency, accountability and anti-corruption measures are included.

After the promulgation of the 2002 Public Administration Act, this national planning process was supplemented with a State Administrative Plan (4 years) (State Administrative Act 2002), under which ministries, departments, provinces and clusters of provinces have developed their goals, indicators, targets and strategies. As illustrated in Figure 11.3, data related to the State Administrative Plan are summarized in scorecards at all levels of the government: the national and ministry level; strategic unit (ministry/cluster/department and provincial cluster/province); and responsible unit, team and individual scorecards. These accountability records are related to performance management agreements or performance agreements signed by the relevant government executives. All of Thailand's participating ministries, departments, universities and provinces have to respond to the strategic and results-based management requirements. They are required to develop their strategic plans including key performance indicators (KPIs) and targets. All have entered into performance agreements with OPDC that involve periodic monitoring. However, it should be noted that while the process is moving along and has already had a positive impact in some areas of government, it has also shown that there are challenges on the road to strategic and results-based management success, including the need for significant reforms in structures and behaviors. Some officials may prefer the "good old ways of doing work," while others are enthusiastic about examining their operations for performance improvement, both for the novelty of the experience and the satisfaction gained from better serving the public interest.

In addition, changing from the traditional planning method to the strategic and results-based management model aims to establish more transparent, open governance, and a civic participation system. In the past, the Thai public sector has been criticized for corruption, especially with regard to development programs or projects. Introducing strategic planning, results-based management, and performance measurement has created a more check and balance system. Through this results-based management system, government sets goals and targets and develops a government scorecard which indicates important performance indicators. The government, then, is required by the Constitution to be accountable for all policy announced and report their annual performance and policy results to Parliament. To manage the results, all responsible ministers (or cabinet members) have to be held accountable and responsible for the delivery of services and goods as indicated in the State Administration Plan. Each ministry develops a four-year administrative plan to guide and manage results. The prime minister, as the head of Cabinet, signs an annual performance agreement with each responsible minister and the minister signs an agreement with the Permanent Secretary or Chief Executive Officer (CEO) of the organization. To achieve the promised targets, limited resources, especially financial resources, must be carefully spent. If resources are leaked out, it means fewer prospects to meet the agreed targets. At the same time, civil servants who are rewarded from their annual performance must carefully spend the allocated budget in order to achieve the agreed results. In theory, both honest politicians and civil servants are checking each other.

In addition, the Public Administrative Act (#5) B.E. 2545 (2002), Section 3/1, and the 2003 Royal Decree on Good Governance indicates that civic participation and participatory governance must be emphasized. This is another channel for the public to get involved and monitor the results of any public organization. Initially, implementation was required at the provincial level; stakeholder groups—civic groups, private sector representatives, local media, academics, etc.—participated in the development of provincial strategic planning and they have been encouraged to monitor and evaluate the development results. In general, if the strategic and results-based management model is continuously and properly implemented, corruption would be reduced and be more difficult to carry out.

Through results-based management, several important indicators were developed and included in the performance agreement every fiscal year. Indicators to curb corruption, for example, were success and completeness of disclosing

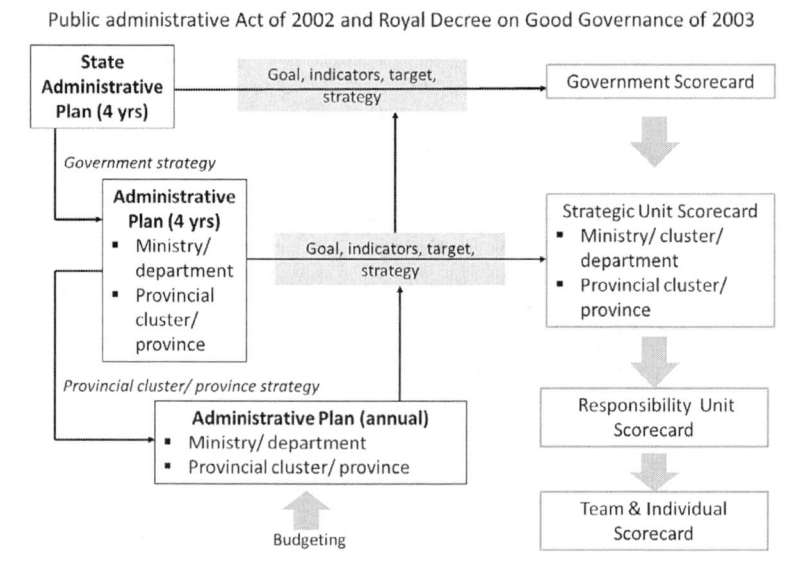

Figure 11.3 Relationship between government strategy and ministry/provincial strategy.

procurement information to the public through the organizational website. Another indicator required all public organizations to develop an action plan to fight corruption and the success of implementing activities were indicated in the plan. With these indicators, outsiders such as auditors and evaluators, could inspect and measure results.

The performance agreements are a modern management tool that helps build a common understanding and expectation between the Cabinet and a responsible minister, and between a responsible minister and top executives of the ministry or departments. The performance agreements are applied to all ministries, government agencies (including public universities), and provinces. The goals, targets, and KPIs are negotiated at the beginning of the fiscal year, conducted by the negotiating committee appointed by the Public Development Commission. Through negotiating processes, annual performance results and KPIs are developed and agreed upon, then, the "performance agreements" are signed between the government (ministers) and ministerial or agency heads (chief executives), also include all provincial governors, at the beginning of each fiscal year to set targets and expected results (see Figure 11.4). The performance agreement aims to ensure performance improvement, to guarantee the expected results and to enforce public accountability and transparency. For the Thai public sector, performance agreements are used to:

- change and improve the culture, methods and processes of public service in the direction of strategic and results-based management;
- improve the performance, budget allocation, monitoring and evaluation of government agencies;
- introduce incentives based on performance-related pay; and
- initiate any important management measure including corruption prevention.

Special measures are necessary to integrated strategic planning and results-based management at the provincial level due to different administrative structures. Therefore, the Cabinet approved the OPDC proposal to change the provincial management processes on July 22, 2003, by implementing the following:

1   All 77 provinces have been divided into 20 sub-regional groupings to realize integrated strategic management at the provincial level. The provincial

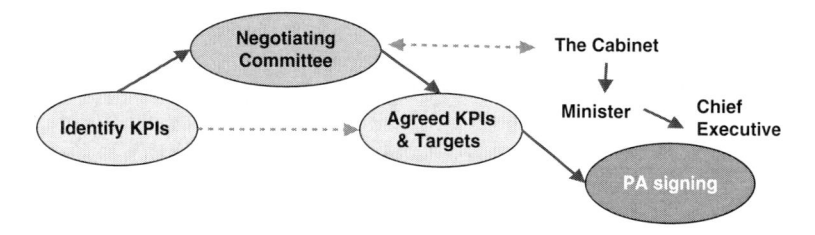

Figure 11.4 Performance agreement process.

cluster groupings have been developed by the OPDC, in collaboration with the Ministry of the Interior, the Office of the Prime Minister, and related government bodies as well as the private sector, to develop a complete approach to integrated administration based on economic, social and geographic factors. The deputy prime minister and inspector-officials of the Office of the Prime Minister are assigned to oversee strategic plan implementation, facilitate and coordinate its development, and monitor progress along with the ministries and departments.

2   Making each provincial "governor" accountable for managing the strategic plan and achieving the expected results in the province and the regional cluster. To successfully oversee the plan, a prime minister regulation was announced sanctioning the devolution of authority to the governor. Ministries and departments are to decentralize authority on directives, permissions and approvals, as well as other authorities, under the following guidelines: facilitation and responsiveness to the needs of the population; timely and efficient public service provision that is finalized at the provincial level; performance in line with government policies; immediate area-based problem solving; and strategic development of the province.

3   It is also essential to improve financial management. Ministries and departments are now being required to include as part of their annual budget arrangement the budget framework proposed by provinces consistent with their strategic development plans. The Budget Bureau must establish and monitor a system that will enable provinces to begin utilizing allocated resources in line with their strategic development plans within sixty days from the date the total budget is realized. Apart from this, provincial governors are also empowered with the flexibility to use remaining funds, and government bodies having remaining funds will be required to transfer full financial management authority to the governor in accordance with the Prime Minister's Office Announcement on Financial Management at the Provincial Level (B.E. 2524).

4   All provinces are required to involve stakeholders and the local population in provincial strategic planning processes and institutionalize participatory governance at the provincial level. This includes informing or providing information about development projects and programs allocated and implemented, listening to the needs and concerns of the local people, and reporting annual performance results to the local community.

The final stage of the strategic and results-based management model is to set up a monitoring and evaluation system. The public manager cascades goals, targets, and KPIs down to all units and individual officials (see Figure 11.5). Ministers and chief executives *monitor and evaluate performance against the performance agreement*; in fact, each agency uses an electronic self-assessment report which all units submit to the OPDC. In this report color codes (green, yellow and red) are applied to provide warning to those KPIs which are in the red, i.e., have not progressed according to the plan.

increasing movement towards efficiency and effectiveness. Furthermore, the process of tracking and measuring performance provides information that can be used to take corrective action and to learn what methods are worth replicating. In the process of implementing performance management systems, governments have found key practices that have improved performance but have also encountered many challenges and obstacles.

In summary, the key success factors from the Thai public sector's experiences in implementing strategic and results-based management are:

- sufficient technical knowhow which the country has accumulated over several decades and through earlier pilot projects in several agencies;
- committed political leaders with a clear public sector improvement policy and direction;
- government gave full support and willing to allocate sufficient resources because all reforms have costs;
- establishing ownership from within is essential, so new change champions must be recruited from both top and middle levels;
- a team at the national level is a crucial mechanism to engineer and drive the reform;
- public organizations have initiated several measures to prevent corruption such as regularly disclosing procurement information, developing a training program to educate public officers, setting up an internal auditing system to monitor performance;
- mass media paid more attention to the annual performance reported; and
- political, civil society and private sector support adds more energy to initiating a strategic management system in the Thai public sector.

However, seven typical obstacles are listed as the follows:

1   uneven integration of the strategic and result-based management with other management systems within the public organizations; it is difficult for public officials to give up their traditional processes or the method they are accustomed to;
2   public organizations and public managers operate under complex and difficult contexts such as policy ambiguity, political uncertainty and intervention, media scrutiny, lateral coordination, and citizen and stakeholder demands;
3   technical difficulties in measuring outcomes as most agencies and their staff have limited skills and knowledge to develop appropriate KPIs which represent outcomes;
4   very few public agencies have fully implemented the strategic management system, especially when it is necessary to use the performance report to reward each individual;

5   implementing the whole system creates a burden of extra work to maintain current systems while adding additional and parallel processes;
6   even though the strategic plan and results-oriented management model were expected to reduce corruption once firmly implemented, amazingly and evidently, the number of corruption cases and behavior has remained basically unchanged. This is due to (a) weakness of civil society and lack of civic participation in monitoring and evaluation, and in accessing the necessary information and (b) the check and balance mechanism introduced by the RBM system is not really functioning;
7   There is resistance to change and a negative mentality among those who must implement the system, which hampers the success of the strategic plan implementation.

Even though Thailand is facing many problems and obstacles, the results-based management system is widely and continuously implemented in public sector organizations. The system and policy has survived across all governments until now; it is still the main system implemented.

In summary, the ongoing strategic and results-based management system in Thailand has already produced some impacts. It is the first time in many decades that such a comprehensive change program has been implemented. The process is however far from complete and will undoubtedly continue for many years. For Thailand, there are many actions needed to fully implement strategic management. One of major impacts is that the process has raised awareness among Thai bureaucracy, initiated many innovative changes and the people support it, which means that future governments will have to continue this policy. It should be noted that an effort to use strategic and results-based management to introduce and institutionalize corruption prevention has not achieved any recognizable success, but there are several signs that there is a light at the end of the tunnel. At least, public organizations have regularly disclosed procurement information, attempted to improve administrative processes and public services to be more transparent and efficient, and been more open to public.

Appendix

Table A11.1 Thailand Corruption Perception Index from 1995 to 2013

Year	Score	Sources	Rank	# of Countries
1995	2.79	7	34	41
1996	3.33	10	37	54
1997	3.06	6	39	52
1998	3.00	11	61	85
1999	3.20	12	68	98
2000	3.20	11	60	90
2001	3.20	12	61	91
2002	3.20	11	64	102
2003	3.30	13	70	133
2004	3.60	14	64	146
2005	3.80	13	59	159
2006	3.60	9	63	163
2007	3.30	9	84	179
2008	3.50	9	80	180
2009	3.40	9	84	180
2010	3.50	9	78	178
2011	3.40	11	80	183
2012	3.70	8	88	176
2013	3.50	8	102	178

Source: www.transparency.org/ and www.transparency-thailand.org (accessed April 15, 2015).

12 Legal system related to corruption control and corruption causes in Thailand

Sirirat Vasuvat

12.1 Introduction

In Thailand corruption is a parasite of society. It has existed for a long time. It has long degraded the Thai nation in terms of national development, its political, administrative, economic and social systems and, most significantly, the security of the nation as a whole, in the worst possible way. Corruption is not only a small bribe gained by an official, it is also the receipt of huge amounts of money by a politician for abusing power in some significant project.

The purpose of this chapter is to provide a practitioner analysis of the situation and problems of the legal system related to corruption control and corruption causes in Thailand, and solutions to them. It has four main topics: the background of corruption in Thailand; current problems relating to corruption in the criminal justice system and their solutions at the investigation, prosecution and trial levels; solutions for these problems; and general measures to prevent corruption.

12.2 Background of corruption in Thailand

On October 14, 1973 many people, including students from schools and universities, united in a campaign to fight for democracy and free the country from military dictatorship, resulting in a catastrophe in Thailand. As a consequence, a number of facts were revealed to the public through the media. Most people found that government servants and state officials had sought personal benefits from their positions and duties on a large scale: some of those who had the power and duty to solve the problem failed to take any form of serious action; some of them even participated in committing the offenses, while others tried to impede and oppose corruption, but were unable to make a breakthrough. Even worse, quite a few of them were so badly harmed that they were deprived of their future. This is not only because at that time the laws to suppress corruption were not effective enough to enable decisive measures to be taken, but because there were many other dark influences that intimidated those whose duty it was to carry out investigations and suppression efficiently, too. Hence, corruption became widely acknowledged as a major issue with a disastrous effect on national development as a whole.

Such awareness of the noxious effects of corruption then began to show up in the form of national policy. The Constitution of the Kingdom of Thailand of 1974,

Section 66, stated: "the State should organize efficient systems of government service and other functions of the state and should take all steps to prevent and suppress the quest for benefits by corrupt means."

Nevertheless, the aftermath of the 1973 uprising split Thai politics down the middle. On the one hand, the incident was viewed as the origin of a representative democratic system. On the other, the protest was regarded as a means through which business barons gained political power. National development plans designed by the central government had widened the income gap in society. The parliamentary system was incapable of meeting the needs of the people, the government lacked freedom to chart a course for the country, and the public was given only a limited say in policymaking.

The government and some members of parliament perceived the need for special legislation and for a special commission to tackle the problem of corruption in particular. Thus, Thailand's first Counter Corruption Act was passed in 1975 and the Office of the Counter Corruption Commission of (OCCC) was established under the Office of the Prime Minister. However the OCCC had very little power to combat corruption because its jurisdiction was limited.

In 1996 the Constitution Drafting Assembly was founded, comprised 99 members directly selected from representatives in the provinces elected by Parliament. This was a significant political development because the Constitution of the Kingdom of Thailand B.E. 2540 (1997), which was enacted a year later, acknowledged the rights and liberties of Thai people to a greater extent than ever before and the Organic Act on Counter Corruption B.E. 2542, passed in 1999, should serve as an effective means to prevent and combat corruption in Thai society, according to the Constitution.

However, in 1997 Thailand suffered a financial crash. In the period leading up to the crisis, Thai people readily adopted Western-style capitalism, which created an internal contradiction because they retained the traditional system of patronage networks, a system built on personal connections to allocate assets and resources. Though personal connections could be innocent, when they became a factor in public affairs they could be deadly because patronage was not based on merit and tended to breed inefficiency and corruption. To avoid this, the decision process must be transparent and open to scrutiny. The people involved, too, must be transparent and open to scrutiny. Citizens must be given free access to all information pertaining to public policies and projects. It was widely acknowledged that the absence of verifiable integrity both within government and in the private sector contributed enormously to the problem, with discussion and analysis of the role of corruption in bringing about the collapse of the country's economic base.

Apart from the 1999 Organic Act on Counter Corruption, the organizations responsible for preventing and combating corruption, as well as ensuring the rights and liberties of the people, were established under the Constitution and were as follows:

1   the Constitutional Court
2   the Election Commission

3   the Ombudsman
4   the State Audit Commission
5   the Administrative Court.

In addition, there were many laws that implemented justice and law enforcement such as:

1   the Official Information Act 1998
2   the Anti-Money Laundering Act 1999
3   the Offenses relating to the Submission of Bids to State Agencies Act 1999 (Thailand 1999)
4   the Management of Partnership Stakes and Shares of Ministers Act 2000.

12.3 Current problems relating to corruption in the criminal justice system and their solutions

There are many forms of corruption in Thailand. One is a corruption network in government procurement, for large and small projects alike. This involves behavior on the part of public sector officials, whether politicians or civil servants, whereby they improperly and unlawfully enrich themselves or their associates through the misuse of the power entrusted to them.

Corruption is seen as a specific type of violation of integrity, a violation of the accepted moral standards and values of political and administrative behavior. A number of integrity violations or forms of public misconduct can be distinguished:

- *corruption: bribing* (misuse of public power for private gain; asking, offering accepting bribes);
- *corruption: patronage* (misuse of public authority to favor friends, family, party);
- *fraud and theft* (improper private gain acquired from the organization; no involvement of external actors);
- *conflict of private and public interest* (personal interest—through assets, jobs, gifts etc.—interferes with public interest);
- *improper methods for good causes* (to use illegal/improper methods to achieve organizational goals).

The agency responsible for countering corruption is the National Anti-Corruption Commission (NACC). To investigate cases of corruption involving politicians, ranking state officials, and members of local administration organizations, the NACC employs *the first law*—the 1999 Organic Act on Counter Corruption.

When the NACC receives complaints about the corruption or malfeasance of unusually wealthy of state officials—the prime minister, ministers, members of the House of Representatives and senators—it appoints a sub-committee or investigator to investigate facts and gather evidence.

According to the Act, when the NACC decides there is a case to answer, the chairman refers the case to the Attorney-General to start legal proceedings and submit the issue to the Supreme Court of Justice's Criminal Division for Persons Holding Political Positions.

Nowadays, there is a new type of corruption called "private corruption"—abuse of power for personal benefit. "Private-to-private" corruption means giving or receiving an improper advantage in the course of business activities of a nature that leads to acts in breach of a person's duties.

The NACC is having trouble coping with counter-corruption, especially at the investigation and prosecution levels. Such problems are related to:

1   *Legislation*

    1.1   In addition to suppressing corruption in accordance with the 1997 Constitution of the Kingdom of Thailand and the 1999 Organic Act on Counter Corruption, the NACC also has duties and missions according to the Offenses Relating to the Submission of Bids to State Agencies Act, passed in 1999. In actual fact, at first neither Act was designed to be under the jurisdiction of the NACC. Therefore, the resulting scope handled by the NACC is wide-ranging and the workload is quite heavy.

    1.2   Some sections of the Organic Act on Counter Corruption stipulate that the NACC performs several duties on its own, which has caused further inconvenience. For example:

- it was determined that only NACC members can chair sub-committees of inquiry, and delays result when there are a large number of cases to be examined;
- only the injured party can request that criminal proceedings are taken against the person holding the political position.

2   *Inspection of assets and liabilities*

Under the Organic Act on Counter Corruption, anyone in a political position such as prime minister, minister, member of the House of Representatives, senators, governor of Bangkok Metropolitan, as well as certain executive members and members of local government organizations, shall submit to the NACC an account detailing their assets and liabilities and those of their spouse and children who have not yet become *sui juris* on the date of submission. The submission must be made within 30 days of the date of taking office, of the date of leaving office and one year after leaving office.

The persons holding a political position and state officials who intentionally fail to submit their accounts on time or submit documents containing false statements or fail to disclose facts which should have been disclosed will be dismissed from their post and be barred from holding a position for five years. This kind of offense must be submitted to the Constitutional Court for a final decision.

If it appears from the inspection that anyone holding a political position has an unusual increase in assets, the NACC Chairman will pass the report to the prosecutor-general for prosecution in the Supreme Court of Justice's Criminal Division for Persons Holding Political Positions so that the proceeds of the unusual increase in assets may devolve on the State.

Moreover, state officials such as the president and vice-president of the supreme court of justice, president and vice-president of the supreme administration court, prosecutor-general, ombudsman and persons holding high ranking positions (director-general level and above) have to submit to the NACC an account detailing their assets and liabilities and those of their spouse and children who have not yet become *sui juris*. The submission must be done within 30 days of the date of taking office, every three years, and within 30 days of leaving office.

Currently, the NACC has trouble inspecting the accuracy and the actual existence of assets and liabilities because of a shortage of real time information systems. The NACC needs the cooperation of other related agencies in both the public sector—Department of Land, Land Transport Department, Revenue Department—and the private sector, e.g., the commercial banks, in gathering all the evidence of intentionally falsifying or omitting particulars of assets and liabilities and in acquiring the relevant supporting documents in time.

Any statement, fact or information obtained as a result of the performance of duties under this Organic Act cannot be disclosed, except by the Cabinet, which is another obstacle to the cooperation of citizens and other professionals in the investigation.

3   *Fact finding, prosecution and trial*

- In conducting the fact-finding inquiry, the NACC must appoint a sub-committee which should consist of one member of the NACC, since there are a large number of cases to be scrutinized.
- The administrative and staffing problems stem from the fact that the organizational structure and staff development plan were only completed in April 2000, after the enactment of the Organic Act on Counter Corruption that confirmed the establishment of a single agency, i.e., the NACC. Consequently, all the work became the responsibility of NACC.

12.4 Solving these problems

The new (2011) Organic Act on Counter Corruption was derived from the Constitution of the Kingdom of Thailand B.E. 2550 (2007). Under the Constitution, the 1999 Organic Act should continue to be effective. In addition, the Chairman of the National Anti-Corruption Commission (NACC) was responsible for supervising and developing the Organic Act in a manner consistent with the Constitution within one year of the Constitution being promulgated.

It should be noted that the 1997 Constitution and the 2007 Constitution provide different rules for the scrutiny of the exercise of state powers. This is especially true for the provisions that allow the NACC to examine a person in a high-ranking position, and to appoint a Provincial Anti-Corruption Committee. Currently, since corruption offenses and misconduct are extremely complicated and fragmented it is necessary for NACC to improve its operational efficiency and enhance its control mechanisms in order to prevent and combat cases of corruption.

Thus, the new Organic Act on Counter Corruption does not only enhance the work of inspection, but it also provides benefits directly to people to participate in preventing and suppressing corruption. These measures have substantially helped to encourage public participation and political accountability.

The 2011 Organic Act contains three amendments to the Organic Act on Counter Corruption B.E. 2542 (1999): (1) Inclusion of a provision for the Provincial Anti-Corruption Commissions; (2) Improvement and enhancement of operational efficiency; and (3) Strengthening of corruption prevention and suppression.

12.4.1   Inclusion of a provision for the Provincial Anti-Corruption Commissions

Pursuant to the Constitution of the Kingdom of Thailand B.E. 2550 (2007), Provincial Anti-Corruption Commissions should be established. The qualifications, selection process, and powers and duties of Provincial Anti-Corruption Commission members are provided by the Organic Act on Counter Corruption.

Under the new Organic Act, Provincial Anti-Corruption Commissions should consist of no less than three members and no more than five members, as determined by the NACC. Provincial Anti-Corruption Commissions are composed of the chair and other qualified members appointed by the NACC. Provincial Anti-Corruption Commission members hold office for a term of four years from the date of their appointment, and serve for only one term. Furthermore, a Selection Committee composed of nine members drawn from representatives of provincial agencies and provincial organizations has to be established.

The duty of the Provincial Anti-Corruption Commissions is to prevent and combat corruption offenses. The provincial anti-corruption commissioners must therefore create mechanisms to facilitate the active involvement and participation of the public. They are responsible for establishing mechanisms to encourage participation by individuals or in collaboration with stakeholders from all sectors to prevent and combat corruption. The Commissions have to cooperate with the government sector to promote honesty and to disseminate knowledge about the prevention of corruption. Furthermore, the provincial commissioners may propose recommendations to prevent corruption that would be useful to the NACC in its fight against corruption. Additionally, they can lighten the work load of the NACC. For example: undertaking the preliminary stage of a fact-finding inquiry into allegations against a state official; gathering preliminary evidence to pass to the NACC for consideration; checking the accuracy and the actual existence of or changes in assets and liabilities of a person that has a duty to submit an account (showing particulars of their assets and liabilities) to the NACC. The NACC is responsible for setting the criteria and procedures the Provincial Anti-Corruption Commissions must comply with.

In addition, members of the Provincial Anti-Corruption Commissions must submit an account to the NACC showing particulars of their assets and liabilities, which may be inspected by the public. A group of at least 5,000 voters has the right to lodge a complaint with the NACC alleging that a provincial commission member has acted unjustly, intentionally violated the Constitution or the law or has been involved in any circumstance which is seriously detrimental to the dignity of their office. If this complaint has foundation, the NACC may decide on the termination of that member's mandate.

12.4.2 Improvement and enhancement of operational efficiency

12.4.2.1 Improvement in the operational efficiency of the inspection of assets and liabilities process

a   The procedures for submitting an account showing particulars of assets and liabilities. Under the 1999 Organic Act, declarers had to submit an account showing particulars of their assets and liabilities and those of their spouse and children who had not yet become *sui juris*, including assets and liabilities in foreign countries and those which were not in the possession of the declarers as they *actually exist on the date of submission*.

However, under the new Organic Act, declarers have to submit an account to the NACC showing particulars of their assets and liabilities, *actually in existence over the duration of their term of office and upon leaving office*. This includes assets and liabilities in foreign countries and those that are not in possession of the declarers. In addition to the submission mentioned above, once they have left office declarers have to resubmit an account showing particulars of assets and liabilities, *actually in existence one year after* they have left office.

b   The declaration of accounts has been revised regarding whose particulars and liabilities are disclosed to the public. Pursuant to the 1999 Organic Act, only the prime minister and the minister had to submit accounts that would be disclosed to the public. However, under the 2007 Constitution, accounts from members of the House of Representatives and the Senate can also be disclosed to the public. However, the accounts of persons holding other positions do not have to be disclosed unless the disclosure will be useful for court hearings and adjudication of cases or unless the account owner consents.

c   The court that has adjudication power over claims that a person holding a political position intentionally fails to submit an account detailing assets and liabilities within the legal time limit, or intentionally submits such accounts containing false statements or concealing facts that should be disclosed. Under these circumstances, instead of referring the matter to the Constitutional Court for a final decision, the new law stipulates that such matters should be submitted to the Supreme Court of Justice's Criminal Division for Persons Holding Political Positions, for further decision.

Consequently, if the Supreme Court of Justice's Criminal Division for Persons Holding Political Positions rules that a person holding a political position has committed the offense of intentionally failing to submit the account detailing their assets and liabilities within the time prescribed by law, or has submitted the account containing false statements or failed to disclose facts that should be stated, such a person shall leave their posts on the date that the court rules in the case. Moreover, any person who has committed such an offence shall be prohibited from holding any political position or holding any position in a political party for five years from the date of the decision.

d   In order to increase the effectiveness of checking the accuracy and the actual existence of or changes in assets and liabilities, the NACC must examine any financial transaction or acquisition of assets and liabilities. In certain circumstances, the NACC can request that such assets will devolve upon the state if;

- there is reasonable cause to suspect or, under the circumstances, it is apparent that, a person has unlawfully acquired of assets or liabilities, or
- any transaction can be reasonably believed to involve the transfer, disposal, removal, concealment or hiding of any property that is connected with an offense, or
- it appears that assets, which are held by another person on the individual's behalf, have increased abnormally.

Under the inspection of assets and liabilities, NACC has the power to request information related to the financial transactions of such a person from the Anti-Money Laundering Office (AMLO) or financial institutions or from a person with a duty to report the financial transaction. Furthermore, in cases where it is necessary to inspect of the accuracy or change of assets and liabilities, the NACC can exercise any of its powers, including the power of the Transaction Committee as specified by the provisions of the Anti-Money Laundering Act.

e   The NACC has had its power increased to undertake temporary seizure or attachment of property, if they suspect that the assets of a person in a political position have seen an unusual increase. In these circumstances, the Chairman shall furnish all existing documents together with the inspection report to the Attorney-General to institute an action in the Supreme Court of Justice's Criminal Division for Persons Holding Political Positions, at the time that the Supreme Court has not made any order.

12.4.2.2 *Corruption suppression*

To facilitate the work of the NACC, make it more efficient and increase its flexibility, revisions have been made to its fact-finding rules and procedures, as follows:

a   Before conducting the "fact-finding inquiry," the NACC must undertake an exploratory exercise. The NACC may entrust the task of gathering evidence that will be duly used in the fact-finding inquiry procedure to the Secretary-General of the National Anti-Corruption Commission (Secretary-General). The Secretary-General may subsequently appoint competent officials to carry out the fact-finding on his behalf.

b   Fact-finding inquiry

- With reference to the 1999 Organic Act, if there is a case to appoint an inquiry sub-committee, one of the NACC members shall be chairman of the sub-committee for all purposes. Nonetheless, under the 2011 amended Organic law, a Commission member is particularly required to act as chairman when conducting a fact-finding inquiry on important matters related to removal from office of and criminal proceedings against persons in political positions.
- The NACC may entrust the task of gathering evidence for criminal proceedings against state officials to a competent official from the Office of the National Anti-Corruption Commission. Moreover, the NACC has the power to determine the rules, procedures and conditions the said official must comply with.
- The NACC or its Chairman is required to submit a motion to the court in certain circumstances, such as the referral of the case to the Supreme Court of Justice's Criminal Department for Persons Holding Political Positions for further decision in a case where a person holding a political position deliberately does not submit an account detailing assets and liabilities or intentionally submits such account containing false statements, or where the Chairman of the NACC refers the case to the Attorney-General to instigate legal proceedings against state officials. But if the Attorney-General holds that there is sufficient evidence to submit the issue to the court and a joint working group of the Attorney-General's office and the NACC is unable to reach a decision as to the prosecution, the NACC shall have the power to appoint an inquiry official. This person must be a practicing barrister or hold a law degree, and have acquired experience relevant to the performance of duties in court proceedings. Such a person will prosecute on the NACC's behalf.

c   A new mechanism has been introduced to improve working functionality. For the purpose of accessing data or information (on a person), the NACC is authorized to request agencies or financial institutions to help the NACC or its sub-committee to inquire into the facts pertinent to the alleged culprit, or a person believed to be involved in the allegation. In a case where the NACC finds that some types of information are inaccessible, it may file a motion requesting an order from the court to access such information.

d   A change has been made to the trial procedures in cases of corruption offenses committed by a state official. In these circumstances, the court has to decide cases on the basis of the inquisitorial system, and its decision is based on the report documents and inquiry files compiled by the NACC. If necessary, the court may conduct further inquiries to gather facts and supporting evidence for the case.

e   Regarding criminal proceedings against state officials, if an alleged culprit has fled during a trial, the periods of prescription are suspended while they are at liberty.

12.4.3   Strengthening of corruption prevention and suppression

12.4.3.1   Protection

a   The NACC may implement measures to protect an injured person, a person who prepares a request or makes an allegation, a deponent, and a whistle-blower who provides any information on corruption offenses or unusual increase in wealth, or any other information that would be useful to the NACC.

b   Regarding protection procedures, the NACC can ask concerned agencies to establish measures to protect the person in (a), who is a witness and must be given protection under the law of witness protection in criminal cases. The NACC can at the same time advise the agency as to whether general or special protection should be provided.

c   Protection may be extended to a person other than the person in (a), if a criminal offense is committed intentionally and such an offense injures the life, body, health, reputation or any right of an ascending or descending relative, spouses, or a person otherwise closely associated with the person defined in (a). The aforesaid person, who testifies or provides the NACC with any clue or information on corruption-related offenses, will be entitled to file a request to the relevant agencies for compensation commensurate with necessity and reasonability.

d   In the case where the person in (a) is a state official and makes a request to the NACC to the effect that they may be treated unfairly or unjustly if they continue to perform their official duties. When the NACC has found convincing evidence of unfair treatment it can submit the case to the prime minister to consider a protection order or other appropriate measures to protect such person.

12.4.3.2   Awards

a   In accordance with the regulations prescribed by the NACC, it may make awards or offer benefits to any person who is not a state official and who makes an allegation or provides any clue or information concerning corruption-related offenses.

b   In the case of a person testifying or providing any clue or information concerning corruption-related offences, the NACC may recommend and submit to the prime minister special salary increments and promotion for that person. The prime minister will consider and decide upon the matter. Moreover, upon the approval of the Council of Ministers and in accordance with the regulations prescribed by the NACC, the individual's merit will be publicly announced and praised as a positive role model for state officials and the people.

c A person, who testifies or provides any clue or information concerning corruption-related offences may make a request to the NACC to submit a petition to the prime minister, when there is convincing evidence that they may be treated unfairly or unjustly if they continue to perform their official duties. In these circumstances, the prime minister will consider a protection order or appropriate measures to protect such person.

12.4.3.3 *Calling a person as a witness*

a Calling a person as a witness is an effective way to encourage and strengthen anti-corruption attitudes. An alleged culprit or a person alleged to have committed an offense with state officials may be called to be a witness.

b A person who has been called as a witness has to testify and to provide information or material facts on a corruption offense. The witness statement will be used as evidence, and the hearing will take place on the basis of this statement. Where the NACC deems it advisable to call someone as a witness, under the rules, procedures and conditions considered by the NACC such person may not be prosecuted for the offense.

12.4.3.4 *Establishing supplementary preventive measures against corruption*

a The government agency will provide information on procurement expenses, particularly the information related to median procurement prices and methods for the calculation of the median price. The procurement information will be stored electronically since it must be available for public inspection.

b Where a government agency enters into a contract with legal person or private individual, such person will become a party to the contract with the state and will also have a duty to disclose to the Revenue Department for inspection an account showing any income and expenses relating to the project that is the subject of the contract with the state.

12.5 General measures to prevent corruption

Although corruption has had a negative impact on Thai society for many decades, it has been uncontrollable. Efforts to deal with corruption in the past may not have been carried out in a systematic manner. Suppression but not prevention of corruption was undertaken. To successfully combat corruption, abuse of power and malpractice, all related agencies in the public sector, private sector and people network will have to fight corruption with determination, patience, and commitment to cooperation. Moreover, the country's leaders should take the corruption problems seriously by giving high and real priority to ratification procedures and to the transposition of the new rules into national legislation. The Commission, the Council and Parliament should seize every opportunity to draw the attention of national authorities to the need to speed up implementation of the agreed rules. Financial resources should be invested in concrete measures to prevent and curb corruption in the country. Such measures include raising awareness of the damaging effects of corruption, and highlighting the political and economic framework conditions which indirectly contribute to countering corruption.

The Thai people must not see money as supreme when it comes to having a better life. Nowadays some Thai citizens do not understand this; they have perceived money as being the basis of power, prestige and fame regardless of how wealth is amassed, and so riches are seen as an end in themselves. Whenever corruption becomes a component of life in Thai social values, society is weakened. Such a troubled society will have poor potential for national development as a whole. Therefore, prevention of corruption needs to be tackled urgently in terms of its root causes in Thai culture and the value structure.

The key element to preventing and suppressing corruption is public awareness. This can be encouraged through public hearings, involvement of the public in brainstorming sessions, debates, meetings and conferences, as well as public investigation. Moreover, honesty is one of the significant elements which should be instilled in Thai citizens' consciousness to counteract corruption. As for the National Anti-Corruption Commission in Thailand, it emphasizes educating people of every age especially the youth, the group of citizens that has been powerful in driving the country's development.

Hence, to successfully eradicate corruption in the long term, the country needs a strong impetus from all related sectors to:

- review and rationalize legislation and administration to enable them to deal with the change in their environment that leads to increasing demands and expectations from the private and public sectors;
- improve the system of oversight that unwaveringly enforces the regulations and laws;
- implement strong social sanctions against corruption;
- create social mechanisms that will make corruption a very difficult and risky business;
- instill citizens with awareness of sound values and self-esteem;
- educate the people to understand the detrimental effect of corruption;
- stimulate the public to be the clean alliance and have the confidence to cooperate in reporting information and giving evidence;
- establish rewards and protection for witnesses;
- build up attitudes, values (what is good to do or bad not to do), morals and ethics (the principles that provide a framework for action) concerning integrity (the quality of acting in accordance ("solidarity") with the values, norms and rules accepted by the body politic and the public); and
- install good governance by reforming the bureaucracy for transparency, efficiency, and accountability.

13 Fighting corruption with strategy

Pedro Nevado and Frederico Cavazzini

13.1 Introduction

Corruption is known for its many faces. It can also take various forms and meanings. Some term it a "tax on economic growth" and nobody knows for certain how much it is worth, but a conservative approach based on worldwide surveys of enterprises and other governance and anti-corruption diagnostic surveys, gives an estimate for annual worldwide bribery at about US $1 trillion dollars.[1] This figure does not cover every form of corruption, such as the global extent of embezzlement in the public sector,[2] which means that a more comprehensive estimate of worldwide corruption would be even higher.

The first studies on the phenomenon, although important and a key step in raising awareness among the general public, were weak in terms of measurement and quantification. Assessments based on perceptions of corruption and governance in countries only surfaced after the mid-1990s, mainly driven by the emerging market investment interests of large multinational companies. As a result of globalization and the growing awareness among multinational companies of the hazardous impact of corruption on investment, growth and poverty reduction and, therefore, on successfully achieving their goals, the phenomenon of corruption became regarded as an effective barrier to global, regional and local economic development.

The pressing need to study and combat corruption is also rooted in the acknowledgement that the predominance of dubious practices in a country undermines both confidence in its private sector and the quality of public institutions, which is neither good for investment nor for development. Generally, an honest investor prefers to avoid markets that collude in illegal forms of wealth generation and is more inclined to invest in more transparent ones, rather than incur the risk of international disapproval and the loss of credibility associated with bribery, for example.

Thus, corruption is not only an obstacle to social development but also to economic growth because it drives the private sector out. When it does not, in most cases, it makes investing in a corrupt country more expensive than in a transparent one. The improvement in quantitative studies and research in this field has provided the means to address the problem more frontally. Indeed, public sector reforms over the last decade seem to have placed strong emphasis on anti-corruption measures. But is it possible to quantify a phenomenon that proliferates worldwide largely due to its "transparency," that is, invisibility? What are the conditions that favor the spread of this socio-economic disease? Is there a trustworthy model that could, to any extent, identify these conditions and predict their occurrence?

In order to discuss this issue, the first section of the chapter reviews the theory on corruption related to the search for a formula to fight corruption, focusing on its most relevant causes and how it is currently measured. Then, an original conceptualized framework to understand and fight corruption is put forward, in which the level of education combined with access to information play a decisive role in sustaining the ability to claim political and social accountability. Based on these main findings, the chapter concludes with a set of recommendations with practical implications.

It should be noted that this study only explores the relationship between the perception of experts with regard to corruption and the level of education and access to information for a sample of sub-Saharan African countries (SSA), as the effects of corruption tend to be more dramatic in these countries. It does not provide a one-size-fits-all formula nor does it aim to identify all the potential variables that influence the intensity of corruption in SSA as measured by the Corruption Perceptions Index. The corruption phenomenon is complex and hard to summarize at such a global level with the available data. Nevertheless, this study provides some preliminary evidence of the above-mentioned relationship which could be further explored in future empirical studies.

13.2   Literature review

13.2.1   *Corruption: what is it and what are its causes?*

According to Llaca (2005), Aristotle was the first to use the word corruption to describe the tyranny, oligarchy and populism associated with the breakdown taking place in royalist and democratic governments. Cicero added the terms bribe and the abandonment of good habits. Thus, corruption could be defined as the renunciation of the ethics, morality, law and good habits of the country where a person lives. In line with Morris (1991), corruption is usually associated to the illegitimate use of public power to benefit a private interest. However, the UN Convention against Corruption typifies corruption as an illegal activity whether in the public or the private sector and therefore considers there is no definition for the concept. Corruption has, nevertheless, existed since the very origins of humankind.

More recently, Senior (2006), after detailed research on more than one hundred definitions and studies on corruption from various authors in the past 30 years, condensed the five most representative elements into his definition of corruption: (a) to secretly provide (b) a good or a service to a third party (c) so that he or she can influence certain actions (d) which benefit the corrupt, a third party, or both (e) in which the corrupt agent has authority. It is a definition somewhat independent of any values, laws, customs, which can therefore be applied to any public or private institution. Thus, it values certain characteristics that for Ocampo (1993) are innate in humans, such as greed and selfishness, for example, although the author also adds contextual causes for corruption, such as elections, lack of control, and opportunity.

As Campos and Pradhan (2007) state, if the expected benefits of a corrupt transaction outweigh its expected costs, an individual will be enticed to perform this transaction. This interpretation becomes important especially when subjective data is considered to be unreliable in the measurement of corruption. However Kaufmann *et al.* (2005) acknowledge the role of information as equally important, whether objective or subjective, in the sense that either always includes some element of uncertainty.

The recognition that all information is relevant, including subjective information, refocuses the fight against corruption around the conditions by which it tends to become more powerful. According to Llaca (2005), corruption is fertilized by the asymmetry in the control of information between the public servant and the common citizen. Hence, personal power in excess may generate inefficiencies in the monitoring processes, therefore promoting corruption, as stated by Batista (2000), as a result of judicial system inefficiencies and operational monitoring. In this regard, Klitgaard *et al.* (1996) believe that corruption is also the result of weak civil society participation, the discretion associated with the centralization of power and distortion of the electoral system, party system and financing of parties. In addition to these socio-economic, legal and political causes, there are also other factors, such as the cultural, for example. Indeed, Klitgaard (1994) suggests there are cultures that encourage corruption and Llaca (2005) uses the Mexican example, where there is some popular admiration for employees who become unlawfully wealthy. In this sense, the culture and traditional forms of organization that reduce the quality and effectiveness of the state are also drivers of corruption (Senior 2006). Furthermore, the idea of "white collar" impunity— that the disclosure of illegal behavior will fall on shallow ground—and that justice is slow and ineffective are cultural products and pre-conceptions of developing societies as more affected by corruption after long years of bad governance and bad rulers.

However, in this relationship between the definition and cause of corruption, Rose-Ackerman (1978, 1999), Klitgaard (1998) and Klitgaard *et al.* (1996) pioneered a systematization of four factors that tend to bring about corruption: monopoly power; a wide margin for discretion, a lack of transparency in decision-making and a lack of accountability for decisions made. This finding has enabled the development of strategies to combat corruption and also the introduction of rational approaches to understanding the motivations that push its practice.

13.2.2   *Corruption: How is it measured today?*

Looking at the benefits obtained, it seems that corruption is easily felt and perceived. However, it is difficult to trace and measure. In recent years, the

World Bank has been actively trying to measure the phenomenon of corruption. Although, as Kaufmann (2005) acknowledges, there are still significant difficulties, with high margins of error. At the end of the 1990s, the World Bank Institute (WBI) developed a set of aggregate indicators that cover various areas of governance, such as control of corruption monitoring, rule of law, government effectiveness, quality of regulation, accountability, and peace and political stability,[3] enabling a macro-level causal relationship between corruption and poor governance to be established.

Furthermore, the Corruption Perceptions Index (CPI), published annually by Transparency International[4] since 1995, although not measuring corruption in an objective manner, does rank it objectively among approximately 180 countries. The ranking is based on triangulated and demanding information from at least three different sources of information, on a scale from 0 to 10, where 0 means a country is perceived as highly corrupt and 10 means very transparent.[5] Thanks to the CPI, not only has it become clear that there is significant correlation between corruption and poverty but that corruption can also be high in developed countries (Transparency International 2008).

The widely cited research on corruption by Mauro (1998a) chooses the International Country Risk Guide (ICRG) as its indicator of corruption. Developed by the PRS Group, this corruption index is based on people's perceptions of governments through a set of 22 components grouped into three major categories of risk: political, financial and economic. However, relying solely on people's perceptions may not provide the big picture in some countries, especially in those where corruption has become a cultural product or where there is a lack of access to information, civic participation and freedom of expression. Their citizens are thus provided with a biased perception of the real situation. Many of these countries are located in the target region of this study (SSA) which is why the ICRG was not chosen as the indicator of corruption.

The Ibrahim Index of African Governance, funded by the Mohamed Ibrahim Foundation, is designed to reflect and monitor the nature of governance in Africa. It uses a number of different indicators to compile an overall ranking of countries, including accountability, education and freedom of expression indicators.

Another contribution to the measurement of corruption is put forward by Klitgaard (1994), who developed an equation that explains the likelihood of corruption according to three variables: monopoly, discretion and accountability. As Klitgaard puts it: corruption is a crime of calculation, not of passion, and people tend to engage in corrupt acts when risks are low, penalties are light and compensation is high (Klitgaard *et al.* 1996, 2000). Based on this premise: C (corruption) = M (monopoly) + D (discretionary power) − A (accountability).

According to Klitgaard *et al.* (1996), corruption tends to be more evident when individuals wield monopoly power over a particular good or service, unlimited discretion to decide who receives the good or service and how much they pay for it, as well as when there is no form of accountability able to control (whether by auditing or monitoring) how these decisions were made. And this rule applies to both the public and private sectors, in rich or poor countries. Closely linked to the three variables influencing corruption in Klitgaard's formula is the concept of transparency. When reinforced by greater participation, transparency contributes to containing monopoly power as well as perverse uses of discretion, while instilling greater accountability in decision-making.

13.2.2.1   A new strategy in the fight against corruption

The variables considered by Klitgaard—monopoly, discretion, and accountability —are sustained by our research and by much of the existing literature. In economics, the term monopoly (from Greek *monos*, one, and *polein*, to sell) is used "when a specific individual or enterprise has sufficient control over a particular product or service to determine significantly the terms on which other individuals shall have access to it" (Friedman 2002: 208). This thus provides fertile ground for corruption to grow, particularly when combined with discretionary power, defined as the ability to make decisions arbitrarily, based on judgments and criteria defined by those making the decision.[6]

Accountability is more than responsibility since it implies that other people are also involved. Accountability means that someone has a stake in whether or not the desired result is achieved. In other words, accountability is a promise to oneself and others to deliver specific, defined results with consequences (Stagl 2009). The greater the absence of rule of law, unable to hold individuals accountable for their actions or to dissolve supremacy relations which jeopardize the right to equality and freedom between two parties, the greater the likelihood that corruption will flourish.

Focusing only on the three original variables, Kiltgaard's formula has importance and validity. It is a simple, straightforward equation. It draws attention to the importance of promoting transparency, participation and accountability at all levels (local, regional and national). Also, it suggests that there are a number of activities that should be carried out by various actors at different levels, rather than concentrated on one or several actors at the same level. Finally, it claims that by changing the incentives, corruption is changed. Hence, Klitgaard's formula is not intended as a mechanism to detect and punish the unethical behavior of individuals or even eradicate corruption. It serves rather to study and identify ways to change the environment that promotes the incidence of corruption.

This framework of corruption can prove very useful for decision-makers developing anti-corruption strategies that meet specific problems by identifying the circumstances that favor the formation of monopolies and discretion and situations where the lack of accountability and transparency increase the risk of corruption (Campos and Pradhan 2007). Nevertheless, it remains too straightforward a mechanism for a phenomenon as complex as corruption. There are other crucial variables in addition to Klitgaard's which should be taken into consideration when implementing strategies to combat corruption.

Despite what Klitgaard's formula may suggest, the existence of only one decision-maker or monopolistic supplier is not in itself a guarantee of highly corrupt activity (monopolistic corruption) nor does market competition equal perfect transparency (competitive corruption). A good example is procurement in the education sector for school construction or provision of equipment, meals, and learning materials, in which corruption can be found before contracts are awarded. It has been found that potential contractors (building contractors and suppliers) offer decision-makers attractive packages, separately or coordinated as a cartel, in order to eliminate competitors.

Even though monopoly creates space for the occurrence of illicit and corrupt activities, perfect competition is not immune to illicit behavior. As pointed out by Savona (1995), both monopolistic and competitive corruption exist and determine the amount of corruption: if the power to influence a decision is exercised by a small group of people, the amount of corruption will be higher than in the case where such power is divided among several decision-makers.

On the one hand, as suggested by Stiglitz (2008), there are always distortions in the free market and, on the other, competition is never completely free, nor are consumers fully informed (Cox 2007). In this sense, equality in consumer decisions does not exist, i.e., the ability to choose is not available to all equally, regardless of the market system operating. Thus:

PROPOSITION 13.1 *Option of Choice. Considering that "the will, in truth, signifies nothing but a power, or ability, to prefer or choose",[7] the lack of that power due to the monopolistic control of goods and services or scarcity of resources means individuals will be deprived of pursuing their interests and benefits and will be confined to the option(s) narrowed down for them.*

As mentioned before, both monopoly and free market competition can lead to adverse and uneven situations. There is no predefined value for the optimal degree of state intervention or market openness for maximizing transparency and social welfare. More important than adopting a more interventionist or more liberal model, there have to be strong institutions, whether there is a minimal state or not, and it is the nature of the markets that defines the form and degree of intervention and not the other way round.

Poor choice options create dependence since not being able to choose confines people to the option(s) narrowed down by another (or others), in most cases, under severe restrictions and often for illicit purposes. However, when there is freedom of choice there is often freedom of information. Hence:

PROPOSITION 13.2 *Freedom of Information. Less informed people, due to deprivation of or difficulty in accessing information, are easily caught in the clutches of corruption. Asymmetric information carries, for example, problems of moral hazard, enabling certain "borrowers" to emerge who encourage struggling institutions to invest in increasingly risky transactions, in turn increasing their dependence. It can actually be one of the key factors causing corruption to proliferate. There can also be problems of adverse selection, in which less attractive investments that are more likely to be unsuccessful drive less risky* *ventures out of the market due to the high cost credit institutions have to face in order to obtain (accurate) information. And last, but not least, "herd behavior" situations can also occur in which the behavior of an individual or group of individuals holding privileged information is followed by others.*

Information brings knowledge and knowledge is power. Therefore, free and easy access to information is an important tool for individual empowerment. Since information and knowledge are two competitive advantage factors, it may be expected that well-informed people will be better positioned to ward off illicit offers with the knowledge of the most effective means to expose corrupt actors and demand rule of law.

Governments can restrict or facilitate information flows through the laws, regulations and codes of conduct they create. Several studies have shown that countries with better information flows often have better quality governance and less corruption (Islam 2006; DiRienzi *et al.* 2007). Higher transparency and access to information are also good for the economy because they provide investors with a better understanding of the behaviors and operations of institutions in a given country and help reduce overall uncertainty, which have been shown to increase investment inflows. The right of access to information within government institutions also strengthens democratic accountability, prevents public power abuses, and improves national resource allocation (Roberts 2002).

Looking at the relationship between democracy and corruption, Treisman (2006) did not find solid evidence that the actual frequency of corrupt interactions is related to democratic institutions. However, there is evidence showing that countries with high levels of democracy and strong free press are perceived to be less corrupt. Also "endogeneity is as great a concern as in the case of economic development. Corruption could itself weaken democratic institutions or could be caused by factors that also undermine democracy" (Treisman 2006: 25).

The use of modern information and communication technologies (ICTs) to improve the efficiency and effectiveness of governance (e-government) has gained increasing popularity, in recent years, due to the acknowledgement of their role in reducing corruption. New technologies such as e-procurement and open data sources, if properly adjusted to the specificities of each sector and made available to the general public represent a valuable tool for good governance. However, these tools are not just about applying technology to existing processes but they entail a more profound reform process which often changes or abolishes long-standing procedures, cultural myths and require a certain level of literacy. Hence:

PROPOSITION 13.3 *Level of Education. Many authors have discussed the impact of corruption in the education sector across the world but few have studied the impact that the level of education in a given country has on its perceived level of corruption. Education is a fundamental human right and a major driver of human and economic development. The moral causes of development lie in a constellation of virtues: labor, power, order, honesty, initiative, thrift, savings,* *spirit of service, honor, courage, work devotion (Moreira 1996) and virtues such as these make a difference between societies and the extent to which they tolerate corruption.*

While we often unfavorably contrast the selfishness of economic actors with the altruism that characterizes the politically and socially involved as a result of a romantic vision of politics, a society based on good habits, morality and ethical values will create an environment ruled by individuals inclined to take actions commonly considered to be good (Fernandes 2009). In this sense, ethics is a tribute to life. It is what gives the fundamental principle of morality, namely, that the right action consists in maintaining, promoting and strengthening life and that destroying, injuring, and restricting life is wrong.[8]

Ethics and education walk hand in hand because the teaching of ethical values and behavior is considered to be a central task of education. As children grow older, they become familiar with corrupt practices but their level of acceptance of such practices will be lower if they realize that bribery and fraud are unethical patterns of behavior. It should be noted, though, that in many developing countries, even among the most educated, petty corruption tends to be more generally accepted (e.g., small bribes) whereas grand corruption (e.g., embezzlement of public funds) tends to be more severely criticized (Chapman 2002).

Education strengthens personal integrity and empowers individuals, just as freedom of information; but while the latter permits access to information, the former helps understand it. Limited access to education—and poor quality—not only inhibits effective accountability and good governance mechanisms but it also leads to a social acceptance of corruption.

The relation between education and economic growth has been the object of several studies in the past. Human capital theories generally acknowledge that education offers a higher probability of obtaining employment, higher productivity and greater wage income. The natural assumption is that investment in education must accelerate economic growth (Blaug 1970).

The number of years of schooling is a leading indicator and contributes to improving people's level of instruction, but for economic growth to take place, it is necessary that this increase in education results in the formation of skilled human capital that is better prepared to produce goods and services, thus incorporating this aggregated knowledge in the productive process (Kenny 2010). Theodore Schultz considers that when the growth of production exceeds the growth of productive factors, it must be the result of human capital investment; he adds that investment in education widens people's range of choices and allows them to increase their level of well-being (Schultz 1961).

Countries with a higher level of human capital tend to achieve higher productivity gains than countries with less human capital, and the rate of technological change and productivity improvement are directly related to the stock of human capital (Hanushek and Woessmann 2010). The stock of human capital is, in turn, determined by the number of years of schooling and level of knowledge attained, among other factors.

For Hanushek, the average student in Ghana or Peru does not achieve the same level of knowledge as the average student in Finland or South Korea, in a given year of schooling, which is why a comparative analysis of this kind should not be conducted on a global scale but within a region. Using the quantitative measure of number of years of schooling assumes that the knowledge gained by both students is equivalent and comes from formal education which does not really apply, for example, to the SSA region. Studies on knowledge formation and cognitive skills show that there are a number of strongly influential external factors to formal schooling and ignoring those factors will distort the analysis of economic growth.

Hanushek's work has shown that cognitive skills are closely related to economic performance over time, not only for individuals but also for countries, with cross-country variations in growth rates largely explained by the level of cognitive skills acquired (Hanushek and Woessmann 2008). In short, modern growth theories highlight human capital as an important input in the creation of new ideas which is a strong enough reason for considering education as a determinant of economic growth.

The relevance of this assumption for our study is that there also seems to be a relationship between corruption and growth, as corruption tends to proliferate in poor economies. The relationship works both ways because corruption increases costs, lowers productivity, discourages investors and concentrates public resources in unproductive projects, ultimately deepening social inequalities and increasing poverty (Mauro 1995). Svendsen (2003) supports these conclusions, arguing that countries with low-level corruption have high GDP levels due to efficient resource provision and Ehrlich and Lui (1999) show that corruption has a negative impact on both growth and GDP per capita. Since corruption and growth are interconnected and education is a determinant of economic growth, what can be said about the relationship between education and corruption?

Cheung and Chan (2008) use several endogenous independent variables (namely, educational, political and economic factors) to examine corruption perceptions in 56 countries and found that both enrollment in tertiary education and GDP per capita can strongly predict corruption perception scores. In other words, the effort educators put into teaching students about social and moral responsibility has a noticeable effect.

Also, Bjørnskov (2003) finds a strong causal link between higher levels of social capital (where education is an indicator) and less corruption. He suggests that social capital can be built by investing in education and other forms of social capital, and improving income redistribution, therefore, reducing corruption.

Again, the relationship between corruption and education can be a two-way street as corrupt practices have a negative impact on the quantity, quality and efficiency of educational services and, consequently, on learning results. Individuals who have a better understanding of their own culture and reality are better equipped to address the complexities of the relations established within the corruption phenomenon and can therefore be more effective when tackling it in their own country.

In this sense, civil society is a crucial element in the fight against corruption because it is itself involved—victim or perpetrator—in corrupt practices. Civil society can, for example, play a monitoring role, disseminate information and demand that corrupt agents be held to account. Sirkku Hellsten and George Larbi (2006) suggest that civic education should be used to spread the values of public service, and the rights and obligations of citizens in society which reinforces the importance of education in the strategy to fight corruption.

13.3 Methodological considerations

This study intends to show that while there is no specific formula to predict the occurrence of corruption, there are variables other than those identified in Klitgaard's equation (monopoly, accountability, discretion) which can and should be considered. It tests the hypothesis that the level of education combined with access to information play a decisive role in sustaining the ability to claim political and social accountability, thus reducing the perception of corruption in a given country.

In order to test this, a corruption index must be selected and regressed on a set of explanatory variables of both a social and economic nature. In addition to education and freedom of expression indexes, other variables such as log GDP per capita, GDP growth and total natural resources rents as a fraction of GDP can be thought of as variables that affect corruption.

It is expected that in countries with high GDP per capita levels and high growth rates there will be less incentives to engage in corrupt activities,[9] and that countries whose economies are dominated by resource extraction industries tend to be more repressive, corrupt and poorly regulated. Our primary interest is in the effects of education and freedom of expression over corruption but the results for the other variables will be discussed as well.

We used a sample of 45 SSA countries[10] (Somalia and Djibouti were excluded due to the systematic lack of data or limited sources of information) for the multiple regressions. The choice for this region was based on the fact that the effects of corruption tend to be more dramatic in SSA in comparison with other regions. Also, the level of knowledge of the average student in SSA and the source of that knowledge (formal, non-formal and informal learning) varies from one region to another, which is why a comparative analysis on a global scale would be hard to conduct and misleading.

It would have been desirable to conduct a time series analysis but data for most variables did not change over time or were based on the most recent reports, so only data for 2011 was gathered (or the closest year available), taken as this study's year of reference.

As mentioned in the previous section, several measures of corruption have been used in modern studies but the most common is the CPI provided by Transparency International, which ranks countries by their perceived levels of corruption, based on expert assessments and opinion surveys. The use of CPI as a solid indicator for empirical studies of corruption does not gather universal consensus, as some critics suggest that the definition of what is legal or illegal is unclear, its statistical value is uncertain and the use of subjective perceptions makes it unreliable.

Yet, the CPI is often used today in published research for analyses on the relationships between corruption, education, and economic variables. Their perception-based scores are believed to be just as strong or even more reliable than any other objective measures, especially in the study of corruption, which is by definition very hard to track and measure. Even when objective data are available, there is often a big gap between the *de jure* rules on which that data is based and the de facto reality that exists. For example, it is illegal for public officials to accept a bribe, whether they are a school teacher or a customs officer, but in many countries, the reality on the ground is very different from the provisions of official legislation.

Looking at the correlation coefficients between different corruption indexes (Transparency International's CPI, Accountability from the Ibrahim Index, and Control of Corruption from the Worldwide Governance Indicators), based on the perceptions provided by enterprise, citizen and expert survey respondents in developed and developing countries (Table 13.1), we see that these indicators are highly correlated, mostly because they use similar data collection methodologies. Therefore, the CPI will be used as the dependent variable in this analysis.

Data on education comes from the Ibrahim Index because its education indicator takes into account more variables (education provision and quality; ratio of pupils to teachers in primary school; primary school completion; progression to secondary school; tertiary enrollment). It also provides a more solid notion of how countries perform and differ from each other, whereas the education component of the Human Development Index strictly focuses on the mean of years of schooling for adults aged 25 years and on the expected years of schooling for children of school-entering age.

To assess freedom of expression, the indicator selected was Freedom of the Press produced by Freedom House. We analyzed other relevant indicators such as Voice and Accountability (Worldwide Governance Indicators) and Freedom of Expression (Ibrahim Index) but since they were strongly correlated (Table 13.2), we opted for the indicator provided by a new source (Freedom of the Press). It should be noted that higher scores in this indicator denote less freedom.

The World Development Indicators (World Bank) provided the data for log GDP per capita (GDPpc), GDP growth (GDPgrowth) and total natural resources

Table 13.1 Correlation coefficients between different corruption indexes

	CPI	*Accountability*	*Control of Corruption*
CPI	1		
Accountability	**0.891**	1	
Control of Corruption	**0.948**	**0.935**	1

Table 13.2 Correlation coefficients between different freedom of expression indexes

	Freedom of Press	Freedom of Expression	Voice and Accountability
Freedom of Press	1		
Freedom of Expression	−0.894	1	
Voice and Accountability	−0.906	0.921	1

Table 13.3 Correlation coefficients of the selected variables

	CPI	Education	FreePress	LogGDPpc	GDPgrowth	Resources
CPI	1					
Education	0.674	1				
FreePress	−0.463	−0.318	1			
LogGDPpc	0.443	0.661	−0.106	1		
GDPgrowth	0.224	0.069	−0.027	−0.037	1	
Resources	−0.383	−0.176	0.286	0.233	0.016	1

rents as a fraction of GDP (resources). Data for the last variable was only available for 2010.

It should be noted that there is no agreement on the "best" indicators to use in the analysis of corruption. In fact, no single model has been developed that can fully cover all the determining factors of corruption, in all its different forms and shapes and, once again, this study will not attempt to do so.

Given the complexity and sectorial permeability of this phenomenon, it makes sense that many different factors will induce or reduce the likelihood of its occurrence and that full consensus on those factors will be hard to achieve. Indicators tend to be chosen based on the specific hypotheses being tested, which is the aim of this study: to determine the impact, if any, that education and access to information in a given country has on the perception of corruption in that same country.

13.4 Results

Before regressing the CPI on a set of explanatory variables, it makes sense to look at the level of correlation between these variables and the dependent variable. Table 13.3 shows that corruption is negatively correlated to education, freedom of expression, GDP per capita, and positively correlated to the total natural resources rents as a fraction of GDP. The correlation between corruption and growth is also negative, although not as expressive as with the other indicators.

It makes sense that countries with higher levels of corruption should be poorer, present obstacles to freedom of expression and suffer from the "resource curse," that is, the paradox that countries rich in natural resources tend to have lower development outcomes and engage in more corrupt activities than countries with fewer natural resources. However, one would expect that lower levels of corruption would be more strongly perceived in fast-growing economies.

Mauro (1995) explains this phenomenon based on the convergence theory which argues that initially poorer economies tend to grow faster which opposes the findings of Ehrlich and Lui (1999) about the negative effect of corruption on both GDP and growth.

The explanatory variables are not strongly correlated among themselves which is positive because the higher the correlation between independent variables, the greater the sampling error of the partials and the more difficult it will be to evaluate their relative importance. Figures 13.1 and 13.2 illustrate the connection between corruption and education and corruption and freedom of expression, which is much stronger in the former. However, it would be too premature to draw any conclusions before considering other variables and see how these two interact and significantly affect corruption or not.

Hence, Table 13.4 shows a set of regressions, each column representing a regression with a new added variable. In the first column, there is a regression using only education as the explanatory variable and the results are positive and highly significant. In other words, countries with a higher level of education have a higher corruption index (which means less perceived corruption).

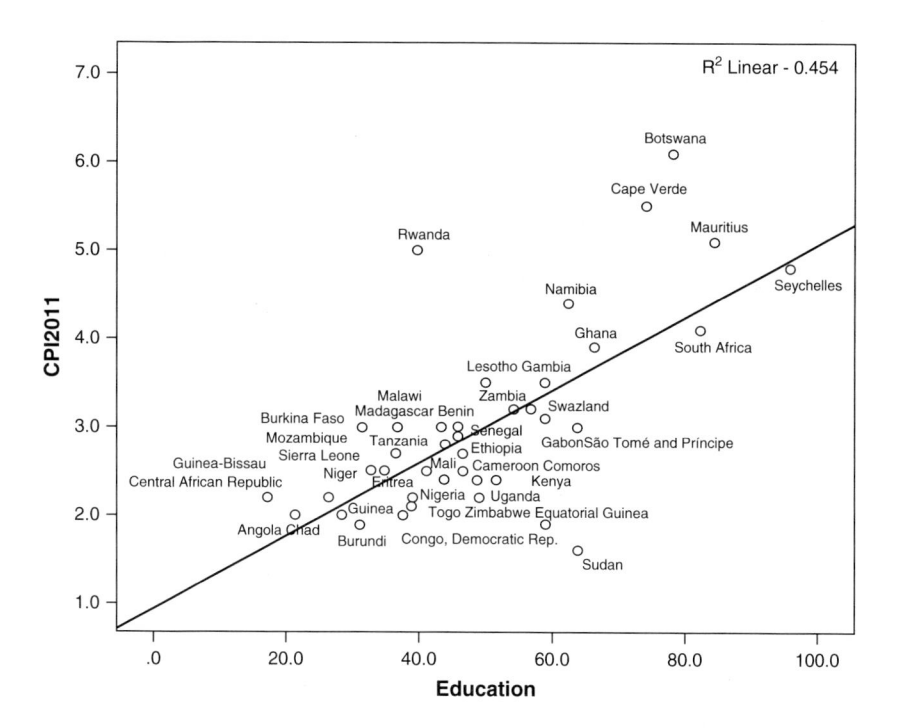

Figure 13.1 Correlation between corruption and education.

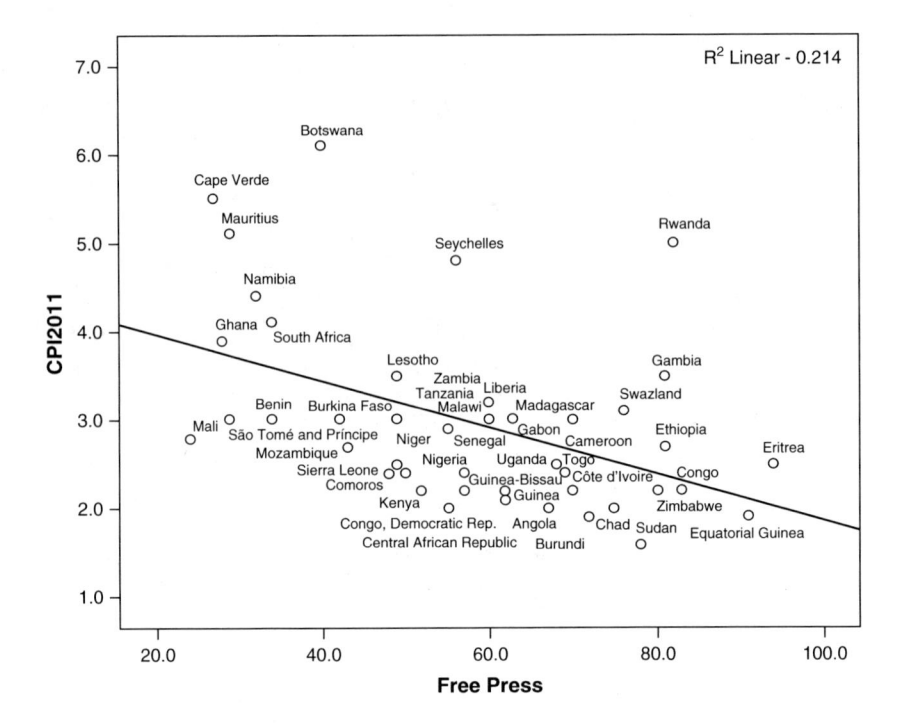

Figure 13.2 Correlation between corruption and free press.

The next column adds the level of freedom of the press and the results again confirm the expectations: countries that score high in this indicator (which means the media is not free) tend to have a low CPI, or are perceived as being less transparent. Education remains a significant explanatory variable of corruption. Next, we consider an economic indicator (GDP per capita) which, as expected, turns out to have a positive effect but not significant. Adding another economic variable (GDP growth) does not affect the significance of education and freedom of the press and only confirms the previous conclusion: in this model, GDP per capita and GDP growth are not significant explanatory variables.

However, in the last column, we take into account the resource curse factor (Resources) which proves to have a negative and significant effect on the CPI, in the sense that countries whose economies rely heavily on natural resource extraction tend to be perceived as more corrupt. While education and freedom of the press remain significant explanatory variables, one interesting aspect is the change in the growth variable which can now provide a significant explanation for changes in perceptions of corruption across SSA countries, if the share of natural resources in those economies is taken into consideration.

Looking at Table 13.4, it becomes clear that education and freedom of the press are consistently two significant explanatory variables of corruption (the beta

Table 13.4 Regressions of corruption (CPI) on education, freedom of expression and other variables

	CPI	CPI	CPI	CPI	CPI
Education beta	.041	.036	.034	.032	**.022**
t statistic	5.98	5.21	3.63	3.47	**2.24**
FreePress beta		−.016	−.016	−.016	**−.013**
t statistic		−2.46	−2.46	−2.53	**−2.11**
LogGDPpc beta			.042	.066	**.213**
t statistic			.330	.529	**1.64**
GDPgrowth beta				.060	**.067**
t statistic				1.73	**2.06**
Resources beta					**−.020**
t statistic					**−2.63**
Constant beta	.940	2.10	1.92	1.58	**1.05**
t statistic	2.62	3.61	2.42	1.97	**1.30**
N	45	45	45	45	**44**
R Square	45%	52%	52%	56%	**60%**

coefficients do not change sign and t statistics are always significant). Also, the inclusion of GDP per capita and growth indicate that there are factors other than income that affect this phenomenon, namely the importance that natural resources have in SSA economies.

13.5 Conclusions

In this chapter, we studied the role of education and freedom of expression as explanatory variables of corruption, measured by the CPI, in a sample of 45 SSA countries for a specific year. The analysis has shown that both variables have, in fact, a significant effect on the countries' perceptions of corruption, as countries with high levels of education and freedom of the press tend to be perceived as less corrupt.

The study also shows that major macroeconomic factors such as GDP per capita and GDP growth which have often been linked to the causes of this phenomenon do not provide the most significant explanations. The exception being made to the relative importance of natural resources in the economy which has reinforced the validity of the resource curse theory.

Overall, the variables considered in this study explain about 60 percent of the variability observed in the CPI, which is not surprising since corruption is a complex, cross-sectorial phenomenon that can take on many different forms and be both a push and pull factor on several other variables. Education and information strengthen personal integrity and empower individuals to make effective use of accountability and good governance mechanisms but, at the same time, the control of corruption enables more effective resource allocation, for instance, in the education sector, or the attainment of good grades without involving bribes.

It should never be forgotten that corruption is a social disease which affects different sectors of a country's economic structure. However, it is a disease that cannot be cured by some unique and magical remedy. One size does not fit all because there are cultural, social, historical, political and economic factors, which inhibit the emergence of a single solution. We can, though, combine some of these factors and identify scenarios propitious to a greater or lesser extent to the practice of corruption.

As with any disease, prevention is the best medicine. When the opportunities for distortion are minimized or eliminated, it is then possible to focus on the most critical areas and fight corruption with strategy.

In spite of the existence of several explanatory variables in the corruption phenomenon, contributions such as Klitgaard's formula to analyze the tendency for corruption remain a powerful and straightforward approach that can only benefit future research. The analysis of such a complex disease requires different angles and approaches but they can all make a contribution and help decision-makers develop a strategy that can change the incentives for corrupt behavior, increase accountability and foster transparency with real and short-term effects for society.

Notes

1 World Bank.
2 Transparency International estimates that political leaders in countries such as Indonesia (Suharto), the Philippines (Marcos), Haiti (Duvalier) and Zaire (Mobutu) may have embezzled several billion dollars.
3 Worldwide Governance Indicators. Washington, DC: World Bank, September 2006.
4 International NGO established in 1993, in Berlin, Germany.
5 The CPI is criticized for two main reasons: the importance the media may give to isolated cases of corruption which influences popular perceptions and the constant change in countries participating in the survey.
6 *The American Heritage Dictionary of the English Language*, Fourth Edition copyright, 2000, by Houghton Mifflin Company.
7 Locke, J. (1689). *An Essay Concerning Human Understanding* (1998, ed.). Book II, Chapter XXI, Penguin Classics, Toronto.
8 Schweitzer, A. quoted in Civilization and Ethics: The Philosophy of Civilization—II (1946).
9 Please note that "less" does not mean "absence," as there are countries with strong GDP growth (e.g., oil-based economies in SSA and the Middle East) and high levels of perceived corruption. The above-mentioned expectation refers to the role of economic development in reducing poverty which is an important incentive to corruption.
10 The countries are Angola, Benin, Botswana, Burkina Faso, Burundi, Cameroon, Cape Verde, Central African Republic, Chad, Comoros, Congo, Côte d'Ivoire, Democratic Republic of Congo, Equatorial Guinea, Eritrea, Ethiopia, Gabon, Gambia, Ghana, Guinea, Guinea-Bissau, Kenya, Lesotho, Liberia, Madagascar, Malawi, Mali, Mauritius, Mozambique, Namibia, Niger, Nigeria, Rwanda, São Tomé and Príncipe, Senegal, Seychelles, Sierra Leone, South Africa, Sudan, Swaziland, Tanzania, Togo, Uganda, Zambia and Zimbabwe.

References

Abed, G.T. and Gupta, S. (2002) *Governance, Corruption, and Economic Performance*, Washington, DC: International Monetary Fund.

Abramovitz, M. (1956) 'Resource and output trends in the United States since 1870', *American Economic Review*, 46: 5–23.

Acemoglu, D. (1995) 'Reward structures and the allocation of talent', *European Economic Review*, 39: 17–33.

Acemoglu, D. (2005) 'Politics and economics in weak and strong states', *Journal of Monetary Economics*, 52(7): 1199–1226.

Acemoglu, D. (2008) *Introduction to Modern Economic Growth*, Princeton and Oxford: Princeton University Press.

Acemoglu, D. and Zilibotti, F. (1997) 'Risk, diversification, and growth', *The Journal of Political Economy*, 105(4): 709–751.

Achwan, R. (2014) 'Reconceptualising political corruption in democratising societies', *Asian Social Science*, 10(11): 201–209.

Ades, A. and Tella, R.D. (1997) 'The new economics of corruption: a survey and some new results', *Political Studies*, 45(3): 496–513.

Afonso, O. (2001) 'The impact of international trade on economic growth', FEP Working Papers n° 106, Porto: Faculdade de Economia, Universidade do Porto.

Agenor, P.R. (2004) 'Does globalization hurt the poor?', *International Economics and Economic Policy*, 1(1): 21–51.

Aghion, P. (2014) *Just the Facts 101. Textbook Key facts, e-Study Guide for: The Economics of Growth: Economics*, UK: Cram101 Textbook Review.

Aghion, P. and Howitt, P. (1992) 'A model of growth through creative destruction', *Econometrica*, 60: 323–351.

Ahmad, E., Ullah, M.A. and Arfeen, M.I. (2012) 'Does corruption affect economic growth?', *Latin American Journal of Economics*, 49(2): 277–305.

Aidt, T.S. (2003) 'Economic analysis of corruption: a survey', *The Economic Journal*, 113(491): F632–F652.

Aidt, T.S. (2009) 'Corruption, institutions, and economic development', *Oxford Review of Economic Policy*, 25(2): 271–291.

Aidt, T.S., Dutta, J. and Sena, V. (2008) 'Governance regimes, corruption and growth: theory and evidence', *Journal of Comparative Economics*, 36(2): 195–220.

Akhter, S.H. (2004) 'Is globalization what it's cracked up to be? Economic freedom, corruption, and human development', *Journal of World Business*, 39(3): 283–295.

Alesina, A. and Rodrik, D. (1994) 'Distributive politics and economic growth', *The Quarterly Journal of Economics*, 109(2): 465–490.

Amaro, F. (2006) *Métodos e Técnicas de Investigação Qualitativa*, in Martins, M. (ed.), *Comunicação e Marketing Político – Contributos Pedagógicos* (pp. 161–176), Lisboa: Instituto Superior de Ciências Sociais e Políticas.

Anderson, J.H. and Gray, C.W. (2006) *Anticorruption in Transition 3: Who Is Succeeding … and Why?*, Washington, DC: World Bank.

Anderson, M. (1971) *Family Structure in Nineteenth Century Lancashire*, Cambridge: Cambridge University Press.

Andvig, J.C. and Fjeldstad, O.H. (2001) 'Corruption. A review of contemporary research', *CMI Reports*: 7. Bergen: Chr. Michelsen Institute.

Andvig, J.C. and Moene, K.O. (1990) 'How corruption may corrupt', *Journal of Economic Behaviour and Organization*, 13(1): 63–76.

Anti-Corruption Council (2011) Report on Pressure and Control Over the Media in Serbia, retrieved from www.antikorupcija-savet.gov.rs/ (accessed April 16, 2015).

Argandoña, A. (2001) 'Corruption: the corporate perspective', *Business Ethics: A European Review*, 10: 163–175.

Arndt, C. and Oman, C. (2006) *Uses and Abuses of Governance Indicators*, Paris: OECD.

Arrow, K.J. (1962) 'The economic implications of learning by doing', *The Review of Economic Studies*, 29(3): 155–123.

Asongu, S. (2014) 'Globalization (fighting), corruption and development: how are these phenomena linearly and nonlinearly related in wealth effects?', *Journal of Economic Studies*, 41(3): 346–369.

Atkeson, A. (1991) 'International lending with moral hazard and risk of repudiation', *Econometrica*, 59(4): 1069–1089.

Attila, J. (2013) 'Globalization and corruption: new evidence', *Oil, Gas and Energy Quarterly*, 541–562.

Auriol, E. (2006) 'Corruption in procurement and public purchase', *International Journal of Industrial Organization*, 24(5): 867–885.

B92 (2012, July 23) *Muz Jelene Trivan posluje sa državom*, retrieved from www.b92. net/info/vesti/index.php?yyyy=2012&mm=07&dd=23&nav_category=206&nav_id= 628778 (accessed April 15, 2015).

Backhouse, R. (1998) *Explorations in Economic Methodology: From Lakatos to Empirical Philosophy of Science*, London: Routledge.

Balestrini, P. (2001) 'Amidst the digital economy, philanthropy in business as a source of competitive advantage', *Journal of International Marketing Research*, 26(1): 13–34.

Banerjee, A.V. and Newman, A.F. (1998) 'Poverty, incentives, and development', *The Review of Economic Studies*, 65(4): 631–653.

Bardhan, P. (1997) 'Corruption and development: a review of issues', *Journal of Economic Literature*, 35: 1320–1346.

Bardin, L. (1977) *L'analyse de contenu*, Paris: PUF.

Barro, R.J. and Sala-i-Martin, X. (2004) *Economic Growth*, Boston: MIT Press.

Bartlett, C.A. (1986) 'Building and managing the transnational: the new organizational challenge', in Porter, M.E. (ed.) *Competition in Global Industries* (pp. 367–401), Boston, MA: Harvard Business School Press.

Batista, A. (2000) *Corrupção no Brasil: Corrupção Fator de Progresso?* [*Corruption in Brazil: Corruption as Factor of Progress?*], São Paulo: Letras & Letras.

Bauhr, M., Nasiritousi, N., Oscarsson, H. and Persson, A. (2010) 'Perceptions of corruption in Sweden', *QoG Working Paper Series*, 8, Göteborg: The Quality of Government Institute.

Baum, C., Schaffer, M. and Stillman, S. (2003) 'Instrumental variables and GMM: estimation and testing', *Stata Journal*, 3(1): 1–31.

Beck, P. and Maher, M. (1986) 'A comparison of bribery and bidding in thin markets', *Economic Letters*, 20: 1–5.

Becker, G.S. (1968) 'Crime and punishment – an economic approach', *The Journal of Political Economy*, 76(2): 169–217.

Becker, G.S. (1974) 'A theory of social interactions', *Journal of Political Economy*, 82: 1063–1093.

Becker, G.S. and Stigler, G.J. (1974) 'Law enforcement, malfeasance, and compensation of enforcers', *The Journal of Legal Studies*, 3(1): 1–18.

Beenstock, M. (1979) 'Corruption and development', *World Development*, 7: 15–24.

Benedict, B. (1968) 'Family, firms and economic development', *Southwestern Journal of Anthropology*, 24: 1–19.

Ben-Porath, Y. (1980) 'The F-Connection: families, friends, and firms and the organization of exchange', *Population and Development Review*, 6(1): 1–30.

Bhagwati, J.N. (1982) 'Directly unproductive, profit-seeking (DUP) activities', *Journal of Political Economy*, 90(5): 988–1002.

Bilhim, J. (2004) *Teoria Organizacional – Estruturas e Pessoas*, Lisboa: Instituto Superior de Ciências Sociais e Políticas.

Bjørnskov, C. (2003) 'Corruption and social capital', Working Paper 03-13, Aarhus School of Business.

Bjørnskov, C. (2011) 'Combating corruption: on the interplay between institutional quality and social trust', *Journal of Law and Economics*, 54(1): 135–159.

Blackburn, K. and Forgues-Puccio, G.F. (2010) 'Financial liberalization, bureaucratic corruption and economic development', *Journal of International Money and Finance*, 29(7): 1321–1339.

Blaug, M. (1970) *An Introduction to the Economics of Education*, London: Allen Lane, Penguin Press.

Blaug M. (2000) 'Endogenous growth theory', *Research Memoranda in History and Methodology of Economics*, 00-7. Universiteit Van Amsterdam, Amsterdam.

Blundo, G. (ed.) (2000) *Monnayer les pouvoirs. Espaces, mécanismes et représentations de La corruption*, Paris: Presses Universitaires de France.

Boerner, K. and Hainz, C. (2009) 'The political economy of corruption and the role of economic opportunities', *Economics of Transition*, 17(2): 213–240.

Bonaglia, F., Braga de Macedo, J. and Bussolo, M. (2001) 'How globalization improves governance', Working Paper No. 181, OECD Development Center.

Bose, N. (2010) 'Corruption and economic growth', in Durlauf, S. N. and Blume, L. E. (eds), *The New Palgrave Dictionary of Economics*, Online Edition. Palgrave Macmillan.

Boycko, Maxim, Shleifer, A. and Vishny, R. (1996) 'A theory of privatization', *Economic Journal*, 106: 309–319.

Brasil (2003) CGU – Controladoria-Geral da União. Portaria n.° 247 de 20 de junho de 2003. Institui em caráter permanente o mecanismo do sorteio público para definição das unidades municipais onde será objeto de fiscalização a aplicação de recursos públicos federais. Brasília, DF, 2003, retrieved from www.cgu.gov.br/AreaAuditoriaFiscalizacao/Arquivos/ExecucaoProgramasGoverno/Portaria%20n%20247%20-%20Municipios.pdf (accessed December 5, 2010).

Brasil (2004a) Decreto N° 5.209 de 17 de setembro de 2004. Regulamenta a Lei n. 10.836, de 09/01/2004, que cria o Programa Bolsa Família. Brasília, DF, retrieved from www.

planalto.gov.br/ccivil_03/_Ato2004-2006/2004/Decreto/D5209.htm (accessed December 20, 2010).

Brasil (2004b) LEI N.° 10.836 de 09 de janeiro de 2004. Cria o Programa Bolsa Família e dá outras providências. Brasília, DF, retrieved from http://www.planalto.gov.br/ccivil_03/_ato2004-2006/2004/lei/l10.836.htm (accessed December 20, 2010).

Brasil (2005) MDS – Ministério do Desenvolvimento Social e Combate à Fome. Instrução Normativa N.° 01 de 20 de maio de 2005. Divulga orientações aos municípios, Estados e Distrito Federal para constituição de instância de controle social do Programa Bolsa Família (PBF) e para o desenvolvimento de suas atividades. Brasília, DF, retrieved from www.mds.gov.br/sobreoministerio/legislacao/bolsafamilia/instrucoesnormativas/2005/Instrucao_Normativa_MDSn1-20-5-05.PDF (accessed December 20, 2010).

Brasil (2010a) CGU – Controladoria-Geral da União. Relatórios de fiscalização de sorteios de municípios n.° 742 a 1667. [Relatório Técnico]. Brasília: Secretaria Federal de Controle Interno, retrieved from www.cgu.gov.br/sorteios/index1.asp (accessed December 2, 2010).

Brasil (2010b) CGU – Controladoria-Geral da União. Licitações fraudadas continuam liderando as irregularidades encontradas pela CGU em municípios [Notícia], retrieved from www.cgu.gov.br/Imprensa/Noticias/2010/noticia08510.asp (accessed July 26, 2011).

Brasil (2010c) MDS – Ministério do Desenvolvimento Social e Combate à Fome. Orientações para a Fiscalização e Controle Social do Programa Bolsa Família. Brasília, DF.

Brasil (2010d) MDS – Ministério do Desenvolvimento Social e Combate à Fome. Sítio do MDS. Brasília, DF.

Brasil (2011) CGU – Controladoria-Geral da União. Sítio Institucional. Brasília, DF, retrieved from www.cgu.gov.br (accessed April 15, 2015).

Brazilian Institute of Geography and Statistics (IBGE) (2010) Instituto Brasileiro de Geografia e Estatística. Censo 2010, retrieved from www.ibge.gov.br/censo2010 (accessed December 24, 2010).

Brooks, C. (2008) *Introductory Econometrics for Finance* (2nd edn), Cambridge: Cambridge University Press.

Brunetti, A. and Weder, B. (2001) 'A free press is bad news for corruption', *Journal of Public Economics*, 87: 1801–1824.

Brytting, T., Minogue, R. and Morino, V. (2011) *The Anatomy of Fraud and Corruption: Organizational Causes and Remedies*, Burlington, VT: Gower.

Buchan, B. and Hill, L. (2014) *An Intellectual History of Political Corruption*, Basingstoke, UK: Palgrave Macmillan.

Buchanan, J.M., Tollison, R.D. and Tullock, G. (eds) (1980) *Toward a Theory of the Rent-Seeking Society*, College Station, TX: Texas A & M University Press.

Burguet, R. and Che, Y.-K. (2004) 'Competitive procurement with corruption', *RAND Journal of Economics*, 35(1): 50–68.

Campos, J., Lien, D. and Pradhan, S. (1999) 'The impact of corruption on investment: predictability matters', *World Development*, 27: 1050–1067.

Campos, J.E. and Pradhan, S. (2007) *The Many Faces of Corruption: Tracking Vulnerabilities at the Sector Level*, Washington, DC: World Bank.

Campos, N.F., Dimova, R. and Saleh, A. (2010) 'Whither corruption? A quantitative survey of the literature on corruption and growth', Center for Economic Policy Research, DP8140.

Caplan, B. (2007) *The Myth of the Rational Voter*, New York: Princeton University Press.

Carmo, H. and Ferreira, M. (1998) *Metodologia da Investigação – Guia para Auto-Aprendizagem*, Lisboa: Universidade Aberta.

Cason, J.W. and Ramaswamy, S. (eds) (2003) *Development and Democracy: New Perspectives on an Old Debate*, Middlebury, VT, Hanover, NH and London: Middlebury College Press, University Press of New England.

Cass, D. (1965) 'Optimum growth in an aggregative model of capital accumulation', *Review of Economic Studies*, 32(3): 233–240.

Centre for International Crime Prevention (CICP) (2001) *United Nations Manual on Anti-Corruption Policy (Draft)*, Vienna: United Nations Office.

CEPAL – Comissão Econômica para América Latina e Caribe. (2010) *Panorama Social de América Latina*, Santiago, Chile: Nações Unidas.

Chapman, D. (2002) *Corruption and the Education Sector. Sectoral Perspectives on Corruption*, Prepared by MSI, sponsored by USAID, DCHA/DG.

Chen, K. (1995) 'As China prospers, so do the children of communist leaders', *The Wall Street Journal*, July 1, 1995, A1, A4.

Cheung, H. and Chan, A. (2008) 'Corruption across countries: impacts from education and cultural dimensions', *The Social Science Journal*, 45(2): 223–239.

Chinhamo, O. and Shumba, G. (2007) 'Institutional working definition of corruption', *Working Paper -1- ACT-Southern Africa Working Paper Series*, retrieved from www.kubatana.net/docs/demgg/act-sa_definition_of_corruption_080731.pdf (accessed April 15, 2015).

CIDA. (2009) *Results-based Management Tool*, Ottowa, Canada: Canadian Internation Development Agency (CIDA).

Cloward, R. and Ohlin, L. (1960) *Delinquency and Opportunity. A Theory of Delinquent Gangs*, New York: Free Press.

CMI. (2009) *U4 Anti-Corruption Resource Centre*, retrieved from www.u4.no. (accessed September 2009).

CMI Report (2007) *Corruption in Serbia 2007: Overview of Problems and Status of Reforms*, retrieved from www.cmi.no/publications/file/2693-corruption-in-serbia-2007.pdf (accessed April 15, 2015).

Coronel, S.S. (2010) 'Corruption and the watchdog role of the news media', in Norris, P. (ed.), *Public Sentinel: News Media and Governance Reform* (pp. 111–136), Washington, DC: World Bank.

Cox, A. (2007) 'Trio norte-americano ganha Nobel de Economia 2007' [North American trio wins Nobel Prize in Economics 2007], *Reuters*, retrieved from http://noticias.uol.com.br/ultnot/reuters/2007/10/15/ult27u63147.jhtm (accessed April 16, 2015).

Crampton, P. (2003) 'Competition and efficiency as organising principles for all economic and regulatory policymaking', OECD, Competition Division, Communication prepared for the First Meeting of the Latin American Competition Forum (April 7–8, 2003), retrieved from www.oecd.org/daf/competition/prosecutionandlawenforcement/2490195.pdf (accessed April 16, 2015).

Creighton, J.L. (2005) *The Public Participation Handbook: Making Better Decisions Through Citizen Involvement*, San Francisco: Jossey-Bass.

Cressey, D. (1953) *Other People's Money: A Study in the Social Psychology of Embezzlement*, Glencoe, IL: Free Press.

Crozier, M. (1963) *Le phénomène bureaucratique*, Paris: Éditions du Seuil.

Crozier, M. and Friedberg, E. (1977) *L'acteur et le système*, Paris: Éditions du Seuil.

Cuervo-Cazurra, A. (2006) 'Who cares about corruption?', *Journal of International Business Studies*, 37(6): 807–822.

Cusson, M. (1998) *La criminologie*, Paris: Hachette.

Das, J. and DiRienzo, C. (2009) 'The nonlinear impact of globalization on corruption', *The International Journal of Business and Finance Research*, 3(2): 33–46.

de Vaal, A. and Ebben, W. (2011) 'Institutions and the relation between corruption and economic growth', *Review of Development Economics*, 15: 108–123.

Demirbag, M., Glaister, K.W. and Tatoglu, E. (2007) 'Institutional and transaction cost influences on MNEs' ownership strategies of their affiliates: evidence from an emerging market', *Journal of World Business*, 42: 418–434.

Deng, X., Zhang, L. and Leverenz, A. (2010) 'Official corruption during China's economic transition: historical patterns, characteristics, and government reactions', *Journal of Contemporary Criminal Justice*, 26(1): 72–88.

Dequech, D. (2007) 'Neoclassical, mainstream, orthodox, and heterodox economics', *Journal of Post Keynesian Economics*, 30(2): 279–302.

Diamond, P. (1965) 'National debt in a neoclassical growth model', *American Economic Review*, 4: 1126–1150.

DiMaggio, P. J. and Powell, W.W. (1983) 'The iron cage revisited: institutional isomorphism and collective rationality in organizational fields', *American Sociological Review*, 48: 147–160.

DiMaggio, P. J. and Powell, W.W. (1991) 'Introduction', in Powell, W. W. and DiMaggio, P. J. (eds), *The New Institutionalism in Organizational Analysis* (1–38), Chicago, IL: University of Chicago Press.

DiRienzi, C., Das, J. Cort, K.T. and Burbridge Jr., J. (2007) 'Corruption and the role of information', *Journal of International Business Studies*, 38(2): 320–332.

Dobson, S. and Ramlogan-Dobson, C. (2010) 'Is there a trade-off between income inequality and corruption? Evidence from Latin America', *Economics Letters*, 107(2): 102–104.

Dollar, D. (2005) 'Globalization, poverty, and inequality since 1980', *World Bank Research Observer*, 20(2): 145–175.

Dreher, A. (2006) 'Does globalization affect growth? Evidence from a new index of globalization', *Applied Economics*, 38(10): 1091–1110.

Driffield, N., Mickiewicz, T., Pal, S. and Temouri, Ya (2010) *Bridging the Gap? Corruption, Knowledge and Foreign Ownership*, CEDI Disscussion Paper 10-01, London: Brunel University.

Duanmu, J.-L. (2011) 'The effect of corruption distance and market orientation on the ownership choice of MNEs: evidence from China', *Journal of International Management*, 17(2): 162–174.

Duvanova, D. (2014) 'Economic regulations, red tape, and bureaucratic corruption in post-communist economies', *World Development*, 59: 298–312.

Dzhumashev, R. (2014) 'The two-way relationship between government spending and corruption and its effects on economic growth', *Contemporary Economic Policy*, 32(2): 403–419.

EC (2014) Report from the Commission to the Council and the European Parliament. EU anti-corruption report, Brussels, February 3, COM(2014) 38 final.

ECLAC (2010) *Estudio Económico de América Latina y el Caribe, 2009–2010*, Santiago de Chile.

Edwards, M. (2008) *Participatory Governance*, retrieved from www.canberra.edu.au/corpgov-aps/pub/issuespaper6-participatory-governance.pdf (accessed May 28, 2012).

Ehrlich, I. and Lui, F. (1999) 'Bureaucratic corruption and endogenous economic growth', *Journal of Political Economy*, 107(6): 270–293.

Eisenhauer, J.G. (2003) 'Regression through the origin', *Teaching Statistics*, 25(3): 76–80.

European Commission (2006) Commission Staff Working Document/Serbia 2006 Progress Report, retrieved from www.delscg.cec.eu.int/en (accessed April 15, 2015).

European Parliament (2011) *European Parliament resolution on the European integration process of Serbia* (2011/2886(RSP), retrieved from www.europarl.europa.eu (accessed April 15, 2015).

Everett, J., Neu, D. and Rahaman, A.S. (2007) 'Accounting and the global fight against corruption', *Accounting, Organizations and Society*, 32: 513–542.

Ewing, K.D. (1992) *Money, Politics and Law*, Oxford: Oxford University Press.

Fehr, E. and Gächter, S. (2000) 'Cooperation and punishment in public goods experiments', *American Economic Review*, 90(4): 980–994.

Fernandes, P. M. (2009) *Corrupção: Definição, Prevenção e Combate – O caso de S. Tomé e Príncipe* [*Corruption: Definition, Prevention and Combat – The case of S. Tomé and Prinicipe*], Master's Degree Thesis. University of Aveiro.

Ferraz, C. and Finan, F. (2005) 'Reelection incentives and political corruption: evidence from Brazilian audit reports', Selected Paper prepared for presentation at the American Agricultural Economics Association Annual Meeting, Providence, Rhode Island, July 24–27, 2005.

Ferraz, C., Finan, F. and Moreira, D.B. (2012) 'Corrupting learning: evidence from missing federal education funds in Brazil', *Journal of Public Economics*, 96(9–10): 712–726.

Ferraz, L.F. (2008) *Programa Bolsa Família: Impactos na Distribuição da Renda*. Monografia (Especialização latu sensu em Orçamento Público) apresentada ao Instituto Serzedello Corrêa – ISC. Brasília, DF.

Ferro, A.R. and Nicolella, A.C. (2007) 'The impact of conditional cash transfer programs on household work decisions in Brazil', in *Population Association of America Annual Meeting*, 2007, New York, retrieved from www.popassoc.org/meetings.html (accessed April 15, 2015).

Field, A. (2000) *Discovering Statistics using SPSS*, London: Sage Publications.

Foddy, W. (1993) *Constructing Questions for Interviews and Questionnaires: Theory and Practice in Social Research*, Cambridge: Cambridge University Press.

Friedman, M. (2002) 'Monopoly and the social responsibility of business and labor', in Friedman, M. (ed.), *Capitalism and Freedom* (pp. 119–136), Chicago: The University of Chicago Press.

Friedrich, C.J. (2002) 'Corruption concepts in historical perspective', in Heidenheimer, A.J. and Johnston, M. (eds), *Political Corruption: Concepts and Contexts* (3rd edn) (pp. 1–23), New Brunswick, NJ: Transaction Publishers.

Galor, O. (2005) 'The demographic transition and the emergence of sustained economic growth', *Journal of the European Economic Association*, 3(2–3): 494–504.

Galor, O. (2011) 'Unified growth theory and comparative development', *Rivista di Politica Economica*, SIPI Spa (2): 9–21.

Gambetta, D. (1988) 'Can we trust trust?', in Gambetta, D. (ed.), *Trust: Making and Braking Cooperative Relations* (pp. 213–237), Oxford: Basil Blackwell.

Gambetta, D. (1993) *The Sicilian Mafia*, Cambridge, MA: Harvard University Press.

Gibbons, K.M. (2010) 'Corruption', *The Canadian Encyclopedia*, Historica Foundation of Canada, retrieved from www.thecanadianencyclopedia.com/articles/corruption (accessed July 2012).

Gigiioli, P. (1996) 'Political corruption and the media: the tangentopoli affair', *International Social Science Journal*, 48: 381–394.

Goel, R.K. and Mehrotra, A.N. (2012) 'Financial payment instruments and corruption', *Applied Financial Economics*, 22(11): 877–886.

Gómez Fortes, B., Cabeza, L. and Palacios, I. (2013) 'Double punishment for regional and national incumbents: the March 2012 regional election in Andalusia', *South European Society and Politics*, 18(4): 591–610.

Goode, W. and Hatt, P. (1952) *Methods in Social Research*, New York: McGraw-Hill.

Graaf, G. (de) (2007) 'Causes of corruption: towards a contextual theory of corruption'. *Public Administration Quarterly*, 31: 39–86.

Gradstein, M. (2004) 'Governance and growth', *Journal of Development Economics*, 73: 505–518.

Granovetter, M. (1985) 'Economic action and social structure: the problem of embeddedness', *American Journal of Sociology*, 91(3): 481–510.

Graycar, A. and Sidebottom, A. (2012) 'Corruption and control: a corruption reduction approach', *Journal of Financial Crime*, 19(4): 384–399.

Graziano, L. (1980) *Clientelismo e Sistema Politico, Il Caso dell Italia*, Milan: F. Angeli.

Greasley, D., Madsen, J.B. and Wohar, M.E. (2013) 'Long-run growth empirics and new challenges for unified theory', *Applied Economics*, 45(28): 3973–3987.

GRECO (2010) Evaluation Report on the Republic of Serbia Transparency of Party Funding, Strasbourg, September 27 to October 1, 2010, retrieved from www.coe.int/greco (accessed April 16, 2015).

Grilo, T. (2005) *A Tematização da Corrupção na Imprensa Escrita Portuguesa (1999–2001)*, Dissertação de Licenciatura em Sociologia, Instituto Superior de Ciências do Trabalho e da Empresa, Lisboa.

Grochová, L. and Otáhal, T. (2013) 'How does corruption in Central and Eastern Europe hurt economic growth? Granger test of causality', *Ekonomicky Casopis*, 61(6): 563–577.

Grossman, G.M and Helpman, E. (1990) 'Trade, innovation, and growth', *American Economic Review*, 80(2): 86–91.

Grossman, G.M. and Helpman, E. (1991) 'Trade, knowledge spillovers, and growth', *European Economic Review*, 35(2–3): 517–526.

Grossman, G.M. and Helpman, E. (1994) 'Protection for sale', *The American Economic Review*, 84(4): 833–850.

Gundlach, E. and Paldam, M. (2009) 'The transition of corruption: from poverty to honesty', *Economics Letters*, 103: 146–148.

Gupta, S., Davoodi, H. and Alonso-Terme, R. (2002) 'Does corruption affect income inequality and poverty', *Economics of Governance*, 3: 23–45.

Habib, M. and Zurawicki, L. (2002) 'Corruption and foreign direct investment', *Journal of International Business Studies*, 33(2): 291–307.

Hair, Jr., J. F., Anderson, R. E., Tatham, R. L. and Black, W. C. (2009) *Análise Multivariada de Dados* (6th edn), São Paulo: Bookman.

Hampton, J.A. (1979) 'Polymorphous concepts in semantic memory', *Journal of Verbal Learning and Verbal Behavior*, 18(4): 441–461.

Handa, S. and Davis, B. (2006) 'The experience of conditional cash transfer in Latin America and the Caribbean', *Development Policy Review*, 24(5): 513–536.

Hanushek, E. and Woessmann, L. (2008) 'The role of cognitive skills in economic development', *Journal of Economic Literature*, 46(3): 607–668.

Hanushek, E. and Woessmann, L. (2010) *The High Cost of Low Educational Performance: The Long-Run Economic Impact of Improving PISA Outcomes*, Paris: OCDE.

Harris, M. and Raviv, A. (1978) 'Some results on incentive contracts with applications to education and employment, health insurance, and law enforcement', *American Economic Review*, 68: 20–30.

Harrison, A. (2006) 'Globalization and poverty', NBER Working Paper No. W12347, National Bureau of Economic Research.

Harrison, E. (2007) 'Corruption', *Development in Practice*, 17(4–5): 672–678.

Harzing, A.W. (2007) *Publish or Perish*, retrieved from www.harzing.com/pop.htm (accessed April 17, 2015).

Harzing, A.W. (2010) *The Publish or Perish Book. Your Guide to Effective and Responsible Citation Analysis*, Melbourne, Australia: Tarma Software Research Pty Ltd.

Hawley, S. (2000) 'Exporting corruption: privatisation, multinationals and bribery', Briefing 19, The Corner House.

Heidenheimer, A.J. (2002) 'Perspectives on the perception of corruption', in Heidenheimer, A.J. and Johnston, M. (eds), *Political Corruption: Concepts and Contexts* (3rd edn) (pp. 141–154), New Brunswick, NJ: Transaction Publishers.

Heidenheimer, A.J., Johnston, M. and LeVine, V.T. (eds) (1993) *Political Corruption. A Handbook*, New Brunswick, NJ: Transaction Publishers.

Heij, C., De Boer, P., Franses, P.H., Kloek, T. and Van Dijk, H.K. (2004) *Econometric Methods with Applications in Business and Economics*, Oxford: Oxford University Press.

Hellman, J. and Kaufmann, D. (2001) 'Confronting the challenge of state capture in transition countries', *Finance and Development*, 38(3), September, retrieved from www.imf.org/external/pubs/ft/fandd/2001/09/hellman.htm (accessed July 2012).

Hellsten, S. and Larbi, G. (2006) 'Public good or private good? The paradox of public and private ethics in the context of developing countries', *Public Administration and Development*, 26(2): 135–145.

Hessami, Z. (2014) 'Political corruption, public procurement, and budget composition: theory and evidence from OECD countries', *European Journal of Political Economy*, 34: 372–389.

Hill, M. and Hill, A. (2005) *Investigação por Questionário*, Lisboa: Edições Sílabo.

Hillman, A.J. and Wan, W.P. (2005) 'The determinants of MNE subsidiaries' political strategies: evidence of institutional duality', *Journal of International Business Studies*, 36(3): 322–340.

Hodgson, G.M. and Jiang, S. (2007) 'The economics of corruption and the corruption of economics: an institutionalist perspective', *Journal of Economics Issues*, XLI: 1043–1061.

Hoover, K. (1991) 'Scientific research program or tribe? A joint appraisal of Lakatos and the new classical macroeconomics', in de Marchi, N. and Blaug, M. (eds), *Appraising Economic Theories: Studies in the Methodology of Research Programmes* (pp. 364–394), Aldershot: Edward Elgar Publishing.

Hu, H. (1989) 'The estimated total size of rent in China's economy', *Comparative Economics and Social Systems*, 5: 10–20.

Huntington, S. (1968) *Political Order in Changing Societies*, New Haven: Yale University Press.

Indexmundi. (2012) Retrieved from Indexmundi: www.indexmundi.com/thailand (accessed April 17, 2015).

International Policy Centre For Inclusive Growth. (2011) 'Cash transfers and social protection', retrieved from www.ipc-undp.org/cct.do (accessed April 15, 2015).

Islam, R. (2006) 'Does more transparency go along with better governance?' *Economics and Politics*, 18(2): 121–167.

Ivanov, A. (2012) 'Why the Russian federation public procurement market does not turn into the market for lemons', *NACC Journal*, Special Issue, 5(2): 37–51.

Jain, A.K. (2001a) *The Political Economy of Corruption*, London: Routledge.

Jain, A.K. (2001b) 'Corruption: a review', *Journal of Economic Surveys*, 15(1): 71–121.

Jancsics, D. (2014) 'Interdisciplinary perspectives on corruption', *Sociology Compass*, 8(4): 358–372.

Javorcik, B.S. and Wei, S.-J. (2009) 'Corruption and cross-border investment in emerging markets: firm-level evidence', *Journal of International Money and Finance*, 28(4): 605–624.

Jensen, M. and Meckling, W. (1976) 'Theory of the firm: managerial behavior, agency costs, and ownership structure', *Journal of Financial Economics*, 3: 305–360.

Johnson, N.D., LaFountain, C.L. and Yamarik, S. (2011) 'Corruption is bad for growth (even in the United States)', *Public Choice*, 147(3–4): 377–393.

Johnston, M. (1997) 'Public officials, private interests, and sustainable democracy: when politics and corruption meet', in Elliott, K. (ed.), *Corruption and the Global Economy* (pp. 61–82), Washington, DC: Institute for International Economics.

Johnston, M. (1998) 'Cross-border corruption: points of vulnerability and challenges for reform' in United Nations Development Programme (UNDP), *Corruption and Integrity Improvement Initiatives in Developing Countries* (pp. 13–23), New York: United Nations.

Johnston, M. (2005) *Syndromes of Corruption. Wealth, Power, and Democracy*, Cambridge: Cambridge University Press.

Joseph, R. (1996) 'Nigeria: Inside the dismal tunnel', *Current History*, May, cited in: http://en.wikipedia.org/wiki/Prebendalism#cite_ref-2 (accessed July 1, 2012).

Joya, L. and Zamot, F. (2002) 'Internet-based reverse auctions by the Brazilian government', *The Electronic Journal on Information Systems in Developing Countries*, 9(6): 1–12.

Justesen, M.K. and Bjørnskov, C. (2014) 'Exploiting the poor: bureaucratic corruption and poverty in Africa', *World Development*, 58: 106–115.

Kadri, N. M. (2009) 'A contribuição dos órgãos de controle na implantação de políticas públicas descentralizadas: programa bolsa família', *II Congresso Consad de Gestão Pública*.

Kaldor, N. (1961) 'Capital accumulation and economic growth', in Lutz, F.A. and Hague, D.C. (eds), *The Theory of Capital* (pp. 177–222), London: St. Martin's Press.

Karhunen, P. (2008) 'Managing international business operations in a changing institutional context: the case of the St. Petersburg hotel industry', *Journal of International Management*, 14(1): 28–45.

Karhunen, P. and Kosonen, R. (2013) 'Strategic responses of foreign subsidiaries to host country corruption: the case of Finnish firms in Russia', *Critical Perspectives on International Business*, 9(1/2): 88–105.

Karhunen, P. and Ledyaeva, S. (2012) 'Corruption distance, anticorruption laws and international ownership strategies in Russia', *Journal of International Management*, 18: 196–208.

Kaufmann, D. (2005) 'Ten myths about governance and corruption', *Finance and Development*, 42(3), Washington, DC: International Monetary Fund.

Kaufmann, D. (2008) 'Capture and the financial crisis: an elephant forcing a rethink of corruption?' *The Kaufmann Governance Post*, November 3, 2008, retrieved from http://thekaufmannpost.net/capture-and-the-financial-crisis-an-elephant-forcing-a-rethink-of-corruption/ (accessed July 2012).

Kaufmann, D., Kraay, A. and Mastruzzi, M. (2005) *Governance Matters IV: Governance Indicators for 1996–2004.* World Bank Policy Research Working Paper No. 3630. Washington, DC: World Bank.

Kaufmann, D., Kraay, A. and Mastruzzi, M. (2007) 'The worldwide governance indicators project: answering the critics', World Bank Policy Research Working Paper No 4149, World Bank.

Kaufmann, D., Kraay, A. and Mastruzzi, M. (2011) 'The Worldwide Governance Indicators (WGI): 1996–2010', retrieved from www.govindicators.org (accessed April 15, 2015).

Kaufmann, D., Kraay, A. and Zoido-Lobatón, P. (1999) 'Aggregating governance indicators', World Bank Policy Research Working Paper 2195.

Keig, D.L., Brouthers, L.E. and Marshall, V.B. (2014) 'Formal and informal corruption environments and multinational enterprise social irresponsibility', *Journal of Management Studies*, 52(1): 89–116.

Kendrick, J. (1956) 'Productivity trends: capital and labor', Occasional Paper 53, National Bureau of Economic Research.

Kenny, C. (2010) 'Learning about schools in development', CGD Working Paper 236. Washington, DC: Center for Global Development.

Keohane, R.O. and Nye, J.S. (2000) 'Introduction', in Keohane, R.O. and Nye, J.S. (eds), *Governance in a Globalizing World* (pp. 1–44), Washington, DC: Brookings Institution Press.

Khan, F. (2007) 'Corruption and the decline of the State in Pakistan', *Asian Journal of Political Science*, 15(2): 219–247.

Khan, M.H. (1996) 'A typology of corrupt transactions in developing countries', *IDS Bulletin: Liberalization and the New Corruption*, 27(2): 12–21.

Khan, M.H. (1998) 'Patron–client networks and the economic effects of corruption in Asia', *European Journal of Development Research*, 10(1): 15–39.

Khoman, S., Mingmaninakin, W., Thosanguan, V., Tantivasadakarn, C., Chetsumon, C., Suntharanurak, S., Nippaya, S. and Suksai, N. (2009) *The World Trade Organisation's Government Procurement Agreement: A Study of Thailand's Preparation for Accession*, research report submitted to the Comptroller-General's Department, Ministry of Finance (in Thai).

Klitgaard, R. (1994) *A Corrupção sob Controle [Controlling Corruption]*, Rio de Janeiro: Editora Jorge Zahar.

Klitgaard, R. (1998) 'Combating corruption', *United Nations Chronicle*, 35(1), Department of Public Information.

Klitgaard, R., MacLean-Abaroa, R. and Parris, H.L. (1996) *A Practical Approach to Dealing with Municipal Malfeasance*, Urban Management Programme, Nairobi: UNDP/UNCHS/World Bank.

Klitgaard, R., Maclean-Abaroa, R. and Parris, H.L. (2000) *Corrupt Cities: A Practical Guide to Cure and Prevention*, Oakland, CA and Washington, DC: Institute for Contemporary Studies and the World Bank Institute.

Klitgaart, R. (1988) *Controlling Corruption*, Berkeley, CA: University of California Press.

Knack, S. and Azfar, O. (2003) 'Trade intensity, country size and corruption', *Economics of Governance*, 4(1): 1–18.

Knight, F.H. (1944) 'Diminishing returns from investment', *Journal of Political Economy*, 52: 26–47.

Koopmans, T.C. (1965) 'On the concept of optimal economic growth', *The Economic Approach to Development Planning* (pp. 225–287), Chicago: Rand McNally.

Kostova, T. (1999) 'Transnational transfer of strategic organizational practices: a contextual perspective', *Academy of Management Review*, 24(2): 308–324.

Kostova, T., Roth, K. and Dacin, T. (2008) 'Institutional theory in the study of multinational corporations: a critique and new directions', *Academy of Management Review*, 33(4): 994–1006.

Kraatz, M.S. and Block, E.S. (2008) 'Organizational implications of institutional pluralism', in Greenwood, R., Oliver, C., Suddaby, R. and Sahlin-Andersson, K. (eds), *The Sage Handbook of Organizational Institutionalism* (pp. 170–197), London: Sage Publications.

Krueger, A. (1974) 'The political economy of the rent-seeking society', *American Economic Review*, 64: 291–303.

Krugman, P. (1991) 'Increasing returns and economic geography', *Journal of Political Economy*, 99(3): 483–499.

Kuhn, T. (1970) *The Structure of Scientific Revolutions*, Chicago: Chicago University Press.

Kunieda, T., Okada, K. and Shibata, A. (2014) 'Corruption, capital account liberalization, and economic growth: theory and evidence', *International Economics*, 139: 80–108.

Kurer, O. (2005) 'Corruption: an alternative approach to its definition and measurement', *Political Studies*, 53: 222–239.

Kurtz, M. and Schrank, A. (2007) 'Growth and governance: models, measures, and mechanisms', *Journal of Politics*, 69(2): 538–554.

La Porta, R., Lopez-de Silanes, F., Shleifer, A. and Vishny, R. (1999) 'The quality of government', *Journal of Law, Economics, and Organization*, 15(1): 222–279.

Lalountas, D.A., Manolas, G.A. and Vavouras, I.S. (2011) 'Corruption, globalization and development: how are these three phenomena related?', *Journal of Policy Modeling*, 33(4): 636–648.

Lambsdorff, J.G. (1999) *The Transparency International Corruption Perceptions Index 1999 – Framework Document*, retrieved from www.transparency.org/files/content/tool/1999_CPI_Framework_EN.pdf (accessed April 17, 2015).

Lambsdorff, J.G. (2007) *The Institutional Economics of Corruption and Reform. Theory, Evidence and Policy*, Cambridge: Cambridge University Press.

Lancaster, K. (1966) 'Change and innovation in the technology of consumption', *The American Economic Review*, 56(1/2): 14–23.

Lasda Bergman, E.M. (2012) 'Finding citations to social work literature: the relative benefits of using Web of Science, Scopus, or Google Scholar', *Journal of Academic Librarianship*, 38(6): 370–379.

Leff, N. (1964) 'Economic development through bureaucratic corruption', *American Behavioral Scientist*, 8(3): 8–14.

Leys, C. (2002) 'What is the problem about corruption?' In Heidenheimer, A.J., and Johnston, M. (eds), *Political Corruption: Concepts and Contexts* (3rd edn) (pp. 59–73), New Brunswick, NJ: Transaction Publishers.

Li, D. and Ferreira, M.P. (2011) 'Institutional environment and firms' sources of financial capital in Central and Eastern Europe', *Journal of Business Research*, 64(4): 371–376.

Li, L. (2012) 'The "production" of corruption in China's courts: judicial politics and decision making in a one-party state', *Law & Social Inquiry*, 37(4): 848–877.

Lind, J.T. and Mehlum, H. (2010) 'With or without u? The appropriate test for a u-shaped relationship', *Oxford Bulletin of Economics and Statistics*, 72(1): 109–118.

Lipovetsky, G. (1996) 'La corruption', *La République des Lettres*, October 1, retrieved from www.republique-des-lettres.fr/280-gilles-lipovetsky.php (accessed May 2009).

Llaca, E.G. (2005) *La Corrupcion: Patologia Colectiva [Corruption: Collective Pathology]*, Ciudad de México: INAP/CNDH/FCPSUAM.

Lovett, S., Simmons, L.C. and Kali, R. (1999) '*Guanxi* versus the market: ethics and efficiency', *Journal of International Business Studies*, 30: 231–248.

Lucas, R.E., Jr. (1988) 'On the mechanics of economic development', *Journal of Monetary Economics*, 22: 3–42.

Lui, F.T. (1985) 'An equilibrium queuing model of bribery', *Journal of Political Economy*, 93(2): 760–781.

Luo, Y. (2011) 'Strategic responses to perceived corruption in an emerging market: lessons from MNEs investing in China', *Business & Society*, 50(2): 350–387.

Maia, A. (2004) 'Os números da corrupção em Portugal', *Polícia e Justiça – Branqueamento de Capitais*, pp. 83–129.

Maia, A. (2008) *Corrupção: Realidade e Percepções – O Papel da Imprensa*, ISCSP – UTL – Tese de Mestrado, Lisboa, in www.bocc.ubi.pt/pag/maia-antonio-corrupcao-realidade-e-percepcoes.pdf (accessed April 17, 2015).

Mair, P. and van Biezen, I. (2001) 'Party membership in twenty European democracies, 1980–2000', *Party Politics*, 7(1): 5–21.

Manojlović, S. (2011a) 'Finansiranje političkih aktivnosti – u susret novom zakonu', *Izbor sudske prakse*, Glosarium, Beograd, 4/2011.

Manojlović, S. (2011b) 'Zakon o finansiranju politickih aktivnosti', *Perspektive implementacije evropskih standarda u pravni sistem Srbije*, Pravni fakultet, Beograd, 2011.

Mashali, B. (2012) 'Analyzing the relationship between perceived grand corruption and petty corruption in developing countries: case study of Iran', *International Review of Administrative Sciences*, 78(4): 775–787.

Mauro, P. (1995) 'Corruption and growth', *Quarterly Journal of Economics*, 110(3): 681–712.

Mauro, P. (1998a) 'Corruption and composition of government spending', *Journal of Public Economics*, 69: 263–279.

Mauro, P. (1998b) 'Corruption: causes, consequences, and agenda for further research', *Finance & Development*, 11–14.

Mayer-Haug, K., Read, S., Brinckmann, J., Dew, N. and Grichnik, D. (2013) 'Entrepreneurial talent and venture performance: a meta-analytic investigation of SMEs', *Research Policy*, 42 (6–7): 1251–1273.

McAfee, P. and McMillan, J. (1987) 'Auctions and bidding', *Journal of Economic Literature*, 25: 699–738.

McMullan, M. (1961) 'A theory of corruption', *Sociological Review*, 9: 181–201.

Mehanna, R.-A., Yazbeck, Y. and Sarieddine, L. (2010) 'Governance and economic development in MENA countries: does oil affect the presence of a virtuous circle?', *Journal of Transnational Management*, 15(2): 117–150.

Méon, P.-G. and Sekkat, K. (2005) 'Does corruption grease or sand the wheels of growth?', *Public Choice*, 122(1): 69–97.

Méon, P.-G. and Weill, L. (2010) 'Does financial intermediation matter for macroeconomic performance?', *Economic Modelling*, 27(1): 296–303.

Merton, R. (1938) 'Social structure and anomie', *American Sociological Review*, 3(5): 672–682.

Michailova, S. and Worm, W. (2003) 'Personal networking in Russia and China: *Blat* and *guanxi*', *European Management Journal*, 21(4): 509–519.

Milenkovic M., Congradin S. and Valtner L. (2009, May 6) Prave donatore zamaskirali nepostoječim firmama ili gubitašima, *Danas*, retrieved from www.danas.rs/vesti/politika/prave_donatore_zamaskirali_nepostojecim_firmama_ili_gubitasima.56.html?news_id=160420 (accessed April 15, 2015).

Miller, S. (2005) 'Corruption', in Zalta, E.N. (ed.), *The Stanford Encyclopedia of Philosophy*, retrieved from http://plato.stanford.edu/archives/fall2005/entries/corruption/ (accessed May 2009).

Millington, A., Ebenhardt, M. and Wilkinson, B. (2005) 'Gift giving, *guanxi* and illicit payments in buyer–supplier relations in China: analysing the experience of UK companies', *Journal of Business Ethics*, 57: 255–268.

Mo, P.H. (2001) 'Corruption and economic growth', *Journal of Comparative Economics*, 29: 66–79.

Moreira, C. (1994) *Planeamento e Estratégias da Investigação Social*, Lisboa: Instituto Superior de Ciências Sociais e Políticas.

Moreira, J.M. (1996) *ética, Economia e Política* [*Ethics, Economy and Politics*]. Porto: Lello e Irmão.

Morgado, M.J. and Vegar, J. (2003) *O Inimigo Sem Rosto – Fraude e Corrupção em Portugal*, Lisboa: Publicações Dom Quixote.

Morris, S.D. (1991) *Corruption and Politics in Contemporary Mexico*, Tuscaloosa, Alabama: University of Alabama Press.

Morris, S.D. (2004) 'Corruption in Latin America: an empirical overview', *SECOLAS Annals*, 36: 74–92.

Murphy, K.M., Shleifer, A. and Vishny, R.W. (1991) 'The allocation of talent: implications for growth', *Quarterly Journal of Economics*, 106: 503–530.

Murphy, K.M., Shleifer, A. and Vishny, R.W. (1993) 'Why is rent seeking so costly to growth?', *American Economic Review Paper and Proceedings*, 83: 409–414.

Myrdal, G. (1968) *Asian Drama: An Inquiry into the Poverty of the Nations*, New York: Random House.

Nassmacher, K. (2003a) 'Party funding in continental Western Europe', in Reginald A. and Tjernström, M. (eds), *Funding of Political Parties and Election Campaigns* (Chapter 7), IDEA Handbook Series: Trydells Tryckeri AB, Sweden.

Nassmacher, K. (2003b) 'Political parties, funding and democracy', in Reginald A. and Tjernström, M. (eds), *Funding of Political Parties and Election Campaigns* (Chapter 1), IDEA Handbook Series: Trydells Tryckeri AB, Sweden.

Nassmacher, K. (2003c) 'The funding of political parties in Anglo-Saxon orbit' in Reginald, A. and Tjernström, M. (eds), *Funding of Political Parties and Election Campaigns* (Chapter 3), IDEA Handbook Series: Trydells Tryckeri AB, Sweden.

Nassmacher, K. (2003d) 'Monitoring, control and enforcement of political finance regulation' in Reginald, A. and Tjernström, M. (eds), *Funding of Political Parties and Election Campaigns* (Chapter 8), IDEA Handbook Series: Trydells Tryckeri AB, Sweden.

Nelson, R. (1998) 'The agenda for growth theory: a different point of view', *Cambridge Journal of Economics*, 22: 497–520.

North, D. (1990) *Institutions, Institutional Change and Economic Performance*, Cambridge: Cambridge University Press.

Nye, J.S. (1967) 'Corruption and political development: a cost–benefit analysis', *The American Political Science Review*, 61(2): 417–427.

Nystrand, M.J. (2014) 'Petty and grand corruption and the conflict dynamics in Northern Uganda', *Third World Quarterly*, 35(5): 821–835.

Oberoi, R. (2014) 'Mapping the matrix of corruption: tracking the empirical evidences and tailoring responses', *Journal of Asian and African Studies*, 49(2): 187–214.

Obstfeld, M. (1994) 'Risk-taking, global diversification, and growth', *American Economic Review*, 84(5): 1310–1329.

Ocampo, L.M. (1993) *En Defensa Propia, como Salir de La Corrupción* [*In Self-Defense: How to avoid corruption?*], Buenos Aires: Editora SudAmericana.

Odi, N. (2014) 'Impact of corruption on economic growth in Nigeria', *Mediterranean Journal of Social Sciences*, 5(6): 41–46.

Odugbemi, S. and Norris, P. (2010) 'Do the news media act as watchdogs, agenda-setters and gate-keepers?' In Norris, P. (ed.), *Public Sentinel: News Media and Governance Reform* (Chapter 15), Washington, DC: World Bank.

OECD (2000) 'Results based management in development co-operation agencies: review of experiences', Working Paper presented to the February 2000 meeting of the WP-EV by the Development Assistance Committee (DAC) Working Party, retrieved from www.oecd.org/dac/evaluation (accessed April 17, 2015).

OECD (2005) *Corruption*, retrieved from www.oecd.org/topic/0,2686,en_2649_37447_1_1_1_1_37447,00.html (accessed April 17, 2015).

OECD (2007) *Integrity in Public Procurement. Good Practice from A to Z*, Paris: Organisation for Economic Co-operation and Development.

OECD (2014) *CleanGovBiz. Integrity in Practice*, Paris: OCED, retrieved from www.oecd.org/cleangovbiz/49693613.pdf (accessed April 18, 2015).

Ohman, M. (2009) 'Practical solutions for the public funding of political parties and election campaigns', in Ohman, M. and Zainulbhai, H. (eds), *Political Finance Regulation: The Global Experience* (Chapter 3, pp. 55–82), Washington, DC: IFES.

Oliver, C. (1991) 'Strategic responses to institutional processes', *Academy of Management Review*, 16(1): 145–179.

Open Society Justice Initiative (2004) *Monitoring Election Campaign Finance: A Handbook for NGOs*, retrieved from www.soros.org/sites/default/files/Handbook_in_full.pdf (accessed April 18, 2015).

Osborne, D. and Gaebler, T. (1993) *Reinventing Government – How the Entrepreneurial Spirit is Transforming the Public Sector*, New York: Penguin Books.

Osborne, P. (ed.) (2002) *Public Management – Critical Perspectives*, New York: Routledge.

Otáhal, T. (2014) 'Mises, Hayek and corruption', *Journal of Business Ethics*, 119(3): 399–404.

Paldam, M. (2002) 'The cross-country pattern of corruption: economics, culture and the seesaw dynamics', *European Journal of Political Economy*, 18(2): 215–240.

Panebianco, A. (1998) *Political Parties: Organisation and Power*, Cambridge and New York: Cambridge University Press.

Pareto, V. (1935) *The Mind and Society*, Volume 4, London: Jonathan Cape.

Park, S.H. and Luo, Y. (2001) '*Guanxi* and organizational dynamics: organizational networking in Chinese firms', *Strategic Management Journal*, 22: 455–477.

Pathmanand, U. (2008) 'Capital group in Thailand after economic crisis', Paper presented at the Economic Crisis seminar, Bangkok.

Pei, M. (2007) 'Corruption threatens China's future', *Carnegie Endowment Policy Brief* No. 55, October 2007, Carnegie Endowment for International Peace, retrieved from http://carnegieendowment.org/2007/10/09/corruption-threatens-china-s-future/g4 (accessed July 30, 2012).

Pellegrini, L. and Gerlagh, R. (2004) 'Corruption's effect on growth and its transmission channels', *Kyklos*, 57(3): 429–456.

Persson, T. and Tabellini, G. (1994) 'Is inequality harmful for growth?', *The American Economic Review*, 84(3): 600–621.

Pešić, V. (2007) 'State capture and widespread corruption in Serbia', CEPS Working Document No. 262.

Pew Research Center (2002) *Global Publics view their countries. What the world thinks in 2002: Chapter 2. Global publics view their countries*, retrieved from www.pewglobal.org/2002/12/04/chapter-2-global-publics-view-their-countries (accessed April 18, 2015).

Philp, M. (2002) 'Conceptualising political corruption', in Heidenheimer, A.J. and Johnstone, M. (eds), *Political Corruption: Concepts and Contexts* (3rd edn), New Brunswick and London: Transaction Publishers.

Pitsoe, V. J. (2013) 'Values education as a social instrument for reducing corruption, poverty and inequality', *Mediterranean Journal of Social Sciences*, 4(13): 745–753.

Poapongsakorn, N. (2011) *Study of Rice Intervention Program to Prevent Corruption*, Bangkok: NACC.

Poeschl, G. and Ribeiro, R. (2010) 'Ancoragens e variações nas representações da corrupção', *Análise Social*, 45(196): 419–445.

Politika (2012, July 28) *Nikolic priznao, Miskovic i Beko cute*, retrieved from www.politika.rs/rubrike/Politika/Nikolic-priznao-Mishkovic-i-Beko-cute.lt.html (accessed April 18, 2015).

Porta, D.D. and Mény, Y. (eds) (1995) *Démocratie et Corruption en Europe*, Paris: Editions La Découverte.

Porter, M.E. (1986) 'Changing patterns of international competition', *California Management Review*, 28(2): 9–40.

Power, T.J. and González, J. (2003) 'Cultura política, capital social e percepções sobre corrupção: uma investigação quantitativa em nível mundial', *Revista de Sociologia e Política*, 21: 51–69.

Prakash, A. and Hart, J. (2000) 'Indicators of economic integration', *Global Governance*, 6(1): 95–114.

Press Online (2010, May 8) *Lider LDP tvrdi da ima milionski biznis – Tajkun Čeda!*, retrieved from www.pressonline.rs/sr/vesti/vesti_dana/story/116365/Lider+LDP+tvrdi+da+ima+milionski+biznis+-+Tajkun+%C4%8Ceda!.html (accessed April 18, 2015).

Pujas, V. (2003) *Les Scandales Politiques en France, en Italie et en Espagne: Constructions, Usagens et Conflits de Légitimité*, Florence: European University Institute.

Quivy, R. and Van Campenhoudt, L. (1988) *Manuel de Recherche en Sciences Sociales*, Paris: Dunot.

Ramsey, F.P. (1928) 'A mathematical theory of saving', *Economic Journal*, 38(152): 543–559.

Ravallion, M. and Wodon, Q. (2000) 'Does child labour displace schooling? Evidence on behavioral responses to an enrollment subsidy', *The Economic Journal*, 110(462): C158–C175.

Rawlings, L.B. and Rubio, G.M. (2003) 'Evaluating the impact of conditional cash transfer programs', *World Bank Policy Research Working Paper*, 3119.

Rebelo, S. (1991) 'Long-run policy analysis and long-run growth', *The Journal of Political Economy*, 99(3): 500–521.

Reginald, A. and Tjernström, M. (eds) (2003) *Funding of Political Parties and Election Campaigns*, IDEA Handbook Series: Trydells Tryckeri AB, Sweden.

Reinert, M. (1993) 'Les "mondes lexicaux" et leur "logique" à travers l'analyse statistique d'un corpus de récits de cauchemars', *Langage et Société*, 66: 5–39.

Riley, S.P. (1999) 'Petty corruption and development', *Development in Practice*, 9(1–2): 189–193.

Rivera-Batiz, L. and Romer, P. (1991) 'International trade with endogenous technological trade', *European Economic Review*, 35: 971–1004.

Roberts, A. (2002) 'Access to government information: an overview of issues', in *Access to Information: A Key to Democracy*. The Carter Center, retrieved from www.cartercenter.org/documents/1272.pdf (accessed April 18, 2015).

Roberts, F.S. (1976) *Discrete Mathematical Models, with Applications to Social, Biological and Environmental Problems*, Englewood Cliffs, NJ: Prentice Hall.

Roman, A.V. and Miller, H.T. (2014) 'Building social cohesion family, friends, and corruption', *Administration & Society*, 46(7): 775–795.

Romer, P. (1986) 'Increasing returns and long-run growth', *Journal of Political Economy*, 94(5): 1002–1037.

Romer, P. (1987) 'Growth based on increasing returns due to specialization', *American Economic Review, Papers and Proceedings*, 77: 56–72.

Romer, P. (1990) 'Endogenous technological change', *Journal of Political Economy*, 98: S71–S102.

Roncarati, M. (2010) 'Governance in the health-care sector: experiences from Asia', *NACC Journal*, Special Issue, 3(2): 16–26.

Rose, A. and Spiegel, M. (2009) 'International financial remoteness and macroeconomic volatility', *Journal of Development Economics*, 89(2): 250–257.

Rose-Ackerman, S. (1975) 'The economics of corruption', *Journal of Public Economics*, 4: 187–203.

Rose-Ackerman, S. (1978) *Corruption: A Study in Political Economy*, London and New York: Academic Press.

Rose-Ackerman, S. (1996) 'Democracy and "grand" corruption', *International Social Science Journal*, 48(149): 365–380.

Rose-Ackerman, S. (1997a) 'The political economy of corruption', in Elliott, K. (ed.), *Corruption and the Global Economy* (pp. 31–60), Washington, DC: Institute for International Economics.

Rose-Ackerman, S. (1997b) 'The role of the World Bank in controlling corruption', *Law & Policy in International Business*, 29: 93–114.

Rose-Ackerman, S. (1999) *Corruption and Government: Causes, Consequences, and Reform*, Cambridge: Cambridge University Press.

Rose-Ackerman, S. (2001) 'Trust, honesty, and corruption: reflection on the state-building process', John M. Olin Center for Studies in Law, Economics, and Public Policy Working Papers. Paper 255, retrieved from http://digitalcommons.law.yale.edu/lepp_papers/255 (accessed April 18, 2015).

Rose-Ackerman, S. and Truex, R. (2013) 'Corruption and policy reform', in Lomborg, B. (ed.), *Global Problems, Smart Solutions: Costs and Benefits* (Chapter 11), Cambridge: Cambridge University Press.

Rosenberg, S. and Jones, R. (1972) 'A method for investigating and representing a person's implicit personality theory: Theodore Dreiser's view of people'. *Journal of Personality and Social Psychology*, 22: 372–386.

Rosenzweig, P. and Singh, J. (1991) 'Organisational environments and the multinational enterprise', *Academy of Management Review*, 16(2): 340–361.

Saastamoinen, A. and Kuosmanen, T. (2014) 'Is corruption grease, grit or a gamble? Corruption increases variance of productivity across countries', *Applied Economics*, 46(23): 2833–2849.

Sah, R.K. (1988) 'Persistence and pervasiveness of corruption: New perspectives', Yale Economic Papers.

Sahlins, M. D. (1965) 'On the sociology of primitive exchange', in Banton, M. (ed.), *The Relevance of Models for Social Anthropology*, New York: Praeger.

Sandholtz, W. and Gray, M. (2003) 'International integration and national corruption', *International Organization*, 57(4): 761–800.

Santos, L.M.V.V. (2010) 'Bolsa familia programme: economic and social impacts under the perspective of the capabilities approach', *13° Bien Congress 2010*. University of London.

Sautu, R. (2004) 'Qué es La corrupción y cómo medirla', in Sautu, R. et al. (2004) *Catálogo de Prácticas Corruptas – Corrupción, Confianza y Democracia* (pp. 38–54), Buenos Aires: Lumiere.

Savona, E. (1995) 'Beyond criminal law in devising anticorruption policies: lessons from the Italian experience', *European Journal on Criminal Policy and Research*, 3(2): 21–37.

Schmookler, J. (1952) 'The changing efficiency of the American economy, 1869–1938', *Review of Economics and Statistics*, 34(3): 214–231.

Schultz, T.W. (1961) 'Investment in human capital', *American Economic Review*, 51: 1–17.

Scott, W.R. (1995) *Institutions and Organizations*, Thousand Oaks, CA, Sage Publications.

Segerstrom, P., Anant, T. and Dinopoulos, E. (1990) 'A Schumpeterian model of the product life cycle', *American Economic Review*, 80: 1077–1092.

Seligson, M. (2006) 'The measurement and impact of corruption victimization: survey evidence from Latin America', *World Development*, 34(2): 381–404.

Senior, I. (2006) *Corruption – The World's Big C*, London: Institute of Economic Affairs.

Serra, D. (2006) 'Empirical determinants of corruption: a sensitivity analysis', *Public Choice*, 126(1–2): 225–256.

Setterfield, M. (2010) *Handbook of Alternative Theories of Economic Growth*, Cheltenham, UK: Edward Elgar Publishing.

Seyf, A. (2001) 'Corruption and development: a study of conflict', *Development in Practice*, 11: 597–605.

Shah, A. and Schacter, M. (2004) 'Combating corruption: look before you leap', *Finance and Development*, 41(4): 40–43.

Shalev, M. and Asbjornsen, S. (2010) 'Electronic reverse auctions and the public sector: factor of success', *Journal of Public Procurement*, 10(3): 428–452.

Shari, B. and Baer, D. (2005) *Money in Politics. A study of Party Financing Practices in 22 Countries*, National Democratic Institute for International Affairs (NDI), USA.

Shi, W. and Hoskisson, R.E. (2012) 'Advantages of foreignness: benefits of creative institutional deviance', in Tihanyi, L., Devinney, T.M. and Pedersen, T. (eds), *Institutional Theory in International Business and Management*. Advances in International Management, 25: 99–125. Emerald Group Publishing.

Shleifer, A. and Vishny, R.W. (1993) 'Corruption', *Quarterly Journal of Economics*, 108(3): 599–617.

Sidel, J.T. (1996) 'Siam and its Twin? Democratisation and Bossism in Contemporary Thailand and the Philippines', *IDS Bulletin*, 27(2): 56–63.

Silva, S.T. (2009) 'On evolutionary technological change and economic growth: Lakatos as a starting point for appraisal', *Journal of Evolutionary Economics*, 19(1): 111–135.

Silva, S.T. and Teixeira, A.A.C. (2009) 'On the divergence of evolutionary research paths in the past fifty years: a comprehensive bibliometric account', *Journal of Evolutionary Economics*, 19(5): 605–642.

Simon, H. (1947) *Administrative Behavior – A Study of Decision-Making Processes in Administrative Organization*, New York: Macmillan.

Simon, H. (1961) *Administrative Behavior* (2nd edn), New York: The Free Press.

Singhapreecha, J. and Boonyasiri, I. (2010) *The Political Economy of Longan Market Intervention*, research report submitted to the National Anti-Corruption Commission, Bangkok (in Thai).

Sloam, J. (2014) "'The outraged young", young Europeans, civic engagement and the new media in a time of crisis', *Information Communication and Society*, 17(2): 217–231.

Soares, S., Osório, R.R.G., Soares, F.V., Medeiros, M. and Zepeda, E. (2007) 'Programas de transferência condicionada de renda no Brasil, Chile e México: Impactos sobre a desigualdade', *Instituto de Pesquisas Econômicas Aplicadas – IPEA*. Discussion Paper no. 1293.

Sodré, A.C.A. and Alves, M.F.C. (2010) 'Relação entre emendas parlamentares e corrupção municipal no Brasil: Estudo dos relatórios do programa de fiscalização da controladoria-geral da união', *RAC – Revista de Administração Contemporânea*, 14(3): 414–433.

Solow, R.M. (1956) 'A contribution to the theory of economic growth', *The Quarterly Journal of Economics*, 70(1): 65–94.

Solow, R.M. (1957) 'Technical change and the aggregate production function', *Review of Economics and Statistics*, 39(3): 312–320.

Sousa, L. (2008) '"I don't bribe, I just pull strings": assessing the fluidity of social representations of corruption in Portuguese society', *Perspectives on European Politics and Society*, 9(1): 8–23.

Sousa, L. and Triães, J. (2007) *Corrupção e Ética em Democracia: O Caso de Portugal*, Lisboa: Centro de Investigação e Estudos de Sociologia – Instituto Superior de Ciências do Trabalho e da Empresa.

Sousa, L. and Triães, J. (2008) 'Corrupção e os Portugueses. Atitudes – Práticas- Valores', Cascais: Rui Costa Pinto Edições.

Stagl, H. (2009) 'Lack of a definition renders accountability meaningless', *EzineArticles*, retrieved from http://ezinearticles.com (accessed April 17, 2015).

State Administration Act 2002. (2002) Retrieved from www.opdc.go.th (accessed May 27, 2012).

Steidlmeier, P. (1999) 'Gift giving, bribery and corruption: ethical management of business relationships in China', *Journal of Business Ethics*, 20: 121–132.

Stiglitz, J. (2008) 'The end of neo-liberalism?' *Project Syndicate*, retrieved from www.project-syndicate.org/commentary/stiglitz101/English (accessed April 18, 2015).

Stojiljković, A. (2008) 'Administrativni izvori finansiranja stranaka', in Milosavljević M. (ed.), *Finansiranje političkih stranaka-između norme i prakse*, CESID, Beograd 2008.

Straub, S. (2008) 'Opportunism, corruption and the multinational firm's mode of entry', *Journal of International Economics*, 74(2): 245–263.

Suls, J. and Wheeler, L. (2000) 'A selective history of classic and neo-social comparison theory', in Suls, J. and Wheeler, L. (eds), *Handbook of Social Comparison: Theory and Research* (pp. 3–19), New York, NY: Plenum Publishers.

Sutherland, E. (1924) *Principles of Criminology*, Chicago: University of Chicago Press.

Sutherland, E. (1945) 'Is white-collar crime crime?', *American Sociological Review*, 10: 132–139.

Svendsen, G. (2003) 'Social capital, corruption, and economic growth: Eastern and Western Europe', Working Paper 03-21. University of Aarhus, retrieved from www.hha.dk/nat/wper/03-21_gts.pdf (accessed April 18, 2015).

Svensson, J. (2003) 'Who must pay bribes and how much? Evidence from a cross section of firms', *Quarterly Journal of Economics*, 118(1): 207–230.

Talbot, C. (2000) 'Performing "performance" – a comedy in three Act', *Public Money & Management*, 20(4): 63–68.

Tangkitvanich, S. et al. (2009) *Costs and Benefits for Thailand of Joining the GPA*, research report submitted to the Comptroller-General's Department, Ministry of Finance (in Thai).

Tanzi, V. (1998) 'Corruption around the world. Causes, consequences, scope, and cures', *IMF Staff Papers*, 45(4): 559–594.

Tanzi, V. and Davoodi, H.R. (1997) 'Corruption, public investment and growth', *International Monetary Fund Working Paper* No. 97/139.

Tebaldi, E. and Mohan, R. (2010) 'Institutions and poverty', *Journal of Development Studies*, 46(6): 1047–1066.

Teixeira, A.A.C. and Grande, M. (2012) 'Entry mode choices of MNCs and host countries' corruption: a review', *African Journal of Business Management*, 6(27): 7942–7958.

Thailand (1999) Act on Offences Relating to the Submission of Bids to State Agencies (1999), retrieved from www.moj.go.th/Law/MojLaw/EngLaw/Act%20Con.

Thailand (2002) Regulation of the Office of the Prime Minister on Procurement 1992, amendment No. 6, 2002.

Thairungroj, S. et al. (2010) 'Thailand: business environment and governance survey', in Office of the Civil Service Commission (eds), *Corruption in Thailand* (pp. 2.1–2.58), Bangkok: P.A. Living (in Thai).

The Economist (2008) 'Happy families: an anti-poverty scheme invented in Latin America is winning converts worldwide', The Americas: Brazil in *The Economist* print edition, February 7, 2008, in: www.economist.com/node/10650663/print.

Tirole, J. (1996) 'A theory of collective reputations with applications to the persistence of corruption and to firm quality', *Review of Economic Studies*, 63(1): 1–22.

Transparency International. (2005) *Corruption Perceptions Index*, retrieved from www.transparency.org (accessed October 31, 2013).

Transparency International. (2008) 'Persistently high corruption in low-income countries amounts to an "ongoing humanitarian disaster"', retrieved from www.transparency.org/news/pressrelease/20080922_persistently_high_corruption_in_low_income_countries (accessed April 28, 2015).

Transparency International. (2009) *Corruption Perceptions Index*, retrieved from www.transparency.org/policy_research/surveys_indices/cpi/2009/cpi_2009_table (accessed February 2010).

Transparency International. (2010) *Corruption Perceptions Index*, retrieved from www.transparency.org/cpi2010/results (accessed July 2012).

Transparency International. (2010/11) *Global Corruption Barometer*, retrieved from http://gcb.transparency.org/gcb201011/results/ (accessed July 2012).

Transparency International. (2012) *Corruption Perceptions Index 2012*, retrieved from www.transparency.org (accessed October 31, 2013).

Transparency Serbia. (2004) *Financing Presidential Electoral Campaign in Serbia*, retrieved from www.transparentnost.org.yu/ (accessed April 15, 2015).

Transparency Serbia. (2006, June 14) *Mediji o korupciji*, retrieved from www.transparentnost.org.rs/ts_mediji/stampa/2006/06JUN/14062006.html (accessed April 15, 2015).

Treisman, D. (2000) 'The causes of corruption: a cross-national study', *Journal of Public Economics*, 76(3): 399–457.

Treisman, D. (2006) 'Fiscal decentralization, governance, and economic performance: a reconsideration', *Economics and Politics*, 18(2): 219–235.

Tullock, G. (1967) 'The welfare costs of tariffs, monopolies and theft', *Western Economics Journal*, 5(3): 224–232.

Tullock, G. (1996) 'Corruption theory and practice', *Contemporary Economic Policy*, 14(3): 6–13.

Tumber, H. and Waisbord, S. R. (2004) 'Political scandals and media across democracies, Volume II', *American Behavioral Scientist*, 47(9): 1143–1152.

Ugur, M. (2014) 'Corruption's direct effects on per-capita income growth: a meta-analysis', *Journal of Economic Surveys*, 28(3): 472–490.

UNCITRAL Model Law (2011) Model Law on Procurement of Goods, Construction and Services with Guide to Enactment.

UNDP. (2010) *Atlas of Human Development in Brazil 2010*, Washington, DC: United Nation Development Plan.

UNDP Serbia (2011) Perception of corruption at the household level, 4th round, November 2011, retrieved from www.undp.org.rs.

United Nations. (2011) 'UN pushes for social schemes to protect poor at mere fraction of national wealth', February 14, 2011, retrieved from www.un.org/apps/news/story.asp?NewsID=37532&Cr=labour&Cr1=#.VLeQkEesVqU (accessed April 18, 2015).

United Nations Economic and Social Council. (2007) *Participatory Governance and Citizen's Engagement in Policy Development, Service Delivery, and Budgeting*, retrieved from www.unpan1.un.org/intradoc/groups/public/documents/un/unpan025375.pdf (accessed June 2, 2012).

United Nations Office on Drugs and Crime (UNODC). (2008) *Corruption*, retrieved from www.unodc.org/unodc/en/corruption/index.html (accessed January 2009).

United Nations Office on Drugs and Crime (UNODC). (2011) *Corruption in Serbia: Bribery as Experienced by the Population*, retrieved from www.unodc.org/.

United Nations Office on Drugs and Crime (UNODC). (2012) *UNODC's Action against Corruption and Economic Crime*, retrieved from www.unodc.org/unodc/corruption/index.html (accessed July 2012).

Uzawa, U. (1965) 'Optimum technical change in an aggregate model of economic growth', *International Economic Review*, 6(1): 18–31.

Van Dooren, W., Bouckaert, G. and Halligan, J. (2010) *Performance Management in Public Sector*, New York: Routedge.

Van Duyine, P., Stocco, E., Bajovic, V., Milenovic, M. and Lojpur, E. (2010) 'Searching for corruption in Serbia', *Journal of Financial Crime*, 17(1): 22–46.

Venice Commission (2007) Opinion on the Constitution of Serbia, adopted by the Commission at its 70th Plenary Session, Venice, March 17–18, 2007, retrieved from www.venice.coe.int.

Vogel, E.F. (1967) 'Kinship structure, migration to the city and modernization', in Dore, R.P. (ed.), *Aspects of Social Change in Modern Japan* (pp. 91–111), Princeton, NJ: Princeton University Press.

Vuković, Đ. (2008) 'Procena koštanja političkih stranaka', in Milosavljević, M. (ed.), *Finansiranje političkih stranaka-između norme i prakse*, CESID, Beograd.

Walecki, M. (2003) 'Money and politics in central and East Europe', in Reginald, A. and Tjernström, M. (eds), *Funding of Political Parties and Election Campaigns* (Chapter 5), IDEA Handbook Series, Sweden: Trydells Tryckeri AB.

Walker, R.M. (2010) *Public Management and Perfromance*, New York: Cambridge University Press.

Wang, Y. and You, J. (2012) 'Corruption and firm growth: evidence from China', *China Economic Review*, 23: 415–433.

Wedeman, A. (2002) 'Development and corruption: the East-Asian paradox', in Gomez, T.E. (ed.), *Political Business in East Asia* (pp. 34–61), London: Routledge.

Wei, S.-J. (1999) 'Does corruption relieve foreign investors of the burden of taxes and capital controls?', Policy Research Working Paper Series 2209, World Bank.

Wei, S.-J. (2000a) 'How taxing is corruption on international investors?', *Review of Economics & Statistics*, 82: 1–11.

Wei, S.-J. (2000b) 'Local corruption and global capital flows', *Brookings Papers on Economic Activity*, 31(2): 303–346.

Weiss, C.H. et al. (1972) *Evaluation Research. Methods for Assessing Program Effectiveness*, Englewood Cliffs, NJ: Prentice Hall.

Williams, A. and Siddique, A. (2008) 'The use (and abuse) of governance indicators in economics: a review', *Economics of Governance*, 9(2): 131–175.

Williams, J. and Beare, M. (1999) 'The business of bribery: globalization, economic liberalization, and the "problem" of corruption', *Crime, Law, and Social Change*, 32(2): 115–146.

Winters, M.S., Testa, P. and Fredrickson, M.M. (2012) 'Using field experiments to understand information as an antidote to corruption', *Research in Experimental Economics*, 15(1): 213–246.

Wolfe, D. and Hermanson, D. (2004) 'The fraud diamond: considering the four elements of fraud', *CPA Journal*, 74: 38–42.

World Bank (2004), *Mainstreaming Anti-Corruption Activities in World Bank Assistance – A Review of Progress Since 1997*, Washington, DC: World Bank.

World Bank (2013) 'Russian economic report: recovery and beyond', Working Paper no. 75578.

World Bank (1997) *Helping Countries Combat Corruption: The Role of the World Bank*, Washington, DC: World Bank.

Wu, J. (2003) 'Corruption control in China', *Strategy and Management*, 2: 7–14.

Yakovlev, A., Allilueva, O., Kuznetsova, I., Shamrin, A., Yudkevich, M. and Jakobson, L. (2010) 'The system of public procurements in Russia: on the road of reform', HSE policy paper.

Zamboni, Y. (2007) 'Participatory budgeting and local governance: an evidence-based evaluation of participatory budgeting experiences in Brazil', retrieved from http://siteresources.worldbank.org/intranetsocialdevelopment/resources/zamboni.pdf (accessed April 18, 2015).

Zhuplev, A. and Shtykhno, D. (2009) 'Motivations and obstacles for small business entrepreneurship in Russia: fifteen years in transition', *Journal of East–West Business*, 15(1): 25–49.

Zimmerman, C.R. (2006) 'Los programas sociales desde La óptica de los derechos humanos: el caso del Bolsa Familia del Gobierno Lula en Brasil', *SUR Revista Internacional de Derechos Humanos*, 3(4), retrieved from www.surjournal.org (accessed April 18, 2015).

Index